W9-CFU-092

Clashing Views
on Controversial
Political Issues

8th edition

Edited, Selected, and with Introductions by

George McKenna
City College, City University of New York

and

Stanley Feingold
Westchester Community College

The Dushkin Publishing Group, Inc.

In memory of Hillman M. Bishop and Samuel Hendel, masters of an art often neglected by college teachers: teaching.

Taking Sides ® is a registered trademark of The Dushkin Publishing Group, Inc.

Library of Congress Catalog Card Number: 92-71146

Manufactured in the United States of America

Eighth Edition, First Printing
ISBN: 1–56134–119–3

 Printed on Recycled Paper

PREFACE

Dialogue means two people talking to the same issue. This is not as easy as it sounds. Play back the next serious conversation you hear between zealots on opposing sides of a controversial issue; listen to them try to persuade one another of the truth, logic, and virtue of their own views and the falsity, irrationality, and downright evil of the others'.

What is likely to go wrong? At the outset, they are unlikely to make clear the nature of the issue, defining or describing it with enough clarity and specificity to make sure that they are both talking about the same area of controversy. As they proceed, they are likely to employ vague, emotion-laden terms without spelling out the uses to which the terms are put. When the heat is on, they may resort to shouting epithets at one another, and the hoped-for meeting of minds will give way to the scoring of political points and the reinforcement of existing prejudices. When, for example, the discussion of affirmative action comes down to both sides accusing the other of "racism," or when the controversy over abortion degenerates into taunts and name-calling, then no one really listens and learns from the other side.

It is our conviction that people *can* learn from the other side, no matter how sharply opposed it is to their own cherished viewpoint. Sometimes, after listening to others, we change our view entirely. But in most cases, we either incorporate some elements of the opposing view—thus making our own richer—or else learn how to answer the objections to our viewpoint. Either way, we gain from the experience. For these reasons we believe that encouraging dialogue between opposed positions is the most certain way of enhancing public understanding.

The purpose of this eighth edition of *Taking Sides* is to continue to work toward the revival of political dialogue in America. As we have done in the past seven editions, we examine leading issues in American politics from the perspective of sharply opposed points of view. We have tried to select authors who argue their points vigorously but in such a way as to enhance our understanding of the issue.

We hope that the reader who confronts lively and thoughtful statements on vital issues will be stimulated to ask some of the critical questions about American politics. What are the highest-priority issues with which government must deal today? What positions should be taken on these issues? What should be the attitude of Americans toward their government? To what extent, if any, does it need to be changed? How should it be organized in order to achieve the goals we set for it? What are these goals? Our conviction is that a healthy, stable democracy requires a citizenry that considers these

i

questions and participates, however indirectly, in answering them. The alternative is apathy, passivity, and, sooner or later, the rule of tyrants.

Plan of the book Each issue has an issue *introduction*, which sets the stage for the debate as it is argued in the YES and NO selections. Each issue concludes with a *postscript* that makes some final observations and points the way to other questions related to the issue. In reading the issue and forming your own opinions you should not feel confined to adopt one or the other of the positions presented. There are positions in between the given views or totally outside them, and the *suggestions for further reading* that appear in each issue postscript should help you find resources to continue your study of the subject. At the back of the book is a listing of all the *contributors to this volume*, which will give you information on the political scientists and commentators whose views are debated here.

Changes to this edition We have considerably revised this eighth edition. There are eight completely new issues: *Is American Government Dominated by Big Business?* (Issue 1); *Does Congress Need to Be Radically Reformed?* (Issue 5); *The Presidency Versus Congress: Should Divided Government Be Ended?* (Issue 6); *Should "Hate Speech" Be Protected?* (Issue 12); *Is the National Debt a National Liability?* (Issue 15); *Does the United States Need Socialized Medicine?* (Issue 16); *Was Roe v. Wade a Mistake?* (Issue 17); and *Should National Self-Interest Be the Basis of American Foreign Policy?* (Issue 19). By popular demand, one issue from an earlier edition has been brought back, *Has Party Reform Succeeded?* (Issue 2), with a new article by Tom Wicker arguing the negative. With many of the issues carried over from the seventh edition, we have changed one or both of the YES and NO selections. In all, there are 27 new selections in this edition. We have also revised the issue introductions and postscripts where necessary.

A word to the instructor An *Instructor's Manual with Test Questions* (multiple-choice and essay) is available through the publisher. A general guidebook, called *Using Taking Sides in the Classroom*, which discusses methods and techniques for integrating the pro/con approach into any classroom setting, is also available.

Acknowledgments We received many helpful comments and suggestions from our friends and readers across the United States and Canada. Their suggestions have markedly enhanced the quality of this edition of *Taking Sides* and are reflected in the totally new issues and the updated selections.

Our thanks go to those who responded with suggestions for the eighth edition:

James J. Boitano
Santa Rosa Junior College

Ken D. Brown
Independence Community
    College

Charles F. Burke
Baldwin-Wallace College

Robert Casier
Santa Barbara City College

Jeff Colbert
University of North Carolina
    at Greensboro

Ed Fleming
Florida Community College–South

Thomas H. Greene
University of Southern California

David Hunter
University Of Georgia

Lisa Langenbach
Lafayette College

George R. Lee
Culver-Stockton College

James Lindeen
University of Toledo

Kathryn L. Malec
Indiana University Northwest

Dennis McNutt
Southern California College

Joseph Melusky
St. Francis College Monastery

Vernon L. Moore
Cosumnes River College

Millard Morgen
College of Marin

David S. Myers
University Of West Florida

Thomas W. O'Connor
Springfield College

Patrick M. O'Neil
Broome Community College

Timothy J. O'Neill
Southwestern University

William Parsons
St. Ambrose University

René Peritz
Slippery Rock University

Carl Pohlhammer
Monterey Peninsula College

Linda K. Richter
Kansas State University

Jack E. Rossotti
American University

Susan Rouder
City College of San Francisco

Allan A. Saxe
University Of Texas at Arlington

Edward Schneier
City College of New York

Charles A. Scudder
West Georgia College

Zachary A. Smith
Northern Arizona University

Kandis Steele
University of Alabama

Gwendolyn J. Sterk
Trinity College

George A. Taylor
Elon College

Kristine Thompson
North Dakota State University

Willard Paul Tice
Oklahoma City University

Paul Weizer
Temple University

John W. Williams
Principia College

George Zilbergeld
Montclair State College

We also appreciate the spontaneous letters from instructors and students who wrote to us with comments and observations. We wish to acknowledge the support given to this project by Rick Connelly, president of The Dushkin Publishing Group. We are grateful as well to Mimi Egan, program manager, for her very able editorial supervision. Needless to say, the responsibility for any errors of fact or judgment rests with us.

George McKenna
City College, City University of New York

Stanley Feingold
Westchester Community College

CONTENTS IN BRIEF

CONTENTS

Political reporter Thomas Byrne Edsall argues that the power of big business
is stronger than ever because of the increasing political sophistication of big
business coupled with the breakdown of political parties. Professor of
business administration David Vogel contends that the power of business
fluctuates with the times and is currently being kept in check by other forces
in U.S. society.

Political scientist William J. Crotty contends that modern reform has opened
up the political process and has given unprecedented influence to each
party's rank and file. Political columnist Tom Wicker concludes that the
presidential nominating process too often fails to produce the candidate who
is most able or most likely to win the greatest popular support.

Common Cause president Fred Wertheimer argues that PACs exert too much
influence over the electoral process, allowing special interests to get the ear of
elected officials at the expense of the national interest. Political analyst
Herbert E. Alexander insists that PACs have made significant contributions
to the American political system.

Media analyst William A. Rusher argues that the media are biased against
conservatives and that news coverage promotes liberal opinions. Professors
Edward S. Herman and Noam Chomsky critique the mass media from the
perspective of the left and find the media to be a "propaganda mill" in the
service of the wealthy and powerful.

Journalists Paula Dwyer and Douglas Harbrecht conclude that the legislative
performance of Congress is dismal, and they identify several areas in which
radical reforms would lead to vast improvement. Political scientist Nelson W.
Polsby believes that "Congress-bashing" is a misguided attack upon the
legislative power and undermines the constitutional separation of powers.

Political scientist James L. Sundquist suggests that a president and Congress from the same party might put an end to governmental deadlocks. Richard P. Nathan, director of the Rockefeller Institute of Government at the State University of New York at Albany, argues that major structural changes in the relationship between the president and Congress are neither necessary nor desirable.

Economist Thomas Gale Moore argues that deregulating economic markets lowers costs, benefits consumers, and makes the American economy more competitive in the world. Journalist David Bollier and political activist Joan Claybrook provide evidence that existing government regulations have prevented serious human and environmental harm in the past, and they argue that the purpose of regulations should not be obscured by economic considerations.

Educator and former judge Robert H. Bork argues that the "original intent" of the framers of the Constitution can and should be upheld by the federal courts, because not to do so is to have judges perform a political role they were not given. Professor of history Leonard W. Levy believes that the "original intent" of the framers cannot be found, and, even if it could, given these changing times, it could not be applied in dealing with contemporary constitutional issues.

Political scientist Stanley C. Brubaker argues that punishment for crime, whether or not it deters crime or rehabilitates criminals, is important because it helps to underscore the community's sense of right and wrong. Editor Linda Rocawich contends that locking people up is inhumane, is often applied in a racially discriminatory manner, and does not deter crime.

Professor of government Walter Berns is convinced that the death penalty has a place in modern society and that it serves a need now, as it did when the Constitution was framed. Social writer Mary Meehan gives a variety of reasons, from the danger of killing the innocent to the immorality of killing even the guilty, why she thinks the death penalty is wrong.

Law professor Stephen L. Carter expresses his concern that affirmative action programs may lower standards and deprive African Americans of the incentive necessary to achieve excellence. Professor of African American studies Herbert Hill argues that affirmative action is necessary to reverse America's long history of racist practices.

Columnist Nat Hentoff is worried that political orthodoxy and "politically correct" speech codes on American college campuses will inhibit discussion of important issues. Professor of law Stanley Fish argues that speech in and of itself has no value, and when its only aim is to humiliate people, it does not deserve protection.

Assistant professor of politics and public affairs Ethan A. Nadelmann contends that drug legalization would help put the criminal drug dealers out of business while protecting the rights of adults to make their own choices, free of criminal sanctions. Political scientist James Q. Wilson argues that drug legalization would vastly increase dangerous drug use and the social ills created by such usage.

Social policy analyst Robert Rector argues that the welfare system undermines the work ethic and discourages the formation of two-parent families. He feels that true welfare reform would encourage personal responsibility and effort. Journalist Barbara Ehrenreich believes that social welfare should not be blamed for the ills of the poor, and she argues that unfettered free enterprise and the consumer culture are responsible for the permissiveness and perceived moral decline of modern America.

Professor of political economics Benjamin M. Friedman believes that the steeply rising national debt of the 1980s led to a sharp decline in the economy, the reversal of which requires radical economic remedies. *Wall Street Journal* editor Robert L. Bartley holds that the significance of the deficit is exaggerated and that it takes attention away from fiscal policies that will enhance our economic growth.

Policy analyst Nancy Watzman argues that the Canadian model of universal medical insurance can be adapted and improved in order to provide superior and less expensive care for all Americans. John C. Goodman, president of the National Center for Policy Analysis, maintains that Americans get more and better health care more promptly than do individuals in countries with compulsory schemes of national health insurance.

Supreme Court chief justice William H. Rehnquist believes that the Court wrongly decided *Roe v. Wade* and that states should have the right to establish their own abortion laws. Supreme Court justice Harry A. Blackmun believes that *Roe* was correctly decided, and he opposes any law that would limit a woman's access to an abortion beyond the limits set in that case.

Edd Doerr, executive director of Americans for Religious Liberty, believes that public schools should promote and reflect shared values, leaving religious instruction and celebration to the home and place of worship. George Goldberg, a writer and lawyer, holds that school prayer and the teaching of religion are permissible as long as all religions are accorded equal treatment.

Alan Tonelson, research director of the Economic Strategy Institute in Washington, D.C., advocates "interest-based" pragmatism in the formulation of American foreign policy and warns against utopian internationalism. Joshua Muravchik, a writer and scholar, warns against "the folly of realism" and argues that *interest* should be understood in the broadest sense, which includes an interest in democracy and human rights.

Foreign policy strategist Edward N. Luttwak believes that Japan and Europe will soon be richer than the United States because of the failure of America's economic policies and social programs. *Wall Street Journal* editor Robert L. Bartley asserts that America is, and will remain, the wealthiest country and that it will continue to play the role of world leader.

INTRODUCTION

Labels and Alignments in American Politics

George McKenna
Stanley Feingold

Liberalism, conservatism, radicalism, pluralism, left wing, right wing, moderate, extremist, radical—do these terms have any meaning? Or are they just descriptive words that are used to rally the faithful and batter the enemy? Are they, as Shakespeare would have said, full of sound and fury but signifying nothing, or do they contain some specific, core meanings? We think that they do have intelligible meanings; however, they must be used thoughtfully. Otherwise, the terms may end up obscuring or oversimplifying positions. Our purpose in this Introduction is to explore the basic, core meanings of these terms in order to make them useful to us as citizens.

LIBERALS VERSUS CONSERVATIVES: AN OVERVIEW

Let us examine, very briefly, the historical evolution of the terms *liberalism* and *conservatism*. By examining the roots of these terms, we can see how these philosophies have adapted themselves to changing times. In that way, we can avoid using the terms rigidly, without reference to the particular contexts in which liberalism and conservatism have operated over the past two centuries.

Classical Liberalism

The classical root of the term liberalism is the Latin word *libertas*, meaning "liberty" or "freedom." In the early nineteenth century, liberals dedicated themselves to freeing individuals from all unnecessary and oppressive obligations to authority—whether the authority came from the church or the state. They opposed the licensing and censorship of the press, the punishment of heresy, the establishment of religion, and any attempt to dictate orthodoxy in matters of opinion. In economics, liberals opposed state monopolies and other constraints upon competition between private businesses. At this point in its development, liberalism defined freedom primarily in terms of freedom *from*. It appropriated the French term *laissez-faire*, which literally means "leave to be." Leave people alone! That was the spirit of liberalism in its early days. It wanted government to stay out of people's lives and to play a modest role in general. Thomas Jefferson summed up this concept when he said, "I am no friend of energetic government. It is always oppressive."

Despite their suspicion of government, classical liberals invested high hopes in the political process. By and large, they were great believers in democracy. They believed in widening suffrage to include every white male, and some of them were prepared to enfranchise women and blacks as well. Although liberals occasionally worried about "the tyranny of the majority," they were more prepared to trust the masses than to trust a permanent, entrenched elite. Liberal social policy was dedicated to fulfilling human potential and was based on the assumption that this often-hidden potential is enormous. Human beings, liberals argued, were basically good and reasonable. Evil and irrationality were believed to be caused by "outside" influences; they were the result of a bad social environment. A liberal commonwealth, therefore, was one that would remove the hindrances to the full flowering of the human personality.

The basic vision of liberalism has not changed since the nineteenth century. What has changed is the way it is applied to modern society. In that respect, liberalism has changed dramatically. Today, instead of regarding government with suspicion, liberals welcome government as an instrument to serve the people. The change in philosophy began in the latter years of the nineteenth century, when businesses—once small, independent operations—began to grow into giant structures that overwhelmed individuals and sometimes even overshadowed the state in power and wealth. At that time, liberals began reconsidering their commitment to the *laissez-faire* philosophy. If the state can be an oppressor, asked liberals, can't big business also oppress people? By then, many were convinced that commercial and industrial monopolies were crushing the souls and bodies of the working classes. The state, formerly the villain, now was viewed by liberals as a potential savior. The concept of freedom was transformed into something more than a negative freedom *from;* the term began to take on a positive meaning. It meant "realizing one's full potential." Toward this end, liberals believed, the state could prove to be a valuable instrument. It could educate children, protect the health and safety of workers, help people through hard times, promote a healthy economy, and—when necessary—force business to act more humanely and responsibly. Thus was born the movement that culminated in New Deal liberalism.

New Deal Liberalism

In the United States, the argument in favor of state intervention did not win a truly popular constituency until after the Great Depression of the 1930s began to be felt deeply. The disastrous effects of a depression that left a quarter of the work force unemployed opened the way to a new administration—and a promise. "I pledge you, I pledge myself," Franklin D. Roosevelt said when accepting the Democratic nomination in 1932, "to a new deal for the American people." Roosevelt's New Deal was an attempt to effect relief and recovery from the Depression; it employed a variety of means, including welfare programs, public works, and business regulation—most of which involved government intervention in the economy. The New Deal liberalism relied on government to liberate people from poverty, oppression, and economic exploitation. At the same time, the New Dealers claimed to be as zealous as the classical liberals in defending political and civil liberties.

The common element in *laissez-faire* liberalism and welfare-state liberalism is their dedication to the goal of realizing the full potential of each individual. Some still questioned whether this was best done by minimizing state involvement or whether it sometimes requires an activist state. The New Dealers took the latter view, though they prided themselves on being pragmatic and experimental about their activism. During the heyday of the New Deal, a wide variety of programs were tried and—if found wanting—abandoned. All decent means should be tried, they believed, even if it meant dilution of ideological purity. The Roosevelt administration, for example, denounced bankers and businessmen in campaign rhetoric but worked very closely with them while trying to extricate the nation from the Depression. This set a pattern of pragmatism that New Dealers from Harry Truman to Lyndon Johnson emulated.

Progressive Liberalism
Progressive liberalism emerged in the late 1960s and early 1970s as a more militant and uncompromising movement than the New Deal had ever been. Its roots go back to the New Left student movement of the early 1960s. New Left students went to the South to participate in civil rights demonstrations, and many of them were bloodied in confrontations with southern police; by the mid-1960s they were confronting the authorities in the North over issues like poverty and the Vietnam War. By the end of the decade, the New Left had fragmented into a variety of factions and had lost much of its vitality, but a somewhat more respectable version of it appeared as the New Politics movement. Many New Politics crusaders were former New Leftists who had traded their jeans for coats and ties; they tried to work within the system instead of always confronting it. Even so, they retained some of the spirit of the New Left. The civil rights slogan "Freedom Now" expressed the mood of the New Politics. The young university graduates who filled its ranks had come from an environment where "nonnegotiable" demands were issued to college deans by leaders of sit-in protests. There was more than youthful arrogance in the New Politics movement, however; there was a pervasive belief that America had lost, had compromised away, much of its idealism. The New Politics liberals sought to recover some of that spirit by linking up with an older tradition of militant reform, which went back to the time of the Revolution. These new liberals saw themselves as the authentic heirs of Thomas Paine and Henry David Thoreau, of the abolitionists, the radical populists, the suffragettes, and the great progressive reformers of the early twentieth century.

While New Deal liberals concentrated almost exclusively on bread-and-butter issues such as unemployment and poverty, the New Politics liberals introduced what came to be known as social issues into the political arena. These included: the repeal of laws against abortion, the liberalization of laws against homosexuality and pornography, the establishment of affirmative action programs to ensure increased hiring of minorities and women, and the passage of the Equal Rights Amendment. In foreign policy too, New Politics liberals departed from the New Deal agenda. Because they had keener memories of the unpopular and (for them) unjustified war in Vietnam than of World War II, they became doves, in contrast to the general hawkishness of the New Dealers. They were skeptical of any claim that the United States must be the leader of the free world or, indeed, that it had any special mission in the world; some were convinced that America was already in decline and must learn to adjust accordingly. The real danger, they argued, came not from the Soviet Union but from the mad pace of our arms race with the Soviets, which, as they saw it, could bankrupt the country, starve our social programs, and culminate in a nuclear Armageddon.

New Politics liberals were heavily represented at the 1972 Democratic national convention, which nominated South Dakota senator George McGovern for president. By the 1980s, the New Politics movement was no longer new, and many of its adherents preferred to be called progressives. By this time their critics had another name for them: radicals. The critics saw their positions as inimical to the interests of the United States, destructive of the family, and fundamentally at odds with the views of most Americans. The adversaries of the progressives were not only conservatives but many New Deal liberals, who openly scorned the McGovernites.

This split still exists within the Democratic party, though it is now more skillfully managed by party leaders. In 1988 the Democrats paired Michael Dukakis, whose Massachusetts supporters were generally on the progressive side of the party, with New Dealer Lloyd Bentsen as the presidential and vice-presidential candidates, respectively. In 1992 the Democrats paired Arkansas governor Bill Clinton, whose record as governor seemed to put him in the moderate-to-conservative camp, with Tennessee senator Albert Gore, whose position on environmental issues could probably be considered quite liberal but whose general image was middle-of-the-road. Both candidates had moved toward liberal positions on the issues of gay rights and abortion.

Conservatism

Like liberalism, conservatism has undergone historical transformation in America. Just as early liberals (represented by Thomas Jefferson) espoused less government, early conservatives (whose earliest leaders were Alexander Hamilton and John Adams) urged government support of economic enterprise and government intervention on behalf of privileged groups. By the time of the New Deal, and in reaction to the growth of the welfare state since that time, conservatives had argued strongly that more government means more unjustified interference in citizens' lives, more bureaucratic regulation of private conduct, more inhibiting control of economic enterprise, more material advantage for the less energetic and less able at the expense of those who are prepared to work harder and better, and, of course, more taxes—taxes that will be taken from those who have earned money and given to those who have not.

Contemporary conservatives are not always opposed to state intervention. They may support larger military expenditures in order to protect society against foreign enemies. They may also allow for some intrusion into private life in order to protect society against internal subversion and would pursue criminal prosecution zealously in order to protect society against domestic violence. The fact is that few conservatives, and perhaps fewer liberals, are absolute with respect to their views about the power of the state. Both are quite prepared to use the state in order to further *their* purposes. It is true that activist presidents such as Franklin Roosevelt and John Kennedy were likely to be classified as liberals. However, Richard Nixon was also an activist, and, although he does not easily fit any classification, he was far closer to conservatism than to liberalism. It is too easy to identify liberalism with statism and conservatism with antistatism; it is important to remember that it was liberal Jefferson who counseled against "energetic government" and conservative Alexander Hamilton who designed bold powers for the new central government and wrote: "Energy in the executive is a leading character in the definition of good government."

Neoconservatism and the New Right
Two newer varieties of conservatism have arisen to challenge the dominant strain of conservatism that opposed the New Deal. Those who call themselves (or have finally allowed themselves to be called) neoconservatives are recent converts to conservatism. Many of them are former New Deal Democrats, and some like to argue that it is not they who have changed, it is the Democratic party, which has allowed itself to be taken over by advocates of progressive liberalism. They recognize, as did the New Dealers, the legitimacy of social reform, but now they warn against carrying it too far and creating an arrogant bureaucracy. They support equal opportunity, as they always did, but now they underscore the distinction between equal opportunity and equality of result, which they identify as the goal of affirmative action programs. Broadly speaking, neoconservatism shares with the older variety of conservatism a high respect for tradition and a view of human nature that some would call pessimistic. Neoconservatives, like all conservatives, are also deeply concerned about the communist threat to America. They advise shoring up America's defenses and resisting any movement that would lead the nation toward unilateral disarmament.

A more recent and more politically active variant of conservatism is called the New Right. Despite the semantic resemblance between the New Right and neoconservatism, the two differ in important ways. Neoconservatives are usually lapsed liberals, while New Rightists tend to be dyed-in-the-wool conservatives—though ones who are determined to appeal to wider constituencies than did the "old" Right. Neoconservatives tend to be academics, who appeal to other similar elites through books and articles in learned journals. The New Right aims at reaching grass-roots voters through a variety of forums, from church groups to direct-mail solicitation. Neoconservatives customarily talk about politico-economic structures and global strategies; New Rightists emphasize the concerns of ordinary Americans, what they call family issues—moral concerns such as abortion, prayer in public schools, pornography, and what they consider to be a general climate of moral breakdown in the nation. These family issues are very similar to the social issues introduced into the political arena by the advocates of progressive liberalism. This should not be surprising, since the rise of the New Right was a reaction to the previous success of the progressive movement in legitimizing its stands on social issues.

Spokesmen for progressive liberalism and the New Right stand as polar opposites: The former regard abortion as a woman's right; the latter see it as legalized murder. The former tend to regard homosexuality as a life-style that needs protection against discrimination; the latter are more likely to see it as a perversion. The former have made an issue of their support for the Equal Rights Amendment; the latter includes large numbers of women who fought against the amendment because they believed it threatened their role identity. The list of issues could go on. The New Right and the progressive liberals are like positive and negative photographs of America's moral landscape. Sociologist James Davison Hunter uses the term *culture wars* to characterize the struggles between these contrary visions of America. For all the differences between progressive liberalism and the New Right, however, their styles are very similar. They are heavily laced with moralistic prose; they tend to equate compromise with selling out; and they claim to represent the best, most authentic traditions of America. This is not to denigrate either movement, for the kinds of issues they address are indeed moral issues, which do not generally admit much compromise. These issues cannot simply be finessed or ignored, despite the efforts of conventional politicians to do so. They must be aired and fought over, which is why we include some of them, such as abortion (Issue 17) and church-state relations (Issue 18), in this volume.

RADICALS, REACTIONARIES, AND MODERATES

The label *reactionary* is almost an insult, and the label *radical* is worn with pride by only a few zealots on the banks of the political mainstream. A reactionary is not a conserver but a backward-mover, dedicated to turning the clock back to better times. Most people suspect that reactionaries would restore us to a time that never was, except in political myth. For many, the repeal of industrialism or universal education (or the entire twentieth century itself) is not a practical, let alone desirable, political program.

Radicalism (literally meaning "from the roots" or "going to the foundation") implies a fundamental reconstruction of the social order. Taken in that sense, it is possible to speak of right-wing radicalism as well as left-wing radicalism—radicalism that would restore or inaugurate a new hierarchical society as well as radicalism that calls for nothing less than an egalitarian society. The term is sometimes used in both of these senses, but most often the word *radicalism* is reserved to characterize more liberal change. While the liberal would effect change through conventional democratic processes, the radical is likely to be skeptical about the ability of the established machinery to bring about the needed change and might be prepared to sacrifice "a little" liberty to bring about a great deal more equality.

Moderate is a highly coveted label in America. Its meaning is not precise, but it carries the connotations of sensible, balanced, and practical. A moderate person is not without principles, but he or she does not allow principles to harden into dogma. The opposite of moderate is extremist, a label most American political leaders eschew. Yet, there have been notable exceptions. When Arizona senator Barry Goldwater, a conservative Republican, was nominated for president in 1964, he declared: "Extremism in defense of liberty is no vice! . . . Moderation in the pursuit of justice is no virtue!" This open embrace of extremism did not help his electoral chances; Goldwater was overwhelmingly defeated. At about the same time, however, another American political leader also embraced a kind of extremism, and with better results. In a famous letter written from a jail cell in Birmingham, Alabama, the Reverend Martin Luther King, Jr., replied to the charge that he was an extremist not by denying it but by distinguishing between different kinds of extremists. The question, he wrote, "is not whether we will be extremist but what kind of extremist will we be. Will we be extremists for hate, or will we be extremists for love?" King aligned himself with the love extremists, in which category he also placed Jesus, St. Paul, and Thomas Jefferson, among others. It was an adroit use of a label that is usually anathema in America.

PLURALISM

The principle of pluralism espouses diversity in a society containing many interest groups and in a government containing competing units of power. This implies the widest expression of competing ideas, and in this way, pluralism is in sympathy with an important element of liberalism. However, as James Madison and Alexander Hamilton pointed out when they analyzed the sources of pluralism in the *Federalist* commentaries on the Constitution, this philosophy springs from a profoundly pessimistic view of human nature, and in this respect it more closely resembles conservatism. Madison, possibly the single most influential member of the convention that wrote the Constitution, hoped that in a large and varied nation, no single interest group could control the government. Even if there were a majority interest, it would be unlikely to capture all of the national agencies of government—the House of Representatives, the Senate, the presidency and the federal judiciary—each of which was chosen in a different way by a different constituency for a different term of office. Moreover, to make certain that no one branch exercised excessive power, each was equipped with "checks and balances" that enabled any agency of national government to curb the powers of the others. The clearest statement of Madison's, and the Constitution's, theory can be found in the 51st paper of the *Federalist*:

> It may be a reflection on human nature that such devices should be necessary to control the abuses of government. But what is government itself, but the greatest of all reflections on human nature? If men were angels, no government would be necessary.

This pluralist position may be analyzed from different perspectives. It is conservative insofar as it rejects simple majority rule; yet it is liberal insofar as it rejects rule by a single elite. It is conservative in its pessimistic appraisal of human nature; yet pluralism's pessimism is also a kind of egalitarianism, holding as it does that no one can be trusted with power and that majority interests no less than minority interests will use power for selfish ends. It is possible to suggest that in America pluralism represents an alternative to both liberalism and conservatism. Pluralism is antimajoritarian and antielitist and combines some elements of both.

SOME APPLICATIONS

Despite our effort to define the principal alignments in American politics, some policy decisions do not neatly fit into these categories. Readers will reach their own conclusions, but we may suggest some alignments to be found here in order to demonstrate the variety of viewpoints.

The conflicts between neoconservatism and liberalism are expressed in the opposed approaches of Linda Rocawich and Stanley Brubaker to the question of how to reduce crime (Issue 9). Brubaker proceeds from the conservative premise that we need to restore the traditional view that punishing criminals is not simply meant to "correct" their behavior, or rehabiliate them, or even to deter future crime, but to make them and everyone else understand that they have done evil. Rocawich, who has a more optimistic view of human nature, thinks that compassion and rehabilitation are better than prisons as means of reducing crime. More difficult to classify is the issue of whether or not the government regulates too much (Issue 7). David Bollier and Joan Claybrook's critique of deregulation is compatible with either New Deal or progressive liberalism, but Thomas Gale Moore's case against regulation is reminiscent of classical liberalism, or libertarianism.

Walter Berns's defense of the death penalty (Issue 10) is almost a purely conservative position. Like other conservatives, Berns is skeptical of the possibilities of human perfection and therefore regards retribution—"paying back" instead of trying to "reform" a murderer—as a legitimate goal of punishment. Issue 11, on affirmative action, has become a litmus test of the new "progressive" liberalism. The progressives say that it is not enough for our laws to become color-blind or gender-blind; they must now reach out to remedy the ills caused by racism and sexism. But conservatives and some New Deal liberals oppose affirmative action, which they regard as a new form of discrimination.

Former federal court of appeals judge Robert Bork's case (in Issue 8) for using "original intent" as the basis of constitutional interpretation is a classic conservative argument, seeking as it does to extract from the thought of the Constitution's founders some authentic guide for interpreting the Constitution today. Leonard Levy's criticism of this approach is liberal in its insistence that the Constitution's meaning must change with the times.

The arguments over welfare (Issue 14) and socialized medicine (Issue 16) are classic liberal-conservative splits. Robert Rector takes the conservative position on welfare and argues that it robs the poor of incentive, and conservative John Goodman contends that socialized medicine would be prohibitively expensive and would lower the quality of health care. On the other side, both Barbara Ehrenreich and Nancy Watzman are unapologetic spokespersons for progressive liberalism. Watzman openly supports the adoption of socialized medicine in the United States, which most New Deal liberals shy away from because it sounds "radical," and Ehrenreich makes no secret of her distaste for capitalism in her support of welfare programs.

The arguments over the national debt (Issue 15) may also divide liberals from conservatives, though the picture has become more cloudy and confused in recent years. Conservatives used to predict dire consequences for the nation if it failed to get its budget into balance, while liberals tended to dismiss debt as largely a bookkeeping item—money Americans owed to themselves. But as deficits soared during the Reagan years, the liberals took over the conservative prophecies of doom, leaving conservatives with the choice of either echoing the former liberal view of the debt as relatively unimportant or of seeking to blame it on liberals. Most conservatives seemed to prefer the latter alternative, though in the selections presented in Issue 15, Robert Bartley holds that the significance of the debt has been greatly exaggerated, which is what liberals used to say during the New Deal.

This book contains a few arguments that are not easy to categorize. The issue of drug legalizations (Issue 13) often divides liberals and conservatives (liberals for legalization, conservatives against it), but it does not always divide so neatly. Conservative editor and writer William F. Buckley, for example, favors drug legalization, while progressive liberal Reverend Jesse Jackson opposes it. The arguments here are usually pragmatic ones: Is it really possible, without incurring excessive social costs, to succeed in banning drugs? Such arguments often cut across liberal-conservative lines, although in our selections, James Q. Wilson, who opposes drug legalization, seems more conservative in his political orientation than does Ethan Nadelmann, who favors legalization.

Issue 17 on the controversial *Roe v. Wade* decision regulating abortion also takes some unpredictable turns. Pennsylvania governor Robert Casey is a liberal Democrat, yet he opposes abortion and sees nothing at all conservative about that position. There are other prominent liberals—columnist Nat Hentoff is one—who also oppose *Roe v. Wade's* legalization of abortion. Although at present most liberals take the pro-choice side, this tendency does not seem to proceed from any logical imperative in the arguments of either side. The selections in Issue 17 are not so much concerned with abortion *per se* as with the question of whether the *Roe v. Wade* decision was mistaken in ruling that abortion rights can be found or implied in the Constitution. Chief Justice William Rehnquist argues that they cannot, while Justice Harry Blackmun, author of the controversial 1973 opinion, insists that the ruling was right then and is right today.

Issue 19, which pits realism against idealism in foreign policy, also does not fit the usual categories of liberal and conservative. The temptation is to say that the realist is conservative and the idealist is liberal. Realism in foreign policy proceeds from a view of human nature similar to that of conservatism: in both cases the view is that self-interest—of nations as well as individuals—is an unvarying law that must constantly be kept in mind. Liberals are more inclined toward belief in change and in a more optimistic view of human nature. But in our selections, Alan Tonelson makes the case for realism, even though he belongs to the liberal camp. Joshua Muravchik, on the other hand, makes the case for a certain kind of liberal idealism based not upon chauvinism but on human rights.

Then there is the argument over "hate speech" (Issue 12). Ordinarily, liberals oppose restrictions on free speech and conservatives tend to support them in certain cases. This, at least, is the way it lines up when the question involves such areas as pornography and inciting to revolution. However, in recent years the issue of "political correctness" on campuses has come close to reversing the positions: Some liberals and leftists on college campuses have supported speech restrictions in cases involving racist, sexist, and homophobic remarks, while most campus conservatives have embraced the liberal position on free speech. In the selections in Issue 12, liberal Nat Hentoff expresses amazement that any liberal could support speech restrictions, while Stanley Fish—whose views are hard to classify but are usually taken to be progressive liberal—is quite ready to justify restrictions on "hate speech."

Obviously one's position on the issues in this book will be affected by circumstances. However, we would like to think that the essays in this book are durable enough to last through several seasons of events and controversies. We can be certain that the issues will survive. The search for coherence and consistency in the use of political labels underlines the options open to us and reveals their consequences. The result must be more mature judgments about what is best for America. That, of course, is the ultimate aim of public debate and decision-making, and it transcends all labels and categories.

UPI/BETTMANN

PART 1

Democracy and the American Political Process

Democracy is derived from two Greek words, dēmos and kratia, and means "people's rule." The issue today is whether or not the political realities of America conform to the ideal of people's rule. Are the people really running the country? Some contend that big business runs the economy and controls the political agenda. Is that a fair charge, or is it based on simplistic premises? Political party reformers have tried to encourage greater participation by voters, but critics charge that well-intentioned reforms have weakened the parties. Another issue generating controversy is the power of pressure groups, particularly that of political action committees (PACs). Do these groups undermine people's rule, or do they help to make democracy work? Finally, in this section, we address the issue of the news media's role in the governmental process.

Is American Government Dominated by Big Business?

Has Party Reform Succeeded?

Do Political Action Committees Undermine Democracy?

Do the News Media Have a Liberal Bias?

1

ISSUE 1

Is American Government Dominated by Big Business?

YES: Thomas Byrne Edsall, from *The New Politics of Inequality: How Political Power Shapes Economic Policy* (W. W. Norton, 1984)

NO: David Vogel, from *Fluctuating Fortunes: The Political Power of Business in America* (Basic Books, 1989)

ISSUE SUMMARY

YES: Political reporter Thomas Byrne Edsall argues that the power of big business is stronger than ever because of the increasing political sophistication of big business coupled with the breakdown of political parties.
NO: Professor of business administration David Vogel contends that the power of business fluctuates with the times and is currently being kept in check by other forces in U.S. society.

Since the framing of the U.S. Constitution in 1787, there have been periodic charges that America is unduly influenced by wealthy financial interests. Richard Henry Lee, a signer of the Declaration of Independence, spoke for many Anti-Federalists, those who opposed ratification of the Constitution, when he warned that the proposed charter shifted power away from the people and into the hands of the "aristocrats" and "moneyites," those who "avariciously grasp at all power and property." Before the Civil War, Jacksonian Democrats denounced the eastern merchants and bankers who, they charged, were usurping the power of the people. After the Civil War, a number of radical parties and movements revived this theme of antielitism. The ferment—which was brought about by the rise of industrial monopolies, government corruption, and economic hardship for western farmers—culminated in the founding of the People's party at the beginning of the 1890s. The Populists, as they were more commonly called, wanted economic and political reforms aimed at transferring power away from the rich and back to "the plain people."

By the early 1900s the People's party had disintegrated, but many writers and activists have continued to echo the Populists' central thesis: that the U.S. democratic political system is in fact dominated by business elites. Wisconsin senator Robert La Follette, who ran for president in 1924 on his own Progressive ticket, charged that the United States had been taken over by a band of "daring unscrupulous men" who had "plotted in violation of the common law, the criminal statutes, and against public right." Unless radical reforms are enacted, he warned, America would soon see "the end of democracy." In the 1930s, another U.S. senator, Gerald Nye, conducted a series of investigations that purported to show that the nation had been manipulated into its involvement in World War I by a conspiracy of "munition-makers." In the 1950s, sociologist C. Wright Mills argued that all the important national decisions in America were made by a "power elite" of generals, corporate chiefs, and high administration officials. There were many differences among such critics, but they all agreed that American public policy is largely dominated by the interests of big business.

The thesis, however, has not gone unchallenged. During the 1950s and the early 1960s, many social scientists subscribed to the *pluralist* view of America. Pluralists admit that there are many influential elites in our society, and that is precisely their point: Because America contains so many groups, the pluralists argue, each group has a tendency to counterbalance the power of the others. Labor groups are often opposed to business groups; conservative interests challenge liberal interests, and vice versa; organized civil libertarians sometimes fight with groups that seek government-imposed bans on pornography or groups that demand tougher criminal laws. No single group can dominate the political system or have a monopoly on power in our pluralist system. Pluralists were not comfortable with calling America a *democracy*, a word that has become invested with emotional connotations, but they did think that rule in America emanates from many centers, so they favored the word *polyarchy* (literally, "rule by many") to describe the operation of the American system.

Pluralism still has its advocates, but since the end of the 1960s the thesis that America is dominated by business elites has acquired new life. Its current advocates, including some former pluralists, agree that corporate influence is now so strong in America that its political and social institutions have lost whatever pluralism they once had. This is the argument advanced by Thomas Byrne Edsall in the following selection. Opposing this view is David Vogel, who contends that the political clout of business has fluctuated in recent times and is now fragmented, defensive, and often quite weak.

YES

Thomas Byrne Edsall

THE NEW POLITICS OF INEQUALITY

In the United States in recent years there has been a significant erosion of the power of those on the bottom half of the economic spectrum, an erosion of the power not only of the poor but of those in the working and middle classes. At the same time, there has been a sharp increase in the power of economic elites, of those who fall in the top 15 percent of the income distribution.

This transfer of power has coincided with an economic crisis: productivity growth, which for the three decades following the Second World War had been the source of a continuing rise in the standard of living, slowed to zero by the end of the 1970s; the median family income, which had doubled in real, uninflated dollars from 1950 to 1973, declined during the next ten years, paralleling a decline in the average factory worker's weekly earnings; and inflation and unemployment, instead of acting as counterbalancing forces, rose simultaneously.

This mounting economic crisis provided an opportunity for newly ascendant representatives of the interests of the business community and of the affluent to win approval of a sea change in economic policy. For nearly fifty years, since the formation of the New Deal coalition in the 1930s, there had been a sustained base of support for both social spending programs and a tax system that modestly redistributed income and restricted the concentration of wealth in the hands of the few. These deeply rooted liberal traditions were abandoned during the late 1970s in favor of policies calling for a major reduction of the tax burden on income derived from capital, and for reductions in domestic spending programs directed toward the poor and the working poor. These shifts in tax and spending policies, in combination with inflation, have had enormous distributional consequences, resulting, for the period from 1980 through 1984, in losses for every income group except the very affluent.

Although the election of Ronald Reagan to the presidency has been the catalyst for much of this alteration of policy, its roots run far deeper. The delicate balance of power between elites and larger groups seeking represen-

From Thomas Byrne Edsall, *The New Politics of Inequality: How Political Power Shapes Economic Policy* (W. W. Norton, 1984). Copyright © 1984 by W. W. Norton & Company, Inc. Reprinted by permission. Notes omitted.

tation in the political process has been changing in almost all quarters, including the Democratic party, the Republican party, the business lobbying community, organized labor, and the intellectual establishment. These changes have been both accelerated and exacerbated throughout the entire electorate by increasingly class-skewed voting patterns. In each of these areas, the changes are resulting in a diminution of the representation of the majority in the development of economic policy, and in the growing leverage of the well-to-do.

Underlying this shift in the balance of political power among economic groups is a changed economic environment that has forced fundamental revisions in political strategies for both political parties. The economic crisis of the past decade has cut to the heart of a tradition in American politics, particularly in Democratic politics, playing havoc with that party's tradition of capitalizing on a growing and thriving economy in order to finance a continuing expansion of benefits for those toward the bottom of the income distribution. Past economic growth had provided the federal government with a fiscal dividend in additional tax revenues with which to finance growth in such broad-based programs as Social Security and Medicare, while simultaneously maintaining popular support, as all wage earners benefited from rising real incomes.

Altered economic circumstances have turned politics into what Lester Thurow has termed a zero-sum process. The balance of power in the competition for the benefits of government has shifted increasingly in favor of those in the top third of the income distribution. In many respects these shifts have pushed the national debate well to the right of its locus ten or twenty years ago. In 1964, the Republican presidential nominee, Senator Barry Goldwater, was decisively defeated while advocating a major reduction in domestic federal spending and a sharp increase in military spending; sixteen years later, Ronald Reagan, one of Goldwater's most ardent supporters, was elected to the presidency on a platform remarkably similar to Goldwater's and succeeded in persuading Congress, including a Democratic House of Representatives, to act into law legislation that would have been politically inconceivable at any time during the previous fifty years.

The roots of this shift to the right are by now deeply imbedded in the political system, severely restricting the scope of choices available to either party, particularly to the Democratic party. Just as the shift to the left in public policy in the early 1960s resulted from fundamental alterations in the balance of power—ranging from rapid postwar economic growth, to the cohesiveness of the liberal-labor coalition, to the political vitality of the civil rights movement—the shift to the right over the past decade has resulted from complex, systemic alterations in the terms of the political and economic debate and in the power of those participating in the debate.

The election of a Democrat to the White House would inevitably slow the conservative initiative; forces pushing the national agenda to the right, however, will retain what amounts to veto power both over the scope of issues admitted to national political discourse and over congressional legislation likely to achieve victory. These conservative forces, as this book will explore, are not only within the Republican party, the right-wing ideological groups, and the business community but within the Democratic party itself. Not only are these forces present in all major elements of the political system; even with economic recovery, lowered inflation, declining unemployment, and growth in the gross national product, the shape of economic and political pressures on the electorate at large would appear to preclude, for at least the near future, the emergence of a consensus in support of a revived liberal agenda. . . .

During the 1970s, the political wing of the nation's corporate sector staged one of the most remarkable campaigns in the pursuit of political power in recent history. By the late 1970s and the early 1980s, business, and Washington's corporate lobbying community in particular, had gained a level of influence and leverage approaching that of the boom days of the 1920s. What made the acquisition of power in the 1970s remarkable was that business achieved its goals without any broad public-political mandate such as that of the 1920s, when probusiness values were affirmed in the elections of 1920, 1924, and 1928. Rather, business in the 1970s developed the ability to dominate the legislative process under adverse, if not hostile, circumstances. Corporate leaders had been closely associated with Watergate and its related scandals, and a reform-minded Democratic party with strong ties to the consumer and environmental movements had gained increasingly large majorities in Congress.

Despite these devastating odds, the political stature of business rose steadily from the early 1970s, one of its lowest points in the nation's history, until, by the end of the decade, the business community had achieved virtual dominance of the legislative process in Congress. The rise of the corporate sector is a case study in the ability of an economic elite to gain power by capitalizing on changes in the political system. In the case of the Democratic party, the shift in the balance of power toward the affluent, the erosion of the labor union movement, and the vastly increased importance of money in campaigns all combined to make Democratic politicians more vulnerable to pressures from the right. In the case of the Republican party, a de facto alliance has emerged between the GOP and much of the business community, a relationship paralleling the ties between the Democratic party and labor but lacking the inherent conflicts characteristic of that liaison. The political ascendancy of the business community, furthermore, has coincided with a sustained and largely successful attack upon organized labor, an attack conducted both in private-sector union representation fights and in legislative battles on Capitol Hill.

In 1978, in the midst of the corporate political revival, R. Heath Larry, president of the National Association of Manufacturers, contended that the single most important factor behind the resurgence of business was "the decline in the role of the party, yielding a new spirit of independence among congressmen—independent of each other, of the president, of the party caucus." Larry's perception of the role of the decline in political parties in the revival of the stature of business was accurate, but his contention that this decline produced increased independence is wrong. In fact, the collapse of political parties and of traditional political organizations, especially those at the local level that formerly had the power to assure or to deny reelection, has been a key factor in a network of forces and developments undermining the independence of politicians and augmenting the strength of the business community.

WEAKENING OF PARTIES

The decline of political organizations, rather than increasing independence, has eliminated a fundamental base of support for those elected to public office, functioning to intensify the elective anxieties of public officials, particularly members of the House and Senate. For a member of Congress, a healthy local political organization traditionally both provided a secure source of backing at election time and served as a conduit, transmitting to the congressman or senator spending the majority of his or her time in Washington the assessment of the local party leadership of public opinion—or the lack of it—on a cross-section of issues. Without this source of information, and without the security provided by the support of a strong local political organization, a House representative or senator becomes highly vulnerable, not only to incessant reelection anxiety but to orchestrated public pressure. Many of the toughest battles in Congress in recent years—legislation to create a consumer protection agency; labor law reform; regulation of used-car dealers and funeral directors; major tax legislation, including the $749 billion tax reduction in 1981, and the 1983 struggle over legislation mandating 10 percent withholding on interest and dividend income—have been fought on this terrain: the organized creation of seemingly spontaneous outpourings of public opinion for or against specific legislative proposals, voiced through coordinated letter writing, telegram, and telephone campaigns—all deluging members of Congress.

This form of lobbying, although centralized, is known as "grass-roots lobbying" and has always been a weapon in the political arsenal, becoming, during the late 1960s and early 1970s, an essential mechanism in strategies to influence congressional decisions in the hands of the environmental movements and of such organizations as Common Cause and Ralph Nader's Congress Watch, organizations that coordinated citizens' grass-roots lobbying campaigns in the successful pressuring of Congress to enact political reforms, health and safety legislation, consumer protection legislation, and environmental conservation legislation. A similar but substantially different form of lobbying has characterized congressional procedures since the days of George Washington: pressure on individual members from local contractors, unions, bankers, chambers of commerce, and developers, to obtain defense, road, dam, and other pork-barrel benefits from the federal government. Pork-barrel lobbying and grass-roots lobbying differ, however, in that pork-barrel lobbying traditionally seeks specific benefits for a congressman's district or state—jobs, buildings, construction products, contract awards—while grass-roots lobbying is an attempt to seek to influence congressional votes on legislation of national importance, legislation that is seen or thought to transcend parochial boundaries.

In the mid-1970s, key leaders of the nation's corporate and trade association network perceived that their institutions and structures were far better suited to grass-roots lobbying than the liberal-reform groups that seemed to have a corner on these tactics. The interest of the constituencies of the liberal-reform organizations in the political process is fluid, rising when issues have high visibility—such as President Nixon's highly controversial Supreme Court nomination of G. Harrold Carswell, the southern judge with a segregationist background whose appointment was opposed by groups ranging from the American Bar Association to the NAACP; or the post-Watergate campaign to enact election reform—and falling when issues are no longer unambiguous.

In contrast, the nation's corporate and trade association communities have a sustained economic interest in the outcome of the legislative and elective process, day in and day out. The basic function of Washington's corporate and trade association lobbying community, a network of well over 150,000 professionals, is not only the defeat or passage of major bills but, in a much more complex process, the shaping of the precise language of legislation and of the committee reports that accompany legislation. This process involves the addition, deletion, and alteration of individual words, paragraphs, and sections of bills as they wend their way from House committee, to House floor, to Senate committee, to the full Senate and then to a House-Senate conference committee. One seemingly minor provision in the 1982 tax bill retroactively legalized corporate sales of investment tax credits from January 1, 1981, to October 20, 1981. This provision, which occupied nine lines out of a 465-page report, in fact sanctioned a controversial $20 million tax deal between Chris Craft Corp. and International Harvester.

Economically driven, sustained interest in the legislative process does not stop with the passage or defeat of legislation. A battle lost on legislation to create a program can be partially redeemed when entirely separate legislation setting the dollar appropriation for the program is later taken up by Congress. An agency empowered to enforce workplace health and safety regulation, without money for an inspection staff, in effect has little or no power. Finally, the way in which a law mandating certain general health and safety requirements will be specifically applied on the production line and on the office floor is determined by the detailed rules and regulations written in the executive branch, and subject in turn to pressure and counterpressure from the White House, Congress, the industry, and the enforcing agency itself.

Just as important as the sustained interest of business in all aspects of the legislative process is the compatibility of the structure of corporations and trade associations with the mechanics of orchestrated grass-roots lobbying. Such diverse major United States companies as General Motors, American Express, Caterpillar Tractor, PepsiCo, Westinghouse Electric Corp., Standard Oil Co. of Ohio, U.S. Steel, Raytheon Company, Squibb Corp., American Airlines, and Allied Chemical Corp. each have networks of plants, suppliers, retailer outlets, subcontractors, salesmen, and distributors in every congressional district in the nation, as well as thousands of dispersed stockholders.

The scope of this leverage was demonstrated during the 1979 debate over legislation to provide federal loan guarantees to the Chrysler Corporation. In the attempt to convince conservative Congressman Elwood R. Hillis, Republican of the Fifth District of Indiana, to vote for the legislation, Chrysler produced for Hillis, as it did for all other members of Congress, a list of all Chrysler suppliers in his district. The list runs to three and a quarter single-spaced pages and includes the names of 436 companies in Hillis's district whose sales to Chrysler totaled $29.52 million, ranging from $6.67 million from the GTR Fiberglass Products Company in Marion to $90 from Leck's Radiator Repair Shop in Hillis's home town of Kokomo. . . .

THE CORPORATE MOBILIZATION

The revival of the political power of business began in 1973 and 1974, initiated in large part by a small group of Washington's most influential corporate lobbyists who began to meet privately to discuss the darkening storm clouds everywhere on the political horizon. Watergate had not only damaged the Republican party, but the taint of corruption had sharply altered the public perception of corporate America. The secret financing for President Nixon's Committee to Re-elect the President in 1972; the case for what was known as the "Townhouse Operation"; channeling unreported money to Republican House and Senate candidates in 1970; the bribes to foreign officials in charge of government contracts—all had come from business executives and from corporate treasuries. Furthermore, American corporations providing weaponry and material for the Vietnam War, ranging from Dow Chemical to the Raytheon Company, had been targeted with extensive and effective negative publicity by the anti-war movement. Public confidence in the chief executives of major corporations fell like a stone from the mid-1960s to the mid-1970s. The percentage of the public describing themselves as having a great deal of confidence in corporate leaders dropped from 51 percent in the 1966–67 period to an average of 20 percent in the 1974–76 period. The rate of decline in confidence was sharper than for any other major institution in the United States, public or private, including the executive branch, the press,

organized labor, and educators—excepting only Congress, which fell from a favorability rating of 42 percent to 20 percent during the same period.

At the same time, Watergate had revived the Democratic party, particularly that wing of the Democratic party supporting the environmental and consumer movements. After losing the 1972 presidential election under the leadership of George S. McGovern, by a 61–39 margin and by 17.9 million votes, the Democrats in 1974 would gain forty-nine House seats and five Senate seats. Before these Democratic gains, and despite the presence of a Republican in the White House, Congress by 1974 had already enacted into law the Environmental Protection Agency (1970), the Occupational Safety and Health Administration (1970), the Consumer Product Safety Commission (1972), the National Traffic Safety Commission (1970), the Mine Safety and Health Administration (1973), increased food stamp funding (1970), a 20 percent Social Security increase (1974), Supplemental Security Income (1972), and the Employee Retirement Income Security Act.

"The danger had suddenly escalated," Bryce Harlow, senior Washington representative for Procter & Gamble and one of the most respected members of the old-line corporate lobbying community, commented later. "We had to prevent business from being rolled up and put in the trash can by that Congress," he said, referring to the Ninety-fourth Congress elected in 1974. The mobilization of business in this critical period, the early and mid-1970s, began at the top. Harlow worked most actively with the elite Washington lobbyists, men like William Whyte of the United States Steel Corporation; Albert D. Bourland, Jr., of General Motors; Don A. Goodall of American Cyanamid Company; and Wayne H. Smithey of Ford Motor Co. These men were an integral part of the Washington establishment, not only representing some of the largest American corporations but conducting their business in such exclusive downtown facilities as the Metropolitan and University clubs. Their roots, however, were in a style of lobbying that no longer worked on Capitol Hill—the cultivation, largely behind closed doors, of a few key holders of power: committee chairmen who could determine with the tap of a gavel or a nod to the staff the content of legislation; cabinet secretaries who could be persuaded over lunch that their employees were pressing a regulatory mandate with too much vigor; and key White House aides whose political currency was the provision of favors for the influential.

By the mid-1970s, however, the decline of party loyalties, congressional reforms weakening the power of committee chairmen, and the diffusion of power to junior members of Congress forced a major alteration in lobbying strategies. "As long as you could go and get the cooperation of the committee chairman and the ranking members, and maybe a few others, you didn't have to have the vast network we are talking about now," Smithey noted. Smithey's reference to a "vast network" describes both the development of grass-roots lobbying as a legislative tactic and a much more pervasive effort to set the terms of the legislative debate in the nation's capital. Not only have the targets of lobbyists changed over the past generation, but the technology of public opinion molding has undergone changes of unprecedented magnitude, producing computerized direct-mail communications in which much of the nation's adult population has been broken down into demographic and "psychographic" profiles. A group or institution seeking to mobilize support or opposition on any issue can seek out ready-made lists of allies in the general public from computer specialists who can then communicate almost instantaneously with any selected constituency via letters produced on high-speed laser printers. If lobbying during the 1950s, in the words of one of the most eminent Washington lobbyists, Charles E. Walker, consisted of personal access to four natives of Texas—President Dwight Eisenhower, House Speaker Sam Rayburn, Senate Majority Leader Lyndon Baines Johnson, and Treasury Secretary Robert Anderson—it currently involves minimally the ability to recognize the interests of 535 members of the House and Senate, an acute sensitivity to potential malleability in public opinion, the cultivation of both print and electronic media, the use of sophisticated technologies both to create and to convey an impression of public sentiment, and the marshaling on Capitol Hill and across the country of legions of newly enlisted corporate personnel.

The effort on the part of the business community to shape the legislative debate has taken place on a number of fronts, one of the most important of which has been the politicization of employees and stockholders. Atlantic Richfield (Arco), for example, spends about $1 million annually on a program in which 15,000 employees are members of politically active local committees. In addition, the nearly 80,000 Arco stockholders, suppliers, and distributors are on a mailing list for company newsletters and publications focusing on political and public policy issues. W. Dean Cannon, Jr., executive vice-president of the California Savings and Loan League, suggested in 1978 to savings and loan firms that they give employees "specific assignments to work in politics" and that an employee's raises "might well be tied directly to his involvement in the political assignment you have given him." During the debate over the 1978 tax bill, officials of a single, mid-sized firm, the Barry Wright Corporation in Watertown, Mass, generated 3,800 letters from its stockholders to members of Congress in favor of a reduction in capital gains taxation.

The politicization of management-level employees is a critical element in achieving effective grass-roots lobbying: an employee who sees a direct economic interest in the outcome of legislative battles will be a far more effective and persistent advocate than an employee who is acting in response only to orders or implied orders from superiors. Stockholders, in turn, represent an ideal target for political mobilization. Only 15 percent of American citizens hold stock, according to liberal estimates by the Securities Industry Association, and those who do are, on average, in the upper-income brackets. They have little or no direct interest in the expansion or maintenance of domestic spending programs, although they have considerable interest in lowering tax rates. In this sense, the economic interests of affluent individuals and of corporations are sharply intertwined. Both stockholders and corporations, for example, share a direct interest in either lowering the capital gains rate or shortening the minimum holding period to qualify for the more favorable capital gains rate. . . .

An equally, if not more, effective use of business money in altering the terms of

the policy debate has been in the total or partial financing of such private institutions engaged in research and scholarship as the American Enterprise Institute; the Heritage Foundation; the Hoover Institution on War, Revolution and Peace; the National Bureau of Economic Research; the Center for the Study of American Business at Washington University in St.Louis, and the American Council for Capital Formation. In a decade during which economic stagnation contributed to the undermining of the intellectual basis of traditional Democratic economic and political strategies, these organizations, among others, have functioned to lay the scholarly and theoretical groundwork for a major shift in public policy favoring business and the higher-bracket taxpayers. . . .

BUSINESS AND ECONOMIC POLICY

The rising political power of business has been associated with the general increase in the number of political action committees [PACs] and with the growing volume of money channeled through them. This line of thinking, in turn, has given rise to charges that Congress, overwhelmed by the flow of cash from the PACs, has become the puppet of special interests, a forum in which every organized group, from doctors to dairymen, can, in return for campaign contributions, receive special antitrust exemption from competition or from taxpayer-financed price supports, or special insulation from the federal regulatory process. The most vocal critic of the system has been Common Cause, the principal reform lobby. "Our system of representative government is under siege because of the destructive role that political action committees or PACs are now playing in our political process," Fred Wertheimer, president of Common Cause, declared in 1983. . . .

These analyses, while both accurate and timely, fail to take into account a number of less frequently reported factors adding to the complexity and subtlety of the current political situation on Capitol Hill. For one, Common Cause and the press have become increasingly effective watchdogs over the legislative process, preventing many of the attempts by special-interest groups to slip through favorable legislation. More important, however, while these analyses, particularly [New Yorker correspondent Elizabeth] Drew's detailed description of the overwhelming concern with fundraising in Congress, accurately portray an essential element of the political process, neither recognizes what has been a major ideological shift in Congress. Business has played a key role in this shift, using not just PAC contributions but increasingly sophisticated grass-roots lobbying mechanisms, the financing of a sympathetic intellectual community, and the expenditure of somewhere in the neighborhood of $1 billion annually on institutional advertising.

This ideological shift in the nation's capital has been pervasive, altering basic tax, spending, and regulatory policies and moving both political parties well to the right over the past decade. Of the various elites that have gained strength in recent years, business has been among the most effective. Not only has it gained from highly favorable tax treatment and from a major reduction in regulation, but government action has increased the bargaining leverage of management in its relations with organized labor. This increased leverage grows out of reductions in unemployment compensation and out of the elimination of the public service job programs, and through the appointment of promanagement officials at such key agencies as the Occupational Safety and Health Administration and at the National Labor Relations Board. The end result is a labor movement that has lost much of its clout at the negotiating table and in the polling booth. . . .

THE WAGES OF INEQUALITY

In the late 1970s, a set of political and intellectual forces began to converge and to gain momentum, joining together in a direction that substantially altered economic policy in the United States. While the forces involved were by no means in agreement as to the specific goals to be achieved, they shared an interest in seeking to change the basic assumptions that have dominated taxation and spending policies in the United States. For nearly fifty years, since the administration of Franklin Delano Roosevelt, two dominant themes of taxation and spending policy have been equity and the moderate redistribution of income. The forces gaining ascendancy in the late 1970s sought to replace such liberal goals with a drive to slow the rate of growth in federal spending in order to increase the availability of money for private capital formation; with a reduction of corporate and individual tax rates, particularly of those rates in the top brackets, in order to provide predicted incentives for work, savings, and investment; and with the paring down of government regulation to facilitate a more productive marketplace. In short, the goal became to influence government policy so as to supplant, in an economic sense, equity with efficiency.

The inherent contradictions between equity, efficiency, redistribution, and investment go to the heart of the conflict in developing economic policy in advanced capitalist democracies. The political resolution of such contradictions determines the balance between competing claims on government: that is, whether government is granted the authority to intervene in the private marketplace in order to correct or to modify inequities inherent in the market system, through a progressive tax rate schedule and through the payment of benefits to the poor; whether it is the role of government to subsidize, encourage, and direct marketplace forces with tax incentives and loan subsidies targeted toward specific industries; or whether government should reduce to a minimum its role in the economy, remaining as remote from and as disengaged as possible from the private sector.

The period from 1977 through the first months of 1982, however, marked a rare moment in American history, when the disparate forces supporting the conservative coalition on these basic economic questions all simultaneously became politically ascendant. Forces coalescing on the political right included a politically revitalized business community; increasing sophistication and centrality among leaders of the ideological new right; the sudden explosion of wealth in the domestic oil community following the 1973 OPEC embargo; the emergence within the academic community and within the major economic research institutions of proponents of tax cuts and of sharp reductions in the tax rate on capital income; a Republican party whose financial resources were exponentially increased by computerized direct-mail and other new political technologies, providing of-

ten decisive access to television, to polling, and to highly sophisticated voter targeting tactics; and the rise of politically conservative evangelical Christian organizations. The emergence of these forces coincided with a series of developments and trends giving conservatism new strength. The business and the new, or ideological, right-wing communities developed a shared interest in the candidates of the Republican party, as such organizations as the Chamber of Commerce and the National Conservative Political Action Committee became de facto arms of the GOP. Voting patterns increased the class bias of voter turnout, as the affluent became a stronger force both within the electorate as a whole and within the Republican party.

Conversely, the forces making up the liberal coalition, represented in large part by major segments of the Democratic party—organized labor, civil rights and civil liberties organizations, political reformers, environmental groups, and feminists—were experiencing increasing disunity. The power of organized labor, essential to any coalition of the left, had been steadily declining. Even more damaging was the emergence of growing inflation and unemployment, a continued decline in the rate of productivity growth, and a drop in the take-home pay of the average worker. This economic deterioration not only splintered the fragile coalition of Democrats that had supported policies of equity and redistribution over the previous forty years but created a growing belief that the nation was caught in an economic crisis that the Democratic party could not resolve, a belief compounded by Democratic disarray.

It was this combination of trends, all favoring the right, that provided the opportunity for a major alteration in public policy. The election in 1980 of Ronald Reagan to the presidency and the take-over of the Senate by the Republican party created the political opportunity for this fundamental realignment, but the groundwork had already been care-fully laid. This groundwork included an increasingly sophisticated political strat-egy capitalizing on the conflicts within the fragile Democratic majority, the care-ful nurturing and financing of intel-lectual support both in academia and within a growing network of think tanks financed by corporations and conserva-tive foundations, and the advance prepa-ration of specific legislative proposals, particularly of tax legislation. . . .

The power shift that produced the fundamental policy realignment of the past decade did not result from a conser-vative or Republican realignment of the voters; nor did it produce such a realign-ment after the tax and spending legisla-tion of 1981 was enacted. Rather, these policy changes have grown out of perva-sive distortions in this country's demo-cratic political process. These distortions have created a system of political deci-sion making in which fundamental is-sues—the distribution of the tax burden, the degree to which the government sanctions the accumulation of wealth, the role of federal regulation, the level of publicly tolerated poverty, and the rela-tive strength of labor and management —are resolved by an increasingly unre-presentative economic elite. To a large extent, these changes have turned the Republican party, in terms of the public policies it advocates, into a party of the elite. For the Democratic party, the politi-cal changes of the past decade have dis-torted the distribution of power and weakened the capacity of the party to represent the interests of its numerous less affluent constituents. Even if the Democrats are victorious in capturing the presidency, there is no evidence that the Democratic party is in any way pre-pared to set an agenda economically ben-efiting its core constituents in the same way that the Republican-conservative movement has been able to define the political debate in recent years to the advantage of its most loyal supporters. As long as the balance of political power remains so heavily weighted toward those with economic power, national economic policy will remain distorted, regardless of which party is in control of the federal government.

NO

David Vogel

FLUCTUATING FORTUNES

THE IMPORTANCE OF TIME

The purpose of this book is not to continue the debate between those who argue that the political position of business is privileged and those who assert that it is not. It is rather to move us beyond it. I offer a new way of looking at the political power of business in contemporary American politics. My central argument is that both perspectives are flawed because they mistakenly assume that the power of business is relatively stable. The pluralists contend that the political power of business is usually counter-vailed by other interest groups, while the critics of pluralism assert that it rarely is. Both contentions are incomplete. The political power of business can and does vary. Furthermore, these variations follow a discernible pattern, which can in turn be explained.

The power of business in American national politics has changed substantially since 1960. The political position of business was relatively secure during the first half of the 1960s, declined significantly between the mid-1960s and mid-1970s, increased between the mid-1970s and early 1980s, and has since slightly eroded. These changes are not unprecedented: the political power of significant segments of American business also declined during both the Progressive Era and the New Deal. This book describes and explains the third major set of fluctuations in the political fortunes of business since the turn of the century.

There is no need to choose between the depictions of business power offered by the pluralists and their critics. The accuracy of each perspective depends on the period in which one is interested. In a number of respects, the political position of business in America could be accurately charac-terized as "privileged" during the 1950s and through the first half of the 1960s. Few issues appeared on the political agenda that threatened business prerogatives, and business exercised virtual power over the resolution of those few issues that did. Correspondingly, American politics between the mid-1960s and mid-1970s more closely resembled the pluralists' description of interest-group competition. The power of business was challenged by both the public-interest movement and organized labor, while public confidence in business dropped dramatically; between 1968 and 1977, the percentage of Americans who believed that "business tries to strike a fair balance between profits and the interests of the public" declined from 70 percent to 15 percent. . . .

It is possible to interpret the ten-year period during which business found itself on the political and ideological defensive as a brief interlude in a political system normally characterized by business dominance. Similarly, the relative resurgence of the influence of business during the next fifteen years, rather than representing a return to the status quo, could instead be viewed as a temporary phenomenon—one shortly to be followed by a backlash from nonbusiness constituencies. My position is that neither period constitutes the norm. While it is true that during this century the years when business has been relatively powerful have been more numerous than those when it has not, it does not necessarily follow that the former state of affairs is the normal one. Rather, as in the case of the business cycle, each "phase" is temporary. Which state of affairs is preferable I leave to the readers' judgment.

POLITICAL POWER AND ECONOMIC CONDITIONS

Because both the pluralists and their critics tend to ignore the extent to which the political influence of business changes over time, they have also overlooked the relationship between political develop-ments and changing economic conditions. . . . These omissions are crucial. The political influence of business has been significantly affected by the long-term performance of the American economy. Over the last three decades, the two have been inversely related. Paradoxically, business has tended to lose political influence when the economy was performing relatively well and has become more influential when the performance of the economy deteriorated.

The relative political power of business is *not* a function of the business cycle. Otherwise, the political power of business would be more unstable than it actually has been. Rather, what *is* critical is the public's perception of the long-term strength of the American economy. The unprecedented increases in both government regulation of corporate social performance and in social-welfare expenditures from the mid-1960s through the early 1970s was made possible by the equally unprecedented economic growth rates of the 1960s. The economy grew at an average rate of 4.5 percent between 1961 and 1968, and between 1965 and 1969 the after-tax rate of return of nonfinancial corporations averaged 9 percent—its highest level since the Second World War. As a result, significant segments of the American middle class began to take both their own prosperity and the success of business for granted. They believed that business could afford to rebuild the inner cities, hire the chronically unemployed, make safer products, clean up air and water pollution, provide all Americans with a healthy and safe working environment and, at the same time, still further improve their own living standards. Politicians from both parties competed with each other to propose policies based on this assumption.

However, during the second half of the 1970s, the American public's perception of the American economy and the continued profitability of the business corporation began to change. The recession of 1974–75 was not simply another downturn in the business cycle. It marked a major discontinuity in the postwar development of American capitalism: rates of economic growth, investment, growth in productivity, and growth in wages and family incomes were all significantly lower in the decade after 1973 than they had been during the preceding one. Between 1975 and 1978, corporate profit rates averaged 5.9 percent, their lowest level since the Second World War. Persistent double-digit inflation, declining real wages and stagnant family income, increased dependence on imported oil, and a dramatic growth in imports in highly visible sectors of the American economy all made the American business corporation, and consequently America itself, suddenly appear economically vulnerable. General Motors, the epitome of arrogant and omnipotent big business during the 1960s, now found itself pleading for government to protect it from Japanese imports; Chrysler, the nation's ninth largest corporation, was on the verge of bankruptcy.

Consequently, the political and social climate became transformed. . . . "Baby boomers," who had played a critical role in organizing and supporting the public-interest movement during the first half of the 1970s, discovered "bracket creep" and became preoccupied with finding well-paying jobs in the private sector or in starting their own companies. The "new class" of college-educated professionals, now worried about their own economic prospects, became more sympathetic to the demands of business to reduce taxes, to slow down the growth of government spending and regulation, and to weaken the power of unions. As a result, the political pendulum shifted. The political position of business once again became relatively privileged: the second half of the 1970s and the early 1980s witnessed a substantial increase in the ability of business to define the terms of political debate and affect governmental decisions.

The economy performed relatively well after 1982. And this in part explains why the political influence of business did not continue to increase throughout the decade: the Reagan administration was unable to deliver on its promises to provide business with significant regulatory relief, and corporate taxes were increased in both 1982 and 1986. But both the rate at which new regulations have been imposed on business and the growth in social welfare expenditures were far less during the 1980s than they were during the 1960s. Politicians from both parties were also more willing to support increased government assistance to industry than they were fifteen years earlier. And these developments in turn can be attributed to the public's continued concern about the apparent ability of American industry to compete successfully in the global economy—particularly vis-à-vis Japanese firms. A poll taken in January 1987 reported that "88 percent of all Americans say that they are concerned that this country is losing its competitive edge and cannot remain the world's pre-eminent economic power." The globalization of the American economy may have created severe economic difficulties for substantial segments of American business, but politically it has been something of a boon.

BUSINESS AND THE POLITICAL SYSTEM

Both pluralists and their critics have also paid insufficient attention to the relationship between the political influence and strategies of business and the changing structure of American politics. Between the mid-1960s and mid-1970s, the American political system changed substantially. One reason why business suffered so many political defeats during this period is that business lobbyists failed to appreciate the extent to which public policy was no longer being made in private negotiations between Washington insiders and a handful of strategically placed representatives and senators. Power within Congress had become more decentralized, the number of interest groups represented in Washington had increased, the role of the media in defining the political agenda and the terms of political debate had expanded, the importance of political parties had declined, and the courts had begun to play a much more active role in making regulatory policy. In a remarkably short period of time, consumer and environmental organizations were able to take advantage of these changes to move from a peripheral position in American politics to become active and effective participants in the making of public policies in the nation's capital.

It took business about seven years to rediscover how to win in Washington. Significantly, when business did become more politically active, it did so in ways that recognized how fundamentally the American political system had changed: it proceeded to imitate the political strategies that had previously been responsible for so many of its defeats. The sponsorship of research studies to influence elite opinion, the attention to the media as a way of changing public attitudes, the development of techniques of grass-roots organizing to mobilize supporters in congressional districts, and the use of ad hoc coalitions to maximize political influence had all been successfully employed, and in some cases even developed, by the public-interest movement. Campaign finance reform, by legalizing the formation of political action committees (PACs), opened another path for business participation in politics. Just as the decentralization of power within Congress during the second half of the 1960s and early 1970s helped reduce the political influence of business, the dramatic growth of business PACs during the second half of the 1970s helped increase it. . . .

MY APPROACH

. . . The interests of business are not monolithic: firms can use politics either to compete with each other or advance their collective interests. Among the most important factors affecting the relative political influence of business since the early 1960s has been the extent to which firms of different sizes and in different industries have been able to work together politically. When business has been unified, its political power has often been extremely impressive. But the degree of business unity also varies over time. With the exception of a relatively brief period between 1977 and 1981, business tended to function as a "community" in name only. Particularly during the 1980s, American business lacked effective leadership. And this, in turn, enabled both politicians and nonbusiness constituencies to play off different segments of business against each other.

This book assumes that it is legitimate to generalize about the political fortunes of business. Admittedly, just as the profit rates of all firms or industries are not affected equally by variations in the business cycle, the political influence of all firms does not vary uniformly. At any given time, some firms or industries have more influence over the decisions of government than others. Nevertheless, the efforts of particular industries and firms to achieve their political objectives do not take place in isolation; they are affected by and in turn affect changes in the relative political influence of other segments of the business community. Thus, the passage of the National Traffic and Motor Vehicle Safety Act in 1966 was not simply a political defeat for the automobile industry: by revealing the political ineptness and the vulnerability of the nation's largest industrial corporation, as well as the political popularity of consumerism, it opened the floodgates for the enactment of scores of additional regulatory statutes over the next decade. Similarly, the defeat of legislation legalizing common situs picketing by the House of Representatives in 1977 was not simply an unexpected political victory for the construction industry and a demoralizing defeat for the building-trade unions: by exposing the political vulnerability of organized labor and the responsiveness of a Congress dominated by liberal Democrats to intensive and sophisticated business lobbying, it encouraged business to become much more politically aggressive.

Momentum is important in politics. Many of the business community's most important political setbacks and gains over the last two decades have come in waves. From 1969 through 1972, Congress enacted the most progressive tax bill in the postwar period, reduced the oil-depletion allowance, imposed price controls on oil, transferred the primary authority for the regulation of both pollution and occupational health and safety from the states to the federal government, established the Consumer Product Safety Commission, and banned the advertising of cigarettes from radio and television. In a comparable span of four years—1978 through 1981—Congress defeated labor-law reform, voted against the establishment of a Consumer Protection Agency, restricted the power of the Federal Trade Commission, deregulated oil prices, delayed the imposition of automobile-emission standards, reduced price controls on natural gas, and enacted two tax bills, the first of which primarily benefited the wealthy and a second which reduced corporate taxes to their lowest level since the Second World War.

It is also characteristic of periods when business finds itself on the defensive that an unusually large proportion of public policies affects relatively large segments of the business community, though not necessarily in an identical manner. Among the most distinctive features of the regulatory statutes enacted during the first half of the 1970s was precisely that they were not directed toward specific industries. Rather, they sought to change the behavior of companies in a wide variety of different industries. This made many business executives much more conscious of their common or class interests, which in turn led to both the formation and revival of political organizations that represented firms in many different industries, such as the Business Roundtable, the United States Chamber of Commerce, and the National Federation of Independent Business.

The history of government intervention is also replete with examples of industry's inability to recognize its self-interest. It is now clear that the business community seriously underestimated the economic consequences of both the Occupational Safety and Health Act and the National Environmental Policy Act. And, in retrospect, the enormous resources the energy industry devoted to the phasing out of federal price controls was ill-advised, since the subsequent decline in the price of oil would have made them obsolete in any event. A similar analysis can be made of the political strategies of other interest groups. The Campaign Reform Act of 1971, which was initiated by organized labor, legalized the use of political action committees—which in turn enhanced the ability of business to participate in the electoral process. In addition, many of the regulatory statutes and rules for which public-interest groups fought so strongly have failed to accomplish their objectives. Indeed, some appear to have made the constituencies in whose name they were enacted actually worse off. . . .

What was the impact of the Reagan administration on the political fortunes of business?

While the business community's influence on public policy during the Reagan administration fell substantially below its expectations, in one respect its relative influence did increase: throughout the 1980s, the political and economic influence of organized labor continued to decline. The cumulative effect of the administration's free trade policies, its disbanding of the air traffic controllers' union, its support for economic deregulation, its unwillingness to restrict hostile takeovers and leveraged buyouts, and its tight monetary policies, as well as

its appointments to the NLRB [National Labor Relations Board], was to weaken the bargaining power of both trade unions and unorganized workers. Real wages declined during the 1980s, and the percentage of workers belonging to unions reached a postwar low of 17.5 percent in 1987—a reduction of 6.5 percent since 1979. There were fewer work stoppages in 1987 than in any year since the Department of Labor started to keep records. Thus the Reagan administration helped business accomplish an objective for which it had been striving since the early 1970s, namely, to reduce labor's claims on its resources. The overall wage share, after increasing by a rate of 0.5 percent between 1966 and 1973, rose by only 0.1 percent between 1973 and 1979. But between 1979 and 1986, it actually declined by 0.4 percent.

The administration also dramatically slowed down the trend toward increased government regulation of corporate social conduct. While it was not able to repeal any of the statutes—or even modify many of the rules—enacted during the previous fifteen years, it certainly affected the rate at which new rules and regulations were promulgated. With a handful of exceptions, the regulatory statutes enacted during the 1980s were virtually all reauthorizations of the laws that had been initially approved during the 1970s: the scope of government controls over corporate social conduct was only marginally greater in 1988 than it had been in 1980. And while enforcement tended to be stricter during Reagan's second term than during his first, in a number of cases it still was less strict than it had been during the 1970s. On balance, the relationship between business and the new social regulatory agencies was much less contentious during the Reagan administration than it had been under its three predecessors.

Third, the 1981 Revenue Act contained the most significant cut in corporate taxes in history. While corporate taxes were increased in 1982, they were significantly lower through 1986 than they had been when Ronald Reagan took office. At the same time, because of the administration's increases in both defense spending and farm subsidies, the amount of direct government assistance to business was far greater under Reagan than it had been under his four predecessors.

On the other hand, the Reagan administration was clearly unable to fulfill its commitment to roll back the increases in government regulation of corporate social conduct that had occurred during the previous four administrations: the "regulatory time bomb" that David Stockman had committed himself to defuse was ticking as loudly in 1988 as it had in 1980. The administration may have succeeded in making significant segments of the American public more skeptical of the virtues of government intervention in a number of policy areas, but its highly visible failure to provide business with "regulatory relief" ironically helped make the government's responsibility to protect the public's health and safety a part of the national consensus. In addition, the 1986 tax reform legislation represented a major political defeat for significant segments of the business community. Finally, much to the frustration of business, the federal budget deficit continued to expand throughout the 1980s; indeed, by 1987, the national debt was more than twice as large as when President Reagan was inaugurated. Why, then, given the popularity of President Reagan, Republican control of the Senate through 1986, a much more probusiness House of Repre-

sentatives, and a politically sophisticated and active business community, was business not more politically influential during the Reagan years? . . .

When the priorities of the administration and business were similar, business did well. Thus, both corporate taxes and nondefense spending were significantly cut in 1981, and the federal government was unresponsive to the demands of organized labor and its liberal allies that the government intervene to ameliorate the impact of the 1981–82 recession, either by establishing a jobs program or restricting imports. Both the administration and the business community agreed on the need to reduce the economic power and political influence of organized labor; as a result, trade unions experienced major setbacks in both areas throughout the 1980s. And the president's desire to reduce the size of government helped reduce the rate at which new rules and regulations were enacted, and in many cases made their enforcement less strict. Finally, both placed major priority during the first half of the 1980s on reducing inflation—an objective whose achievement represented one of the administration's most important accomplishments in the area of economic policy.

But business and the Reagan administration were able to work extremely well together only in 1981. Afterward, their priorities and interests diverged. In 1982, the president decided that a tax increase was needed, and after his reelection in 1984 he committed his administration to a sweeping reform of the nation's tax laws. The result of both decisions was to increase the effective corporate tax rate. In the area of social regulation, business depended on the Reagan administration to take the initiative in proposing major statutory changes. But the administration had other priorities: in 1981 and 1982, it was more concerned about the budget and taxes, and in 1983 and 1984, it was preoccupied with preventing the Democrats from making a campaign issue out of its disastrous management of the EPA [Environmental Protection Agency]. In a sense, the administration undermined the position of business twice, initially through its zealotry in attempting to change the direction of regulatory policy and then by moving in the opposite direction to defuse the political fallout that resulted. The business community remained, on the whole, strongly committed to reducing the federal deficit. But this flew in the face of the administration's firm commitment to increase defense spending substantially and to keep individual tax rates low. As a result, the deficit continued to increase.

Many of the president's disagreements with business stemmed from a tension between his own conservative ideology and the economic interests of the private sector. The president was persuaded that a substantial increase in defense spending was necessary if the United States was to reassert its preeminence in world affairs; business, on the other hand, was more interested in reducing the size of the budget deficit. Likewise, it was precisely the president's desire to strengthen the role of the market in allocating capital that led him to support a major reduction in the granting of tax preferences to business in 1986. The administration's resistance to virtually all of the pleas of particular industries for protection from imports as well as its unwillingness to restrict hostile takeovers also stemmed from the president's free-market orientation. In many respects, Reagan was not

so much probusiness as he was antigovernment.

A second factor had to do with the performance of the economy. Although Reagan did preside over the worst recession in the postwar period shortly after he took office, the economy recovered strongly after 1982. Between 1983 and 1987, economic growth averaged 3.4 percent and inflation averaged only 3.8 percent. Equally significant, the recovery was a continual one. By the fall of 1988, the economy had begun to approach the previous postwar record for consecutive months of growth set in the 1960s. This performance was not impressive enough to rekindle the economic euphoria of the 1960s or early 1970s. Real family income increased only modestly, and the magnitude of the trade deficit created considerable public anxiety about the long-term competitiveness of American industry. Nonetheless, the success of Reaganomics was sufficient to make politicians less deferential to the demands of business. It is unlikely that Congress would have increased the size of the superfund or raised corporate taxes so significantly in 1986 had the economy not recovered from both the stagflation in the late 1970s and the recession of the early 1980s.

A third factor contributing to the limited political effectiveness of business after 1981 was its own political division. The business community was unable to sustain the degree of unity and political cohesion that had served it so well between 1977 and 1981. With only a handful of exceptions, business lobbying after 1981 was not characterized by the kind of broad coalitions that had proved so effective in the late 1970s. To be sure, corporations and trade associations continued to form alliances; indeed, more than one hundred distinctive business coalitions were established during the 1980s. But more frequently than not, these new coalitions found themselves opposed by coalitions formed by other companies and trade associations. They also frequently sought to enlist nonbusiness constituencies as members in order to enhance their own legitimacy and effectiveness. In addition, 1980 and 1982 marked the high point of business political unity with respect to campaign contributions. In 1984 and 1986, a significant share of corporate spending was directed less at changing either the partisan or ideological composition of Congress than at securing advantages for particular segments of the business community. In 1986, nearly fifty percent of corporate and trade association PAC contributions went to Democrats.

In short, the focus of business political activity changed during the 1980s. Compared to the 1970s, a relatively small share of the political efforts of business was devoted to defending the interests of business as a whole or of particular industries from challenges from either the public-interest movement or organized labor. Rather, more of it was directed at advancing the economic interests of particular segments of the business community—often at the expense of other firms. In effect, the Washington office became another profit center; government relations became an integral component of economic competition. Companies originally came to Washington in the early 1970s primarily to defend themselves. But, once having invested so much in learning how the political process works, many decided to use their political skills to help them gain advantages over their competitors, domestic as well as foreign. As a result, the political agenda became increasingly dominated by the requests of particular firms and industries for changes in public policies that would enhance their competitive positions. . . .

THE DYNAMICS OF BUSINESS POLITICAL INFLUENCE

How powerful is American business? The question itself is misconceived. There is little point in continuing to debate whether the managers and owners of American enterprises exercise political influence disproportionate to their share of the American population. Rather than analyzing the power of business in the abstract, we need to understand its exercise in dynamic terms: What, in fact, makes business as a whole, or segments of business, more or less powerful?

One of the most crucial factors that has affected the relative political influence of business is the public's perception of the long-term strength of the American economy. The relative political influence of business—particularly vis-à-vis public-interest groups—declined as a result of the strong performance of the American economy from the early 1960s through 1973. The 1974–75 recession did not immediately reverse this decline. This was due both to the scandals associated with Watergate that allowed the Democrats to make substantial gains in the 1974 congressional elections and the depth of public hostility to the oil industry following OPEC's oil embargo. But by 1978, business had regained the political initiative. Not only was it able to block the major legislative proposals of both organized labor and the public-interest movement but it began to make significant progress in achieving its own legislative goals. The perennial shortage of energy was now attributed in part to price controls, and in 1978, Congress began to phase them out, while the sluggish growth of business investment, coupled with stagflation, helped persuade Congress to reduce the capital-gains tax in 1978 and corporate income taxes three years later. The continued stagnation of the economy also gave credibility to the complaints of business about the cost of government regulation. Significantly, the high point of business's political influence during the last two decades coincided with the most severe postwar recession.

In turn, the relatively strong performance of the economy following the 1981–82 recession helped make it more difficult for business to further the political gains it had achieved between 1978 and 1981. It is unlikely that the Tax Reform Act of 1986 would have been enacted had the economy experienced another downturn in the mid-1980s, and a third energy crisis might well have made it more difficult for the environmental movement to continue to occupy the moral high ground following the Gorsuch-Watt scandals. On the other hand, the dramatic growth in foreign competition during the 1980s placed the issue of competitiveness on the political agenda and facilitated the efforts of some sectors of American business to secure government assistance in order to compete more effectively with foreign companies and countries.

A second critical factor that affects the relative political influence of business is the degree of cooperation among different firms and industries. One reason so many industries suffered so many political setbacks between the mid-1960s and early 1970s is that they received no assistance from other sectors of the business community. The automobile industry in 1966 and again in 1970, the textile indus-

try and the meat packers in 1967, the cigarette companies in 1970, and the manufacturers of pesticides in 1972 each fought more or less alone. The only industries that were politically active were those whose members were directly affected by regulatory legislation. Likewise, many of the major political victories experienced by business between 1977 and 1981 can be attributed to the ability of a large number of firms, trade associations, and business organizations to work closely together—an effort that reached its climax with the passage of the Revenue Act of 1981. However, after 1981, the business community was less effective than it otherwise might have been because of divisions both within and among industries.

When business is both mobilized and unified, its political power can be formidable. But while the former is now the norm, the latter occurs relatively infrequently. Large numbers of firms were able to work together effectively only for approximately five years. The class consciousness of American business, like that of the American working class, is limited: companies generally tend to become aware of their common interests only when they are faced with a common enemy. In a number of respects, the 1970s were an unusual decade: a significant proportion of political issues affected the interests of business as a whole. As a result, by the end of the decade, companies and trade associations had learned the importance of cooperating with one another. But during the 1980s, as during the 1960s, relatively few issues united the business community. Instead, companies and industries generally pursued relatively narrow goals: corporate public affairs became another form of economic competition. In short, business is not a monolith: the extent of its political unity, like the extent of its political influence, fluctuates.

The political influence of business is also affected by the dynamics of the American political system. Prior to the mid-1960s, business did not need to become politically active to remain influential in Washington. The centralized structure of congressional decision making, along with the prevailing ideological consensus regarding the appropriate role of the federal government, effectively limited any expansion of government controls over the private sector. Over the next decade, both the institutional and the ideological barriers to increased government intervention were eroded, requiring business to play the game of interest-group politics in order to regain its influence. The political resurgence of business was in turn facilitated by a change in the laws governing campaign spending, the increased fragmentation of decision making in Congress, and an increase in public hostility to government.

However, politicians do not simply react passively to either changing economic conditions or interest-group pressures. They also have their own priorities and preferences, which are in turn shaped by both their ideology and their desire to be reelected. The Democratic senators who played a critical role in enacting consumer and environmental legislation during the 1960s and early 1970s, and who challenged the oil industry in the mid-1970s, were responding less to lobbying by public-interest groups than to their perception of the changing preferences of their constituents. President Johnson viewed consumer and environmental regulation as a way of maintaining the momentum of the Great Society without increasing government expenditures, and President Nixon's support for

both occupational safety and health legislation and the strengthening of the Clean Air Act Amendments of 1970 was dictated by electoral considerations. In 1983, Ronald Reagan, motivated by the same considerations as Richard Nixon in 1970, hastily abandoned his effort to provide business with regulatory relief, lest the Democrats use the scandals at EPA to challenge his reelection bid. On occasion, politicians can transform the political agenda on their own. There was virtually no public interest in the issue of tax reform during the mid-1980s. It was placed on the political agenda because Ronald Reagan, supported by a handful of key congressional leaders from both parties, decided to make it the major political priority of his second term.

To paraphrase Karl Marx, business does make its own political history, but it does so in circumstances that are largely beyond its control. Since the mid-1960s, business has tended to be politically effective when its resources have been highly mobilized, when companies share similar objectives, when the public is critical of government, when the economy is performing relatively poorly, and when its preferences coincide with those of powerful politicians. But with the exception of the first, the ability of business to influence each of these contingencies is limited. There are many important issues on which it is simply impossible for substantial numbers of firms and business associations to agree. Business investment decisions are only one of the number of factors that affect the performance of the economy and, in any event, managers and owners are hardly likely to deliberately slow down the economy or reduce their company's profits so that their lobbyists can become more effective. Business certainly can, through both its campaign spending and influence over the climate of public and elite opinion, affect the preferences of politicians. But politicians' calculations are influenced by many considerations other than the desire to placate business. On balance, business is more affected by broad political and economic trends than it is able to affect them.

POSTSCRIPT

Is American Government Dominated by Big Business?

Vogel's brand of pluralism is a linear kind: he says that the power of business ebbs and flows in American history. Business was dominant in the 1950s, in retreat during the 1960s and early 1970s, dominant again in the early 1980s, and is now once again on the defensive. The only change Edsall sees is the increasing political sophistication of business and a corresponding breakdown in countervailing forces. For Edsall, the pattern of business influence since the 1970s points diagonally upward; for Vogel, the pattern is cyclical, with busines influence currently at a downturn, at least in comparison with that of other interests.

Social science literature contains a number of works discussing the issues of pluralism and corporate power. Charles E. Lindblom was one of those early pluralists who made the journey all the way over to elite theory. His earlier book, written with political scientist Robert A. Dahl, was *Politics, Economics, and Welfare* (Harper, 1953). His repudiation of pluralism was complete by the time he published *Politics and Markets: The World's Political-Economic Systems* (Basic Books, 1977). Lindblom may have been influenced by some of the critiques of pluralism that appeared in the 1960s, including Peter Bachrach, *The Theory of Democratic Elitism* (Little, Brown, 1967), and Theodore Lowi, *The End of Liberalism* (W. W. Norton, 1969). Recent works arguing that corporate elites possess inordinate power in American society include Michael Schwartz, ed., *The Structure of Power in America* (Holmes & Meier, 1987), and G. William Domhoff, *The Power Elite and the State* (Aldine de Gruyter, 1990).

One way of evaluating the pluralist and elitist perspectives on who rules America would be to study them in terms of concrete examples. We might ask, for example, what significant events have occurred in America over the past 20 years. The list might include the civil rights revolution, the women's movement, the establishment of stricter environmental laws, the withdrawal of U.S. forces from Vietnam, the legalization of abortion, the Camp David accords, the Panama Canal treaties, the deregulation of the airline industry, the savings and loan crisis, the soaring budget deficits, the Persian Gulf War, and the new friendly relationship between the United States and the former Soviet Union. Were all these the work of one elite "establishment" or did they result from an interaction of groups in the political arena?

ISSUE 2

Has Party Reform Succeeded?

YES: William J. Crotty, from *Decision for the Democrats: Reforming the Party Structure* (Johns Hopkins University Press, 1978)

NO: Tom Wicker, from "Let Some Smoke In," *The New York Times Magazine* (June 14, 1992)

ISSUE SUMMARY

YES: Political scientist William J. Crotty contends that modern reform has opened up the political process and has given unprecedented influence to each party's rank and file.
NO: Political columnist Tom Wicker concludes that the presidential nominating process too often fails to produce the candidate who is most able or most likely to win the greatest popular support.

The present party alignment of Democratic and Republican parties became fixed shortly before the Civil War, nearly a century and a half ago. Since then the parties have enjoyed great popular support. People tended to identify themselves—as well as their families, regions, and ethnic groups—with one of the major parties. A striking change, however, has taken place in recent years: One-third of all adult Americans now consider themselves to be independent, refusing to identify with either party, and that proportion is increasing among young voters.

The decline of party support relates to such events as the Vietnam War and the Watergate scandal and the ways in which they reflected unfavorably upon the parties. Party decline may also stem from television's increasing influence. Television often makes party politics look either suspicious or ridiculous. It also focuses upon the personality of the campaigner, which weakens the tie of party loyalty. The increasing mobility and sophistication of Americans weakens their ties to family, birthplace, and social class, all of which once supported party bonds as well.

Liberals and conservatives alike often deplore the absence of meaningful ideological choice between the major parties. Liberals have additionally bemoaned what they perceived to be the undemocratic processes by which the parties choose their candidates, particularly the candidate for president. Simmering resentment came to a boil at the Democratic convention in

Chicago in 1968. Bitterness within the convention, protests in the streets outside it, and the use of excessive force against the demonstrators broke the party apart, and it was unable to completely put itself together before the presidential election. However, the ill-fated convention did adopt a mandate for procedural changes whose impact has changed the presidential nominating process, and with it the character of the national parties.

Reforms initiated by a party commission went into effect at the Democratic convention in 1972. One of the major reforms called for proportional representation of women, blacks, and young people in the state delegations. This was nearly achieved at the 1972 convention, but at the price of excluding many party leaders, including prominent elected officials, from seats in the convention. Another major reform required apportionment of delegate votes in accordance with the support each candidate received in the caucus or primary at which the delegates were chosen.

The Democratic reforms led many states to abandon the convention and caucus methods of delegate selection in order to comply with the national party's requirements, which affected the Republican delegate selection process as well. One result is that, whereas 17 states held primaries in 1968, 39 states and the District of Columbia did so in 1992. As the reformers predicted, party meetings were opened up to more members, the influence of party bosses was reduced, the rules for delegate selection were made specific where they had previously been vague, and minority points of views received a hearing previously denied to them in party councils.

Perhaps the most significant consequence of the changes has been the diminished importance of the national convention. It has been reduced to a mere ratifying body for the candidate chosen in the primaries. In five of the six presidential elections since the reforms were adopted, the successful Democratic candidate received fewer than half of the primary votes but more than any other single candidate.

Despite the fact that incumbent president Jimmy Carter received barely more than half the primary vote in 1980, widespread dissatisfaction with his nomination, as well as with that of Republican nominee Ronald Reagan, suggested that within both parties there were leaders who might have commanded broader support within party ranks as well as with independent voters. In 1988 a majority of voters indicated that they wished they had had an alternative to the major party candidates.

These events have led some observers of American politics to ask whether or not the reforms need reforming. Should we modify the present nominating process, go back to the old convention of party leaders, devise a new method of nomination, or stick with the present system?

William J. Crotty, who helped to fashion the post-1968 reform, believes that the reform has worked well and should be preserved. Tom Wicker favors moving toward a nominating convention in which the delegates could debate the choice of a candidate.

YES   William J. Crotty

DECISION FOR THE DEMOCRATS

The year 1968 seemed predestined for sorrow. It suffered from the accumulated grievances of the preceding years which were exacerbated by two
assassinations, riots, and an administration hellbent on pursuing a major war
while denying that this was its intent. It experienced a government out-of-
touch with its public and neglectful, to the point of being scornful, of any
and all dissent from its policies, and it witnessed a frustration born of
attempting a challenge through conventional means destined to be mocked
by a system unresponsive at best, closed at worst, to its pressures. The result
was the explosions that shook the nation during the Chicago convention.

The "why" of Chicago is relatively easy to document. Far more difficult is
tracing and evaluating the response of the political parties. The reaction of
the parties, and especially the Democratic party, to the upheavals was
unprecedented by any standard: it resulted in nothing less than an attempt
to reshape fundamental structural mechanisms to better accommodate a
diversity of views, to provide a fully representative and "open" convention,
and to modernize, in line with democratic principles, procedures notoriously
unreceptive to change. Whether these ambitious goals were achieved, and at
what price, is another story. It is possible, though, that the reforms emanat-
ing from the convention are of far greater substantive importance than
anything to emerge from that fateful election year. . . .

Party reform took second place to a lackluster general election campaign in
the fall. The Humphrey campaign meandered, spiritually and organiza-
tionally, toward a November decision. The Nixon drive concentrated on
packaged media presentations, carefully worded slogans designed to reassure an anxious electorate, and the presentation of a low political profile
engineered to take advantage of the divisiveness within the Democratic
ranks and the schisms in a tired electorate. The voters did not appear
inclined to award any of the contenders with a decisive plurality. Everyone
appeared relieved when the unhappiest of election years finally drew to its
inevitable close.

While the victorious Republican candidate readied himself for his oath of
office, another inauguration of sorts was being prepared for January, though

From William J. Crotty, *Decision for the Democrats: Reforming the Party Structure* (Johns
Hopkins University Press, 1978), pp. 32–40. Copyright © 1978 by Johns Hopkins University
Press. Reprinted by permission.

this one received considerably less press and public attention. The efforts of a broken and dispirited party to reexamine its unhappy immediate past and to remedy its ways to insure, in the words of George McGovern, that the events of 1968, and particularly the gross abuses that occurred at the Chicago convention, would never happen again, do not constitute an especially interesting story. Yet defeat—especially after an election year so debilitating for a party—can lead to a period of profound change and, in time, to a spiritual regenesis. This had happened to the Republicans after a bitter defeat in 1912, and, on a more superficial level, after their loss in 1964. In a different manner, a defeat was about to trigger a profound transformation of Democratic party pro-cedures, one without precedent in the history of the American two-party experience. . . .

The reforms introduced a remarkable era to American politics. More was attempted, and accomplished, than can truthfully be said to have been envisioned in the decades since the Progressive movement of the early 1900s. Remarkably, the reforms had been initiated and executed by a political party that perceived itself to be in trouble. In contrast to earlier attempts at political change, the intent was to strengthen and preserve an institution of incomparable value to the American political system rather than to destroy or replace it.

The changes introduced were many. The traditional priorities of American party structure had been reversed. The national party units had attempted, with some success, to establish a code of fair and decent behavior and to have it prevail in the conduct of party business. A sense of rationality had been introduced into an incredibly complex system, and

an aura of openness and equity had begun to prevail in several areas—changes in the presidential nominating process, the most significant of the national parties' duties, appeared to be an excellent foreboding of future changes in all aspects of party operations. A series of organizational structures and institutional values, little changed since the formation of the political parties over a century and a quarter earlier, were giving way to a new sense of national purpose and, it was hoped, a relevancy and responsiveness to constituent pressures, responsibilities neither party had acquitted impressively over the years.

The political implications of what the reforms were attempting to accomplish were never far from mind. The work of the reformers would effectively open the party in two regards. First, it would permit new groups to enter and make their views as to policy or candidates felt without depending on the goodwill or sponsorship of party elders whose favor they would have had to curry. Second, it would develop the foundation for establishing a permanent set of rules that would treat all with an impartiality previously unknown in party circles. It is too much to argue that such objectives were achieved by the first, and more than likely the most decisive, of the reform bursts, but a substantial beginning had been made.

Party processes were given a new legitimacy at a time when parties had begun to appear increasingly irrelevant to the solution of the main problems besetting American life and when both party and the political system more broadly needed whatever support they could muster. In these terms then—and they are impressive—the reform movement, and most significantly the achievements of the McGovern-Fraser Commission, had accomplished a good deal. In its own way the reform era constituted a revolution in party operations, notable as much for its impact on traditional modes of thinking as on the structures it placed in question. One would be hard pressed to find comparable moments of achievement in the long history of political parties in this nation.

WHAT REFORM ACCOMPLISHED

The ramifications of the reform period were many. A listing of the accomplishments and their broader implications would include the following.

Opening the Party

The party was opened and, in the process, made more responsive to and representative of its rank and file. The new openness was meant to extend to all aspects of the party organization. The effort was made, for example, by the Sanford Commission, to extend procedural guarantees of fair play to party organizations from the local to the national levels. The party charter set standards and established guidelines for all manners of party deliberations. The Sanford Commission, in conjunction with the McGovern-Fraser, O'Hara, and, to a lesser extent, Mikulski commissions, attempted to restructure party institutions to make them more responsive to grassroots sentiments.

The most notable success in opening the party to influence from the rank and file was the transformation of the presidential nominating process. The work of the McGovern-Fraser Commission, of course, was responsible for turning a relatively closed nominating process, controlled primarily by the party regulars, into one directly reflective of the concerns of those party members who chose to participate in delegate selection.

Rearranging Power Distributions Within the Party

In the process of opening presidential nominations, the power relationships within the Democratic party were rearranged. Gaining increased influence were the party activists and candidate supporters who worked during presidential election years to advance a cause, an issue, or a presidential contender with whom they identified. For the most part, these tended to be the professional people—lawyers, businessmen, teachers—and the young persons, blacks, housewives, and minority groups attracted to the party during the significant prenominating races. Losing influence were the power-wielders of the pre-1972 period: the party regulars, elected officials (governors, congressmen, senators, mayors, state legislators), party organizational personnel (state chairmen, national committee representatives, county chairmen), and the "fat cats," as they were called, of the business world who sought influence in politics by bankrolling candidates and campaigns and on whom the party had been heavily dependent. Also losing power in the new alignment favored by the reform procedures were the southern states and their parties, which were experiencing transformations, and the old-line factions and interest groups at the state and national levels, which had at least been consulted on nominations. These latter groups had held, in many cases, a negative veto over both candidates for the presidential nomination and the issues treated in the party platform.

The most dramatic example of the last category would have to be the labor unions. . . . The AFL-CIO continued to be a significant contributor to the congressional campaigns of Democratic candidates, but its concern with the national party affairs lessened. . . .

The Nationalization of the Party

The reform movement altered the power distributions within the Democratic party in an even more fundamental way. The historic relationship between the national party and its local and state units was altered, and before reform had run its course, dramatically reversed. Traditionally, the national party exercised little real power in party matters. This role was reserved for the state and local units, the party agencies presumed to be closest to the voter. The national party appendages were relatively inactive. They occasionally provided skilled services to state and local parties in such areas as registration, polling, and getting-out-the vote campaigns, but their contributions seldom went beyond the level of rudimentary back-up support. The national parties, of course, did hold their semiannual national committee meetings, but these were uneventful gatherings of no particular significance to the parties at any level. The national party also supervised the arrangements for the quadrennial national convention. Here the power over the convention scheduling and agenda could be significant to the faction controlling the national chairmanship at the time. The national party, however, had little concern over such basic practices as delegate apportionment formulas, controlled by the state parties and influenced by local political customs and power arrangements.

All of this changed abruptly, and more than anyone could ever have predicted, because of the McGovern-Fraser Commis-

sion. Building on the precedent established by the (Richard) Hughes Special Equal Rights Committee, the McGovern-Fraser Commission required the state parties to enact changes demanded by itself, the offspring of the national party. . . .

Extending the Rule of Law to Party Affairs

Implicit in the proposals throughout the reform period was the effort to protect the interests of the individual party member and to extend and safeguard his influence in party deliberations. The intention was to remove, insofar as was possible, control over participation from the whim and caprice of individuals who happened to be in authority in a given place at a particular time. To a large extent, such an effort ran counter to the customary political efforts of using every available instrument to gain a political edge, however small, and certainly counter to the experience of the Democratic party. Traditionally, the party had resolved differences in a political give-and-take between contending party factions or candidates in any manner the combatants might devise. Manipulating rules or enforcing selective by-laws [were] among the many stratagems a party faction might use to gain its ends.

This effort to abolish the regulars' control over participation was not good enough for the reformers. They not only wanted an inclusiveness and an intraparty democracy in political decision-making, but they also sought an impartiality in party rules and procedures that was foreign to the historic practices of the Democrats.

The emphasis can be seen in all aspects of the reform movement. The McGovern-Fraser Commission's rules attempted to establish a model of fairness and openness in delegate selection that set the tone for future developments. The O'Hara Commission created elaborate procedures for resolving credentials committee challenges that assured clear standards of performance impartially assessed through a series of mechanisms similar to those employed by the courts. There would be briefs and counterbriefs, set times and dates for the selection meetings and for the various steps involved in adjudicating any disagreements, hearings of facts by qualified officers, and appeals made to a credentials committee and, potentially at least, to the national convention. The Credentials Review Commission carried the process a step further by attempting to provide a continuing assessment of the applicability and relevance of state party rules to the national party's reform guidelines.

Less successfully, the O'Hara Commission made efforts to open the flow of information to the individual delegates and to advance their control over presiding officials within the convention. Most dramatic of all, the Charter Commission wrote a party constitution for party affairs and established a judicial council, modeled after the Supreme Court, to codify and apply party rulings in all disputes brought before it. The Charter Commission's actions are perhaps the ultimate steps, if they prove to be feasible, in instituting the rule of law within party councils.

REFORM AS A CONTINUING PROBLEM

One other result of the reform movement may be less obvious. The reformers extensively reviewed party processes and then rewrote the rules of behavior for the totality of national party activities. As a consequence, the reform era opened questions, once presumed settled either for better or worse or at least removed from immediate political debate, to continual reassessment. The success of the reformers in overhauling party procedures within a very few years invites others to try. The public and the party membership have now been conditioned to such reassessments. Such activity is accepted as a legitimate national party function and the authority of the party to engage in such exercises—including the enforced implementation of its directives—is no longer a subject of contention. There is much to be gained by a restructuring of procedure by any party faction that might control the national party apparatus, a national convention, or simply a reform commission. The process invites attempts at duplication. In fact, because the impressive changes brought by the McGovern-Fraser Commission serve as a model of what could be accomplished, repeated attempts to introduce new reforms (in these situations, changes intended to favor one faction or candidate) may be difficult to avoid.

For the most part, the original review of procedures and the changes introduced by the reformers were badly needed. The presidential nominating process had evolved over generations, with little rationale or logic underlying the diverse procedures utilized in the states. The reformers contended that the process was closed and arbitrary and that it gave unfair advantage to the party regulars who controlled the processes. In this broad sense, the reformers' claims were not contested by the regulars (although, of course, the measures proposed by the reformers were less well received).

No particular rules governed the operations of the national convention and its management, and the procedures were open to gross abuse. The bylaws applying to local, state, and national party organs were complex, often unrecorded, and openly manipulated by those in power. Such problems demanded some type of ordering. The reform movement attempted to accomplish this task.

The work of the McGovern-Fraser Commission and, in the wake of the post-1972 election, the Mikulski and Compliance Review commissions, indicates that no area of presidential selection can remain off limits to reevaluation and potential modification. . . .

DEBATING THE MERITS

The controversies created by the reforms are not likely to abate. The reform movement raised fundamental questions about American political parties that are not easily answered and that go to the very essence of what political parties in the United States are, or should be, about. What is a political party for? Whom does it serve? What does (or should) it stand for? Whom should it represent (and how should these groups, interests, and individuals be represented)? Implicit in the controversy is the question of the adaptability and adequacy of political parties—institutions developed in another age—in dealing with the pressures and problems of late-twentieth-century American life. Are political parties relevant to the major concerns of contemporary American society? If not, can they be made relevant?

THE RESPONSE OF THE REGULARS

The answers that the Democratic party regulars and reformers would give to these questions should be clear enough at this juncture. The party regulars would contend that political parties are quite adequate to the demands made upon them. They would say that 1968 and its problems were exceptions to the long and basically successful exercise of party authority. If a little care is taken, the problems of that election year need not be repeated.

Political parties are electoral coalitions intended for winning elections. The achievement of this end is, by all odds, their most significant function, and all other obligations are secondary at best. The regulars would contend that a party should, of course, represent the best interests of its members, but they would go on to argue that the most effective way to do this is by winning elections. The way to pick the candidates most likely to be victorious is to give the decisive role in party affairs (including presidential nomination contests) to party and elective officeholders. These individuals have the greatest stake in the party's success as well as the knowledge and experience necessary to select the most formidable nominees representative of the party's long-run interests.

THE RESPONSE
OF THE REFORMERS

Reformers would be more skeptical of the claims made on behalf of the political party. They would argue that the party has not served its membership well, that its procedures are out-dated and discriminatory, and that it has not adapted to a changing electorate and an evolving society. Their perception of the 1968 election year and its attendant difficulties would be quite different from that of the regulars. They would see that election year and the Democratic prenomination difficulties and national convention as symbolic of the internal decay that has been spreading within the party system. The 1968 election year was simply a manifestation of how serious the problems have become.

The reformers have little faith in the party regulars. They openly question the breadth of the regulars' concerns and the extent to which they accurately reflect, or possibly even consider, the sentiments of the party rank and file. Reformers differ with the party regulars on where a party's major obligations lie, and they contest the wisdom, competence, and representativeness of the party regulars. They see no particular value in entrusting the fate of the national party or control over its presidential decision-making process to an elite with which they have so little in common and which they believe to be out of touch with its constituency and with national political currents.

The reformers would argue that the grass-roots party members should be represented in all party bodies and should, to the furthest extent possible, control their deliberations. To enlarge upon this belief, reformers feel that party members who participated in the presidential primaries and caucuses should have a controlling voice in the concerns of the process. The reformers believe in a participant-oriented party, accessible to those who cared to identify with it and take part in its activities, and open to influence from below. And they seek a party that would best represent and implement as precisely as possible the views and wishes of its membership.

The conception of an open, participant-oriented party responsive to and dependent on the good will of its rank and file is at odds with the regulars' view of a quasi-closed organization led by a somewhat inaccessible and self-perpetuating elite that would look out for the party's best interests. In fact, an open party that entrusts ultimate power over, for example, the choice of a presidential nominee to the individual party member acting in a primary or a caucus at the local level makes the need for indirect representation through local or state party organizations or elected officeholders extraneous. The reformers want a direct correspondence between the individual party member and national-level decisions, a relationship that deemphasizes the role and contributions of any intermediate agencies.

The reformers would also reject winning office as the sole end of a political party. Instead, they would contend that a party serves many functions and that perhaps its most important is adequately to represent the views of its members and to funnel these into governmental decision-making. Unless a political party responsively addresses its members' concerns about pressing social issues, its victories will be hollow. They believe that a political party has to be in direct touch with, and representative of, its grass-roots sentiments. Anything less means that the political party is not fulfilling its obligations.

The reformers would emphasize a broad set of party goals and activities (witness the party charter) than the regulars. They would argue that a party should attempt to fulfill a number of functions, from educating its membership on the issues of the day to campaigning for office, and that it should have permanent organizations active throughout the year with full-time professional staffs to serve the needs of its members. These party organizations should be open to direction from the rank and file.

While they favor a more ambitious program and a more highly institutionalized (and open) party structure, the reformers would be more skeptical of the party's operations and the adequacy of its contributions to contemporary society. They would want the party to engage in more activities while at the same time being more demanding in their assessments of the relevance and value of what the party undertakes. And they would insist (as they did) that to reach any of these goals, the Democratic party would have to be thoroughly restructured. The regulars, of course, would disagree on each and every point.

TWO MODELS OF REPRESENTATION

The two sides in the reform issues are operating from different models of political behavior. They are applying different standards of acceptable political conduct and accountability. The two models have little in common. The party regulars are advocating "a taking care of" (to borrow Hanna Pitkin's terminology) concept of representation that sees party regulars and the established interest group leaders within the Democratic coalition as the best conservators of the interests of the party and its members. . . .

The reformers would argue that a system that directly reflects rank-and-file views and allows the grass-roots participants control over party decisions, particularly over the critical choice of a presidential nominee, is not only preferable but is the only type of procedure that will meet their concept of democratic accountability.

To the extent that direct control over party decision-making is not feasible, the reformers would opt for an "agent" theory of representation. The representative chosen by the individual party members would be given limited independence. On the major issues facing the party, he would be carefully instructed on how to perform in order to best fulfill his sponsor's wishes.

The two conceptions of representation have little in common. The issues raised, both in theoretical and practical terms, are fundamental to one's definition of a political party and the relevance of its contributions to a society. They deal with the nature of the party and its continued existence. Add to these concerns the groups displaced by the turmoil caused by the reforms and the stakes being contested in the fight for control of a national party and its nominating processes, and it is not difficult to see why the debate over reforms has continued.

The reformers won the initial battle and much of what they accomplished cannot be reversed. Nonetheless, the basic differences between the competing conceptions of what a political party is (or should be) and the manner in which it should fulfill its obligations are essentially irreconcilable. At a minimum, however, political parties in the future may be judged by stricter standards of performance than in the past. Political parties should be continually called upon to prove their relevance and justify their contribution by a public that is increasingly skeptical of their value.

The reform movement accomplished a great deal in a short period of time. It managed to breathe new life into moribund party structures and to center debate on the operation of these agencies. Political parties are seldom the focus of public concern. They have grown episodically over the last century and a half to fill immediate needs. They are of immense concern quadrennially, when the various presidential contenders and their supporters attempt to bend them to their will. Between presidential elections a short-term interest is being replaced by a more customary apathy. It can be argued that during the interim between elections the hulking organizational monster that constitutes the remnants of the national party only fitfully serves any function of consequence to the electorate.

The reform movement attempted to resurrect an interest in party activities per se and to revitalize party structures and adapt them to modern concerns. . . .

Political parties had changed little in form or activity since their inception. One factor, however, had become increasingly clear: they had become spiritually exhausted and increasingly less relevant functionally to the operation of a modern democracy. The demand for organizations adequately executing the duties the parties are supposed to perform cannot be quarreled with. Critical concerns of any democratic nation include the mobilization of voters behind representative candidacies of similar policy persuasion; the selection and promotion of the most able within its ranks to positions of public responsibility; the effective representation of the views of its members; the day-to-day scrutiny of the acts of those in office; and the provision of sensible policy and candidate alternatives to an electorate it educated to the implications of official behavior. Both parties performed these functions with increasingly less ability.

In truth the parties became fractious, warring tribes, divorced from their bases of support and slavishly dependent on a president chosen from their ranks. They responded more to organized pressures and financial strength than they did to the mass of their membership. A review of party history during the last few troubled decades would make it appear that the party supporters were an inconvenience to be suffered and catered to only during national election campaigns.

Such foreboding might never have arisen above the level of irrelevant speculation had it not been for 1968. The fury unleashed by the obvious abuse of official party machinery and the ugly picture of party operations that resulted convinced most people within and without the Democratic party that change was overdue. The forces that would propel reform had been set in motion, but the events of that election year proved the catalyst. Beyond a doubt, the immediate need for remedial action had been demonstrated. Change was required; the need had been dramatized in a manner that would create the necessary reform constituency, and people were available and willing to devote themselves to the effort. So began the attempt to democratize one of the nation's oldest and most significant political institutions.

NO   Tom Wicker

LET SOME SMOKE IN

Despite his obvious problems of "electability," Gov. Bill Clinton of Arkansas has moved inexorably into position to win the Democratic Presidential nomination. Republicans have little choice except to renominate George Bush, despite his equally obvious vulnerabilities.

These seemingly inevitable major-party candidates may be the main reason why Ross Perot, until recently an unknown figure in national politics, suddenly looks like a man of destiny to so many voters.

The stars were not always so nearly fixed in their course. In an earlier, less-regulated era, the out-of-power Democrats, at least, could have urged a strong candidate to make a late entry into the nominating campaign. If none responded, national convention delegates, under prodding from party leaders alarmed by Clinton's problems and Perot's potential, could have nominated someone other than the front-runner.

Neither option is more than a theoretical possibility for the Democrats this year. Even if somebody other than Governor Clinton looked promising, Democratic Party "reforms" since 1968 have all but guaranteed that his primary victories, together with the party's system of awarding delegates in proportion to a candidate's share of primary votes, will insure his nomination on the first ballot.

Some Democrats—dourly contemplating the loss of four of five Presidential elections since the reform era began after 1968—have had enough of this "automated" process, as it has been called by Nelson Polsby, a political scientist at the University of California at Berkeley. They'd like to return to a more "deliberative" system.

However, that would mean reneging on a reformed nominating process touted for two decades as more "open and democratic" than it used to be. Whether or not such openness is a good thing, or actually has been achieved, few Democrats would dare advocate anything carrying the scent of the bad old days of party "bosses" and "smoke-filled rooms."

From Tom Wicker, "Let Some Smoke In," *The New York Times Magazine* (June 14, 1992). Copyright © 1992 by The New York Times Company. Reprinted by permission.

More and more Democrats, nevertheless, are asking themselves some hard questions. What, for example, is the virtue of a nominating process that effectively closes the list of possibilities three or four months before the convention? What's "open" or "democratic" about rules that effectively prevent some in the party from reconsidering what others of its members did in the early primaries, even when—as in 1992—polls show that so many Democrats are clearly dissatisfied with the results of those primaries?

Why foreclose California, the most populous state in the union, whose rich haul of electoral votes may be ripe this year for Democratic plucking, from any effective role in choosing the party's Presidential nominee? By the time the California primary rolled around two weeks ago, Clinton had the nomination all but in the bag.

Where, anyway, is it written in the Constitution or in American political history or practice that no one need apply for the Presidency unless he or she has made it through a torturous obstacle course of state primaries—37 of them this year?

Why does everyone have to run the same gantlet to win a party's Presidential nomination? And if everyone does, won't the field soon be limited (if it isn't already) to those men or women who most desperately want to be President, who are willing to pay the high personal price of achieving that goal—subjecting themselves and their families, for instance, to the considerable rigors and indignities of a year or more of primary campaigning in 37 states?

Why should such obsessed persons, no matter how bold, be the only ones our political parties may consider for the highest office in the nation?

ON APRIL 23, 1968, IN THE AFTERSHOCK OF the withdrawal of the Democratic incumbent, Lyndon Johnson, from one of the most turbulent Presidential campaigns in American history, Eugene McCarthy won the Pennsylvania primary by more than 300,000 votes—71.6 percent of the Democratic total. The primary, however, was a nonbinding "beauty contest," and the state's Democratic leader, Mayor James H. Tate of Philadelphia, steered most of the delegates to Vice President Hubert H. Humphrey, who was not even on the ballot.

Political potentates like Tate had been doing that sort of thing routinely throughout the history of American party politics. But in that year of protests—against the war in Vietnam, L.B.J., the draft, the universities, the establishment, the second-class status of black Americans—the routine seemed doubly outrageous. Because of Pennsylvania and other such "atrocities," the legions of young people who had flocked into the Democratic Party to oppose the war and support Gene McCarthy—or, later, Robert Kennedy—demanded a new "participatory politics," a greater public voice in a more open process of choosing Presidential nominees.

Leaders like Mayor Tate and Mayor Richard Daley (the elder) of Chicago nevertheless controlled the 1968 national convention. Blandly asserting their dominance-as-usual, they duly nominated Humphrey for President, though he had entered no primaries at all. Perhaps chastened, however, by Humphrey's loss in November to Richard M. Nixon, the Democrats finally responded to continuing calls for "participatory politics." Ultimately, a number of reforms were developed by a commission led by George McGovern, who in 1972 became the party's nominee and Nixon's second victim.

After 1968, the McGovern Commission decreed, delegates to the Democratic National Convention were to include women and members of minority groups in fair proportion to their presence in a state's population. Presidential candidates were to be awarded a share of each state's delegates in proportion to the number of votes the candidate received in that state's primary or state convention.

Most significantly, as was to become apparent, these delegates were to be selected by the various state parties through "open and democratic" processes that ultimately would have to gain the approval of the Democratic National Committee and the national convention's credentials watchdogs. Banned outright was the selection of convention delegates in a caucus of party officials, or by primary ballots on which only the names of delegate candidates appeared.

These McGovern rules were designed to tip the balance of power in the nomination process from party bosses and machines to the voting public. No longer, for example, could the Georgia party chairman, in consultation with only the Governor, choose the state's entire delegation (with little regard to race or sex) and have it in place long before the national convention, awaiting the highest bid from Presidential candidates who had to come, hats figuratively in hands, seeking Georgia's delegates.

John F. Kennedy—like most nominees before him—had won the Democratic race in 1960 mostly by gaining the backing of state delegations, sometimes by personal or political appeal, often by making alliances with state officials and leaders who controlled or influenced members of their delegations. Kennedy

won only two significant primaries, in Wisconsin and West Virginia—and the latter was important primarily for its demonstration to dubious Democrats in nonprimary states that a Roman Catholic could win in a Protestant electorate.

The McGovern rules caused this "old politics" of Presidential nominating to disappear after 1968. State party leaders, looking at the new complexities and uncertainties of choosing delegates under unfamiliar rules, saw only one thing clearly: the legitimacy of their state's delegates was out of their control. It would be determined by the national party and convention.

Many such leaders wanted no part of this threatening new process, and the result was a startling proliferation of candidate primaries. They appeared to be the most obvious means of "open and democratic" candidate selection, and their results were almost certain to be approved at the national level.

From 17 Democratic state primaries in 1968—many, like Pennsylvania's, not binding, some, like California's, winner-take-all—the number grew to 23 in 1972. As years and elections passed, more states joined the primary parade. Now three-quarters of the states apportion their convention delegates via a public vote.

Republicans, with less enthusiasm for participatory politics, were forced to go along in some cases by changing state laws; their primaries increased from 16 to 22 by 1972, and more have been added since. More important, Republican fund-raising scandals in 1972—the year of Creep (Committee for the Re-Election of the President) and Watergate—influenced passage of new laws to regulate election finance. Notably, these changes provided for Federal subsidy of primary campaigns, nominating conventions and

Presidential elections, and for limitations on amounts that could be spent by candidates who accepted Federal funds.

Taken together, campaign-financing reform and the new reliance of the parties on candidate primaries resulted in the "automation" cited by Nelson Polsby. The automated nominating system has the virtue of giving little-known or underfinanced candidates—Jimmy Carter in 1976, Paul Tsongas in 1992—an opening in the relatively low-cost state contests in Iowa and New Hampshire, which have become so important. Proportional awarding of delegates increases the clout of minorities in the nominating process, though not necessarily in the ultimate election.

Some party pros also like the fact that the early primaries can give the party an early nominee, and thus extra time to make the case against a Republican opponent. But Michael Dukakis's early triumph did not do the Democrats much good in 1988; nor, many fear, will Bill Clinton's April clinching this year.

Governor Clinton has raised the most money to be matched by Federal subsidy, put together the best organization, waged the most effective primary campaigns and won the most primaries in the most regions. Why, then, do so many Democrats view his impending nomination with so much trepidation?

Governor Clinton no doubt would be more highly esteemed by more Democrats if questions about his marital problems and Vietnam draft status had not arisen. Even if these "character" issues had never been raised, however, an automated Presidential nomination was likely to prove unsatisfactory to many who must support a nominee if he or she is to win in November.

That's because participatory primaries are not necessarily the most "open and democratic" means of choosing delegates or a nominee. The widespread perception that they are probably results from Americans' theological faith in "free elections" as a means of political choice.

Voters in early primaries in a few states, however, are not representative of a national party, much less the national electorate; witness the fate of Michael Dukakis. Nor do primary voters necessarily reflect even their state party's overall makeup. A winner may be backed by little more than a highly motivated faction.

If several competent candidates are entered in a primary, one may come in first with a relatively small vote—and still reap the enormous publicity benefits of winning. Several candidates together may receive far more votes than that single candidate who comes in first—but without the support of a majority. Thus, had only two candidates entered the contest, the putative winner might well have lost.

As was the case even in the hotly contested New York primary this year, voter turnout may be abysmally low. Primaries tend, moreover, to yield great advantages to glamorous or charismatic candidates, to those most adept at providing sound bites and photo-ops to a voracious press, to organizations with plenty of money to buy television spots, to candidates who have been publicized for coming in first in other states and to users of hit-and-run tactics that damage an opponent without giving him or her sufficient opportunity to respond.

Those who benefit for such reasons, however, may not meet the political standards of voters in other states, or those who backed the losers, or those who refused or neglected to vote in a primary. None of this is likely to help the winner when it really matters, on Election Day in November; and all of it can diminish the national party acceptability of the winner of a string of early primaries.

But these deficiencies of primaries will make little difference to a winner's bonanza of headlines and TV interviews. They will make no difference whatever in the delegate total he or she will have amassed, in low turnout or high, and no matter how small the "winning" percentage of a state's primary vote, or how questionable the tactics that may have been used.

And if the voting public, or some portion of it, chooses among candidates in a primary, these voters do not really choose delegates. Those who are to fill the seats at the national convention are chosen, instead, by candidates, as they fill the numerical quota they won in the primary. Thus, the McGovern rules actually have shifted the power to select delegates from party officials (sometimes called "bosses") to candidates.

It's not apparent that the candidates are better qualified to choose than the party officials, or that they are more public-spirited; and the delegates they pick are as beholden to those who anointed them as any delegate ever was to Boss Flynn of the Bronx. Most, in fact, are pledged by state law, at least on the first ballot. That such delegates might be persuaded to turn to a "dark horse" or to a late-blooming candidacy is a forlorn hope indeed.

NO REFORMS CAN RELIEVE BILL CLINTON of the burden of his 1968 draft problems; nor can any produce a candidate who would necessarily be more electable in November. But the problems his impending nomination present to many in his party might have been circumvented in a more deliberative nominating process—one that could be put in place of today's automation by permitting state parties once again to select delegates by any method they choose.

This proposal evokes anguished cries about a return to the smoke-filled room, with all-white, all-male delegations again dominating national conventions. For the Democratic Party, at least, in which women and minorities are firmly established in the hierarchy, this is implausible; participation once granted is not easy to curtail. Moreover, not all states that, under the McGovern rules, have moved to primary selection would abandon that method if permitted.

But enough might to produce a more representative mix of delegates. Many states would still use the participatory primary, despite its shortcomings; some would turn to perhaps less "open" but more deliberative processes relying on the knowledge, experience and preference of elected and state party officials. If some of the latter did deliberate in smoke-filled rooms, their efforts would be balanced by the primary states. In turn, the deliberators would balance some of the less helpful primary results.

Above all, the delegations of an increased number of nonprimary states might provide a roadblock at the convention against the bandwagon of a candidate who had piled up victories and delegates in early but unrepresentative primaries. They could keep a convention open for deliberation, compromise and astute ticket-making, in place of an automated nominee ratified on the first ballot.

DON'T HOLD YOUR BREATH, HOWEVER, FOR a reform movement that can be portrayed as retreating from participatory politics, re-creating bosses and machines and yielding to the old politics. Any political process has its winners and losers, and the automated nominating process of the post–1968 era is no different. Those who benefit from it will not easily give it up—not, perhaps, until the Democrats lose a few more Presidential elections with nominees chosen in unrepresentative primaries.

POSTSCRIPT

Has Party Reform Succeeded?

Many voters in recent elections indicated after voting that they wished they had had a different choice. Expressing concern with the process, the reforms have been reformed every four years since the presidential nominating reforms were introduced in 1972. States have altered their primaries and caucuses, and superdelegates (members of Congress and other national leaders) have been added. But these and other changes have not altered the stated purpose nor the practical consequences of the reforms. That purpose has been to make the process more democratic by giving weight to the preferences of the electorate in the primaries and caucuses. James W. Ceaser, *Reforming the Reforms: A Critical Analysis of the Presidential Selection Process* (Ballinger, 1982), sees the reforms as seeking the replacement of "representation" (that is, selection by party leaders) with "direct democracy" (that is, selection by the voters themselves).

The consequence has been that the national convention has been little more than a ratifying body, with the decision already assured by the commitments of the elected delegates. Crotty defends this enhancement of party democracy, while Wicker deplores the fact that it deprives concerned party leaders of the opportunity to deliberate in making their party's best choice for candidate.

Perhaps the most influential critiques of the reforms and defenses of the traditional nominating role of the party organizations have been Everett Carll Ladd, Jr., *Where Have All the Voters Gone?* (W. W. Norton, 1978), and Nelson W. Polsby, *Consequences of Party Reform* (Oxford University Press, 1983). Terry Sanford, *A Danger of Democracy: The Presidential Nominating Process* (Westview Press, 1981), urges the selection of thinking delegates who will have the time and means to examine the candidates.

Larry M. Bartels, in *Presidential Primaries and the Dynamics of Public Choice* (Princeton University Press, 1988), examines the momentum provided by early primary victories, as well as the likely consequences of regional primaries or a one-day national primary. Reaching different conclusions, John G. Geer, *Nominating Presidents: An Evaluation of Voters and Primaries* (Greenwood Press, 1989), studies voters in the nominating process and proposes a series of grouped primaries and a preferential ballot for primary voters.

One aspect of the nomination process that has never been reformed is the manner in which the presidential nominee chooses the vice presidential candidate, often at the convention itself, and without any public debate. One of the newest and most interesting examinations of this process is Jules Witcover, *Crapshoot: Rolling the Dice on the Vice Presidency* (Crown, 1992).

ISSUE 3

Do Political Action Committees Undermine Democracy?

YES: Fred Wertheimer, from "Campaign Finance Reform: The Unfinished Agenda," *THE ANNALS of the American Academy of Political and Social Science* (July 1986)

NO: Herbert E. Alexander, from "The Case for PACs," A Public Affairs Council Monograph (1983)

ISSUE SUMMARY

YES: Common Cause president Fred Wertheimer argues that PACs exert too much influence over the electoral process, allowing special interests to get the ear of elected officials at the expense of the national interest.
NO: Political analyst Herbert E. Alexander insists that PACs have made significant contributions to the American political system.

Half a century ago, American folk humorist Will Rogers observed that it took a lot of money even to *lose* an election. What would Will Rogers say if he were alive today?

The cost of television as a medium of communication and persuasion has greatly increased the expenditures in election campaigns. In 1984, campaign expenditures for the presidential election totaled $325 million, $50 million more than in the previous election. The cost of campaigning for Congress is also rising dramatically. Campaign spending on House and Senate races totaled $450 million in 1986, more than double the amount spent in 1978. Money, said a prominent California politician, is the "mother's milk of politics."

More controversial than the amount of money spent in politics is its source. Political action committees have become a major factor in financing American election campaigns. PACs (as they are called) have proliferated in recent years, with more than 100 new special-interest groups being founded each year. It is estimated that there are now more than 4,100 PACs, representing almost every conceivable political interest.

By raising money from political sympathizers, association members, and public solicitations, PACs have provided the funds with which candidates reach the public. It is estimated that PACs spent more than $80 million on campaigns in 1982, when there was no presidential election. In 1984 at least 10 incumbent senators (in both parties) received more than $300,000 in PAC money. Some members of Congress have taken no chances on winning an existing PAC's approval and have created their own. The Congressional Club, founded by Republican senator Jesse Helms of North Carolina, raised nearly $5 million in 1983 alone.

Legislators are divided on the influence of PACs. Democratic representative Barney Frank of Massachusetts has said: "You can't take thousands of dollars from a group and not have it affect you." But Republican congressman Henry Hyde of Illinois offers a different perspective. "The more PACs proliferate," he says, "the less influence any individual PAC has. . . . Their influence is diminished by their proliferation."

Critics argue that PAC money in recent years probably influenced congressional votes on bills to maintain high dairy price supports and to defeat legislation that would have required warranties on used cars. On the other hand, defenders of PACs maintain that they are less interested in influencing members of Congress opposed to their points of view than in electing new members who are sympathetic.

PACs are not a new phenomenon. Pressure groups, or factions, as founding father James Madison called them, have always been part of the political process. To eliminate them would be to destroy liberty itself. What Madison hoped for was the broadest participation of interest groups, so that compromises among them would result in an approximation of the national interest.

Has this happened? In the following selections, Fred Wertheimer, president of Common Cause, a self-styled citizens' lobby, argues that the opposite has occurred. In his view, the proliferation of PACs has given special interests the power to override the national interest. Disputing this view is Herbert E. Alexander, who points out a number of significant contributions PACs have made to the American political system.

YES

Fred Wertheimer

CAMPAIGN FINANCE REFORM: THE UNFINISHED AGENDA

Our democracy is founded on the concept of representation. Citizens elect leaders who are given responsibility to weigh all the competing and conflicting interests that reflect our diversity and to decide what, in their judgment, will best advance the interests of the citizenry.

It is obviously a rough system. It often does not measure up to the ideal we might hope to attain. But we continue to place our trust in this system because we believe our best chance at governing ourselves lies in obtaining the best judgment of elected representatives.

Unfortunately, that is not happening today. We are not obtaining the best judgment of our elected representatives in Congress because they are not free to give it to us. As a result of our present congressional campaign financing system—and the increasing role of political action committee (PAC) campaign contributions—members of Congress are rapidly losing their ability to represent the constituencies that have elected them.

We have long struggled to prevent money from being used to influence government decisions. We have not always succeeded, but we have never lost sight of the goal. Buying influence violates our most fundamental democratic values. We have long recognized that the ability to make large campaign contributions does, in fact, make some more equal than others. . . .

CONGRESSIONAL CAMPAIGN FINANCING

The last decade of congressional campaign financing has been marked by an exponential increase in the number of PACs formed by corporations, labor unions, trade associations, and other groups. In 1974 there were 608 PACs. Today there are more than 4000.

This explosion in PACs can be traced to congressional action—and inaction—in 1974. Ironically, at the very time when members of Congress were acting to clean up presidential elections, they opened the door for PACs to

From Fred Wertheimer, "Campaign Finance Reform: The Unfinished Agenda," *THE ANNALS of the American Academy of Political and Social Science* (July 1986). Copyright © 1986 by the American Academy of Political and Social Science. Reprinted by permission of Sage Publications, Inc.

enter the congressional arena in an unprecedented way. The key to the PAC explosion was a provision attached to the 1974 law by labor and business groups, over the opposition of Common Cause and other reform advocates, that authorized government contractors to establish PACs. In addition, by creating public financing for presidential campaigns, but not for congressional races, the 1974 amendments focused the attention and interest of PACs and other private campaign donors on Congress.

The resulting growth in PACs was no accident, and it certainly was not a reform. The growth of PACs, moreover, is certainly no unintended consequence of the 1974 law—the provision was included to protect and enhance the role of PACs in financing campaigns, and it has.

This tremendous increase in the number of PACs has not resulted in balanced representation in Washington. As Senator Gary Hart, Democrat of Colorado, has told the Senate:

> It seems the only group without a well-heeled PAC is the average citizen—the voter who has no special interest beyond low taxes, an efficient government, an honorable Congress, and a humane society. Those are the demands we should be heeding—but those are the demands the PACs have drowned out.

In fact, the increasing number of PACs has largely served to increase the ability of single interests to bring pressure to bear on a congressional candidate or a member of Congress. There are more than 100 insurance company PACs, more than 100 PACs sponsored by electric utilities, and more than 300 sponsored by labor unions. Representative David Obey, Democrat of Wisconsin, has observed that frequently in Washington:

an issue affects an entire industry and all of the companies and labor unions in that industry. . . . When that occurs, [and] a large number of groups which have made substantial contributions to members are all lobbying on the same side of an issue, the pressure generated from those aggregate contributions is enormous and warps the process. It is as if they had made a single, extremely large contribution.

The increase in the number of PACs, not surprisingly, has also produced a tremendous increase in PAC contributions to congressional candidates. In 1974, PACs gave $12.5 million to congressional candidates. By the 1984 elections, their contributions had exceeded $100 million, an eightfold increase in ten years.

PAC money also represents a far more important part of the average candidate's campaign funds than it did ten or so years ago. In 1974, 15.7 percent of congressional candidates' campaign money came from PACs; by the 1984 election, that proportion had increased to 30 percent.

Yet these numbers only begin to tell the story. The increased dependence on PAC contributions has been greatest for winners, those individuals who serve in Congress and who cast votes that shape our daily lives. In the Ninety-ninth Congress (1985–86), over 150 House members received 50 percent or more of their campaign funds from PACs, including 20 of the 27 committee chairs and party leaders. House winners in the 1984 election received an average of 41 percent of their campaign dollars from PACs. Of all winning House candidates in the 1974 election, only 28 percent received one-third or more of their campaign funds from PACs. By 1984, that figure had grown to 78 percent.

For senators, PAC contributions are also becoming a more important source of campaign dollars. Senators elected in 1976 received a total of $3.1 million from PACs; Senate winners in the 1984 election raised $20 million from OACs. In the 1984 elections, 23 winning Senate candidates raised more than $500,000 each from PACs.

Some have suggested that the growth in PACs is an important new form of citizen involvement in the political process. Yet PAC participation is often likely to be more of an involvement in the corporate process or the union process or the trade association process than it is in the political process. University of Minnesota professor Frank J. Sorauf has noted:

> To understand political participation through PACs, we need also to note the nature of the participation. Some of it is not even political activity; buying a ticket in a raffle, the proceeds of which go to a PAC, a party, or a candidate, does not qualify as a political act by most standards. Even the contributory act of writing a check or giving cash to a PAC is a somewhat limited form of participation that requires little time or immediate involvement; in a sense it buys political mercenaries who free the contributor from the need to be personally active in the campaign. It is one of the least active forms of political activity, well suited to the very busy or to those who find politics strange, boring, or distasteful.

In fact, the growth of PACs and the increased importance of PAC money have had a negative effect on two different parts of the political process—congressional elections and congressional decision making. First, PAC money tends to make congressional campaigns less competitive because of the overwhelm-

ing advantage enjoyed by incumbents in PAC fund-raising. The ratio of PAC contributions to incumbents over challengers in 1984 House races was 4.6 to 1.0; in the Senate, incumbents in 1984 enjoyed a 3.0 to 1.0 advantage in PAC receipts. On the average, 1984 House incumbents raised $100,000 more from PACs than did challengers. This $100,000 advantage was true even in the most highly competitive House races, those in which the incumbent received 55 percent or less of the vote. In these races, incumbents received an average of over $230,000 from PACs; their challengers received less than $110,000. The advantage enjoyed by incumbents is true for all kinds of PAC giving—for contributions by labor groups, corporate PACs, and trade and membership PACs.

Second, there is a growing awareness that PAC money makes a difference in the legislative process, a difference that is inimical to our democracy. PAC dollars are given by special interest groups to gain special access and special influence in Washington. Most often PAC contributions are made with a legislative purpose in mind. The late Justin Dart, former chairman of Dart Industries, once noted that dialogue with politicians "is a fine thing, but with a little money they hear you better." Senator Charles Mathias, Republican of Maryland, has stated:

> An official may not change his or her vote solely to accommodate the views of such contributors, but often officials, including myself, will agree to meet with an individual who made a large contribution so the official can hear the contributor's concerns and make the contributor aware these concerns have been considered. . . . Since an elected official has only so much time available, the inevitable result of such special

treatment for the large contributor is that other citizens are denied the opportunity they otherwise would have to confer with the elected official.

Common Cause and others have produced a number of studies that show a relationship between PAC contributions and legislative behavior. The examples run the gamut of legislative decisions, including hospital cost containment, the Clean Air Act, domestic content legislation, dairy price programs, gun control, maritime policies, and regulation by the Federal Trade Commission of professional groups or of used-car sales.

PAC gifts do not guarantee votes or support. PACs do not always win. But PAC contributions do provide donors with critical access and influence; they do affect legislative decisions and are increasingly dominating and paralyzing the legislative process.

In the last few years, something very important and fundamental has happened in this country—and that is the development of a growing awareness and recognition of the fact that the PAC system is a rotten system that must be changed. We know that concern is growing when Irving Shapiro, former chairman and chief executive officer of duPont and the former chairman of the Business Roundtable, describes the current system of financing congressional campaigns as "an invidious thing, it's corrupting, it does pollute the system." . . .

CONCLUSION

In the spring of 1973, Common Cause chairman John Gardner told the SenateCommerce Committee that "there is nothing in our political system today that creates more mischief, more corruption, and more alienation and distrust on the part of the public than does our system of financing elections. Despite major progress in improving the presidential campaign-financing system, that observation remains true today with regard to the congressional campaign-financing system. As former Watergate special prosecutor and current Common Cause chairman Archibald Cox has observed, inaction has resulted in "a Congress still more deeply trapped in the stranglehold of special interests which threatens to paralyze the process of democratic government." Congress needs to complete the reforms begun in the wake of Watergate by fundamentally transforming its own campaign-financing system and by making other adjustments needed to preserve the integrity of presidential public financing, campaign reporting requirements, and limitations on contributions by individuals and PACs.

A consensus has been reached in this country that PACs are inimical to our system of representative government. The question now remaining is whether that public consensus can be translated into congressional action.

No solution that may be adopted will be final and perfect. We will always need to reevaluate and adjust any campaign finance system. The presidential public financing system demonstrates the need for periodic adjustments. But more important, the experience of presidential public financing shows us that fundamental improvement in our campaign finance laws is indeed attainable.

We can and must have a better system for financing congressional campaigns. Representative government is at stake.

NO

Herbert E. Alexander

THE CASE FOR PACs

Seen in historical perspective, political action committees represent a functional system for political fund raising that developed, albeit unintentionally, from efforts to reform the political process. PACs represent an expression of an issue politics that resulted from attempts to remedy a sometimes unresponsive political system. And they represent an institutionalization of the campaign fund solicitation process that developed from the enactment of reform legislation intended to increase the number of small contributors.

Despite the unforeseen character of their development, PACs have made significant contributions to the political system:

1. *PACs increased participation in the political process.* The reform efforts that spawned PACs were designed to allow more voices to be heard in determining who will become our nation's elected officials. Thanks in part to PACs, that goal has been achieved.

Although it is difficult to determine how many individuals now participate in the political process through voluntarily contributing to political action committees, some useful information is available. The survey of company PACs by Civic Service, Inc., found that in the 1979–1980 election cycle more than 100,000 individuals contributed to the 275 PACs responding to the survey, and that the average number of donors to those PACS was 388. By extrapolation, it appears that all corporate PACs active in the 1979–1980 cycle received contributions from at least 210,000 individuals.

The largest conservative ideological group PACs, which rely on direct mail solicitations, received about 1.3 million contributions in 1979–1980, though individuals may well have contributed to more than one of those groups. It is difficult to estimate the total number of persons who gave to professional and membership association PACs, though information about specific groups is available. For example, an official of the National Association of Realtors PAC estimated that his group had 80,000 contributors in 1979, 87,000 in 1980, 92,000 in 1981 and about 95,000 in 1982. It is more difficult still to estimate the number of contributors to labor PACs, although here, too, information is available regarding specific groups. According to a National

From Herbert E. Alexander, "The Case for PACs," a Public Affairs Council monograph. Copyright © 1983 by the Public Affairs Council. Reprinted by permission.

Education Association official, for example, the NEA PAC received donations from about 600,000 persons in the 1979–1980 election cycle.

Surveys taken between 1952 and 1976 indicate that from 8 to 12 percent of the total adult population contributed to politics at some level in presidential election years, with the figure standing at 9 percent in 1976. According to a survey by the Center for Political Studies at the University of Michigan, however, 13.4 percent of the adult population—about 17.1 million persons—gave to candidates and causes during the 1979–1980 election cycle. Survey data suggest that the increase registered in 1980 is due to the increased number of persons giving to interest groups. Of those surveyed, 6.8 percent gave to candidates, 3.8 percent gave to parties, and 6.8 percent gave to interest groups. Since those figures add up to well over 13.4 percent, it is obvious that a significant number of persons contributed in two or all three categories.

2. *PACs allow individuals to increase the impact of their political activity.* PACs and their interest group sponsors not only encourage individual citizens to participate in the electoral process, they provide them with a sense of achievement or effectiveness that accompanies taking part in political activity with like-minded persons rather than merely acting alone.

3. *PACs are a popular mechanism for political fund raising because they respect the manner in which society is structured.* Occupational and interest groups have replaced the neighborhood as the center of activities and source of values and the ideologically ambiguous political parties as a source of political action. Individuals seem less willing to commit themselves to the broad agenda of the parties; they are interested mainly in single issues or clusters of issues. PACs, organized on the basis of specific occupational or socioeconomic or issue groupings, allow individuals to join with others who share their values and interests and to undertake action to achieve the political goals they perceive as most important to them.

4. *PACs and the interest groups they represent serve as a safeguard against undue influence by the government or by the media.* By energetically promoting their competing claims and views, such groups prevent the development of either a single, official viewpoint or a media bias. They demonstrate the lively pluralism so highly valued and forcefully guaranteed by the framers of the Constitution.

5. *PACs have made more money available for political campaigns.* By helping candidates pay the rising costs of conducting election campaigns, PACs help to assure the communication of the candidates' views and positions and thus to clarify campaign issues. They also encourage individuals without wealth to run for office.

6. *PACs have contributed to greater accountability in election campaign financing.* Corporations are legitimately concerned about public policy, but prior to the FECA they were uncertain about the legality of providing financial support to candidates who would voice their concerns. That many corporations resorted to subterfuges to circumvent the law is common knowledge. By sanctioning the use of PACs by corporations, the law has replaced the undisclosed and often questionable form of business participation in politics with the public and accountable form practiced by corporate and other business-related PACs today. However much money now is derived from corporate PACs, it is not clear that corporate PAC money today is greater proportionally than was business-derived money when

there were no effective limits on giving and when disclosure was less comprehensive.

HOW PACSs CAN RESPOND

PACs enjoy a growing constituency, but, in view of current anti-PAC publicity and endeavors, PAC supporters must engage in a concerted educational effort regarding their methods and goals if PACs are to avoid being restricted in their ability to participate in the political process. That effort should include, certainly, responding with specific and accurate information to criticisms made of PACs and making plain the many values PACs bring to the political process.

Educational efforts also might include using the methods of PAC opponents to the advantage of the PAC movement. For example, PAC opponents frequently correlate PAC contributions and legislative outcomes and conclude that the contributions resulted in specific legislative decisions. PAC critics publicized widely the fact that maritime unions contributed heavily to some members of the House Merchant Marine Committee who favored a cargo preference bill introduced in 1977 and supported by the unions. They implied the committee members were influenced by the contributions to report out a favorable bill. PAC supporters did little to discover and publicize the committee members' other sources of funds. The American Medical Association Political Action Committee, for example, contributed to every incumbent on the House Committee, yet AMPAC and the medical practitioners who support it had no vested interest in the cargo preference bill or in other legislation considered by the committee. Nor was much publicity given to the fact that

the two committee members who received the greatest financial support from the unions represented districts in which there is a significant amount of port activity and that consequently they would understandably be responsive to maritime interests.

When critics use simplistic correlations to demonstrate undue PAC influence on the decisions of legislators, PAC supporters should endeavor to present the whole campaign finance picture: What percentage of the legislators' campaign funds came from the interest group or groups in question? Did those groups also contribute to other legislators whose committee assignments gave them no formative role in legislation of particular interest to the groups? Did groups with no special interest in the legislation in question contribute to the legislators dealing with it at the committee or subcommittee level? What factors in the legislators' home districts or states might have influenced the legislators' decisions? What non-monetary pressures were brought to bear on the legislators?

It also might be useful for PAC supporters to publicize "negative correlations," which would demonstrate that PAC contributions often do not correlate with specific legislative decisions.

PAC supporters also should question the unarticulated assumptions at the basis of much of the anti-PAC criticism.

• Money is not simply a necessary evil in the political process. By itself money is neutral; in politics as in other areas its uses and purposes determine its meaning.

• There is nothing inherently immoral or corrupting about corporate or labor contributions of money, any more than any other private contribution of funds.

• All campaign contributions are not attempts to gain special favors; rather, contributing political money is an important form of participation in a democracy.

• Money is not the sole, and often not even the most important, political resource. Many other factors affect electoral and legislative outcomes. (At the close of the 97th Congress, for example, an immigration reform bill that reportedly had widespread support in the House and the Senate died because of the effective lobbying efforts of employees, labor unions and minorities who believed they would be adversely affected by it; few, if any, campaign contributions were involved in the effort to forestall the legislation.)

• Curbing interest group contributions will not free legislators of the dilemma of choosing between electoral necessity and legislative duty. Even if PACs were eliminated, legislators would still be confronted with the sometimes conflicting demands between doing what will help them remain in office and serving what they perceive as the public good.

• A direct dialogue between candidates and individual voters without interest group influence is not possible in a representative democracy. Politics is about people, their ideas, interests and aspirations. Since people seek political fulfillment partly through groups, a politics in which supportive groups are shut out or seriously impaired is difficult to conceive.

There is danger, clearly, in our pluralistic society if groups are overly restricted in their political activity. It is useful to recall that five of the most significant movements of the last two decades—the civil rights movement, the Vietnam peace movement, the political reform movement, the women's rights movement, and the movement toward fiscal restraint—originated in the private sector, where the need for action was perceived and where needed interest organizations were established to carry it out. *These movements would not have taken place if like-minded citizens had not been permitted to combine forces and thereby enhance their political power.*

One hundred and fifty years ago, de Tocqueville recognized that in America "the liberty of association [had] become a necessary guarantee against the tyranny of the majority." The freedom to join in common cause with other citizens remains indispensable to our democratic system. The pursuit of self-interest is, as Irving Kristol has pointed out, a condition, not a problem.

POSTSCRIPT

Do Political Action Committees
Undermine Democracy?

Interestingly, both Alexander and Wertheimer couch their arguments in terms of democratic values: open government, fairness to all, and popular participation. Alexander claims that PACs bring a wide variety of groups into the political process, give new groups a chance to be heard, and let corporations openly contribute funds instead of resorting to back-channel routes. Wertheimer pins much of his argument on the need for equality in the democratic process, and he worries that PACs make some voters "more equal" than others.

Edward Roeder has edited a useful directory of PACs that supplies information about their sources, their funds, and whom they support. See his *PACs Americana: The Directory of Political Action Committees and Their Interests*, 2d ed. (Sunshine Service, 1986). Larry Sabato's *PAC Power* (W. W. Norton, 1984) is a comprehensive overview of PACs: what they are, how they operate, and their impact. Frank J. Sorauf's *What Price PACs?* (Priority Press, 1985) studies PAC financing and its implications today. For an excellent general study of interest groups, including PACs, see Graham K. Wilson's *Interest Groups in the United States* (Clarendon Press, 1981).

Other countries succeed in setting strict limits on campaign spending. Can America do it without inhibiting political expression? Should we substitute public financing of congressional elections? Or do we accept PACs as a vigorous expression of political freedom? In short, do PACs undermine or do they underline democracy?

ISSUE 4

Do the News Media Have a Liberal Bias?

YES: William A. Rusher, from *The Coming Battle for the Media: Curbing the Power of the Media Elite* (William Morrow, 1988)

NO: Edward S. Herman and Noam Chomsky, from "Propaganda Mill," *The Progressive* (June 1988)

ISSUE SUMMARY

YES: Media analyst William A. Rusher argues that the media are biased against conservatives and that news coverage promotes liberal opinions.
NO: Professors Edward S. Herman and Noam Chomsky critique the mass media from the perspective of the left and find the media to be a "propaganda mill" in the service of the wealthy and powerful.

"A small group of men, numbering perhaps no more than a dozen 'anchormen,' commentators and executive producers . . . decide what forty to fifty million Americans will learn of the day's events in the nation and the world." The speaker was Spiro Agnew, vice president of the United States during the Nixon administration. The thesis of Agnew's speech, delivered to an audience of midwestern Republicans in 1969, was that the television news media are controlled by a small group of liberals who foist their liberal opinions on viewers under the guise of "news." The upshot of this control, said Agnew, "is that a narrow and distorted picture of America often emerges from the televised news." Many Americans, even many of those who were later shocked by revelations that Agnew took bribes while serving in public office, agreed with Agnew's critique of the "liberal media."

Politicians' complaints about unfair news coverage go back much further than Spiro Agnew and the Nixon administration. The third president of the United States, Thomas Jefferson, was an eloquent champion of the press, but after six years as president, he could hardly contain his bitterness. "The man who never looks into a newspaper," he wrote, "is better informed than he who reads them, inasmuch as he who knows nothing is nearer to truth than he whose mind is filled with falsehoods and errors."

The press today is much different than it was in Jefferson's day. Newspapers then were pressed in hand-operated frames in many little printing shops around the country; everything was local and decentralized, and each paper averaged a few hundred subscribers. Today, newspaper chains have taken over most of the once-independent local newspapers. The remaining independents rely heavily on national and international wire services. Almost all major magazines have national circulations; some newspapers, like *USA Today* and the *Wall Street Journal*, do too. Other newspapers, like the *New York Times* and the *Washington Post*, enjoy nationwide prestige and help set the nation's news agenda. Geographical centralization is even more obvious in the case of television. About 70 percent of national news on television comes from three networks whose programming originates in New York City.

A second important difference between the media of the eighteenth century and the media today has to do with the ideal of "objectivity." In past eras, newspapers were frankly partisan sheets, full of nasty barbs at the politicians and parties the editors did not like; they made no distinction between "news" and "editorials." The ideal of objective journalism is a relatively recent development. It traces back to the early years of the twentieth century. Disgusted with the sensationalist "yellow journalism" of the time, intellectual leaders urged that newspapers cultivate a core of professionals who would concentrate on accurate reporting and who would leave their opinions to the editorial page. Journalism schools cropped up around the country, helping to promote the ideal of objectivity. Although some journalists now openly scoff at it, the ideal still commands the respect—in theory, if not always in practice—of working reporters.

These two historical developments, news centralization and news professionalism, play off against one another in the current debate over news "bias." The question of bias was irrelevant when the press was a scatter of little independent newspapers. If you did not like the bias of one paper, you picked another one—or you started your own, which could be done with modest capital outlay. Bias started to become an important question when newspapers became dominated by chains and airwaves by networks, and when a few national press leaders like the *New York Times* and the *Washington Post* began to emerge. When one news anchor can address a nightly audience of 25 million people, the question of bias is no longer irrelevant.

But *is* there bias? If so, *whose* bias? These are the central questions. Defenders of the press usually concede that journalists, like all human beings, have biases, but they deny that they carry their biases into their writing. Journalists, they say, are professionals, trained to bring us news unembellished by personal opinion. They conclude that bias is in the eye of the beholder: left-wingers think the press is conservative, right-wingers call it liberal; both are unhappy that the press is not biased in *their* direction.

Both the Left and the Right disagree. The Left considers the press conservative because it is tied in with big business, indeed *is* a big business. The Right insists that the bias of the press is overwhelmingly liberal because most reporters are liberal. In the following selections, William A. Rusher argues that the media are biased against conservatives, and Edward S. Herman and Noam Chomsky develop a critique of the media from a leftist perspective.

YES

William A. Rusher

THE COMING BATTLE FOR THE MEDIA

It is the conviction of a great many people, not all of them conservative by any means, that news presentation by the media elite is heavily biased in favor of liberal views and attitudes.

It is important, right at the outset, to specify precisely what is being objected to. This is a free country, and journalists are every bit as entitled to their private political opinions as the rest of us. But the average newspaper or television news program, and certainly those we have categorized as the "media elite," purport to be offering us something more than the personal opinions of the reporter, or the chief editor, or even the collective opinions of the journalistic staff. In one way or another, to one extent or another, they all profess to be offering us the "news"—which is to say, an account of as many relevant events and developments, in the period in question, as can be given in the space or time available. Moreover, in offering this account, the media we are discussing implicitly claim to be acting with a reasonable degree of objectivity. Their critics sharply challenge that claim.

But just how much objectivity is it reasonable to expect? The question is more complicated than it may at first appear. There is a school of thought—popular, perhaps naturally, among a certain subcategory of journalists themselves—that a journalist is, or at least ought to be, a sort of vestal virgin: a chalice of total and incorruptible objectivity. But this, of course, is nonsense, and is certainly not expected by any reasonable person.

Journalists too are, after all, sons and daughters of Adam. Their conception was far from immaculate; they share our taint of Original Sin. They were born into our common society, received the same general education we all received, and had roughly the same formative experiences. How likely is it that, simply by choosing to pursue a career in journalism, they underwent some sort of miraculous transformation, to emerge shriven and pure, purged of all bias and dedicated henceforth solely to the pursuit of the unvarnished Truth? . . . Just how does one go about demonstrating that the media elite are, in the matter of their private opinions, overwhelmingly partial to liberal policies and liberal political personalities? A general impression, based on familiarity with their work-product as on display in the *New York Times* or the *Washington Post*, in *Time* or *Newsweek*, or on the evening news programs of one or another of the major networks, is absolutely worthless. You will be told that your perception is distorted by your own partiality to conservative policies and personalities. You will be assured that the liberals complain just as loudly as conservatives about maltreatment by the media (though on inspection it turns out to be the harder left—e.g., Alexander Cockburn—that complains; liberals typically, and understandably, complain very little about distortion by the media elite). You will be referred to news stories in which there was no liberal bias, and to news presentations well and truly balanced—shining exceptions that merely emphasize the rule.

There is, in fact, only one way to ascertain with precision anyone's political leaning, inclination, or prejudice, and that is to interview him or her in depth. Moreover, if the intention is to evaluate the opinions of an entire group, the sample interviewed must be large enough to be dependably representative. Fortunately there have recently been several conscientious surveys of the political views of America's media elite, and the results are thoroughly unambiguous. . . .

[A] remarkable survey, whose results were published in 1981 . . . was conducted in 1979 and 1980 by two professors of political science—S. Robert Lichter of George Washington University and Stanley Rothman of Smith College—as part of a larger inquiry into the attitudes of various elites, under the auspices of the Research Institute on International Change at Columbia University. The survey itself was supervised by Response Analysis, a survey research organization.

Lichter and Rothman began by defining the following organizations as America's "most influential media outlets": three daily newspapers—the *New York Times*, the *Washington Post*, and the *Wall Street Journal;* three weekly newsmagazines—*Time, Newsweek,* and *U.S. News and World Report;* the news departments of four networks—CBS, NBC, ABC, and PBS; and the news departments of certain major independent broadcasting stations.

Within these organizations they then selected at random, from among those responsible for news content, individuals to be approached for interviews. In the print media, these included "reporters, columnists, department heads, bureau chiefs, editors and executives responsible for news content." In the electronic media, those selected included "correspondents, anchormen, producers, film editors and news executives." . . .

It transpires that, of those who voted in these elections at all (and this was 82 percent in 1976, when all but the youngest among those interviewed in 1979–80 would have qualified), *never less than 80 percent of the media elite voted for the Democratic candidate.* . . .

Like many American liberals, the media elite accept the essential free-enterprise basis of the United States economy, but they are devoted to welfarism. Over two thirds (68 percent) believe "the government should substantially reduce the income gap between the rich and the poor," and nearly half (48 percent) think the government should guarantee a job to anyone who wants one.

On sociocultural issues, the media elite's support for liberal positions is overwhelming. Ninety percent believe it is a woman's right to decide whether or not to have an abortion. A solid majority

(53 percent) can't even bring itself to affirm that adultery is wrong.

There is far more to the Lichter-Rothman survey than the above brief sample of its findings, but the basic thrust of the study is unmistakable: America's media elite are far to the left of American public opinion in general on the great majority of topics. . . .

THE EFFECT ON THE "NEWS"

Proving statistically that the media's demonstrated liberalism influences their handling of the news is no simple matter. The media clearly aren't going to do us the favor of admitting it, and the formidable human capacity for self-delusion makes it likely that many members of the media don't even realize it, at least not fully. A good many of them undoubtedly think their selection and treatment of stories is governed solely by their acute "news sense," where any objective observer would detect bias. And even when a member of the media knows full well that his handling of news stories is influenced by his biases, he is naturally prone to minimize that influence and make excuses for the residue.

Adding to the difficulty is the fact that evidence of bias, liberal or otherwise, is almost inevitably somewhat subjective. One man's "bias" is another man's "robust journalism," etc. Obvious as the bias may be to many thoughtful people, how can one nail it down?

One of the earliest and still one of the best efforts to do so was made by Edith Efron in her book *The News Twisters* (Nash, 1971). It is said that medieval philosophers had a high old time arguing over how many teeth a horse has, until some spoilsport ended the game by

going out and actually counting them. That was essentially Efron's solution, too. . . .

[Rusher quotes extensively from Efron's discussion of her methodology. She counted the number of words used in prime-time TV news programs that could be classified "for" and "against" the three major candidates for president in 1968: Alabama governor George Wallace (running as an independent), Democrat Hubert Humphrey, and Republican Richard Nixon. —Eds.]

Efron then sets forth, in bar-graph form, the total number of words spoken for and against the three presidential candidates on the three major networks during the period under study. In the case of George Wallace, the result was as follows:

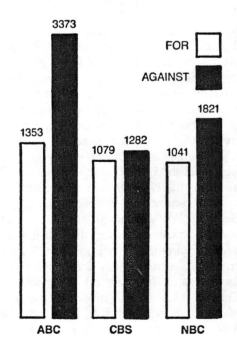

THE EFFECT ON THE "NEWS"

FOR □

AGAINST ■

ABC   CBS   NBC

3373   1353   1079   1282   1041   1821

In the case of Hubert Humphrey, the graph looked like this:

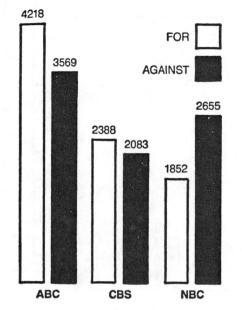

In the case of Richard Nixon, this was the result:

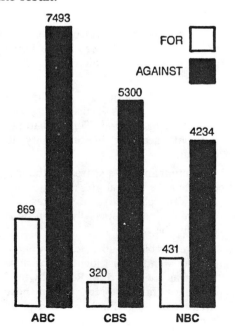

Now, how can the statistics regarding Nixon be interpreted, save as a product of bias? Bear in mind that this was long before Watergate—indeed, that in the next election (1972) Nixon would be re-elected by a landslide. Yet in 1968 the words spoken *against* Nixon on ABC (the network with the smallest imbalance in this respect) outnumbered the words spoken *for* him by nearly nine to one. At NBC the negative proportion was almost ten to one. At CBS it actually exceeded sixteen to one. . . .

Maura Clancey and Michael Robinson conducted another comprehensive study of the media's bias in reporting the "news," in connection with the 1984 presidential election, under the auspices of George Washington University and the American Enterprise Institute. . . .

Clancey and Robinson summed up their findings as follows:

There may be some questions about the validity of our measure, but there can be no question about the lopsidedness of what is uncovered. Assuming that a piece with a positive spin equals "good press," and assuming that negative spin equals "bad press," Ronald Reagan and George Bush proved overwhelmingly to be the "bad press" ticket of 1984. Figure 1 [see next page] contains the number of news seconds we scored as good press or bad press for each of the candidates. Ronald Reagan's bad press total was *ten times greater* than his good press total. (7,230 seconds vs. 730). In other words, his "spin ratio" was ten-to-one negative.

George Bush had a spin ratio that defied computation—1,500 seconds of "bad press" pieces and zero seconds of good press.

Walter Mondale and Geraldine Ferraro, on the other hand, had slightly *positive* spin ratios—1,970 seconds of

Figure 1

News seconds

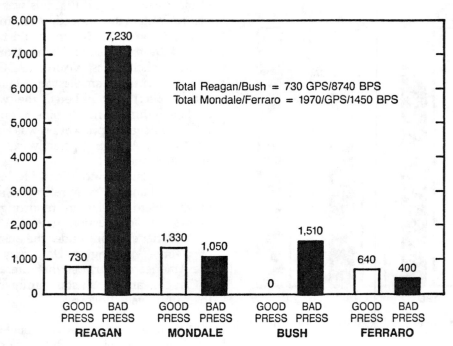

Total Reagan/Bush = 730 GPS/8740 BPS
Total Mondale/Ferraro = 1970/GPS/1450 BPS

good press about themselves as people or potential leaders, and 1,450 seconds of bad press. Given what we know about the bad news bias of television, the fact that anyone, let alone any ticket, got more positive spin than negative is news indeed.

But Clancey and Robinson are not even prepared to concede that their own lopsided results in 1984 conclusively demonstrated a liberal bias on the part of the media. On the contrary, they suggest, "liberal bias is not the only explanation, or even the best."

Instead, they posit the existence of what they call "the four I's"—non-ideological reasons for the bad press admittedly accorded Reagan and Bush in 1984. These are:

"Impishness"—a human tendency to want to turn a walkaway into a horse race "to keep one's own work interesting."

"Irritation"—annoyance at what the media perceived as Reagan's glib one-liners and his alleged "Teflon coating" (i.e., his seeming invulnerability to criticism).

"Incumbency"—a sense that the media have "a special mission to warn Americans about the advantages any incumbent has," especially when he is winning big.

"Irrevocability"—the feeling that a double standard is justified because 1984 was the last time Reagan would ever face the electorate. Under those circumstances, giving him a bad press became "a near-messianic mission."

Defenders of the media may well wonder whether pleading them guilty to the above unpleasant set of impulses would actually constitute much of an improvement over admitting that they have a liberal bias. But they can be spared that painful decision, because "the four I's" simply don't survive careful inspection. In pure theory they might explain the media's astonishing bias against Reagan in 1984, but not one of them applies to the equally well-established instance of bias discussed earlier: the media's treatment of Nixon in the 1968 campaign.

That campaign was no "walkaway" for Nixon; it was one of the closest presidential elections in United States history—43.4 percent for Nixon, 42.7 for Humphrey, and 13.5 for Wallace. And Nixon was certainly no Reagan, either in his mastery of glib one-liners or in possessing a "Teflon coating." Moreover, he was not the incumbent, or even the nominee of the incumbent's party. And 1968 was *not* the last time Nixon could or would face the electorate. Yet the media gave him the same biased treatment that Reagan received in 1984. The conclusion is unavoidable that the media's conduct had the same basis in both cases: a liberal bias neatly congruent with the demonstrated liberal preferences of the overwhelming majority of the media elite.

NO

Edward S. Herman
and Noam Chomsky

PROPAGANDA MILL

It is a primary function of the mass media in the United States to mobilize public support for the special interests that dominate the Government and the private sector.

This is our conclusion after years of studying the media. Perhaps it is an obvious point—but the common assumption seems to be that the media are independent and committed to discovering and reporting the truth. Leaders of the media claim that their news judgments rest on unbiased, objective criteria. We contend, on the other hand, that the powerful are able to fix the premises of discourse, decide what the general populace will be allowed to see, hear, and think about, and "manage" public opinion by mounting regular propaganda campaigns.

We do not claim this is all the mass media do, but we believe the propaganda function to be a very important aspect of their overall service.

In countries where the levers of power are in the hands of a state bureaucracy, monopolistic control of the media, often supplemented by official censorship, makes it clear that media serve the ends of the dominant elite. It is much more difficult to see a propaganda system at work where the media are private and formal censorship is absent.

This is especially true where the media actively compete, periodically attack and expose corporate and governmental malfeasance, and aggressively portray themselves as spokesmen for free speech and the general community interest. What is not evident (and remains undiscussed in the media) is the severely limited access to the private media system and the effect of money and power on the system's performance.

Critiques of this kind are often dismissed by Establishment commentators as "conspiracy theories," but this is merely an evasion. We don't rely on any kind of conspiracy hypothesis to explain the performance of the media; in fact, our treatment is much closer to a "free-market" analysis.

From Edward S. Herman and Noam Chomsky, "Propaganda Mill," *The Progressive* (June 1988). Adapted from *Manufacturing Consent: The Political Economy of the Mass Media* by Edward S. Herman and Noam Chomsky (Pantheon Books, 1988). Copyright © 1988 by Edward S. Herman and Noam Chomsky. Reprinted by permission of Pantheon Books, a division of Random House, Inc.

Most of the bias in the media arises from the selection of right-thinking people, the internalization of preconceptions until they are taken as self-evident truths, and the practical adaptation of employees to the constraints of ownership, organization, market, and political power.

The censorship practiced within the media is largely self-censorship, by reporters and commentators who adjust to the "realities" as they perceive them. But there are important actors who do take positive initiatives to define and shape the news and to keep the media in line. This kind of guidance is provided by the Government, the leaders of the corporate community, the top media owners and executives, and assorted individuals and groups who are allowed to take the initiative.

The media are not a solid monolith on all issues. Where the powerful are in disagreement, the media will reflect a certain diversity of tactical judgments on how to attain generally shared aims. But views that challenge fundamental premises or suggest that systemic factors govern the exercise of State power will be excluded.

The pattern is pervasive. Consider the coverage from and about Nicaragua. The mass media rarely allow their news columns—or, for that matter, their opinion pages—to present materials suggesting that Nicaragua is more democratic than El Salvador and Guatemala; that its government does not murder ordinary citizens, as the governments of El Salvador and Guatemala do on a routine basis; that it has carried out socioeconomic reforms important to the majority that the other two governments somehow cannot attempt; that Nicaragua poses no military threat to its neighbors but has, in fact, been subjected to continuous attack by the United States and its clients and surrogates, and that the U.S. fear of the Nicaraguan government is based more on its virtues than on its alleged defects.

The mass media also steer clear of discussing the background and results of the closely analogous attempt of the United States to bring "democracy" to Guatemala in 1954 by means of a CIA-supported invasion, which terminated Guatemalan democracy for an indefinite period. Although the United States supported elite rule and organized terror in Guatemala (among many other countries) for decades, actually subverted or approved the subversion of democracy in Brazil, Chile, and the Philippines (again, among others), is now "constructively engaged" with terror regimes around the world, and had no concern about democracy in Nicaragua so long as the brutal Somoza regime was firmly in power, the media take U.S. Government claims of a concern for "democracy" in Nicaragua at face value.

In contrast, El Salvador and Guatemala, with far worse records, are presented as struggling toward democracy under "moderate" leaders, thus meriting sympathetic approval.

IN CRITICIZING MEDIA BIASES, WE OFTEN draw on the media themselves for at least some of the "facts." That the media provide some information about an issue, however, proves absolutely nothing about the adequacy or accuracy of media coverage. The media do, in fact, suppress a great deal of information, but even more important is the way they present a particular fact—its placement, tone, and frequency of repetition—and the framework of analysis in which it is placed. That a careful reader looking for a fact can sometimes find it, with diligence and a skeptical eye, tells us nothing about whether that fact received the attention and context it deserved, whether it was intelligible to most readers, or whether it was effectively distorted or suppressed.

The standard media pattern of indignant campaigns and suppressions, of shading and emphasis, of carefully selected context, premises, and general agenda, is highly useful to those who wield power. If, for example, they are able to channel public concern and outrage to the abuses of enemy states, they can mobilize the population for an ideological crusade.

Thus, a constant focus on the victims of communism helps persuade the public that the enemy is evil, while setting the stage for intervention, subversion, support for terrorist regimes, an endless arms race, and constant military conflict—all in a noble cause. At the same time, the devotion of our leaders—and our media—to this narrow set of victims raises public patriotism and self-esteem, demonstrating the essential humanity of our nation and our people.

The public does not notice media silence about victims of America's client states, which is as important as the media's concentration on victims of America's enemies. It would have been difficult for the Guatemalan government to murder tens of thousands over the past decade if the U.S. press had provided the kind of coverage it gave to the difficulties of Andrei Sakharov in the Soviet Union or the murder of Jerzy Popieluszko in Poland. It would have been impossible to wage a brutal war against South Vietnam and the rest of Indochina, leaving a legacy of misery and destruction that may never be overcome, if the media had not rallied to the cause, portraying murderous aggression as a defense of freedom.

Propaganda campaigns may be instituted either by the Government or by one or more of the top media firms. The campaigns to discredit the government of Nicaragua, to support the Salvadoran elections as an exercise in legitimizing democracy, and to use the Soviet shooting down of the Korean airliner KAL 007 as a means of mobilizing support for the arms buildup were instituted and propelled by the Government. The campaigns to publicize the crimes of Pol Pot in Cambodia and the allegations of a KGB plot to assassinate the Pope were initiated by the *Reader's Digest*, with strong follow-up support from NBC television, *The New York Times*, and other major media companies.

Some propaganda campaigns are jointly initiated by the Government and the media; all of them require the media's cooperation.

THE MASS MEDIA ARE DRAWN INTO A SYMbiotic relationship with powerful sources of information by economic necessity and reciprocity of interest. The media need a steady, reliable flow of the raw material of news. They have daily news demands and imperative news schedules. They cannot afford to have reporters and cameras at all places where important stories may break, so they must concentrate their resources where significant news often occurs, where important rumors and leaks abound, and where regular press conferences are held.

The White House, the Pentagon, and the State Department are central nodes of such news activity at the national level. On a local basis, city hall and the police department are regular news beats for reporters. Corporations and trade groups are also regular and credible purveyors of stories deemed newsworthy. These bureaucracies turn out a large volume of material that meets the demands of news organizations for reliable, scheduled flows. They also have the great merit of being recognizable and credible because of their status and prestige.

Another reason for the heavy weight given to official sources is that the mass media claim to be "objective" dispensers of the news. Partly to maintain the image of objectivity, but also to protect themselves from criticism of bias and the threat of libel suits, they need material that can be portrayed as presumptively accurate. This also reduces cost: Taking information from sources that may be presumed credible reduces investigative expense, whereas material from sources that are not *prima facie* credible, or that will draw criticism and threats, requires careful checking and costly research.

The Government and corporate bureaucracies that constitute primary news sources maintain vast public-relations operations that ensure special access to the media. The Pentagon, for example, has a public-information service that involves many thousands of employees, spending hundreds of millions of dollars every year and dwarfing not only the public-information resources of any dissenting individual or group but the aggregate of *all* dissenters.

During a brief interlude of relative openness in 1979 and 1980, the U.S. Air Force revealed that its public-information outreach included 140 newspapers with a weekly total circulation of 690,000; *Airman* magazine with a monthly circulation of 125,000; thirty-four radio and seventeen television stations, primarily overseas; 45,000 headquarters and unit news releases; 615,000 hometown news releases; 6,600 news media interviews; 3,200 news conferences; 500 news media orientation flights; fifty meetings with editorial boards, and 11,000 speeches. Note that this is just the Air Force. In 1982, *Air Force Journal International* indicated that the Pentagon was publishing 1,203 periodicals.

To put this into perspective, consider the scope of public information activities of the American Friends Service Committee and the National Council of the Churches of Christ, two of the largest nonprofit organizations that consistently challenge the views of the Pentagon. The Friends' main office had an information services budget of less than $500,000 and a staff of eleven in 1984–1985. It issued about 200 press releases a year, held thirty press conferences, and produced one film and two or three slide shows. The Council of Churches office of information has an annual budget of about $350,000, issues about 100 news releases, and holds four press conferences a year.

Only the corporate sector has the resources to produce public information and propaganda on the scale of the Pentagon and other Government bodies. These large actors provide the media with facilities and with advance copies of speeches and reports. They schedule news conferences at hours geared to news deadlines. They write press releases in usable language. They carefully organize "photo-opportunity" sessions.

In effect, the large bureaucracies of the powerful subsidize the mass media, and thereby gain special access. They become "routine" news sources, while non-routine sources must struggle for access and may be ignored.

Because of the services they provide, the continuous contact they sustain, and the mutual dependency they foster, the powerful can use personal relationships, threats, and rewards to extend their influence over the news media. The media may feel obligated to carry extremely dubious stories, or to mute criticism, to avoid offending sources and disturbing a close relationship. When one depends on authorities for daily news, it is difficult to call them liars even if they tell whoppers.

Powerful sources may also use their prestige and importance as a lever to deny critics access to the media. The Defense Department, for example, refused to participate in discussions of military issues on National Public Radio if experts from the Center for Defense Information were invited to appear on the same program. Assistant Secretary of State Elliott Abrams would not appear on a Harvard University program dealing with human rights in Central America unless former Ambassador Robert White were excluded. Claire Sterling, a principal propagandist for the "Bulgarian connection" to the plot to assassinate the Pope, refused to take part in television programs on which her critics would appear.

The relation between power and sourcing extends beyond official and corporate provision of news to shaping the supply of "experts." The dominance of official sources is undermined when highly respectable unofficial sources give dissident views. This problem is alleviated by "coopting the experts"—that is, putting them on the payroll as consultants, funding their research, and organizing think tanks that will hire them directly and help disseminate their messages.

The process of creating a body of experts who will confirm and distribute the opinions favored by the Government and "the market" has been carried out on a deliberate basis and a massive scale. In 1972, Judge Lewis Powell, later elevated to the Supreme Court, wrote a memo to the U.S. Chamber of Commerce in which he urged business "to buy the top academic reputations in the country to add credibility to corporate studies and give business a stronger voice on the campuses."

During the 1970s and early 1980s, new institutions were established and old ones reactivated to help propagandize the corporate viewpoint. Hundreds of intellectuals were brought to these institutions, their work funded, and their output disseminated to the media by a sophisticated propaganda effort.

The media themselves also provide "experts" who regularly echo the official view. John Barron and Claire Sterling are household names as authorities on the KGB and terrorism because the *Reader's Digest* has funded, published, and publicized their work. The Soviet defector Arkady Shevchenko became an expert on Soviet arms and intelligence because *Time*, ABC television, and *The New York Times* chose to feature him despite his badly tarnished credentials. By giving these vehicles of the preferred view much exposure, the media confer status and make them the obvious candidates for opinion and analysis.

Another class of experts whose prominence is largely a function of their serviceability to power consists of former radicals who have "come to see the light." The motives that induce these individuals to switch gods, from Stalin (or Mao) and communism to Reagan and free enterprise, may vary, but so far as the media are concerned, the ex-radicals have simply seen the error of their ways. The former sinners, whose previous work was ignored or ridiculed by the mass media, are suddenly elevated to prominence and anointed as experts.

MEDIA PROPAGANDA CAMPAIGNS HAVE generally been useful to elite interests. The Red Scare of 1919–1920 helped abort the postwar union-organizing drive in steel and other major industries. The Truman-McCarthy Red Scare of the early 1950s helped inaugurate the Cold War and the permanent war economy, and also weakened the progressive coalition that had taken shape during the New Deal years.

The chronic focus on the plight of Soviet dissidents, on enemy killings in Cambodia, and on the Bulgarian Connection helped weaken the Vietnam Syndrome, justify a huge arms buildup and a more aggressive foreign policy, and divert attention from the upward distribution of income that was the heart of the Reagan Administration's domestic economic program. The recent propaganda attacks on Nicaragua have averted eyes from the savageries of the war in El Salvador and helped justify the escalating U.S. investment in counterrevolution in Central America.

Conversely, propaganda campaigns are *not* mobilized where coverage of victimization, though it may be massive, sustained, and dramatic, fails to serve the interests of the elite.

The focus on Cambodia in the Pol Pot era was serviceable, for example, because Cambodia had fallen to the communists and useful lessons could be drawn from the experience of their victims. But the many Cambodian victims of U.S. bombing *before* the communists came to power were scrupulously ignored by the U.S. press. After Pol Pot was ousted by the Vietnamese, the United States quietly shifted its support to this "worse than Hitler" villain, with little or no notice in the press, which once again adjusted to the official political agenda.

Attention to the Indonesian massacres of 1965–1966, or to the victims of the Indonesian invasion of East Timor since 1975, would also be distinctly unhelpful as bases of media campaigns, because Indonesia is a U.S. ally and client that maintains an open door to Western investment. The same is true of the victims of state terror in Chile and Guatemala—U.S. clients whose basic institutional structure, including the state terror system, were put in place by, or with crucial assistance from, the United States.

No propaganda campaigns are mounted in the mass media on behalf of such victims. To publicize their plight would, after all, conflict with the interests of the wealthy and powerful.

POSTSCRIPT

Do the News Media Have a Liberal Bias?

As the opposing arguments in this issue indicate, we can find critics on both the Left and the Right who agree that the media are biased. What divides such critics is the question of whether the bias is left-wing or right-wing. Defenders of the news media may seize upon this disagreement to bolster their own claim that "bias is in the eye of the beholder." But it could also mean that the news media are unfair to both sides. If that were true, however, it would seem to take some of the force out of the argument that the news media have a distinct ideological tilt.

Edward Jay Epstein's *News From Nowhere* (Random House, 1973) remains one of the great studies of the factors that influence television news shows. A study by S. Robert Lichter et al., *The Media Elite* (Adler & Adler, 1986), tends to support Rusher's contention that the media slant leftward, whereas Ben Bagdikian's *The Media Monopoly* (Beacon Press, 1983) and Mark Hertsgaard's *On Bended Knee: The Press and the Reagan Presidency* (Schocken, 1989) lend support to Chomsky and Herman. A more recent Robert Lichter book, coauthored with Linda Lichter and Stanley Rothman, is *Watching America* (Prentice Hall, 1991), which surveys the political and social messages contained in television "entertainment" programs. Lichter has also written a media textbook with Thomas Dye and Harmon Ziegler entitled *American Politics in the Media Age*, 4th ed. (Brooks-Cole, 1992). David Halberstam's *The Powers That Be* (Knopf, 1979), a historical study of CBS, the *Washington Post*, *Time* magazine, and the *Los Angeles Times*, describes some of the political and ideological struggles that have taken place within major media organizations.

Edward Jay Epstein's book, previously cited, uses as an epigraph a statement by Richard Salant, president of CBS News in the 1970s: "Our reporters do not cover stories from *their* point of view. They are presenting them from *nobody's* point of view." Most probably, Salant had not intended to be facetious or ironic, but the statement so amused Epstein that he parodied it in the title of his book: *News From Nowhere*!

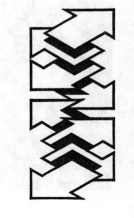

The White House/Official Photograph

PART 2

The Institutions of Government

The Constitution provides for three governing bodies: the president, Congress, and the Supreme Court. Over the years, the American government has generated another organ with a life of its own: the bureaucracy. In this section, we examine issues that concern all the branches of government (executive, legislative, and judicial). Many of these debates are contemporary manifestations of issues that have been argued since the country was founded.

Does Congress Need to Be Radically Reformed?
_____

The Presidency Versus Congress: Should Divided Government Be Ended?
_____

Does the Government Regulate Too Much?
_____

Should the Federal Courts Be Bound by the "Original Intent" of the Framers?

ISSUE 5

Does Congress Need to Be Radically Reformed?

YES: Paula Dwyer and Douglas Harbrecht, from "Congress: It Doesn't Work. Let's Fix It," *Business Week* (April 16, 1990)

NO: Nelson W. Polsby, from "Congress-Bashing for Beginners," *The Public Interest* (Summer 1990)

ISSUE SUMMARY

YES: Journalists Paula Dwyer and Douglas Harbrecht conclude that the legislative performance of Congress is dismal, and they identify several areas in which radical reforms would lead to vast improvement.
NO: Political scientist Nelson W. Polsby believes that "Congress-bashing" is a misguided attack upon the legislative power and undermines the constitutional separation of powers.

"It could probably be shown by facts and figures that there is no distinctly native American criminal class except Congress."

"Congress—these, for the most part, illiterate hacks whose fancy vests are spotted with gravy, and whose speeches, hypocritical, unctuous, and slovenly, are spotted also with the gravy of political patronage."

The first quotation was written by American novelist Mark Twain in 1897; the second by social critic Mary McCarthy in 1961. What would they say today in the wake of congressional scandals involving check-bouncing in the House of Representatives' bank, illegal activities in the House post office, and kickbacks and bribes paid to members of Congress by powerful interests wanting to influence legislative action?

Public opinion polls have long confirmed that the public generally holds negative opinions of Congress. There is a widespread belief that Congress is a clumsy and unwieldy institution, if not simply corrupt. The structure of Congress impresses its critics as being a horse-and-buggy vehicle in a jet age.

Power is fragmented among many committees in the absence of national parties, which might impose discipline on legislators and coherence on legislation. Within the committees, the chair usually has great power; until recently, committee heads were chosen strictly on the basis of seniority (length of service) rather than for their leadership abilities. Woodrow Wilson called America "a government by the chairmen of standing committees of Congress." Although much power has since shifted to the president, congressional chairs remain subject to few checks.

Perhaps the decline of Congress in this century is partly due to its outmoded structure, but it is easy to see how the Great Depression, two world wars, the Korean, Vietnam, and Persian Gulf wars, and the containment of Soviet communism contributed to the decline. The president initiates foreign policy and makes military judgments, and he can act with the speed and secrecy that cannot exist in a representative legislature. Moreover, we can identify with the president as a person, while Congress remains a faceless abstraction for most Americans.

But our framers did not intend, and few Americans want, an all-powerful executive. They wanted representative government, and the framers created elaborate checks and balances to ensure that no branch of government would have unrestrained power. However much we may gripe about the shortcomings of Congress and deadlocks between it and the president, there is little likelihood that the constitutional separation of powers between Congress and the president will be abandoned.

Critics argue that legislative logjams would be broken if the president were given a line-item veto, that is, the ability to veto part of a bill while accepting the remainder. Defenders of Congress maintain that this would effectively undermine the separation of powers, making for a too-powerful president.

Critics also favor term limits for members of Congress. This would reduce the advantages of incumbency, evident in the superior campaign funding and greater name recognition of long-term Congress members. Defenders of Congress argue that this ignores the value of experience and expertise, as well as the public's right to choose.

For all our criticism of Congress, its supporters maintain that the voting public is at fault if Congress falls short. Less than half of the electorate votes for Congress in a presidential year, and less than one-third in a midterm election. If the American people want to change Congress, they have only to vote its members out.

In the following selections, Paula Dwyer and Douglas Harbrecht examine the susceptibility of Congress to special interests, its immersion in trivial issues, its failure to deal effectively with budget deficits, the savings and loan scandal, and other major issues. Their conclusion is that sweeping reforms are necessary in order to make Congress more effective. Nelson W. Polsby defends Congress because he believes in the constitutional separation of powers. He sees many alleged reforms of Congress as serious attacks upon the nature of our political system. *Can Representative Government Do the Job?* was the title of a thoughtful 1945 book, and a half-century later many Americans remain uncertain about the answer to that question.

YES

Paula Dwyer and
Douglas Harbrecht

CONGRESS: IT DOESN'T WORK.
LET'S FIX IT.

Take a walk on Capitol Hill these days, and you can't help but notice the strangers. Mingling with the bustling young Hill aides and gawking tourists are animated intellectuals from Poland, Hungary, and Czechoslovakia. For months, Eastern European politicians have descended on Congress, intent on adapting American democratic principles to their fledgling governments. But if the visitors seem perplexed at times, it's more than just cultural differences. A close look at U.S. legislative mechanics these days can deflate the idealistic dreams of even the most determined European reformer.

Just ask Marian Lemke, a 27-year-old adviser to Poland's Solidarity government. Since January, he's been working as a Capitol Hill intern. Here are some of the scenes that Lemke and his fellow pilgrims have witnessed:

• Just four days after Nicaraguans voted to throw out their Sandinista government, the Senate is working late, locked in furious debate over a resolution deploring Daniel Ortega's slowness to relinquish power. This is the 63rd such congressional effort since 1980 to impose U.S. will on tiny Nicaragua. It is nonbinding and, outside the insular world of Washington, utterly irrelevant. As the haranguing builds to fever pitch, an exasperated Senator John C. Danforth (R-Mo.) rises to ask his battling colleagues: "Why can't we just shut up for a change?"

That night, the Senate takes up another nonbinding resolution, this one calling for an end to the baseball players' lockout. Enraged by the windy speeches, Senator Warren B. Rudman (R-N.H.) complains: "We're wasting everyone's time, and we just look like fools." The measure passes 82–15.

• Earlier that day, 15 jubilant senators rush before the TV cameras to announce a "historic" breakthrough on clean-air legislation. The bipartisan group doesn't mention that it has taken 12 years to reach this agreement, despite rising concern about acid rain and foul air.

From Paula Dwyer and Douglas Harbrecht, "Congress: It Doesn't Work. Let's Fix It," *Business Week* (April 16, 1990). Copyright © 1990 by McGraw-Hill, Inc. Reprinted by special permission.

• That same week in the House, Speaker Thomas S. Foley (D-Wash.) looks over his schedule and remarks sardonically: "We have another heavy week." House members authorize the Agriculture Dept. to produce sterile screwworms for sale overseas, change the name of a lake in Kansas, approve two new statues in the Capitol, and vote yet another national education study, the umpteenth such survey in recent years.

The lessons are not lost on Lemke. "Congress is really a huge bureaucracy," he concludes, noting that Poland's new parliament took just two weeks to enact 14 sweeping measures to convert the country to a market economy. "It would be impossible to transfer your political system to Poland."

That may be a lucky break for the Poles. The U.S. Congress now works about as well—and as cleanly—as a Polish steel mill. It huffs, it puffs, and it belches fire. But Congress produces very little tangible value.

E PLURIBUS NIL

This once proud institution is paralyzed by cynicism and a corrupting quest for campaign dollars. Partisan sniping and issue-ducking are so pervasive that basic congressional functions—such as approving the budget and appropriating funds—have become too tough to manage. Legislators increasingly rely on contrivances, such as automatic spending cuts, as a substitute for judgment. Yet, even with Congress on autopilot, recurring budget crises cause the government to totter on the verge of shutdown at least once a year.

Political action committees (PACs) representing powerful special interests increasingly dominate congressional elections,

driving members into a frenzied money chase that leaves little time for problem-solving. "I've become acclimated to everything but fund-raising," says freshman Representative Harry A. Johnston (D-Fla.). "The day you're elected, you start raising money [again]. It's immoral."

Since 1976, the cost of the average House campaign has risen from $80,000 to $380,000. A heated contest, such as the 1988 battle between Representative Robert J. Lagomarsino (R-Calif.) and California State Senator Gary Hart, can run almost $3 million. The cost of an average Senate race, meantime, has jumped from $600,000 to $3.9 million per candidate. A big-time duel, such as the 1984 battle between Jesse Helms (R-N.C.) and Democrat James B. Hunt, can total $25 million.

Dependence on interest-group money has other unpleasant side effects. It is at the core of congressional ethics scandals such as last year's toppling of House Speaker Jim Wright (D-Tex.) and this year's inquiry into the role five prominent senators played in aiding controversial savings and loan operator Charles H. Keating Jr. The flood of money also helps immobilize Congress, since lawmakers in search of their PAC fix are reluctant to antagonize competing interests. And PAC contributions serve as an unnatural prop for incumbents, denying Congress needed new blood. Some 98% of House members now win reelection, many by running content-free campaigns that further erode the influence of the national parties. In 1988, PACs gave $115 million to congressional incumbents, only $17 million to challengers. "I question why we even have elections anymore," says Fred Wertheimer, president of Common Cause, a Washington-based campaign-reform group.

So, apparently, do voters. Since 1960, participation in congressional elections has dropped from 58% to 45% during Presidential election years. In midterm elections, the figure is now an abysmal 30%.

Congress' ills can be fixed. . . . But the problems have become so ingrained that more and more Americans consider them endemic. Lasting solutions will not come until this dangerous complacency is replaced by the will to begin a top-to-bottom overhaul of the institution.

'CRIMINAL CLASS'

With its rich history of logrolling, pettifoggery, and corruption, Congress has never exactly been at the top of Americans' ethical hit parade. (Mark Twain once called Congress home to the only "distinctly native American criminal class.") But more recently, its ratings have plunged. Surveys taken by pollster Louis Harris & Associates find that the percentage of Americans expressing a "great deal" of confidence in Congress has tumbled to 15%, down from 28% in 1984.

In their defense, lawmakers assert that Congress was designed to be reactive. Political scientists add that there's plenty of blame to go around for recent failures to tackle the nation's problems. "Ronald Reagan is Congress' role model," says Thomas E. Mann of the Brookings Institution. "He demonstrated you could be politically successful while creating a fiscal mess."

What's puzzling to many is that Capitol Hill has become steadily less responsive to national needs even as legislators have become more qualified. "Congress has a spectacular amount of individual talent," laments former House Rules Committee Chairman Richard Bolling

(D-Mo.). "But institutionally it has great difficulty performing."

The nation is paying a steep price for this legislative impotence. For two decades, ticket-splitting voters have been inclined to give Democrats control of Congress and Republicans a virtual lock on the White House. In an era of divided government, the Hill must play a much larger role to have any impact on policy. But Congress isn't rising to the task.

At some other time, perhaps, the current congressional drift might be accepted as merely another phase in a long historical cycle of activism and repose. But facing such fundamental problems as sagging international competitiveness, third-rate schools, and inadequate health care systems, America can ill afford the Hill's sclerosis.

As the cold war recedes, attention is shifting to the global struggle for economic supremacy. And America's competitors, notably West Germany and Japan, arrive at political consensus far faster than the fractious, crisis-driven U.S. system. On the eve of a new century, the U.S. is saddled with the problems of a superpower—and the legislature of a banana republic. Says Representative Lee H. Hamilton (D-Ind.): "We face a crisis of democracy."

If that sounds like political hyperbole, consider the following:

Shaking Down Business

If you're like most citizens, you probably think lawmakers mostly pass laws and such. Silly you. Some have discovered that it can be wildly lucrative to make a halfhearted legislative feint in the direction of certain industries, then back off.

In every Congress since 1978, the House and Senate Banking Committees have made a fitful run at restructuring the financial industry by attempting to overhaul the 1933 Glass-Steagall Act. But reform is hopelessly deadlocked because of the conflicting interests of big banks, small banks, insurance companies, and securities firms. Yet the committees go through the motions year after year—and then squeeze contributions from jittery PACs. Other favorite scams: the effort to "reform" product-liability laws, now 13 years old, and the perennial hints that tax-writing committees may limit the mortgage-interest deduction, which bring anguished shrieks from real estate agents and home-builders. "It's all ginned up," shrugs one veteran lobbyist.

Ducking the Issues

With the rise of negative campaigning, many members are concluding that it's safer to duck hard issues than to make unpopular choices. Increasingly, they lob difficult decisions to outside contractors. The model was the 1982 Social Security commission. Confronting an explosive Social Security funding shortfall, the panel came up with a solution that gave Congress the political cover it needed to raise payroll taxes and trim benefits.

More often than not, however, the commissions founder in partisan bickering. The 1989 National Economic Commission took 15 months and $1 million to produce a report that did not even contain a consensus plan for cutting the deficit. This year, the Bipartisan Commission on Comprehensive Health Care devoted nine months and $1.5 million to propose a $66 billion "solution" to the health needs of the uninsured and elderly. The report was pronounced dead on arrival because feuding panelists omitted any reference to funding.

While committees are busy shunting their responsibilities off on commissions

and task forces, individual members increasingly dodge problems by falling back on boosterism. A favorite pastime is passing commemorative resolutions, proclaiming everything from "National Prom Recognition Day" to "National Dairy-Goat Awareness Week." Since 1926, when Congress officially enshrined Mother's Day, such valentines have risen to about 200 a year. Representative Claudine Schneider (R-R.I.) reckons that Hill staffers spent more than 30,000 hours working on such resolutions during the 99th Congress.

A vivid example of congressional spinelessness occurred when lawmakers last year repealed a year-old law designed to shield the elderly from the high costs of major illness. Catastrophic insurance had strong bipartisan support. But when a small but vocal group of well-off seniors rose in revolt over the plan's progressive taxes, panicky legislators didn't bother to revise the program. They just chucked it—denying catastrophic insurance to the elderly poor. "Five percent of the elderly swung us around like a dead cat," fumes Senator Alan Simpson (R-Wyo.).

Too Little, Too Late

The Hill has always responded more to crises than to reasoned debate. The result is periodic stampedes that lawmakers later regret. "Congress either does nothing or it overreacts," says Kenneth M. Duberstein, former Chief of Staff in the Reagan White House. Lately, though, the crises seem to be getting bigger and costlier to fix.

The nation's thrift industry has been going bust for a decade, pushed under by a combination of uneven deregulation, poor business practices, and inadequate supervision. By 1987, it was apparent that the Federal Savings &

Loan Insurance Corp. would go broke unless it got a quick infusion of funds. But some key lawmakers were hooked on contributions from S&L owners. The thrift operators didn't want FSLIC to get enough money to shut them down. So their friends in Congress stalled the legislation for a year, then made sure that the sum appropriated was inadequate.

This interference drove up the cost of the S&L mess by billions. When Congress and the Bush Administration finally dealt with the problem, it required the costliest bailout in American history. In 1989, the Hill struggled to enact a $50 billion rescue plan that will shutter 30% of the nation's thrifts. But industry experts estimate the actual cost of the mess at $167 billion to $200 billion. Sooner or later—probably later—Congress will have to come up with more money.

But when Congress appears to be doing a good job, as in exposing the Housing & Urban Development Dept. influence-peddling scandal, it's often late on the scene. The House Government Operations housing subcommittee, headed by Representative Tom Lantos (D-Calif.), uncovered massive Reagan-era corruption at HUD. But Lantos is the first to admit that Congress should have begun looking under the rocks earlier, while the abuses were going on. Legislators were too busy issuing attention-grabbing press releases that lambasted Reagan's budget cuts.

Punting on the Budget
In 1985, lawmakers frustrated by huge Reagan-era deficits passed the Gramm-Rudman Act, which mandated steady reductions in red ink and a balanced budget by fiscal 1991. But Congress has never met those annual goals honestly. Instead, it either revises looming targets or decides that certain spending, such as

part of last year's S&L bailout, won't count against the ceiling. Now some members are coming to view Gramm-Rudman's automatic spending cuts—intended to enforce discipline—as a convenient way to avoid making painful choices. In the face of all this maneuvering, the real deficit remains enormous. Most independent budget analysts think it will top $160 billion in fiscal 1990.

The Hill's annual obsession with sidestepping deficit targets has crippled its ability to conduct other business and contributed to congressional craveness. Most years, lawmakers spend much of their time on inconclusive budget debates and then, at yearend, stuff most pending legislation into a huge catchall spending bill. This year's budget shenanigans aren't deviating much from the script. Congress has yet to begin serious work on a fiscal 1991 tax-and-spending blueprint. The prospect is for another year of budget chaos.

One senator who tired of the game was Budget Committee Chairman Lawton Chiles. The Florida Democrat, now 60, retired in 1988. "I was like Chicken Little, warning people that we would have to pay a terrible price for the budget deficit," he sighs. "I finally hung it up and came home."

Baronial Congress
In 1946, the last time the Hill underwent major reorganization, 34 House and Senate committees were run by powerful senior members. Today Congress has 47 committees, but it also has 244 subcommittees, each with its own staff and territorial imperatives. In the '40s subcommittees were ad hoc bodies that had little real power. These days, the Hill's unofficial slogan is, "Every man a baron."

Drug policy director William J. Bennett, to cite one example, must answer to 90 committees and subcommittees. When Bennett asked the House leadership recently to set up an informal meeting with members who have a stake in drug issues, 60 lawmakers showed up. Monster conference committees, once a rarity, are now commonplace. In 1987, the conference on omnibus trade legislation included 201 House and Senate members. Says former White House Counsel Lloyd N. Cutler: "The House can't come to the conference table anymore with fewer than 100 members."

Naturally, the bigger the Hill gets, the more slowly it moves. A key reason for the failure to enact child-care legislation in 1989, despite solid backing, was a turf battle between two powerful Democratic committee chiefs. Overlapping jurisdiction is a major reason that measures involving health care, energy, and the environment have so much trouble passing. The House Judiciary Committee has both a subcommittee on crime and on criminal justice. No one seems to know why. There are select committees on aging, hunger, children, and narcotics—panels that have no legislative authority but offer a tempting podium for grandstanding.

Much of the impetus for proliferating committees came from a post-Watergate rebellion. Reformers weakened the seniority system, undercutting the leadership and entrenched committee chairs and diffusing power to younger members. To appease the Young Turks, subcommittees were doled out like candy. "On the surface, spreading power around looked like a great idea," reflects Robert D. Loevy, a political scientist at Colorado College. "But nobody sees the big picture anymore. Nobody is able to broker compromises."

The Imperial Staff

Congress' bureaucratic empire is maintained by an army of invisible aides— 31,000 staffers are on the congressional payroll. Numbers alone don't tell the story. Rather, it's the power these largely faceless aides command, and their lack of accountability that is at issue.

As lawmakers focus more on raising reelection money, their subordinates have been ceded wide latitude to draft legislation, plot strategy, handle lobbyists, and even to decide how to vote. "Too much is being done by anonymous people," says former Senate Majority Leader Howard H. Baker Jr.

Consider a complex measure known in Washington-ese as "Section 89." In the name of tax equity, this amendment mandated that employers give both low-paid workers and better-paid managerial employees equivalent health benefits. It was written by a House Ways & Means aide and put into the 1986 tax reform law without debate or review by lawmakers. Only when business discovered how nightmarishly difficult it would be to comply with the directive and a huge outcry went up was the law repealed.

Last year, the public was outraged when Congress voted itself a $12 million pay raise. Yet no one complained when lawmakers approved a $210 million increase in Congress' $2 billion administrative budget. The House's professional and support-staff costs went from $400 million to $422 million. Top salary for a committee staff director is now $90,000, although most midlevel aides earn $30,000 to $60,000.

Unlike an underperforming corporate board, Congress' insular barons are in no fear of a Boone Pickens or Carl Icahn shaking things up. For that, the voters— the same folks that the can't-do Congress is alienating in droves—must demand accountability and restructuring. "Congress needs to return to its role as a policy-making agency," says Baker. "It must stop acting like an aggregation of bureaucrats, pseudo-Presidents, and pseudo-Secretaries of State."

Privately, many lawmakers share this assessment. But after years of congressional decline, only a howl of rage from the voters will make Congress sit up and listen. Until then, Marian Lemke and the other Europeans eagerly rushing to study Congress will probably learn more about empty gestures, budget gimmickery, and political evasion than the stuff of which great democracies are made.

HOW TO GET THE HILL HUMMING AGAIN

Can Congress remake itself? Can it modernize its creaky procedures and end its intoxication with special-interest money? The experts say it can.

In reporting on the breakdown on Capitol Hill, *Business Week* interviewed more than 150 current and former government officials, lobbyists, and political scientists. From those discussions emerged a reform agenda that could attack some of the Hill's biggest problems. If lawmakers ever get serious about fixing what ails Congress, they could start here:

Shrink the Empire
The Hill could get by with fewer full committees and half of its existing subcommittees. For instance, the House Education & Labor Committee has three education subcommittees and five on employment issues. In the Senate, 47 of 55 Democrats head committees or subcommittees. Each House member now gets 18 full-time staff aides, Senators up to 40. That, too, should be halved.

If downsizing reduces the ability of Congress to hold hearings and engage in other forms of theatrics, that's fine. Members could use the freed-up time for problem-solving. Congressional leaders might issue a formal list of legislative priorities at the beginning of each session—and try to stick to it.

Fix the Budget Process
The ineffectual Budget Committees should be replaced with panels made up of the leadership and the chairmen of key committees. This arrangement gives Hill leaders a direct stake in implementing any budget blueprint. True, it gives the leadership enormous power—but with it comes enormous responsibility.

Next, Congress should replace its annual budget deliberations with a two-year plan that operates on a strict pay-as-you-go method. The longer cycle would free members from endless tax and spending harangues. Last year, 70% of Senate floor votes involved the budget. "I can't envision anything that would do more to improve the lives of members," declares New Mexico Senator Pete V. Domenici, ranking Republican on the Senate Budget Committee. The pay-as-you-go idea would require that any new spending program be paired with a revenue source or an off-setting spending cut. And all federal receipts and expenditures should appear in the budget, ending the game of not counting any spending that Congress wants to hide.

Finally, Congress should no longer be allowed to cram a year's worth of legislation into a single catchall measure—and present it to the President as a take-it-or-leave-it package. Lawmakers should be forced to enact regular appropriations bills each year. That would make continuing resolutions, stopgap measures that give the government temporary spending authority, unnecessary. Hill leaders could guarantee action on appropriations by requiring Congress to stay in session until all 13 money bills are passed. "The hammer is there," says Representative Peter A. DeFazio (D-Ore.). "The leadership has just been reluctant to use it."

Junk Gramm-Rudman

Congress has found enough ways to evade the Gramm-Rudman Act's deficit targets to make the law meaningless. When lawmakers want to spend money that would exceed the deficit ceilings, they simply vote to exclude the outlays from the Gramm-Rudman calculation. As part of any drive to restructure budget procedures, the statute should be repealed. Says Thomas E. Mann, a Brookings Institution political scientist: "The charade of Gramm-Rudman has to end. It has only served to introduce deceit into budget policy."

Curb PAC Donations

Political action committees can now give each candidate up to $5,000 per election, with no limit on the total PAC money a candidate can accept. To reduce the influence of special interests, Congress should limit total PAC contributions to any House candidate to $100,000. Senate races could be subject to higher limits based on state population.

PACs should also be prohibited from contributing after the election to help winners retire debts. Most such contributions come from groups that bet on the wrong candidate and are trying to curry favor with the winner. Leadership PACs also should be banned. These committees are created by Hill power-brokers solely to shower money on other members to win political IOUs.

Reform Campaign Spending

It's time for Congress to impose some rational limits on spending as well. Reining in the cost of campaigns will not be easy. The U.S. Supreme Court has said that campaign expenditures are a form of free speech and ruled that any limitations must be voluntary. In Presidential elections, candidates who accept public funding must agree to live within spending limits, but no such restrictions have been imposed on House and Senate races.

Efforts to clean up campaign finance laws have run into a partisan stalemate. Democrats want a system based on Presidential elections—public funding in exchange for spending caps. But Republicans have mastered the art of raising vast sums of money from millions of small donors. The GOP believes its best hope for winning control of Congress lies in using this fund-raising advantage against Democrats, who rely more heavily on PACs. So Republicans want to rein in political action committees, while leaving total spending unchecked.

Any proposal that tilts toward one party is doomed. The solution lies in blending the two approaches, and there are some promising ways that could be done. For example, a bipartisan Senate task force is weighing a recommendation for "flexible" spending limits based on each state's voting-age population. It's worth trying.

Of course, such cash-rich incumbents as Senator Phil Gramm (R-Tex.), who has already raised $10 million for his 1990 race, could ignore the cap. But big spenders could be made to pay a price. Any candidate who doesn't accept spending caps would risk criticism for being in thrall to the fat cats. The law could also give advantages to challengers who live within the caps. As a condition of license renewal, broadcasters could be required to give challengers facing free-spending opponents reduced advertising rates. And the Postal Service could give a similar break on postage.

End Guaranteed Incumbency

Young conservatives, led by House Minority Whip Newt Gingrich (R-Ga.), want to limit members to three consecutive terms. But that would deny voters the right to reelect talented lawmakers.

The problem of unhealthy incumbency rates could be addressed more intelligently by making it easier for challengers to raise money. Norman J. Ornstein of the American Enterprise Institute suggests that "serious" challengers—those who have raised at least $25,000—be given federal matching grants. Ornstein also favors lifting the $2,000-per-election-cycle limit on individual giving to candidates—but only for donations that go to challengers. Larry J. Sabato, a political scientist at the University of Virginia, has a similar idea. He would create an incentive pool of cash for challengers and pay for it by permitting taxpayers to earmark $1 or $2 of their tax refunds.

What about incumbents? Congress should give up subsidized postal rates for all mass mailings during an election year. And members ought to be required to zero-out their campaign treasuries after each election. As things now stand, six House members have amassed campaign surpluses in excess of $1 million, and several others are close behind. Huge postelection war chests intimidate potential challengers. Any surplus should be returned to contributors.

Strengthen Parties

Strong national parties can inject passion, ideas, and discipline into our politics. But in the television age, political organizations are withering.

The parties need to play a larger role in congressional campaigns. Although no one advocates a return to machine politics, more muscular national parties could discipline wayward members and demand some loyalty to their platforms.

Rather than being curbed, as some reformers advocate, party-run registration and get-out-the-vote drives should be encouraged. But because there is no ceiling on contributions to these so-called "party building" efforts, all gifts and spending should be disclosed. Parties would gain clout if they were given the job of dispensing discounted airtime and reduced postal rates to candidates who accept spending caps. Stronger parties also could protect candidates from the pet agendas of special interests. Says David W. Brady, a Stanford University political scientist: "There has to be a way for the parties to say, 'Hey, do this and we'll look out for you.' "

Incumbents will wince at many of these changes, but they are essential if Congress is to become the great deliberative body it was intended to be. This was, after all, the institution that established the system of national credit in the 1790s, tamed rapacious trusts at the turn of the century, banned child labor, and passed the landmark Civil Rights Act in 1964. These grand compromises showed Congress at its best. To regain that past glory, lawmakers will have to take a cue from Corporate America and begin restructuring.

NO

Nelson W. Polsby

CONGRESS-BASHING FOR BEGINNERS

On a shelf not far from where I am writing these words sit a half a dozen or so books disparaging Congress and complaining about the congressional role in the constitutional separation of powers. These books date mostly from the late 1940s and the early 1960s, and typically their authors are liberal Democrats. In those years Congress was unresponsive to liberal Democrats and, naturally enough, aggrieved members of that articulate tribe sought solutions in structural reform.

In fact, instead of reforms weakening Congress what they—and we—got was a considerably strengthened presidency. This was mostly a product of World War II and not the result of liberal complaints. Before World War II Congress would not enact even the modest recommendations of the Brownlow Commission to give the president a handful of assistants with "a passion for anonymity," and it killed the National Resources Planning Board outright. After World War II everything changed: Congress gave the president responsibility for smoothing the effects of the business cycle, created a Defense Department and two presidential agencies—the NSC and the CIA—that enhanced the potential for presidential dominance of national security affairs, and laid the groundwork for the growth of a presidential branch, politically responsive to both Democratic and Republican presidents.

CONGRESS AND THE GORING OF OXEN

Though it took time for the presidential branch to grow into its potential, the growth of this branch, separate and at arm's length from the executive branch that it runs in the president's behalf, is the big news of the postwar era—indeed, of the last half-century in American government. It is customary today to acknowledge that Harry Truman's primary agenda, in the field of foreign affairs, was quite successfully enacted even though Congress was dominated by a conservative coalition, and what Truman wanted in the way of peacetime international involvement was for the United States quite unprecedented. Dwight Eisenhower's agenda was also largely international

From Nelson W. Polsby, "Congress-Bashing for Beginners," *The Public Interest*, no. 100 (Summer 1990), pp. 15–23. Copyright © 1990 by National Affairs, Inc. Reprinted by permission.

in its impact. Looking back, it seems that almost all Eisenhower really cared about was protecting the international position of the United States from diminution by Republican isolationists. Everything else was expendable.

Congress responded sluggishly and in its customary piecemeal fashion. It was right around John Kennedy's first year in office that liberals rediscovered that old roadblock in Congress, a "deadlock of democracy," as one of them put it. It was Congress that had thwarted the second New Deal after 1937, the packing of the Supreme Court, and Harry Truman's domestic program; it was Congress that had stalled civil rights and buried Medicare; it was Congress that had sponsored the Bricker Amendment to limit the president's power to make treaties. Are memories so short that we do not recall these dear, departed days when Congress was the graveyard of the forward-looking proposals of liberal presidents? Then, Congress was a creaky eighteenth-century machine unsuited to the modern age, and Congress-bashers were liberal Democrats.

To be sure, Congress had a few defenders, mostly Republicans and Dixiecrats, who found in its musty cloakrooms and windy debates a citadel (as one of them said) of old-time legislative virtues, where the historic functions of oversight and scrutiny were performed, where the run-away proposals of the presidency could be subjected to the sober second thoughts of the people's own elected representatives, and so on.

Why rehash all this? In part, it is to try to make the perfectly obvious point that Congress-bashing then was what people did when they controlled the presidency but didn't control Congress. And that, in part, is what Congress-bashing is about

now. Today, Republicans and conservatives are doing most (although not all) of the complaining. It is worth a small bet that a fair number of editorial pages claimed that the separation of powers made a lot of sense during the Kennedy-Johnson years—but no longer say the same today. On the other side, backers of FDR's scheme to pack the Court have turned into vigorous defenders of the judicial status quo since Earl Warren's time [Warren was chief justice of the United States, 1953–1969].

There is nothing wrong with letting the goring of oxen determine what side we take in a political argument. In a civilized country, however, it makes sense to keep political arguments civil, and not to let push come to shove too often. There is something uncivil, in my view, about insisting upon constitutional reforms to cure political ailments. What liberal critics of Congress needed was not constitutional reform. What they needed was the 89th Congress, which, in due course, enacted much of the agenda that the Democratic party had built up over the previous two decades. History didn't stop with the rise of the presidential branch and the enactment of the second New Deal/New Frontier/Great Society. President Johnson overreached. He concealed from Congress the costs of the Vietnam War. He created a credibility gap.

This, among other things, began to change Congress. The legislative branch no longer was altogether comfortable relying on the massaged numbers and other unreliable information coming over from the presidential branch. They began to create a legislative bureaucracy to cope with this challenge. They beefed up the General Accounting Office and the Congressional Research Service. They

created an Office of Technology Assessment and a Congressional Budget Office.
They doubled and redoubled their personal staffs and committee staffs.

Sentiments supporting this expansion
began, oddly enough, after a landslide
election in which the Democratic party
swept the presidency and both houses of
Congress. So mistrust between the
branches in recent history has by no
means been entirely a partisan matter.
Nevertheless, Richard Nixon's presidency, conducted entirely in unhappy
harness with a Democratic Congress, did
not improve relations between the two
branches of government. Johnson may
have been deceitful, but Nixon, especially after his reelection in 1972, was
positively confrontational.

It was Nixon's policy to disregard comity between the branches. This, and not
merely his commission of impeachable
offenses, fueled the impeachment effort
in Congress. That effort was never wholly
partisan. Republicans as well as Democrats voted articles of impeachment that
included complaints specifically related
to obstruction of the discharge of congressional responsibilities.

It is necessary to understand this recent history of the relations between
Congress and the president in order to
understand the provenance of the War
Powers Act, the Boland Amendment, numerous other instances of congressional
micromanagement, the unprecedented involvement of the NSC in the Iran-*contra*
affair, and like manifestations of tension
and mistrust between Congress and the
president. These tensions are, to a certain degree, now embedded in law and
in the routines of responsible public officials; they cannot be made to disappear
with a wave of a magic wand. They are,
for the most part, regrettable in the con-

sequences they have had for congressio-
nal-presidential relations, but they reflect
real responses to real problems in these
relations. Congressional responses so far
as I can see, have been completely legal,
constitutional, and—in the light of historical circumstances—understandable. The
best way to turn the relations between
the legislative and the presidential
branches around would be for the presidential side to take vigorous initiatives to
restore comity. As head of the branch far
more capable of taking initiatives, and
the branch far more responsible for the
underlying problem, this effort at resto-
ration is in the first instance up to the
President.

PRESIDENT BUSH AND
THE ITEM VETO

In this respect, President Bush is doing a
decent job, giving evidence of reaching
out constructively. It is not my impression that the Bush administration has
done a lot of Congress-bashing. After all,
what Bush needs isn't a weakened Congress so much as a Republican Congress.
Over the long run (though probably not
in time to do Bush much good) Republicans are bound to regret despairing of
the latter and therefore seeking the former. We have seen enough turns of the
wheel over the last half-century to be
reasonably confident that sooner or later
Republicans will start to do better in
congressional elections. The presidential
item veto, the Administration's main
Congress-bashing proposal, won't help
Republicans in Congress deal with a
Democratic president when the time
comes, as sooner or later it will, for a
Democrat to be elected president.

The item veto would effectively take
congressional politics out of the legisla-

tive process, and would weaken Congress a lot. It would encourage members of Congress, majority and minority alike, to be irresponsible and to stick the president with embarrassing public choices. It would reduce the incentives for members to acquire knowledge about public policy or indeed to serve.

By allocating legislative responsibilities to Congress, the Constitution as originally (and currently) designed forces representatives of diverse interests to cooperate. Because what Congress does as a collectivity matters, legislative work elicits the committed participation of members. The item veto would greatly trivialize the work product of Congress by requiring the president's acquiescence on each detail of legislation. Members would lose their independent capacity to craft legislation. Their individual views and knowledge would dwindle in importance; only the marshalling of a herd capable of overturning a veto would matter in Congress.

The item veto is, in short, a truly radical idea. It is also almost certainly unconstitutional. To espouse it requires a readiness to give up entirely on the separation of powers and on the constitutional design of the American government. There are plenty of people, some of them well-meaning, who are ready to do that. I am not, nor should people who identify themselves as conservatives or liberals or anywhere in the political mainstream.

The separation of powers is actually a good idea. It gives a necessary weight to the great heterogeneity of our nation— by far the largest and most heterogeneous nation unequivocally to have succeeded at democratic self-government in world history. It would take a medium-sized book to make all the qualifications and all the connections that would do justice to this argument. The conclusion is worth restating anyway: the item veto is a root-and-branch attack on the separation of powers; it is a very radical and a very bad idea.

TERM LIMITATIONS

Less serious in its impact, but still destructive, is the proposal to limit the terms of members of Congress. This proposal relies heavily for its appeal upon ignorance in the population at large about what members of Congress actually do. For in order to take seriously the idea of limiting congressional terms, one must believe that the job of a representative in Congress is relatively simple, and quickly and easily mastered. It is not.

The job of a member of Congress is varied and complex. It includes: (1) Managing a small group of offices that attempt on request to assist distressed constituents, state and local governments, and enterprises in the home district that may have business with the federal government. This ombudsman function gives members an opportunity to monitor the performance of the government in its dealings with citizens and can serve to identify areas of general need. (2) Serving on committees that oversee executive-branch activity on a broad spectrum of subjects (such as immigration, copyright protection, telecommunications, or health policy) and that undertake to frame issues of national scope for legislative action. This entails mastering complicated subject matter; working with staff members, expert outsiders, and colleagues to build coalitions; understanding justifications; and answering objections. (3) Participating in general legislative work. Members have to vote on everything, not merely on the work of their own committees. They have to inform themselves of the merits of bills, and stand ready to cooperate with colleagues whose support they will need to advance their own proposals. (4) Keeping track of their own political business. This means watching over and occasionally participating in the politics of their own states and localities, and mending fences with interest groups, friends and neighbors, backers, political rivals, and allies. (5) Educating all the varied people with whom they come in contact about issues that are high on the agenda and about reasonable expectations of performance. This includes the performance of the government, the Congress, and the member.

Plenty of members never try to master the job, or try and fail, and these members would be expendable. The objection might still be raised that constituents, not an excess of constitutional limitations, ought to decide who represents whom in Congress. But that aside, what about the rather substantial minority of members who learn their jobs, do their homework, strive to make an impact on public policy, and—through long experience and application to work—actually make a difference? Can we, or should we, dispense with them as well?

It is a delusion to think that good public servants are a dime a dozen in each congressional district, and that only the good ones would queue up to take their twelve-year fling at congressional office. But suppose they did. In case they acquired expertise, what would they do next? Make money, I suppose. Just about the time that their constituents and the American people at large could begin to expect a payoff because of the knowledge and experience that these able members had acquired at our expense, off they would go to some Washington law firm.

And what about their usefulness in the meantime? It would be limited, I'm afraid, by the greater expertise and better command of the territory by lobbyists, congressional staff, and downtown bureaucrats—career people one and all. So this is, once again, a proposal merely to weaken the fabric of Congress in the political system at large, and thereby to limit the effectiveness of the one set of actors most accessible to ordinary citizens.

The standard objection to this last statement is that members of Congress aren't all that accessible. Well, neither is Ralph Nader, who has long overstayed the dozen years that contemporary Congress-bashers wish to allocate to members. Neither is the author of *Wall Street Journal* editorials in praise of limitations. And it must be said that a very large number of members take their representational and ombudsman duties very seriously indeed. This includes holders of safe seats, some of whom fear primary-election opposition, some of whom are simply conscientious. A great many of them do pay attention—close attention— to their constituents. That is one of the reasons—maybe the most important reason—that many of them are reelected. Much Congress-bashing these days actually complains about high reelection rates, as though a large population of ill-served constituents would be preferable.

CONGRESSIONAL SALARIES

While we have Ralph Nader on our minds, it is certainly appropriate to pay our disrespects to his completely off-the-wall effort, temporarily successful, at the head of a crazed phalanx of self-righteous disk jockeys and radio talk-show hosts, to deprive members of Congress of a salary increase. The issue of congressional salaries is a straightforward one. Many members, being well-to-do, don't need one. But some do. The expenses of maintaining two places of residence—in Washington and at home—make membership in Congress nearly unique and singularly expensive among upper-middle-class American jobs. Here is the point once more: it is a job, requiring skill and dedication to be done properly. Moreover, membership in Congress brings responsibilities. National policy of the scope and scale now encompassed by acts of the federal government requires responsible, dedicated legislators. People with far less serious responsibilities in the private sector are ordinarily paid considerably better than members of Congress. Think, for example, how far down the organizational chart at General Motors or at CBS or at some other large corporation one would have to go before reaching executives making what members of Congress do, and compare their responsibilities with those of Congress and its members. Actually, most corporations won't say what their compensation packages are like. But at a major auto company, people who make around $100,000 a year are no higher than upper middle management, and certainly don't have responsibilities remotely comparable to those of members of Congress.

There is a case for decent congressional salaries to be made on at least two grounds: one is the rough equity or opportunity-cost ground that we ought not financially to penalize people who serve, and the second is the ground of need for those members who have the expense of families or college educations to think of, and who have no extraordinary private

means. The long-run national disadvantage of failing to recognize the justice of these claims is of course a Congress deprived of people for whom these claims are exigent, normal middle-class people with family responsibilities and without money of their own. These are not the sorts of people a sane electorate should wish to prevent from serving.

Members of Congress, knowing very well of the irrational hostilities that the proposal of a congressional pay raise can stir up, have taken the unfortunate precaution of holding hostage the salaries of federal judges, who are now ludicrously underpaid by the admittedly opulent standards of the legal profession and senior civil servants. An unhealthy impasse has been created owing, at bottom, to Congress-bashing of the most unattractive kind, which exploits the ignorance of ordinary citizens of the dimensions of the members' working lives, and incites citizens to a mindless social envy, in which it is assumed that paying a decent professional salary to professional officeholders is automatically some sort of rip-off.

Members of Congress now make about $98,000. The bottom salary for major-league baseball players is $100,000. Some law firms in New York start new graduates of good law schools at $90,000 or more. How can we argue that members of Congress and others at the top of the federal government should not be paid at least a modest premium above these beginners' wages? There is, evidently, no talking sense to the American people on this subject.

I believe we can dismiss out of hand the charge that large numbers of members individually, or Congress collectively, live in a world all their own, divorced from realities of everyday life.

The sophomores who have written attacks of this sort in recent years in the *Atlantic, Newsweek,* and elsewhere simply don't know what they are talking about. They abuse their access to large audiences by neglecting to explain the real conditions that govern the lives of members, conditions that provide ample doses of everyday life.

No doubt scandals involving various members have in recent times made Congress as an institution vulnerable to criticism. But much of this criticism is irresponsible and irrelevant. Suppose we were to discover instances of cupidity, unusual sexual activity, and abuses of power among the rather sizable staff of an important daily newspaper? Or a symphony orchestra? Or, God forbid, a university? I suppose that would shake our confidence in at least part of the collective output, but one would hope for relevant discriminations. One might distrust the ticket office, perhaps, but not the symphony's performance of Mozart; the stock tips, perhaps, but not the Washington page; the basketball program, but not the classics department. I do not think that the existence of scandal excuses us from attempting to draw sensible conclusions about institutions and their performance.

This sort of balanced and discriminating analysis isn't what proposals for item vetoes, limitations on terms of service, or depressed rates of pay are all about. They are about the ancient but now slightly shopworn American custom of Congress-bashing.

POSTSCRIPT

Does Congress Need to Be Radically Reformed?

Few commentators, including members of Congress, have unqualified praise for how Congress works. Nor does anyone have a constitutional alternative to Congress. The practical question, then, is: What does it take to make Congress work well?

Nothing less than a fundamental constitutional change could lead to a more effective exercise of congressional power, according to James Mac-Gregor Burns. He has argued this thesis most recently in *The Power to Lead: The Crisis of the American Presidency* (Simon & Schuster, 1984). Philip Stern is unremitting in his criticism of Congress's dependency on PACs and private financing, and the ways in which this influences legislative behavior, in his book *The Best Congress Money Can Buy* (Pantheon Books, 1988).

Arthur Maass dissents from the critics in *Congress and the Common Good* (Basic Books, 1984). He describes, analyzes, and defends the role of Congress in the democratic political process.

An illuminating study of how members of Congress actually function can be found in Burdett Loomis's *The New American Politician: Ambition, Entrepreneurship, and the Changing Face of Political Life* (Basic Books, 1988). Loomis takes an inside look at members of Congress who were elected in 1974 and follows their legislative careers over the next decade, providing insights into where Congress has succeeded and where it has failed.

Two former aides to members of Congress have written thoughtful accounts and appraisals of their experiences. Mark Bisnow, *In the Shadow of the Dome: Chronicles of a Capitol Hill Aide* (William Morrow, 1990), is sympathetic to the institution and the dedication of its members. John L. Jackley, *Hill Rat: Blowing the Lid Off Congress* (Regnery Gateway, 1992), is a biting attack on the scruples and skills of members of Congress. Students seeking up-to-date information on Congress and legislative issues will find the *Congressional Quarterly Weekly Report* and the annual *Congressional Quarterly Almanac* to be reliable sources.

Perhaps before asking what is wrong with *Congress,* we should ask what is wrong with *us.* Far fewer than half of all American adults actually vote to elect Congress and more than 95 percent of all members of the House of Representatives have been reelected in most recent elections. If the caliber of Congress depends in large part on the concern of voters, we must consider how to motivate the American people to desire and to elect a better Congress.

ISSUE 6

The Presidency Versus Congress: Should Divided Government Be Ended?

YES: James L. Sundquist, from *Constitutional Reform and Effective Government* (Brookings Institution, 1986)

NO: Richard P. Nathan, from "The Presidency After Reagan: Don't Change It—Make It Work," in Larry Berman, ed., *Looking Back on the Reagan Presidency* (Johns Hopkins University Press, 1990)

ISSUE SUMMARY

YES: Political scientist James L. Sundquist suggests that a president and Congress from the same party might put an end to governmental deadlocks.
NO: Richard P. Nathan, director of the Rockefeller Institute of Government at the State University of New York at Albany, argues that major structural changes in the relationship between the president and Congress are neither necessary nor desirable.

The founders of America set up Congress and the presidency in such a way as to invite conflict. The two branches are elected by different constituencies and for different terms of office. This would not necessarily lead to conflict if the president and Congress were tending to different tasks. But oftentimes they are dealing with the same matter, though approaching it from different perspectives. As political scientist Richard Neustadt once remarked, what the founders gave us was not separation of power but "a government of separated institutions *sharing* power." Both Congress and the president are involved in the legislative process, both make foreign policy decisions, and both are responsible for appointments to the federal judiciary. Seldom can either branch act effectively without the other, yet they are often in conflict.

Most modern democratic governments are structured differently. In parliamentary systems the chief executive, usually called a premier or prime minister, is elected by the majority in parliament and is the leader of the party that controls the parliament. The executive and legislative branches thus share common political interests, and the executive is virtually assured that any major piece of legislation he or she submits to parliament will be passed. There is no need for an executive veto because the parliament would never pass a bill opposed by the executive. This system seems to work fairly well in most democratic countries. Why did the United States not adopt it?

James Madison, often called "the father of the Constitution," insisted that our system was deliberately and carefully crafted to produce tension between the branches of government; the idea was to prevent any single branch—legislative, executive, or judicial—from assuming all power. That, Madison said in the *Federalist Papers*, would be "the very definition of tyranny." The great safeguard against that eventuality was to give each branch both the means and the will to prevent encroachments by the other branches. "Ambition," he said, "must be made to counteract ambition." Such devices as the president's veto and the Senate's power to reject appointments and treaties are among the many checks by which each branch can reject the encroachments of the other. It may be, Madison confessed, a dark reflection on human nature that such devices are necessary to preserve liberty, "But what is government itself but the greatest of all reflections on human nature? If men were angels, no government would be necessary."

People need to be governed, then, and they also need to be protected from the "ambition" of those who govern them. The framers provided ample means for implementing the second of these propositions, that of protecting the American people from a government that would abuse its power. The question today is whether they gave enough attention to the affirmative task of governing. Is our system of divided government equal to the task?

Historian Henry Steele Commager once characterized checks and balances as "a harmonious system of mutual frustration," and political scientist James MacGregor Burns claimed that it was partly to blame for what he called "the deadlock of democracy." Numerous proposals have been made for bringing the branches into a more harmonious relationship. One, long favored by Burns and other political scientists, is to make the political parties more philosophically consistent and their leadership stronger. That way, if the president and Congress are in the same party, they can work together more closely. The problem is that for the past 40 years Americans have gotten into the habit of "ticket-splitting," which means voting for a president from one party and a Congress from the other. In such a context, a stronger party system would probably exacerbate tensions between the branches.

Such considerations have led to the proposal for a "team ticket," a single ticket bracketing together the senator, the representative, and the presidential candidate from each party. This would end ticket-splitting by forcing voters to pick their senators and representatives on the same ticket as they pick the president (just as they now vote for president and vice president on a single ticket). The team ticket would result in unified party control of both branches. Such a proposal would be a radical departure from the system bequeathed to us by the framers and would probably require a constitutional amendment. Nevertheless, in the selections that follow, James L. Sundquist suggests that it deserves consideration, for something must be done to end the deadlock between the branches. Richard P. Nathan criticizes this proposal as a radical and an unnecessary departure.

YES

James L. Sundquist

FORESTALLING DIVIDED GOVERNMENT

Those who believe that a basic weakness of the United States government is the recurrent conflict and deadlock between the executive and legislative branches must turn, at the outset, to the problem of divided government.

When one party controls the executive branch and the opposing party has the majority in one or both houses of the Congress, all of the normal difficulties of attaining harmonious and effective working relationships between the branches are multiplied manifold. For, by the nature of party competition in a democracy, the business of political parties is to oppose each other. Competition between the two major parties in the United States is a constant of political life—and it must be, as a safeguard against abuse of power and as the means of assuring the citizenry a genuine choice of leaders and of programs. In an overriding emergency, partisan competition may be set aside, but only temporarily. As soon as the crisis is surmounted, the competition must resume.

When government is divided, then, the normal and healthy partisan confrontation that occurs during debates in every democratic legislature spills over into confrontation between the branches of the government, which may render it immobile. The president and the Congress always promise as their terms begin to collaborate unselfishly across the party boundary, but the dynamics of party competition inevitably thrust them into conflict, with each party mobilizing resources of the branch that it controls to advance its partisan program and defeat the proposals of its adversary. When the president sends a recommendation to the opposition-controlled Congress, the legislators are virtually compelled to reject or profoundly alter it; otherwise, they are endorsing the president's leadership as wise and sound— and, in so doing, strengthening him or his party for the next election. Conversely, if the congressional majorities initiate a measure, the president must either condemn it and use his veto or else acknowledge to the nation the prudence and creativity of his political opponents.

There have been, of course, times when political adversaries have collaborated across the chasm that separates the branches. Much of the fabric of the

From James L. Sundquist, *Constitutional Reform and Effective Government* (Brookings Institution, 1986). Copyright © 1986 by the Brookings Institution. Reprinted by permission. Notes omitted.

Western alliance that sustains the post-war world was woven at a time of divided government, in 1947–48, when President Truman and leaders of Republican congressional majorities—notably Senator Arthur H. Vandenberg of Michigan—together committed the nation to the Marshall Plan, the North Atlantic Treaty, the Truman Doctrine, and major programs of military and economic aid to allies overseas. But this was the exception, explained by the clear menace of a hostile and aggressive Soviet Union and an extraordinary degree of consensus in the country at large that the spread of communism had to be stemmed. Much more typical was the country's experience during the short presidency of Gerald Ford, when the Democratic Congress took foreign policy into its own hands, refusing to support commitments the Nixon administration had made to South Vietnam, wrecking negotiations with the Soviet Union over a trade agreement, and thwarting the president's foreign policy in Cyprus, Angola, and elsewhere. Observers may debate whether the president or the Congress had the superior policy, in each instance, but what is not contestable is that when the two branches pursue divergent policies, the country can have no foreign policy at all. The deadlock was equally pronounced on domestic matters. President Ford exercised his veto no fewer than sixty-three times in his twenty-nine-month tenure, sparing hardly any important measure, as recriminations flowed back and forth between the White House and the Capitol.

Periods of divided government have recurred throughout American history, but until the midtwentieth century they were relatively rare. During the first hundred years after the Republican party was formed in 1854 and Democratic-Re-publican competition became the structure of American politics, only twice did an incoming president have to confront an opposition majority in either house of the Congress. President Rutherford B. Hayes faced a Democratic House after the 1876 election, and Grover Cleveland had to contend with a Republican Senate at the outset of his first term. On a dozen occasions, the midterm election gave the opposition control of one or both houses, but a president could normally count on at least two years of undivided party government. Since 1954, however, the concept of what is normal has had to be reversed. Between that date and 1986, Republican presidents have occupied the White House most of the time—for twenty of the thirty-two years—but the Democrats have organized the House during the entire period and the Senate during all of the twenty-six year span from 1955 through 1980. President Eisenhower had to deal with Democratic majorities in both houses during all of his last six years in office. So did Presidents Nixon and Ford for all of their eight years. And President Reagan confronted a Democratic House during his first six years.

In the Eisenhower years, the president's foreign policy received bipartisan support, but on the domestic side the period was unproductive. The president and his Democratic opponents quarreled over what to do about education, health insurance, housing, jobs, water pollution, and many other questions. Each side had the capacity to block initiatives by the other; neither a Republican nor a Democratic program could be enacted, and action on pressing domestic issues had to await the establishment of unified Democratic control after the election of 1960. The Nixon-Ford years, likewise, saw the emasculation of such presidential initiatives as the family assistance plan and the New Federalism, and by the end of Nixon's first term relations between the branches had degenerated into open warfare. In his second term, Nixon wrote in his memoirs, "I had thrown down a gauntlet to Congress, the bureaucracy, the media, and the Washington establishment and challenged them to epic battle." The Congress took up the challenge and, even after forcing Nixon out of office, continued the battle with his successor. President Reagan, confronting a Democratic House, did succeed in driving through his radical economic program, but his victories were confined, for the most part, to his first year in office. After that, relations steadily deteriorated, and by the third year the government was once again reduced to ineffectiveness. The House—and to some extent the Republican-controlled Senate as well—was resisting further domestic budget cuts, and it was frustrating the president's foreign policy, particularly in Central America. But the government's impotence was reflected most dramatically in its incapacity to cope with gigantic and unprecedented budget deficits. As the revenue shortfall reached $200 billion annually, the president and spokesmen for both parties in both houses of the Congress separately warned the nation of impending disaster, but together they could not muster the will to act.

Nor, in a divided government, could anyone be held accountable. In the 1984 election, the Democrats could—and did—charge the president with responsibility for the record deficits, but he in turn could—and did—blame the Democratic House. Yet both parties were entirely right in denying responsibility, because neither *was* responsible. And the voters, having declined in 1980 and 1982 to vest

an undivided authority in either party, could not in 1984 register a clearcut approval or disapproval of what had happened, and so set the future course of government, by either returning a responsible party to office or turning it out of office. An electoral verdict on the conduct of a divided government is perforce a muddy and a muddled mandate. . . .

THE PRESIDENTIAL-CONGRESSIONAL TEAM TICKET

The most direct and effective, but most arbitrary, way to end ticket-splitting between candidates for president and Congress would be simply to prohibit it. Each party's candidates for president, vice president, senator, and representative could be bound together as a slate—or team ticket, as it has been called—with the voter casting a single vote for the team of his or her choice.

The team ticket would be less than a foolproof protection against divided government, to be sure. Since only one-third of the Senate seats are filled in each presidential election, a lopsided Senate majority—such as the Democratic majorities of the 1960s—would not be overturned in a narrow presidential election won by the opposition candidate (assuming that the system of staggered six-year terms is not altered . . .). And even in the case of the House, where all the seats are at stake in each election, a slim mathematical possibility would exist that in a close election the winning presidential candidate might not carry a majority of House districts. Nevertheless, the prospects for unified party control of the government would be tremendously enhanced. Divided government following a presidential election would become the kind of rarity it was during the first century of Republican-Democratic competition.

Beyond that, the team ticket would have a profound effect on the conduct of politicians of the majority party in office. Throughout a president's first term, the chief executive and legislators of the winning party would recognize that when reelection time came around they would stand or fall together. Congressmen of the president's party would be at pains to enhance the president's success, since they as well as he would be dependent on the public's acceptance of his record in office. Would this produce a Congress too docile, too subservient to exercise its responsibility to oversee, and where necessary investigate, the executive branch? Certainly—at least until a president was reelected and entered his lame-duck second term—the congressmen would lose a measure of their independence, as is the case in parliamentary countries where members are forced to run on the party record. Members would no longer be free to score political points in their home states or districts by opposing, and embarrassing, a president of their own party. They could no longer denounce their leader and reject party discipline altogether, as leading senators and representatives have done so often in the past, reducing their party's program to a shambles. They would have to accept the president's leadership, like it or not, as long as he remained the party's likely nominee for reelection.

Nevertheless, in their own interests, individual legislators would be forced to oppose the president where his policies and programs appeared likely to undercut support for the party in a particular state or district. Their incentive to make the president's record look good would extend to the prevention of mistakes,

and their oversight and investigative powers would still be important for that end. If the president persisted in a locally unpopular course, dissenting legislators would have the recourse always available in any democracy when party discipline becomes intolerable—to bolt the party and either join another party or form a new one. . . .

The Challenge to Tradition

The idea of a team ticket has one notable precedent. Since the formation of parties in the United States, candidates for president and vice president have been bound together; the voter casts a single ballot for a slate of electors committed to one or another party's presidential–vice presidential team. No one has been heard to advocate a right for voters to split their ticket for those two offices.

Nevertheless, to further restrict the voter's right of choice would do violence to a tradition that has been cherished by the American polity ever since progressive reformers introduced the secret ballot. One may anticipate the response of typical southern ticket-splitters in 1984 had it been suggested that, in order to support President Reagan for a second term, they be required to vote to oust their friendly and effective Democratic congressman. Or if they wanted to retain their congressman in office, that they be forced to accept Walter Mondale and Geraldine Ferraro. And these southern voters have their counterparts in every region, who split tickets in both directions and would defend vehemently their right to do so. If those voters had thought about divided government at all, they would be apt to see its adverse consequences as remote and speculative—and of a kind that could be averted if only the responsible officials would put aside partisanship and do their duty in the national interest—while the restriction on their freedom to vote as they please would be immediate, clear, and personally felt. . . .

Clearly, proponents of the team ticket will have an enormous task persuading typical voters that giving up their freedom to split their tickets will be good for the country, and for them. The Democrats who had no fear of divided government in five midterm elections, and who may even have preferred it, will have to be persuaded that unified control by the Republican party will somehow produce better government. Few partisan Democrats, surely, would admit to such a probability—least of all the party activists who have contributed the leadership, the effort, and the money to press for Democratic congressional victories while a Republican president was in the White House. The argument can assuredly be made that, with united Republican control, one party could be held indisputably accountable for the exercise of power, and that that would be healthy and beneficial for the political system as a whole, and hence good for everybody. But to make the argument is not to predict that many Democrats would be persuaded, or that the party would abandon its campaign. And Republicans are no more likely to yield to the logic of the claim. When Democratic presidents have been in office, there has been no evidence of slackening in the desire of Republican partisans to regain control of the Congress at midterm.

If the party activist and the rank-and-file partisan voter would be difficult to persuade, the average member of Congress, as noted earlier, would be even more so. For every winner in general elections, of course, there is a loser. For every incumbent senator or representa-

tive who survived only because of ticket-splitting, there is a candidate of the other party who would have been elected if the practice had been forbidden. Southern Republicans, for example, should find great merit in the team-ticket idea. Indeed, if the scheme had been in place over the past thirty years, the entire Republican party would have benefited, for it would have been the majority party in the Congress during many of the years when it was in fact consigned to what seemed to be perpetual minority status. That assumes, as seems likely, that the support given the team ticket would have come closer to that accorded its presidential candidates in 1956, 1968, 1972, 1980, and 1984 than to the much lower level of support given its nominees for Congress. Even if the Republicans had won the White House on only four of those five occasions (the 1968 election having been the only close one), they would have gained from having had the opportunity to enact their party program unobstructed by the opposition.

It is the incumbent members of Congress who vote, however, not the opponents they defeated. And those whose own political careers, or whose colleagues' careers, were saved by ticket-splitting are not likely to step forward quickly to outlaw the practice. Adoption of the team ticket would therefore depend, in all likelihood, on bypassing the Congress in the constitutional amendment process. That has never been done, but it can be. On petition of two-thirds of the state legislatures, the Congress must call a constitutional convention, which submits its proposed amendments directly to the states for ratification—and that method would have to be used to accomplish any of the changes . . . that might be perceived by sitting members of the Congress to be against their interest. . . . However, the state legislators who would have to initiate such a convention have much in common with congressmen. Many of them, too, have survived through ticket-splitting in state elections, and their outlook might not differ greatly from that of their counterparts in Washington.

An electoral system should never be judged, of course, according to the degree of comfort and convenience it accords political candidates and officeholders. It should be measured by its effects on the performance of the political system as a whole. And from that perspective, . . . the very features that discommend the team ticket idea to members of Congress are its merit. By requiring a party's presidential and legislative candidates to share a common success or failure at the polls, it would compel them to work together once elected. Inevitably, some members of Congress would be dragged to defeat by a presidential candidate unpopular in their states or districts. Occasionally, a presidential candidate might be dragged down, too. But one candidate's loss would be another's gain. And, if reducing conflict and averting deadlock would benefit the political system as a whole, the public at large would gain immensely from an end to divided government as the normal circumstance, and from the incentives to party cohesion and cooperation that the team ticket would provide.

NO

Richard P. Nathan

THE PRESIDENCY AFTER REAGAN: DON'T CHANGE IT—MAKE IT WORK

Ronald Wilson Reagan was not a great president, but perhaps greatness may not be possible without a major national crisis. He was, however, a very successful president, serving out two full terms and leaving office as a respected national leader with a great reservoir of good will among the people, much as was the case with Dwight David Eisenhower. The purpose of this chapter is to examine both the Reagan presidency as an institution and the case for making fundamental changes in the office.

The presidency is much more than one person; "it is," said Albert De Grazia, "a Congress covered with skin." We need to assess presidents in these terms as the leaders of a large system. Actually, there were two Reagan presidencies: a first term, during which the Reagan system worked relatively smoothly, considering the immensity of the challenge; and a second term, in which the presidency as an institution fell short of this earlier standard. I derive lessons from both of them to argue in favor of keeping the presidency as an institution in its present form and against those who want basic constitutional changes in the office.

This is not to say that we should take a head-in-the-sand attitude toward all modifications in the role of the president and the office of the presidency. I distinguish two types of changes: (1) constitutional—in the role, term, and duties of the president and the principle of the separation of power; and (2) procedural—in the organization and staffing of the office of the president and in the selection process for the presidency. Changes of the latter type may indeed be desirable. In fact, they are happening all the time.

I take specific issue with the scholarly opinion among some contemporary presidency watchers, much of which opinion dates from the Carter years, that we should make fundamental alterations in the American presidency. These opinions can be identified easily by associating them with Lloyd N. Cutler, a distinguished Washington attorney and counsel to President Carter; and government expert James L. Sundquist. My position is that we

From Richard P. Nathan, "The Presidency After Reagan: Don't Change It—Make It Work," in Larry Berman, ed., *Looking Back on the Reagan Presidency* (Johns Hopkins University Press, 1990). Copyright © 1990 by Johns Hopkins University Press. Reprinted by permission. Some notes omitted.

should not adopt their proposals for constitutional changes that vary the basic character of the American presidency.

THE BASIC CHARACTER OF THE PRESIDENCY

The presidency is a quintessentially American institution. Its operation reflects the competitive, often confrontational, style and spirit of American government. It can and often does work well as the focus for policy-making and in its execution of the American governmental system despite the inevitable criticisms leveled at presidents and the rocky moments that are bound to occur. For much of the first term of Ronald Reagan's presidency (to the surprise of many president watchers) Reagan operated successfully to get his way in this intense political milieu. I can best convey the spirit of my assessment with an anecdote.

A newspaper reporter interviewing people about a primary election asked a man on the street how he would vote. "Oh, I never vote," the man replied, "it just encourages them."

The reason many people think this story is funny is that it has a familiar ring to it, reflecting the idea that in the United States politics is not the most venerated of professions. We love to make fun of, and trouble for, our politicians, perhaps out of envy for the excitement of their work and the attention they receive when they are riding high.

Personally, my bias is that I think we are too hard on our politicians. The fear that voting "just encourages them" reflects the tendency that bad press for politicians is good press for the media; many citizens know more about the foibles than the fineness of our political leaders. We do not give enough credit to the thousands of men and women who dedicate their lives to the profession of politics in this country.

The pluralistic American political system and culture have much to do with this love-hate relationship with our politicians. The character of U.S. politics makes every citizen a potential political player and critic. In De Tocqueville's terms, our political system is "full of striving and animation," but at the same time it is responsive and vibrant in a way De Tocqueville clearly admired.

The framers of the Constitution may have had a little secret among themselves—which James Madison never recorded—to the effect that they should make the presidency a beguiling office. They surely did so. The dominant view in the literature is that the framers resisted assigning a clear strong role to the presidency because of their fear of England's last powerful king, George III, against whom the colonists saw themselves fighting the Revolutionary War. Tom Paine called George III "the Royal Brute of Britain." The king stood in the minds of the framers as a symbol of the dangers of lodging executive power in a single person. As a result, some of the framers did not want to have an executive; and Forrest McDonald says that one fourth of the delegates at the constitutional convention advocated a plural executive. McDonald added that the lack of a knowledge base and different opinions among the delegates were the reasons for "the curious manner" in which executive powers are divided and distributed in the U.S. Constitution.

The result is that Article II created a relatively weak executive branch in terms of the president's relationships with the Congress. In his brilliant study of the Jeffersonian presidencies, James Sterling

Young said that when it came to presidential leadership of Congress, the president's cupboard was bare:

> It seems beyond argument that the Constitution provided a wholly inadequate vehicle for presidential leadership of Congress. That the framers made the Chief Executive independent of the representative body was no inconsiderable accomplishment in a nation whose colonial experience gave every reason for mistrusting executive power. Nothing would have been more out of character with the organizing principles of the Constitution than for the framers to have admitted into it the concept of presidential leadership of the executive branch.

The original conception of the American national government put the force of government in the legislature. Article I of the Constitution, dealing with the legislative branch, is the longest and most specific article. It contains the enumerated powers of the new national government, which are explicitly assigned to the Congress.

Now in the twentieth century, this earlier conception that regarded the presidential office as having a limited role in the political process has been supplanted by a greatly strengthened presidency that has acquired new and broad powers. The Rooseveltian communications power of the modern presidency, the executive budget, the creation of the executive office, and the expansion of its staff and duties have all contributed to the growth in the role of the modern president as a policy initiator and leader. Under and since the FDR presidency, the fear has often been expressed that now an "imperial presidency" threatens our liberties and our political system.

There is also another contemporary view that rises to the surface in periods of stress. It was evident with Lyndon Johnson during the Vietnam War; with Jimmy Carter on his retreat to Camp David to ponder the national malaise; with Richard Nixon in the Watergate affair; and with Ronald Reagan for much of his second term. At the height of the Iran-contra affair, Larry Speakes, serving as the chief White House spokesman for President Reagan, said, referring to the presidency, "when you stumble, you're immobilized." His comment reflects this second view of the presidency as a vulnerable and isolated office, beset by pressures and inflated expectations; this is a view that coexists, often in the same formulation, with the idea of an imperial presidency.

Elements of the opinion of an isolated and vulnerable presidency can be seen in some of the proposals for changes in the office. Lloyd Cutler, in a now famous 1980 article in *Foreign Affairs*, emphasized what he saw as the perennial problem of stalemate in the American policy process. The focus of his analysis was Jimmy Carter's failure to win ratification of the SALT II treaty—not necessarily a good example since, historically, the Senate has ratified about 1,000 treaties and has turned down twenty, only five in this century. Unfortunately for Jimmy Carter, the Soviets invaded Afghanistan just before the SALT II treaty came up for a vote.

Lloyd Cutler's essential complaint is that the existing system prevents the government from "making those decisions *we* all know must be made." The problem with this analysis is the assumption that there is a group of people that knows what is best and that the political process, in synthesizing the values and views of the citizenry, is unable to do what that omniscient "we" know should be done.

Another reason, according to Cutler, for reform of the presidency is the related tendency for the American political system to reflect "a sort of permanent centrism." I do not so much quarrel with this part of Cutler's analysis as I would raise a question about whether this tendency is a weakness at all. One can argue quite to the contrary that it is the very key to the stability and longevity of the American constitutional system.

On the basis of his analysis, Lloyd Cutler calls for changes that would convert the presidency into an office resembling that of the prime minister in a parliamentary form. Among his chief recommendations are permitting as many as half of the members of the Cabinet to be chosen from among sitting members of the Congress; allowing for a vote of confidence during each presidential term; and changing the duration of presidential and congressional terms so that they are coterminous.

In much the same way as Lloyd Cutler, James L. Sundquist, in a Brookings Institution book on constitutional reform published in 1986, takes aim at the condition of divided government in which one party controls the Congress and the other the executive branch. Under these conditions, he says, "the normal difficulties of attaining harmonious and effective working relationships between the branches are multiplied manifold." Sundquist urges reforms similar to those advocated by Cutler.

I base my case against these and similar non-quick constitutional fixes on two arguments:

1. The Edmund Burkean argument: be very careful about changing institutions.

[Burke, 1729–1797, was a British statesman and orator.]

2. The experience of the Reagan presidency offers guidance for the future which supports the conclusion that the presidency can and does work. This is, I believe, the major thrust of this chapter.

An important idea associated with the Burkean argument fits the subject at hand: Burke's respect for institutions. Referring to the dangers of institutional change, Burke said, "By this unprincipled facility of changing the state as often and as much, and in as many ways, as there are floating fancies or fashions, the whole chain of continuity of the commonwealth would be broken. No one generation could link with another. Men would become little better than flies of summer."

I believe it is just as well that no important political leaders are currently pressing for constitutional changes of the type advocated by Cutler and Sundquist. Many politicians would like to amend the Constitution to require a balanced budget (a dubious constitutional tenet), to permit prayer in the schools, or to ban abortions, but as far as I know, no important active politician supports opening the Pandora's box of constitutional change to permit congressmen to serve in the Cabinet, to provide for votes of confidence, or to have combined executive-congressional tickets.

In dealing with the second argument, I wish to draw on Ronald Reagan's experience to support the position on the presidency taken here and as stated in the chapter title. The modern president is the nation's most powerful leader, a teacher, and a human being all wrapped up in one. He must be skillful in structuring and managing the office if the institution is to succeed and stay on an even keel amid the great pressures that swirl around it. The president cannot let the machinery take on a life of its own. He must be in control, but he cannot control everything. The fact that there is constant political bargaining in our governmental system does not mean that we cannot make important decisions; however, decisions take skill and time and they often require a triggering event or issue to produce broad agreement on a new or significantly changed course of action.

The first term of the Reagan administration was a good period for the American presidency in which the office and the officeholder stood in high regard and in which Reagan's policies had a profound effect on many areas of our national life.

More than anything else, Ronald Reagan was viewed at the outset of his presidency as a great communicator—although in point of fact, I do not believe this was or is his strongest suit. Reagan's greatest strengths, as demonstrated by the experience of his first term, are three-fold: (1) his excellent sense of timing; (2) his ability to select and deploy effectively his chief subordinates; and (3) what Fred Greenstein calls "his propensity to act on principles" and to stick to them.

PRINCIPLES OF EFFECTIVE PRESIDENTIAL LEADERSHIP

There are three principles about the way the presidency works which I believe were the keys to the effectiveness of the presidency in Reagan's first term.

The first principle is that the president must be *selective* in choosing the issues on which his or her personal decisions and leadership are required. This, of course, is where Carter and Nixon were said to have had their greatest problems: they were not very selective; both were detail men. As presidents, they tended to take too many subjects and issues to themselves. In Carter's case, so the barbs went, he was said to view the role of the presidency as being similar to that of the captain of a nuclear submarine.

The second principle for organizing the presidency is that the president must *consider dissenting views* but not allow them to swamp the system and prevent action. The Bay of Pigs fiasco very early in Kennedy's presidency is a case in which dissent could not get through. Afterward, the President said, "How could I have been so off base?"; but it was too late.

The third, and I believe most important, principle is that in dealing with the issues the president selects for his own attention and leadership, he must have a *balanced group of trusted advisors* who bring a range of experience and viewpoints to dealing with them. There are a number of dimensions to presidential issues which need to be represented in the advice of the president's associates. One is the capital "P"olitical dimension in the broad sense of what the times call for and what the public wants. A second dimension is that of intellectual or substantive input. A third is the political dimension with a small "p" in the sense of getting things done, working with friends, and watching out for opponents and detractors.

Reagan's first-term troika of Edwin Meese, James Baker, and Michael Deaver was a balanced and smooth-working system in these three-dimensional terms. Edwin Meese represented the "P"olitical dimension—what Reagan was about, and what he had stood for. He had been a close associate of the President's when he was governor of California and knew the agenda and the man in these terms. James Baker, although not an intellectual or scholarly person in his own right, brought to the group substantive ideas as well as a keen organizational sense in handling issues and executing decisions. Michael Deaver was the keeper of the political person—i.e. with a small "p." Although I was not privy to the inner workings of the Reagan White House, I understood Deaver's role to be that of the person who knew both of the Reagans (Mr. and Mrs.) in terms of their personal preferences; their work style; preferred schedule; whom they liked and whom they did not; with whom they wanted to share time, when, and on what basis.

It needs to be remembered that this threesome—despite the destructive problems Meese and Deaver later faced—brought the needed range of inputs to the President's decisions and winnowed out opinions that could disrupt or distort the presidential decision process. I credit Reagan himself for this system; the presidency cannot be delegated. This blend of people and process would not have worked had it not above all reflected the style and personality of the President.

To underline this theory of *how* the presidency works *when* it works, I submit that Nixon, with his very strong intellect and deep substantive knowledge, failed to have this kind of a balance of political, substantive, and personal inputs. When he was off base, his worst instincts tended to predominate because so many of the people around him shared his uneasy view of the world. I have always believed that if a balanced group of advisors had been involved in the planning of Nixon's reelection campaign, the Watergate break-in would not have occurred. If Melvin Laird or Elliott Richardson had been in the room when John Mitchell and others were discussing campaign shenanigans, the planning group very likely would not have considered the Watergate caper as a fit subject for discussion, much less approval.

The theory of how the presidency works when it works well, grounded in these three principles, is supported in Reagan's case by what happened in his second term. In order to keep James Baker on his team, Reagan made a decision that cost him dearly because it went against these principles. Reagan picked Secretary of the Treasury Donald Regan to be the White House chief of staff. In terms of the institution of the presidency, this was a serious error for which the President was clearly and personally responsible, and which now, in retrospect, he must regret mightily. Donald Regan was not suited to this position, much less capable of replacing a three-person system. He demonstrated in this office—as he had done beforehand—tendencies to mistrust independent-minded people and particularly politicians, which was a fatal flaw in a person in so central a political role. . . .

My thesis, to reiterate, is that despite this rocky period and the reversals it involved, Ronald Reagan had more than his share of successes and good moments in office. No president can fail to be controversial. Success in the presidency is appreciated more in hindsight than in the present tense. That Reagan has weaknesses is undeniable. My argument is that for much of his tenure and in a number of areas, Ronald Wilson Reagan demonstrated qualities that made the office, especially in the first term, work well. . . .

CONCLUSION

I am not arguing that any alterations in the way the presidency operates are ill advised—only that our standards and aspirations should be human-scaled and that in this spirit, fundamental constitutional changes in the office should not be adopted at this time. I said earlier, and I repeat, that procedural changes in the operation of the presidency and changes in the presidential selection process are being made all the time, and in many cases they are needed. As an example, I believe we have overstaffed both the executive office of the president and the Congress and that this top-heaviness makes it harder for the two branches to work together. The two branches often appear, as British political expert James Douglas has suggested, like two huge armies that are extremely hard to maneuver on the field. However, changes in the procedures and staffing of the Congress or the presidency are a far cry from constitutional changes that alter the separation of powers and the role and structure of either.

In sum, my balance sheet for the Reagan presidency shows many pluses; and to me, they support my thesis: we should not fundamentally change the presidency as an institution of the American governmental system. It can be made to work, not perfectly; but, as Edmund Burke surely would have asked, what does work perfectly?

NOTE

Appreciation is expressed to James Ceasar, John J. DiIulio, James Douglas, Fred I. Greenstein, and John Lago for assistance in the preparation of this paper.

POSTSCRIPT

The Presidency Versus Congress: Should Divided Government Be Ended?

Sundquist assumes that a president and a congressional majority from the same party could work together harmoniously and efficiently. That assumption is open to question, or at least to qualification. During his administration in the late 1970s, Jimmy Carter had a congressional majority from his party, but his legislative success rate was modest at best. A productive relationship between the president and Congress depends upon a number of factors, not the least of which is the skill of those who serve as the president's liaison with the legislative branch. In that respect many observers thought that Carter was not very well served.

Wilfred E. Binkley's classic historical study of the presidency and Congress, appropriately entitled *President and Congress*, 3rd ed. (Vintage Books, 1962), is still useful for studying the ebbs and flows of presidential and congressional hegemony. *The Fettered Presidency* (American Enterprise Institute, 1989), edited by L. Gordon Crovitz and Jeremy A. Rabkin, is a collection of essays that argue that modern Congresses have prevented presidents from exercising their proper functions. Hedrick Smith's *The Power Game: How Washington Works* (Random House, 1988) is an inside look at how key Washingtonians in the executive and legislative branches play politics. *The Reagan Legacy: Promise and Performance* (Chatham House, 1988), edited by Charles O. Jones, and *The Bush Presidency: First Appraisals* (Chatham House, 1991), edited by Colin Campbell et al., include accounts of legislative-executive relations under Reagan and Bush.

Regardless of who occupies the White House, it seems likely that there will always be tension between the president and Congress. Senators and representatives serve their states or districts, but the president and vice president are the only elected officials in this country whose political survival depends upon what the nation as a whole thinks of them. Inevitably, then, they must look at issues from a different perspective than that of the various members of Congress. There is a political fault line between the branches—can it ever be bridged or even eliminated?

McKenna and feingold, Taking Sides

Dushkin, 1993

ISSUE 7

Does the Government Regulate Too Much?

YES: Thomas Gale Moore, from "Regulation, Reregulation, or Deregulation," in Annelise Anderson and Dennis L. Bark, eds., *Thinking About America: The United States in the 1990s* (Hoover Institution Press, 1988)

NO: David Bollier and Joan Claybrook, from "Regulations That Work," *The Washington Monthly* (April 1986)

ISSUE SUMMARY

YES: Economist Thomas Gale Moore argues that deregulating economic markets lowers costs, benefits consumers, and makes the American economy more competitive in the world.
NO: Journalist David Bollier and political activist Joan Claybrook provide evidence that existing government regulations have prevented serious human and environmental harm in the past, and they argue that the purpose of regulations should not be obscured by economic considerations.

Government regulation of economic decision-making is as old as the Interstate Commerce Commission, which was established in 1887 to regulate railroad rates. The Sherman and Clayton Antitrust Acts of 1890 and 1914, respectively, as well as the law establishing the Federal Trade Commission in 1914, were also designed to outlaw unfair methods of business competition.

Congress later established regulatory agencies to set standards for natural (or socially useful) monopolies, such as electric power companies and radio and television stations. Between 1920 and 1940, Congress set up the Federal Power Commission, the Federal Communications Commission, and the Civil Aeronautics Board. The national government also created the Federal Reserve System in 1913 and the Securities and Exchange Commission in 1934 (after the stock market crash) to regulate the investment of capital in industry and general banking practices.

Although governmental regulation of commerce on behalf of the public interest was introduced as early as the Pure Food and Drug Act of 1906 (now administered by the Department of Health and Human Services), most activity within this area is relatively recent. The Equal Employment Opportunity Commission was established in 1965. The Environmental Protection Agency, the Occupational Safety and Health Administration, and the National Highway Traffic Safety Administration were all created in 1970. The Consumer Product Safety Commission was set up in 1973, and the Office of Surface Mining Reclamation and Enforcement (within the Department of the Interior) came into being in 1977. With these and other newly established agencies, the federal government assumed wide-ranging responsibility to protect all persons against certain hazards that unrestrained private economic enterprise might otherwise create.

The rules written by these regulatory bodies have changed our lives in many ways, altering the food we eat, the cars we drive, and the air we breathe. Their defenders have applauded the protection that has been provided against profit-motivated predators who would otherwise adulterate our food, threaten our safety, and pollute the environment in order to maximize profits.

On the other hand, many investigators have joined businessmen in condemning government's movement into these areas. Critics make the following arguments: (1) Regulation inhibits production by suppressing innovation and discouraging risk taking, which results in declining employment. (2) Regulation invariably overregulates by setting standards for every aspect of manufacturing when it could set overall objectives that businesses could meet in whatever ways they devise. Some economists maintain that government would accomplish more by assessing fees or taxes to discourage certain activities rather than fixing rigid standards. (3) Regulation costs to businesses are passed on to the consumer and increase government payrolls. If government regulation drives a company out of business, the standard of living for those affected will go down. That is to say, the costs outweigh the benefits.

Different values will result in different assessments of the consequences of regulation or deregulation. The regulation of lumbering and mining to protect the environment, for example, pits those who place a higher value on environmental preservation, and who therefore tend to support regulation, against those who put economic well-being first, who tend to oppose regulation.

But sometimes deregulation can lead to results that cost a great deal of money. Deregulating the savings and loan (S&L) industry tempted many S&Ls into making high-profit but risky investments, and when the borrowers defaulted, the federal government stepped in to pick up the tab at a total cost of roughly half a trillion dollars. Seen from a different standpoint, however, S&L bailout was not the result of deregulation but of incomplete deregulation: the federal government stopped supervising the banks but continued to insure them.

No serious analyst advocates regulation of all social enterprises or of none, but Thomas Gale Moore believes that most regulation is likely to do more harm than good, and David Bollier and Joan Claybrook offer what they believe is clear proof that many government regulations protect the health, safety, and welfare of the public.

YES

Thomas Gale Moore

REGULATION, REREGULATION, OR DEREGULATION

The 1990s will see an increasingly competitive world. The United States, which for most of the post–World War II period has been the dominant economy, experienced a real loss of competitiveness in the first half of the 1980s. Over the last twenty years Japanese industry has become known worldwide for its quality and innovativeness. In addition the rise in the value of the dollar from 1980 to 1985 and the growing perception that U.S. goods may not embody the most up-to-date technology have reduced the U.S. share of world trade.

With the reversal in the value of the dollar in the second half of the 1980s, it became apparent that U.S. manufacturing was still highly competitive. In fact the evidence from 1983 on was of a vibrant, strong economy, which despite a large trade deficit was employing more people and generating more jobs than any other economy in the world. Europe, in contrast, enjoyed a large and growing trade surplus but failed to reduce its unemployment or add jobs. Only in Great Britain, which adopted a policy of privatization and of encouragement of business, was economic growth vigorous.

The United States followed two polices in the 1980s that strongly contributed to superior economic performance. The Reagan administration led a successful effort to reduce marginal tax rates to the lowest levels since the 1920s. The top individual marginal tax rate, which was 70 percent in 1980, was reduced through two major tax acts to 28 percent in 1988. The corporate rate was lowered from 46 to 34 percent.

The other factor contributing to U.S. economic performance was the low and decreasing level of government control over markets. During the 1960s and first half of the 1970s U.S. government regulation had been growing, but this trend slowed and in important aspects reversed around the middle of the 1970s. In much of the rest of the world, however, governments continued to believe that they could do better than competitive markets. Recently a number of other countries have been following the U.S. lead in deregulating such industries as airlines and telecommunications.

From Thomas Gale Moore, "Regulation, Reregulation, or Deregulation," in Annelise Anderson and Dennis L. Bark, eds., *Thinking About America: The United States in the 1990s* (Hoover Institution Press, 1988). Copyright © 1988 by the Board of Trustees of the Leland Stanford, Jr., University. Reprinted by permission. Notes omitted.

From the mid-1970s to the mid-1980s the federal government carried out a remarkable bipartisan program of reducing economic regulation of many industries. Starting with commissions on stock transactions, air freight, and airlines, deregulation was extended to motor carriers, railroads, oil prices, intercity buses, long-distance telecommunications and interest rates on savings accounts. In the anti-trust area, during the Reagan administration the Department of Justice took actions to revise and clarify merger guidelines, encourage productivity-enhancing joint research and development efforts, and, by dismissing the IBM case, remove the implicit condemnation of bigness per se. In the main this deregulation did not extend to environmental, safety, or social regulation, although the Reagan administration did slow the growth of government intervention in these areas. Even for economic regulation the agenda is incomplete. Financial markets remain under strict controls, although less regulated than in 1975; motor carriers are still subject to Interstate Commerce Commission (ICC) regulation; only a portion of natural gas sold at the wellhead is free from federal restrictions.

Nevertheless, the partial deregulation of the U.S. economy has worked to improve the competitiveness of our industry. Transportation, banking, and communication costs have declined. The growth and partial freeing of financial markets have lowered the cost of capital. Over the last seven years inflation has reduced the extent to which the minimum wage prices low-skilled labor out of the market. The United States has also been fortunate in not following Europe's example of regulating the labor market through rules designed to protect jobs. Laws that inhibit layoffs inhibit hiring; laws that mandate health benefits impose higher costs and less flexibility on labor markets; attempts to protect jobs in one industry cost jobs in another.

Partly as a consequence of deregulation and resisted efforts to extend regulation, productivity in U.S. manufacturing has increased at an annual rate of 5 percent since 1982. Overall employment has grown by about fifteen million. With only a modest growth in wage rates, unit labor costs in 1986 and 1987 (through the third quarter) actually declined in manufacturing. Adjusted for the sharp 1986 appreciation of foreign currencies, Japanese and Western European unit labor costs rose about 20 to 40 percent.

But there is significant room for improvement. Except for reduced control over broadcasting content, a speedup of Federal Drug Administration new drug approvals, and an increased use of trade-offs in the control of air pollution, there has been little movement toward making safety, environmental, or social regulation less burdensome. In fact legislation has been enacted limiting the energy requirements of most household appliances. Although controls on natural gas uses have been eliminated, federal restrictions on the fuel efficiency of new cars have continued despite declining petroleum prices.

PROGRESS ON DEREGULATION

Pressure is growing for reregulation of many of the industries deregulated in whole or part in the earlier period. Some claim that abolishing the Civil Aeronautics Board (CAB) was a major mistake, whereas others point to the huge benefits for consumers. Nevertheless, the evidence clearly shows that decontrol reduced fares, increased competition, and improved the frequency and availability of individual flights.

A Brookings Institution study concluded that airline passengers gain about $6 billion a year in 1977 dollars (or about $11.5 billion in 1988 dollars) from deregulation. Contrary to the predictions of those who opposed deregulation, most small towns have more service now than before decontrol. Airlines have improved efficiency and thus can offer more and deeper discounts while making a good return on their investment. Of course not all airlines are in the black, but in any competitive industry some firms will do worse than others. Safety has continued to improve in the decade since airline deregulation started.

Decontrol, however, has brought problems. The very success of the experiment has led to a tremendous burgeoning of travel. The number of passengers has risen 74 percent since 1977 and the number of flights, 30 percent. Unfortunately this rapid growth, together with the illegal air traffic controllers' strike in 1981, the subsequent firing of the strikers, and the slow rebuilding of the system, has led to increased congestion and concern about safety. There is little reason for concern about decreased safety as a result of deregulation, but there are real problems with congestion and delays.

Some have suggested bringing back the CAB. Legislation has been introduced to prevent airlines from buying and selling operating rights. The most likely prospects include legislation to require that airlines compensate passengers for lost or delayed baggage, report on-time performance, and have the Federal Aviation Administration (FAA) limit takeoffs and landings at certain airports. These requirements, if enacted, would move the airline industry back toward regulation. The result would undoubtedly mean higher fares, lower capacity, and less-frequent service. Thus the benefits of greater competition would be sacrificed to reduce congestion and delays.

A more promising solution would be to introduce variable landing fees. Higher charges for landing and taking off at peak times would push those more flexible about their travel time away from the most congested periods. Another promising change would be to privatize part or all of the air traffic control system. Currently air traffic controllers are government employees whose job security limits the FAA's ability to assign them where they are most needed. Moreover, an airport wishing to expand capacity cannot be sure that the FAA will increase tower personnel and equipment enough to accommodate the increase in traffic. Privatization of airways and airports would be a natural sequel to airline deregulation. . . .

Less well known is the success of the 1984 divestiture of the Bell operating companies from AT&T. Despite advance planning, there were initial difficulties with the quality of service and other adjustment problems. Now, in 1988, most of these problems seem to be behind us, although there is considerable pressure to modify the conditions limiting the activities of the regional Bell operating companies. Although no one has done a rigorous assessment, service quality appears to be as good as it ever was. Since the decree breaking up AT&T, competition in the industry has greatly increased. At least four new long-distance companies offer nationwide service for residential and business customers, and a handful of others provide service exclusively for business. Some five hundred interexchange carriers, providing connections between exchanges, compete with AT&T. Together they have installed nearly twice as many circuit miles as Ma Bell. Consequently interexchange rates have declined over 30 percent since divestiture. The long-distance companies have been competing by offering new services for residential and business users.

The manufacturing market has also become much more competitive. Before the decree Western Electric had most of the market to itself. Six large new international firms and over a hundred new smaller firms now offer residential telephones, key systems, private branch exchanges, central office switches, and transmission equipment. Prices have dropped sharply, and many innovative products not previously offered are now available. The former assistant attorney general for antitrust, William Baxter, estimated that "the per-line price of key telephone systems would decrease by 25 percent in 1985 alone, at the same time as technological advances made such systems more versatile than ever before. In the market for telecommunications equipment, the per-line price of certain central office switching equipment has been cut in half."

REGULATORY REFORM AGENDA

It is vital in the 1990s to maintain the gains that have already been achieved from deregulation. Reregulation of transportation, communication, or energy would be a tragedy. Where regulation is incomplete, such as trucking and natural gas, it should be perfected. In addition, regulatory reform should be extended to Corporate Average Fuel Economy (CAFE) standards, financial institutions, and environmental regulation.

CAFE Standards

Among the least known but most pernicious regulations are the CAFE standards. These regulations, intended to reduce fuel consumption, have required automobile manufacturers to sell cars that on average meet or exceed a specific mileage-per-gallon standard. For the last few years the CAFE standard has been 27.5 miles per gallon. If the average vehicle sold failed to meet that standard, the manufacturer would be fined $5.00 per tenth of a mile under for each car sold. Thus if a producer sold a million vehicles and missed the standard by 0.2 miles per gallon (that is, its cars averaged 27.3 miles per gallon), it would be fined $10 million. This standard applies separately to domestically produced and imported vehicles.

Whether the CAFE standards have had much effect until recently is questionable. During most of the period since their implementation, gasoline prices alone have been high enough to encourage consumers to demand fuel-efficient vehicles. But the drop in oil prices in the last few years has reduced gasoline prices to consumers considerably, and many are purchasing bigger, more comfortable, safer cars with lower fuel efficiency than smaller vehicles. General Motors (GM) and Ford have had trouble meeting the current standard and have successfully petitioned the National Highway Traffic Safety Administration to reduce it, though only temporarily. The auto companies are in danger of having to pay heavy fines in the future.

When firms exceed the standard, they get credit toward years when they fall short. Most Japanese companies, which sold mainly fuel-efficient small cars in the past, have built up considerable mileage credits and are now in an excellent position to import large cars to the U.S. market without CAFE constraint. By contrast, to meet the CAFE standard GM and Ford must offset sales of large cars with sales of small ones by raising and lowering prices respectively. Thus the CAFE standard acts as a tax on domestic manufacturers of large cars, a market where the United States has a comparative advantage, and favors Japanese imports. It may be undesirable to discriminate against imports, but it is certainly not sensible to discriminate against U.S. producers and in favor of imports.

Financial Markets
On October 19, 1987, the Dow Jones Average on the New York Stock Exchange plunged 22.6 percent, the second largest fall in history (a collapse in 1914 was larger). The next day the stock market in Tokyo fell 15 percent, the London market dropped 12 percent, Sydney plummeted 25 percent, and Hong Kong closed for the week. If before the debacle the public did not understand that we operate in a world capital market, it did afterward. The same firms operate in each of the major capital markets and trade around the clock and around the globe. Banks, securities firms, investment bankers, insurance companies, and individual borrowers and lenders buy and sell in all these markets. Foreign currency and gold can be bought 24 hours a day, and many other securities can be purchased in one market and sold in another after the first has closed.

The worldwide integration of capital markets has increased competition between markets, between government regulations in various countries, and between individual players in the markets. An early example of this competition was the development of the Eurodollar market in the late 1950s and early 1960s, created primarily to avoid U.S. interest rate ceilings and reserve requirements.

Interest rate ceilings have now been eliminated, but U.S. firms are handicapped by considerably more controls than exist in many of the most competitive markets worldwide. Restrictions on interstate banking in the United States have led to the balkanization of financial firms. Whereas elsewhere banks can operate throughout a country, in the United States until recently a bank was confined to its state of origin and sometimes to its original location. Consequently many U.S. banks do not compete directly with each other. The economies of very large size have been denied to all but a few U.S. banks in New York and California. Banks in other states are unable to achieve sufficient scale to compete adequately in world markets.

Although federal law still permits states to exclude or control competition from out-of-state banks or even to limit or prohibit branching, many states are opening their markets to either regional or nationwide banking. This trend is likely to continue, and ultimately U.S. banks will be permitted to operate throughout most of the country. As a result our institutions will gain a much stronger deposit base to compete in world financial markets.

Under the Glass-Steagall Act, passed in the 1930s as a consequence of the banking collapse, commercial banks are prohibited from entering the investment banking field and other financial markets. Conversely investment bankers, brokers, insurance companies, and other such institutions are barred from commercial banking. Similar restrictions exist in some other international markets, but not in such major ones as London or Frankfurt.

There are legitimate concerns about banks entering other markets. Because of deposit insurance, which protects depositors from losses, creditors of the banks (depositors) have little interest in whether the bank is soundly managed. Banks typically have only a small equity position compared with their liabilities (deposits). If bad management or ill luck take a bank's equity toward zero, managers face a strong temptation to make risky loans. If such loans are profitable, the firm can rebuild its equity base. If the loans lose value, the taxpayers, who have implicitly guaranteed the bank, must cover the losses.

The problem resulting from the deposit guarantee is inherent and cannot be totally eliminated by regulation. If the bank is permitted to enter other lines of business, regulation to protect the government (taxpayer) guarantee becomes much more difficult. This is why most proposals to abolish Glass-Steagall have required noncommercial banking activity to be carried out in a separately incorporated subsidiary. This precaution would most likely provide adequate protection for the taxpayer and prevent reckless behavior.

Environmental Regulation

A clean environment is high on nearly everybody's agenda, yet there is considerable dissatisfaction with current controls. The costs of the controls are high and the results meager. Although the nation's air and water have been getting cleaner, Congress's utopian objectives have in almost all cases been postponed.

A more significant problem has been the unwillingness of Congress to allow environmental regulation to have a significant impact on important interest groups. Basically it has attempted to se-

cure a cleaner environment without making any existing identifiable group pay the cost. Congress has been willing to throw money at pollution and to prescribe costly standards for future investments where no existing interest is hurt but not to impose costs on known participants.

Nevertheless, private expenditures on pollution abatement have been costly. In 1984, the latest year for which there are data, total expenditures on abatement ran to $51.6 billion (in 1982 dollars). In addition, environmental regulations have also reduced measured productivity in U.S. industry. Moreover, the air pollution laws and their amendments have effectively discouraged the construction of new heavy industrial facilities or power plants and have made it more expensive to build such facilities in areas of the country that are in compliance with the ambient air pollution standards. Since clean-air laws also require the use of expensive scrubbers to remove sulfur from smokestacks but give no credit for burning clean coal, coal-mining jobs are preserved at high economic and environmental cost.

Because of these restrictions, U.S. industry is less efficient and uses older plants. Power companies refrain from building new cleaner plants and simply maintain the existing ones, which must meet much less stringent standards.

Complicating the issue is the ongoing debate over the harm various pollutants cause. For example, acid rain is identified with the acidification of lakes, the deterioration of forests, and the impairment of agriculture. The National Acid Precipitation Assessment Program (NAPAP) released an interim report in September 1987 on the effects of acid rain. The report identifies three subareas where acidic deposition has contributed to acidification of between 2 and 12 percent of lake areas and concludes that "overall, the number of historical trends analyses in the United States documenting loss of fish populations as a result of acidic deposition is low."

On the effect of acid rain on forests, the report concludes that "results to date suggest negligible impact from acid rain on the foliage of plantations and low-elevation forests." The report also finds that "at current deposition levels, there is no detectable effect of acidic deposition on crop yield; however, there may be a net fertilizer benefit from nitrogen deposition on the order of $100 million per year."

Even when there is a documented problem, many regulations appear excessively stringent. For example, medical evidence indicates that ozone levels above fifteen parts per billion can cause damage to exercising individuals with respiratory problems. The Environmental Protection Agency has set the ozone standard at twelve parts per billion. Although such a standard might be prudent, compliance requires that no monitor in a city measure more than twelve parts per billion for more than three periods of one hour each over a three-year period. Thus a city could have twenty measuring stations, nineteen of which show not one hour in a three-year period in which the level of ozone exceeds eleven parts per billion; but if the twentieth station registers four one-hour periods over the limit during three years, the city is considered not in compliance.

CONCLUSION

In the long run the only way to maintain a vibrant, strong economy that can compete in the world is to preserve its flexible markets. The lessons of other countries that have experimented with market intervention and the lessons that the United States has learned from regulating and then deregulating industries are that free and uncontrolled markets work best. Regulation may be necessary in some situations—to protect the environment, to provide safe working conditions and safe products, and to protect against financial fraud and manipulation. But it is important to be cautious and ensure that the cure is less harmful than the disease. The beneficiaries of regulation and of regulatory regimes are often special interests rather than the general public. The deregulation of transportation, energy, telecommunications, and some financial services has lowered costs, benefited consumers, and made the U.S. economy more competitive, but it is still incomplete. The 1990s will be the critical decade for maintaining these gains and accomplishing what remains to be done in the automobile industry, banking and finance, and the environment. Continuing the trend toward deregulation is critical to U.S. jobs and to the U.S. position in world markets.

NO   David Bollier and Joan Claybrook

REGULATIONS THAT WORK

When Jonas Salk discovered a vaccine for polio, the news was welcomed by *The New York Times* as "one of the greatest triumphs in the history of medicine." The serum's widespread use lowered the incidence of polio from 21,000 cases in 1952 to fewer than 900 in 1962. Thanks to Salk, proclaimed the cover of *Time* magazine, "generations will grow up free."

Salk's considerable achievement drew praise because it was the work of one easily identifiable hero against a disease that was widely known and feared. We are not so quick to support great potential strides in public health when they are made by the federal government and when they take on not bacterial but man-made killers. In 1984, for example, the Environmental Protection Agency proposed a new rule to reduce the amount of lead in regular gasoline. The rule, which went into effect in March 1985, will protect an estimated 50,000 children from brain damage due to airborne lead. But because those responsible for this regulation were anonymous bureaucrats, and because the hazard being fought was not an identifiable "disease," there were no brass bands—only a quick blip on the evening news.

Regulators have not always been quick to respond to health and safety hazards, and when they have, the results often have been disappointing. In many cases, however, the federal government has made great strides toward removing or at least reducing dangers that affect us all. These success stories have gone unsung, particularly in the present conservative climate, where it has become fashionable to denounce all regulation as inherently meddlesome. With a president in office who has shown himself unabashedly hostile to regulation and a Congress entering the tight-fisted era of Gramm-Rudman, it's worth considering instances where federal regulators, no less than Dr. Salk, have saved American lives. Herewith, we submit ten regulations that have made a difference.

I. SAFE DRUGS: PRE-MARKET TESTING

There's a reason why you cannot buy "Hamlin's Wizard Oil" or "Warner's Safe Cure for Diabetes" at your corner drug store. Nearly 50 years ago, the

From David Bollier and Joan Claybrook, "Regulations That Work," *The Washington Monthly,* vol. 18, no. 3 (April 1986). Copyright © 1986 by The Washington Monthly Company, 1611 Connecticut Avenue, NW, Washington, DC 20009; (202) 462-0128. Reprinted by permission of *The Washington Monthly.*

Food and Drug Administration determined that these once-popular "medicines" were worthless and banned their sale. Ever since, consumers have been spared costly frauds and, more importantly, serious illness, drug addiction, blindness, and death caused by quack medicines.

In 1938, 100 people, many of them children, experienced slow, agonizing deaths from a special elixir used to treat streptococcal infection. The next year Congress gave the FDA authority to review and approve drugs before they go on the market. The FDA now requires the pharmaceutical companies to perform rigorous tests, the results of which the FDA scientists review. Although drug companies often complain about the lengthy process, the FDA's drug approval system has saved thousands of lives and prevented millions of adverse drug reactions.

Between 1959 and 1961, for example, approximately 10,000 babies in more than 20 countries were born with serious deformities because their mothers had taken a new sedative, thalidomide, during pregnancy. American women who obtained the medicine from Canada and Europe or participated in investigational tests were affected as well. A skeptical FDA medical officer withheld full approval, preventing tens of thousands of birth defects in the U.S. The FDA has screened out other medications that have caused deaths and injuries overseas. For example, it refused to approve isoproterenol inhalers—used to relieve asthma—which caused the death of 3,500 children in England and Wales in the 1960s. It also banned Stalinon, an ineffective treatment for boils that killed more than a hundred patients in a small French town in 1954, and Aminorex, an appetite suppressant marketed in Europe, which caused an epidemic of primary pulmonary hypertension and 26 deaths.

II. SAFE FOOD: SLAUGHTERHOUSE INSPECTIONS

The serious problems with meat slaughterhouses and packinghouses first came to public attention in the early 1900s when Upton Sinclair's muckraking novel, *The Jungle*, and subsequent congressional hearings revealed revolting conditions: filth on meat, standing water that could breed disease, inadequate toilet facilities for workers, and meat-borne diseases. Much of the burden for preventing such conditions falls on the Department of Agriculture (USDA) slaughterhouse inspection program. First, the department must approve the blueprints of a new plant to ensure that it meets sanitation standards. Water supplies, for example, must be safe from contamination, and slaughterhouses no longer may have wooden floors, which can rot, spawning disease. USDA inspectors check cattle, sheep, swine, goats, and other livestock for diseases that may be difficult to detect after slaughter, like rabies and listeriosis. For the slaughter, the USDA stipulates methods that are both sanitary and humane. Don Houston, administrator of the Food Safety and Inspection Service, notes, "We have very specific procedures that a company must follow to make sure that manure is not released on the carcass. For certain cuts, you have to tie off certain body orifices, etc." To be sure that the standards are adhered to, USDA inspects carcasses after the slaughter.

Data on diseased carcasses is collected daily and fed into the USDA's Livestock Disease Reporting System, which monitors disease patterns and checks how thoroughly inspections are being performed. With this specific information, inspectors can identify diseases that are confined to certain parts of the country or breeds of livestock.

Budget cuts have reduced the Food Safety and Inspection Service inspector corps by 300 to roughly 7,300, while the number of plants they need to inspect has gone up by 200.

III. SAFE CARS: AUTO RECALLS

Before 1966, auto manufacturers who produced defective cars had nothing to fear from the federal government. Only state product liability laws put pressure on them to warn consumers or to correct defects, and the pressure was minimal. When cars needed to be recalled, a manufacturer simply sent letters to customers suggesting that they take advantage of the company's "customer relations program" to bring their cars to the dealer for a general checkup; no mention was made of a defect that might threaten the car owners' safety.

Since the creation of the National Highway Traffic Safety Administration (NHTSA) in 1966, the industry no longer can leave motorists in the dark. Automakers must now inform each car owner specifically about safety-defect recalls. During the Carter administration, the NHTSA set up a toll-free hotline for car owners to find out if their automobile, or any of its components, has been recalled. They can also use the hotline to report a problem with their car. By compiling defect complaints by year, model, and make of vehicle and combining this data with the hundred thousand or more complaint letters the agency receives each year, the NHTSA can spot previously undetected problems. When a

number of similar complaints are lodged, the agency begins an investigation that may lead to a recall.

Recalls have had a direct impact on public safety. Since 1966 more than 100 million vehicles and equipment with potentially dangerous defects have been recalled by manufacturers. For example, NHTSA forced the recall of eight million Firestone 500 tires after it had documented at least 50 deaths and several hundred injuries resulting from a design defect in which the steel belt did not bond to the tire carcass.

Unfortunately, today recalls rarely make the news. Since Reagan took office, NHTSA has made an average of 154 recalls annually for six million automobiles compared to an average of 244 recalls for 7.2 million automobiles in the previous ten years.

IV. SAFE DRIVING: MOTORCYCLE HELMETS, SEAT BELTS, AND AIR BAGS

The probability of a motorcyclist being killed is 10 to 15 times greater per mile than that of a passenger in an automobile, and about 70 percent of motorcycle fatalities are from head injuries. One way to fight these grim odds is to wear a helmet: unhelmeted riders are at least three times more likely to incur a fatal head injury than helmeted riders. In 1966 the NHTSA started leaning on the states to require motorcyclists to wear helmets. States that failed to enact helmet laws could be penalized by reductions in precious federal highway funds. By the end of 1975, all but three states had complied.

The success of this regulation is, sadly, easy to measure. In 1976, Congress struck the helmet law requirement from the books, allowing states to repeal their helmet laws without loss of federal funds. Over the next three years, deaths from motorcycle crashes jumped 48 percent, or 1,832 more fatalities, a disproportionate number occurring in the 27 states that had either repealed or weakened their helmet laws. Only then did states take the message to heart and stop repealing the laws. Libertarians point to motorcycle helmet laws as an example of government intrusion into personal decision-making. The real question, though, is whether it is in society's interest to pass a law that can save 1,832 lives.

In 1974 the Department of Transportation took a major step toward protecting car passengers by requiring air bags or automatic seat belts. But as the federal government retreated from motorcycle helmet laws, it also tried to dump the passive restraint standard. After the U.S. Supreme Court, in 1983, overruled Reagan and ordered the federal standard reissued, Reagan added a new twist. Transportation Secretary Elizabeth Dole announced that the requirement would be rescinded if states comprising two thirds of the population passed by April 1989 seatbelt laws that meet certain criteria. The auto industry has launched a $20 million campaign to enact the laws and avoid the passive restraint requirement.

Twenty states have passed seatbelt laws, but none of the laws meet the minimum criteria. The Insurance Institute for Highway Safety estimates that in New York, the first state to pass a mandatory seatbelt law, motor vehicle fatalities declined by 9 percent in the first nine months after passage (that is 75 lives saved). It is estimated that, if instituted nationally, seat belt laws could save 4,400 deaths and prevent 73,000 injuries annually. But statistics from the states that have passed the laws show an increase in seatbelt use immediately after passage and then a decline as enforcement slackens. Usage averages below 50 percent.

While seatbelts are better than nothing, air bags offer protection to car occupants who do not use seatbelts (teenagers and drunk drivers are least likely to wear seatbelts and most likely to have an accident) and provide those who do wear seatbelts the head and facial protection needed in a crash over 20 miles per hour. Passive restraints (including air bags) could save 9,000 lives and prevent more than 150,000 injuries annually, twice the estimates for seatbelts alone.

V. CLEAN AIR: INDUSTRIAL POLLUTION

Before the 1970 Clean Air Act, American industry dismissed air pollution as either negligible or the inevitable price of progress. "Particulates"—better known as smoke, soot, and invisible dust—poured into the air, aggravating asthma and heart disease and carrying carcinogens, toxic gases, and heavy metals into people's respiratory systems. Electric utilities burned high-sulfur coal and oil; owners of apartment buildings vented incinerator smoke into the open skies; factories, refineries, printing plants, and other industrial enterprises had become so accustomed to pollution-prone production methods that the prospect of cleaning up the air seemed unlikely.

In barely a decade, though, the EPA has made dramatic progress in cleaning up the air. The particulate levels in Birmingham, Alabama, for example, were more than double the primary health standard in 1972. By mid-1976, annual emissions from stationary sources had dropped 83 percent, from 155,000 tons to 26,000 tons. Sulfur dioxide levels in Washington, D.C. are now half their 1960 levels and the pulp and paper mills of New Hampshire and Maine pour less than one-tenth of the particulates into the air than they did prior to 1970.

The EPA has three tools for reducing air pollution. The "new source performance standards" require that a new factory have the most modern pollution control devices. As new plants with stricter controls gradually replace old ones with less effective, obsolete controls, a region's air quality improves over time. The EPA established industry-by-industry standards, but in 1982 the Reagan administration removed 12 types of industries from the list of those needing regulation.

The "emissions offsets" require that if a company in an already highly polluted area is opening a new facility that will increase the pollution, it has to reduce pollution within its existing facility or convince another polluter to reduce its output. Thus, when General Motors proposed a new assembly plant in Oklahoma City, it, with the help of local officials, paid local oil companies to reduce their pollution emissions. The offset policy successfully allows polluters to establish a market price for "pollution rights." Air pollution has become a commodity that companies can buy, sell, trade, and even bank, and businesses have an incentive to efficiently meet the EPA's pollution standards. The Reagan administration, however, has drastically weakened the offset program. By making some changes within the regulations, the administration has enabled companies to get away with increasing the pollution level a certain amount and not having to use state-of-the-art pollution control technology.

The third tool is the EPA's "prevention of significant deterioration" program, which keeps industries that dislike strict cleanup requirements in one state from relocating to cleaner regions of the country and start polluting there. The EPA requires industries to abide by especially tough pollution standards in areas without major pollution problems.

VI. CLEAN AIR: LEAD STANDARDS

Lead can cause irreversible brain damage, kidney problems, anemia, mental retardation, seizures, and even death. Children are especially vulnerable, particularly those from poor families, who are more exposed to peeling paint and automobile pollution. (They are also likelier to suffer from poor nutrition, which aggravates the effects of lead poisoning.) Lead poisoning kills several hundred children each year and causes learning deficiencies in thousands more.

Because lead is a multi-source pollutant—it is transmitted through the air and in food, paint, and soil—the federal government's response has had to take several forms. With prodding by the FDA, food manufacturers voluntarily have reduced the amount of lead in metal containers or have switched to glass containers when possible. The FDA has put special emphasis on packaging foods for babies and young children in lead-free containers. As a result, there was an approximately 40 percent decrease in the amount of lead in canned foods from 1977 through 1982.

The fight against lead in paint has been a mixed success. On the one hand, the Lead-Based Paint Poisoning Prevention Act of 1971 has reduced the lead content of new paint products to .06 percent. (During the 1950s the lead content of house paint was as high as 60 percent.) On the other hand, 28 million buildings remain with walls covered by lead-based paint. The act directed a federal effort to reduce lead hazards in existing buildings, but this has been hampered by scientific uncertainties, limited funding, and the magnitude of the problem. Environmental Action reports that more than one half of the 61 cities that had lead testing programs in 1981 have had their funding reduced and 14 cities have eliminated their programs.

It is in the battle against airborne lead that regulators have been most successful. Airborne lead has been the easiest to control because 80 percent originates from one source—motor vehicle exhaust. For decades, auto emissions contained lead because gasoline refiners found it a cheap, simple way to boost the octane of low-grade fuels to prevent engine knocking. Lead probably would have remained the octane-booster of choice if Congress hadn't decided to clean up the nation's air. When it was discovered that only a few tankfuls of leaded gasoline could ruin the most promising emission-control device—the catalytic converter—it was clear that lead would have to be controlled. So, starting in 1975, when new cars were required to be equipped with catalytic converters, refiners were forced to invest in technology to produce high-octane gasoline without lead. By 1984 only 45 percent of the gasoline sold in the nation was leaded. Under current law, this figure is expected to drop to 18 percent by 1990, as pre-1975 cars are retired from use.

But the EPA wasn't interested just in protecting its catalytic converters; it also was concerned about reducing the amount of lead in the air. So in 1973 the agency initiated regulations requiring a progressive reduction in the lead content of "regular" (leaded) gasoline as well. By March 1985 the EPA had set the acceptable level of lead in regular gasoline at 0.1 gram per gallon—down from 2.2 grams per gallon prior to 1973. The agency has proposed regulations banning all lead in gasoline in 1988; the true test of its commitment to reducing lead content is whether it issues the final regulation. This would help prevent more than 1,000 strokes and 5,000 heart attacks among those who suffer from high blood pressure.

While lead exposure remains a serious health problem, the switch to unleaded gasoline and the reduction of lead content in regular gasoline have made the air safer to breathe, especially in urban areas. In a study conducted between 1976 and 1980, the Centers for Disease Control found a remarkable 36.7 percent decline in the overall mean blood-lead level in the U.S. population.

One other benefit: cars that run on unleaded gasoline can run three to five times longer without an oil change. A 1984 EPA study estimated that reduction of lead to 0.1 gram per gallon could save car owners as much as $660 million annually in auto maintenance costs.

VII. CLEAN WATER: TECHNOLOGY STANDARDS

By the late 1960s it had become apparent that existing environmental laws had not prevented rampant abuse of the nation's waters. The food, textile, paper, chemical, coal, oil, rubber, metals, machinery, and transportation industries were spewing out an estimated 25 trillion gallons of waste water each year. In one notorious case, the Reserve Mining Company of northern Minnesota was dumping an average of 67,000 tons of iron ore tailings into Lake Superior daily.

Galvanized by the glare of public attention and concern, Congress in 1972 approved amendments to the Federal Water Pollution Control Act that fundamentally changed the way the government regulates water pollution. Previously, states had set water quality standards for individual bodies of water. Although logical in theory, in practice that approach resulted only in protracted battles over the definition of standards and little progress. The 1972 amendments cut through this regulatory Gordian knot by establishing uniform, technology-based standards. The amendments authorized construction of sewage treatment plants and required industry to use the "best practicable technology" to control pollution and to apply to local environmental agencies for dumping permits.

Less than a decade later, dramatic improvements were visible throughout the country. Lake Erie, once considered dead, now attracts hundreds of thousands of fishermen each year. The Detroit River also had been considered a dead river after years of absorbing sewage, chemicals, oil, acid, garbage, and paper sludge. A quarter-inch film of oil covered much of the shoreline and large greaseballs frequently washed ashore. By 1975, the discharge of oil and grease into the river was reduced an estimated 82 percent from 1963 levels. In all, from 1972 to 1977 the regulations reduced industrial discharge of six major pollutants by 69 percent or more. The Clean Water Act reauthorization is now before a House-Senate conference committee; the Reagan administration has threatened to veto the bill unless it phases out the program to build sewage treatment facilities.

VIII. WORKPLACE SAFETY: ASBESTOS

Prior to the 1970 creation of the Occupational Safety and Health Administration (OSHA), government and industry contended that they held little responsibility for the 14,000 workers who were killed and the two million who were disabled in industrial accidents every year. OSHA changed that, issuing regulations under the belief that companies have a responsibility to remove unreasonable workplace hazards.

Among the most significant OSHA regulations are those limiting worker exposure to asbestos. Airborne asbestos fibers can cause cancer and asbestosis, a lung disease that resembles emphysema. Because asbestos was unregulated until 1972, an estimated 8,200 to 9,700 workers will die each year during the rest of this century from asbestos-related cancers.

In 1972, in response to overwhelming medical evidence and a petition from the AFL-CIO, OSHA limited asbestos dust levels in the workplace to two million fibers per cubic meter. A study issued in 1975 showed that the regulation was saving hundreds, and perhaps thousands, of lives each year. Unfortunately another study showed that a cancer risk continued at levels as low as 100,000 fibers per cubic meter.

The Reagan administration was uninterested in toughening the asbestos standards until the EPA scandals of 1983 focused attention on its environmental record. In 1984, one standard was proposed but then struck down in court. OSHA has since proposed a new, permanent standard of 200,000 fibers per cubic meter. If this limit goes into effect and is properly enforced, thousands of workers will be spared an unnecessary cancer risk. Even the weak asbestos standards in effect, however, probably will not be well enforced if the administration's past OSHA record is any indication. A 1984 study showed that OSHA's inspection record had improved since the early days of the administration, but there are still serious gaps. Follow-up inspections, for example, were down 87 percent from the Carter administration and penalties for serious health and safety violations had declined 33 percent.

IX. WORKPLACE SAFETY: VINYL CHLORIDE

Vinyl chloride and a related resin, polyvinyl chloride, both found in plastics, can cause liver cancer. In 1912 about 10,000 workers were routinely exposed to vinyl chloride, while the emissions from the plants endangered those who lived within a five-mile radius. The general public was exposed to vinyl chloride through plastic bottles, plastic wrap, hair spray, insecticides, and disinfectants.

In 1972, again responding to a petition from the AFL-CIO (and one from the United Rubber Workers), OSHA reduced the permissible exposure level of vinyl chloride from 500 parts to one part per million. The affected companies protested that the regulation would cost them $90 billion and that thousands of workers would be thrown out of work. In fact, the changes required ended up costing only $300 million and no jobs were lost. And the technology developed to comply with the standard actually improved productivity. One study predicted that there would be 2,000 fewer cancer deaths in the last quarter of this century as a result of the regulation.

X. SAFE PRODUCTS: HAZARDS TO CHILDREN

The most conscientious parent cannot detect every hazard in poorly designed playground equipment, cribs, and infant strollers. And even when parents are not as vigilant as they should be, their children shouldn't be the ones to suffer. That is why, contrary to the antiregulatory cries of the "pro-family" conservatives, few federal agencies can surpass the Consumer Product Safety Commission (CPSC) for serving and protecting children.

In the 1920s only one out of ten childhood deaths was due to accidental injury. By the 1970s the ratio had risen to one in three. While this increase in part reflects a decline in disease-related deaths, it also reflects the proliferation of new products over the past 60 years.

The CPSC requires that drugs, furniture polish, drain cleaners, paint solvents, and vitamins containing iron be sold in containers with child-resistant safety caps. In 1981 one doctor told a congressional committee, "A decade ago, before safety packaging was really efficiently introduced, 500 children under the age of five died annually. In 1977, 51 children died." According to the CPSC, aspirin deaths alone were down more than 83 percent seven years after the child-proof container regulations were adopted.

Other hazards to children that have been reduced by CPSC regulations:

• Crib rails were sometimes so low that babies could fall to the floor; in some cribs the spaces between spindles and slats were just large enough for a baby's head to slip through, creating the danger of strangulation; some cribs had ill-fitting mattresses, which could lead to suffocation. To prevent these dangers, CPSC regulations have saved an estimated 50 lives a year, cutting design-related crib deaths in half.

• Playpens have safer folding mechanisms and have been redesigned to reduce the chances of asphyxiation from webbing or padded vinyl top rails. These voluntary regulations are expected to eliminate some 1,190 serious injuries annually.

• Strollers are now more stable and have locking devices that are less likely to crush infants' hands. The voluntary standards will prevent approximately 8,000 injuries a year.

• Pacifiers used to be extremely hazardous. In 1978, after some infants choked to death, the CPSC issued standards for pacifiers and banned those that failed to meet them. More recently, the CPSC got manufacturers to reduce significantly or eliminate cancer-causing nitrosamines in pacifiers.

Despite the success of this tiny, $36 million commission, in 1981 the Reagan administration, arguing that the market would ensure product safety, unsuccessfully proposed abolishing it and has since moved to cut back its funding. Since Reagan came into office, the CPSC staff has been reduced by 41 percent. From 1981 to 1983 inspections dropped 45 percent, recalls decreased by two-thirds, and investigations of injuries declined 28 percent. The commission also has had to scale back efforts to make upholstery flame-retardant and kerosene heaters safer.

In addition to restoring the inspectors to the CPSC, Congress could take an inexpensive but effective step toward protecting children by requiring toy manufacturers to describe on box labels what hazards a product might pose to children. Currently, manufacturers must list recommended ages, but do not have to explain, for example, that young children may gag on pieces from a rattle.

ETHICS NOT DOLLARS

The Reagan administration has launched a full-scale attack on health and safety protections that save lives and prevent injuries. Often the administration's approach has been to revoke these regulations on the grounds that there are less costly solutions. The ascendency of the economic paradigm in assessing federal regulation tends to obliterate the memory of why regulations are needed in the first place. It seeks to substitute a specious economic test for a distinctly moral criterion for regulation—prevention of human and environmental harm.

While conservative critics of regulation might view this notion of regulation as quaint and uninformed, it is the underlying reason why public support for specific regulatory programs remains so strong. A 1982 Louis Harris survey found: "Anti-regulation opinion outnumbers opinion favoring more regulation by a ratio of two to one. However, this indicator of opinion at a general or abstract level does not translate into public disfavor with all concrete forms of regulation. Quite the contrary, consumers strongly support specific types of regulation. . . . Virtually no support is found for rolling back or dismantling consumer protection regulation."

POSTSCRIPT

Does the Government Regulate Too Much?

Any consideration of social regulation by government must assess both costs and benefits. Society must ask how much it is willing to pay to avoid a given risk, just as workers will demand increased wages for taking greater risks. Most people are likely to agree that there are some benefits that merit the cost and some costs that outweigh the benefits. But that agreement is theoretical; in practice, people differ both in their values and their assessments of needs. Ardent environmentalists believe that industry cannot be allowed to do irremediable harm to the air, water, other species, and the Earth's atmosphere, while their critics believe, with equal conviction, that the dangers are exaggerated and that a possible loss to the environment must be weighed against the loss of jobs and living standards that would result from curbed economic activity.

Focusing on the Environmental Protection Agency and the Federal Trade Commission, Richard A. Harris and Sidney M. Milkus, *The Politics of Regulatory Change: A Tale of Two Agencies* (Oxford University Press, 1989), provide an illuminating study of how the regulatory process works. Looking at the efforts by Presidents Reagan and Bush to deregulate, they speculate: "Deregulation may be so difficult to accomplish not because regulatory policy is so fragmented, but because it is so coherent."

Believing that deregulation has succeeded, Susan J. Tolchin and Martin Tolchin, *Dismantling America: The Rush to Deregulate* (Oxford University Press, 1983), deplore the consequences. Since their book was published, the deregulation efforts begun by former president Reagan were continued in the Bush presidency by the Council on Competitiveness, headed by Vice President Dan Quayle, who used that executive body to pressure regulatory agencies to abandon regulation in various economic and environmental areas.

The world is a dangerous place. The supporters of governmental regulation believe that in the absence of such controls we will face greater hazards and that more dangers will be loosed upon us by unscrupulous entrepreneurs. The opponents hold that we will more surely be strangled by red tape and impoverished by the regulatory costs that make prices higher when they do not actually make production unprofitable. It is tempting to counsel moderation between the extreme principles, but it is difficult to apply moderation in practice. Take, as an example, the debate on the development of nuclear energy for nonmilitary uses. Neither side would be happy with a compromise that means limited utilization of atomic power. Such a policy would not fulfill the hopes of those who see nuclear energy as a solution for the energy crisis, and it would not allay the fears of those who see it as a threat to the lives of millions of people living near nuclear plants. Yet it is possible that, in this area as in others, the give and take of politics will dictate solutions that are unsatisfactory to all concerned and thus keep the issue of regulation alive.

ISSUE 8

Should the Federal Courts Be Bound by the "Original Intent" of the Framers?

YES: Robert H. Bork, from "The Case Against Political Judging," *National Review* (December 8, 1989)

NO: Leonard W. Levy, from *Original Intent and the Framers' Constitution* (Macmillan, 1988)

ISSUE SUMMARY

YES: Educator and former judge Robert H. Bork argues that the "original intent" of the framers of the Constitution can and should be upheld by the federal courts, because not to do so is to have judges perform a political role they were not given.

NO: Professor of history Leonard W. Levy believes that the "original intent" of the framers cannot be found, and, even if it could, given these changing times, it could not be applied in dealing with contemporary constitutional issues.

Although the Supreme Court has declared fewer than 100 acts of Congress unconstitutional, judicial review (the power to exercise this judgment) is a critical feature of American government. It extends to all law—not simply federal law—and includes not only statutes but the actions of all agents of governmental power.

The power of judicial review consists not only of a negative power to invalidate acts contrary to the Constitution but also (and far more frequently) of a positive power to give meaning and substance to constitutional clauses and the laws enacted in accordance with constitutional power. Finally, individual cases have impact and reverberation, which may profoundly influence the future direction of law and behavior. To take a prominent example, when the Supreme Court reinterpreted the equal protection clause of the Constitution's Fourteenth Amendment in 1954, it changed forever the legal and social patterns of race relations in the United States.

Some limitations on judicial review are self-imposed, such as the Court's refusal to consider "political questions"—that is, questions better decided by the elective branches rather than the courts. But it is the Supreme Court that decides which questions are political. The Supreme Court has been notably reluctant to curb a president's extraordinary use of emergency power in wartime and has done so rarely.

Still other limitations on judicial review derive from the judicial process, such as the requirement that the party bringing a case to court (any court) must have sufficient "standing" as an aggrieved party to be heard. Some laws do not appear to give any contesting party the basis for bringing a suit. Other laws rarely present themselves in an appropriate form for judicial decision, such as the ordinary exercise of presidential power in foreign relations. These exceptions qualify, yet do not really negate, the spirit of French statesman Alexis de Tocqueville's observation of nearly a century and a half ago that "scarcely any political question arises in the United States that is not resolved, sooner or later, into a judicial question."

Judicial review is exercised by state courts and lower federal courts as well as by the United States Supreme Court, but the last word is reserved to the latter. Because its power is so vast and is exercised in controversial areas, the judiciary is subject to considerable criticism. Critics have argued that the framers of the Constitution did not intend for so great a power to be possessed by so unrepresentative (unelected) an organ of government. The Court has been chided for going too far, too fast (for example, law enforcement agencies protest measures dealing with the rights of accused persons) and for not going far enough, fast enough (for example, by civil rights activists working for racial equality). In the 1930s, liberals castigated the "nine old men" for retarding social progress by invalidating New Deal measures. In the 1950s, conservatives pasted "Impeach Earl Warren" (then chief justice) stickers on their car bumpers, and they bemoaned the Court's so-called coddling of communists and criminals. More recently, liberal critics have viewed the Supreme Court headed by chief justices Warren E. Burger and William H. Rehnquist as being less sympathetic to enforced integration, women's rights, the defense of accused persons, and the protection of socially disapproved expression.

The Supreme Court professes to decide these issues on the basis of constitutional principles. One view, argued in the following selection by Robert H. Bork, is that the Court should uphold the "original intent" of the framers as it is found in the Constitution and its amendments. To do otherwise is to engage in political decision-making, which is not the Court's business.

The other view, upheld by Leonard W. Levy, is that we cannot find the "original intent" of the framers because the framers (and ratifiers) differed among themselves, and, even if we could find it, we could not be bound by it in finding new solutions to new problems.

YES

Robert H. Bork

THE CASE AGAINST POLITICAL JUDGING

What was once the dominant view of constitutional law—that a judge is to apply the Constitution according to the principles intended by those who ratified the document—is now very much out of favor among the theorists of the field. In the legal academies in particular, the philosophy of original understanding is usually viewed as thoroughly passé, probably reactionary, and certainly—the most dreaded indictment of all—"outside the mainstream." That fact says more about the lamentable state of the intellectual life of the law, however, than it does about the merits of the theory.

In truth, only the approach of original understanding meets the criteria that any theory of constitutional adjudication must meet in order to possess democratic legitimacy. Only that approach is consonant with the design of the American Republic.

When we speak of "law," we ordinarily refer to a rule that we have no right to change except through prescribed procedures. That statement assumes that the rule has a meaning independent of our own desires. Otherwise there would be no need to agree on procedures for changing the rule. Statutes, we agree, may be changed by amendment or repeal. The Constitution may be changed by amendment pursuant to the procedures set out in Article V. It is a necessary implication of the prescribed procedures that neither statute nor Constitution should be changed by judges. Though that has been done often enough, it is in no sense proper.

What is the "meaning" of a law, that essence that judges should not change? It is the meaning understood at the time of the law's enactment. What the Constitution's ratifiers understood themselves to be enacting must be taken to be what the public of that time would have understood the words to mean. It is important to be clear about this, because the search is not for a subjective intention. If, for instance, Congress enacted a statute outlawing the sale of automatic rifles and did so in the Senate by a vote of 51 to 49, no court would overturn a conviction under the law because two senators in the majority later testified that they had really intended only to prohibit the *use* of such rifles. They said "sale" and "sale" it is. Thus, the common objection to the philosophy of original understanding—that Madison kept his notes of the convention at Philadelphia secret for many years—is off the mark. He knew that what mattered was public understanding, not subjective intentions.

Law is a public act. Secret reservations or intentions count for nothing. The original understanding is thus manifested in the words used and in secondary materials, such as debates at the conventions, public discussion, newspaper articles, dictionaries in use at the time, and the like.

THE SEARCH FOR THE INTENT OF THE LAW-maker is the everyday procedure of lawyers and judges when they apply a statute, a contract, a will, or the opinion of a court. To be sure, there are differences in the way we deal with different legal materials, which was the point of John Marshall's observation in *McCulloch v. Maryland* that "we must never forget, that it is a *constitution* we are expounding." By that he meant narrow, legalistic reasoning was not to be applied to the document's broad provisions, a document that could not, by its nature and uses, "partake of the prolixity of a legal code." But in that same opinion he also wrote that a provision must receive a "far and just interpretation," which means that the judge is to interpret what is in the text and not something else. And, it will be recalled, in *Marbury v. Madison* Marshall based the judicial power to invalidate a legislative act upon the fact that a judge was applying the words of a written document. Thus, questions of breadth of approach or of room for play in the joints aside, lawyers and judges should seek in the Constitution what they seek in other legal texts: the original meaning of the words.

We would at once criticize a judge who undertook to rewrite a statute or the opinion of a superior court; and yet such judicial rewriting is often correctable by legislatures or superior courts, whereas the Supreme Court's rewriting of the Constitution is not correctable. At first glance, it seems distinctly peculiar that there should be a great many academic theorists who explicitly defend departures from the understanding of those who ratified the Constitution while agreeing, at least in principle, that there should be no departure from the understanding of those who enacted a statute or joined a majority opinion. A moment's reflection suggests, however, that Supreme Court departures from the original meaning of the Constitution are advocated *precisely because* those departures are not correctable democratically. The point of the academic exercise is to be free of democracy in order to impose the values of an elite upon the rest of us.

It is here that the concept of neutral principles, which Herbert Wechsler has said are essential if the Supreme Court is not to be a naked power organ, comes into play. Wechsler, in expressing his difficulties with the decision in *Brown v. Board of Education*, said the courts must choose principles which they are willing to apply neutrally; to apply, that is, to all cases that may fairly be said to fall within them. This is a safeguard against political judging. No judge will say openly that any particular group or political position is always entitled to win. He will announce a principle that decides the case at hand, and Wechsler has no difficulty with that if the judge is willing to apply the same principle in the next case, even when it means a group favored by the first decision is disfavored by the second.

When a judge finds his principle in the Constitution as originally understood, the problem of the neutral derivation of principle is solved. The judge accepts the ratifiers' definition of the appropriate ranges of majority and minority freedom. The "Madisonian dilemma" (essentially, the conflict of majority rule with minority rights) is resolved in the way that the Founders resolved it, and the judge accepts the fact that he is bound by that resolution as law. He need not, and must not, make unguided value judgments of his own.

This means, of course, that a judge, no matter on what court he sits, may never create new constitutional rights or destroy old ones. Any time he does so, he violates the limits of his own authority and, for that reason, also violates the rights of the legislature and the people. When a judge is given a set of constitutional provisions, then, as to anything not covered by those provisions, he is, quite properly, powerless. In the absence of law, a judge is a functionary without a function.

This is not to say, of course, that majorities may not add to minority freedoms by statute, and indeed a great deal of the legislation that comes out of Congress and the state legislatures does just that. The only thing majorities may not do is invade the liberties the Constitution specifies. In this sense, the concept of original understanding builds in a bias toward individual freedom. Thus, the Supreme Court properly decided in *Brown* that the equal protection clause of the Fourteenth Amendment forbids racial segregation or discrimination by any arm of government, but, because the Constitution addressed only governmental action, the

Court could not address the question of private discrimination. Congress did address it in the Civil Rights Act of 1964 and in subsequent legislation, enlarging minority freedoms beyond those mandated by the Constitution.

THE NEUTRAL DEFINITION OF THE PRINCIPLE derived from the historic Constitution is also crucial. The Constitution states its principles in majestic generalities that we know cannot be taken as sweepingly as the words alone might suggest. The First Amendment states that "Congress shall make no law . . . abridging the freedom of speech," but no one has ever supposed that Congress could not make some speech unlawful or that it could not make all speech illegal in certain places, at certain times, and under certain circumstances. Justices Hugo Black and William O. Douglas often claimed to be First Amendment absolutists, but even they would permit the punishment of speech if they thought it too closely "brigaded" with illegal action. From the beginning of the Republic to this day, no one has ever thought Congress could not forbid the preaching of mutiny at sea or disruptive proclamations in a courtroom. One may not cry "Fire!" in a crowded theater.

But the question of neutral definition remains and is obviously closely related to neutral application. Neutral application can be gained by defining a principle so narrowly that it will fit only a few cases. Thus, once a principle is derived from the Constitution, its breadth or the level of generality at which it is stated becomes of crucial importance. The judge must not state the principle with so much generality that he transforms it. The difficulty in finding the proper level of generality has led some critics to claim that the application of the original under-standing is actually impossible. That sounds fairly abstract, but an example will make clear both the point and the answer to it.

In speaking of my view that the Four-teenth Amendment's equal protection clause requires black equality, Dean Paul Brest said:

> The very adoption of such a principle, however, demands an arbitrary choice among levels of abstraction. Just what is "the general principle of equality that applies to all cases"? Is it the "core idea of *black* equality" that Bork finds in the original understanding (in which case Allan Bakke [a white who sued because a state medical school gave preference in admissions to other races] did not state a constitutionally cognizable claim), or a broader principle of "*racial* equal-ity" (so that, depending on the precise content of the principle, Bakke might have a case after all), or is it a still broader principle of equality that en-compasses discrimination on the basis of gender (or sexual orientation) as well?
>
> . . . The fact is that all adjudication requires making choices among the levels of generality on which to articulate principles, and all such choices are in-herently non-neutral. No form of con-stitutional decision-making can be salvaged if its legitimacy depends on satisfying Bork's requirements that principles be "neutrally derived, de-fined, and applied."

If Brest's point about the impossibility of choosing the level of generality upon neutral criteria is correct, we must either resign ourselves to a Court that *is* a "naked power organ" or require the Court to stop making "constitutional" decisions. But Brest's argument seem to me wrong, and I think a judge commit-ted to original understanding can do what Brest says he cannot. We may use Brest's example to demonstrate the point.

The role of a judge committed to the philosophy of original understanding is not to "*choose* a level of abstraction." Rather, it is to find the meaning of a text—a process which includes finding its degree of generality, which is part of its meaning—and to apply that text to a particular situation, which may be diffi-cult if its meaning is unclear. With many if not most textual provisions, the level of generality which is part of their meaning is readily apparent. The problem is most difficult when dealing with the broadly stated provisions of the Bill of Rights. It is to the latter that we confine discussion here. In dealing with such provisions, a judge should state the principle at the level of generality that the text and his-torical evidence warrant. The equal-pro-tection clause was adopted in order to protect freed slaves, but its language, being general, applies to all persons. As we might expect, the evidence of what the drafters, the Congress that proposed the clause, and the ratifiers understood themselves to be requiring is clearest in the case of race relations. It is there that we may begin in looking for evidence of the level of generality intended. Without meaning to suggest what the historical evidence in fact shows, let us assume we find that the ratifiers intended to guaran-tee that blacks should be treated by law no worse than whites, but that it is un-clear whether whites were intended to be protected from discrimination. On such evidence, the judge should protect only blacks from discrimination, and Allan Bakke would not have had a case. The reason is that the next higher level of generality above black equality, which is racial equality, is not shown to be a constitutional principle, and, therefore, there is nothing to be set against a current legislative majority's decision to favor blacks. Democratic choice must be accepted by the judge where the Constitution is silent. The test is the reasonableness of the distinction, and the level of generality chosen by the ratifiers determines that. If the evidence shows the ratifiers understood racial equality to have been the principle they were enacting, then Bakke *would* have a case.

To define a legal proposition or principle involves simultaneously stating its contents and its limits. When, for instance, you state what *is* contained within the clause of the First Amendment guarantee of the free exercise of religion, you necessarily state what is *not* contained within that clause. Because the First Amendment guarantees freedom of speech, judges are required reasonably to define what is speech and what is its freedom. Where the law stops, the legislator may move on to create more; but where the law stops, the judge must stop.

The neutral or nonpolitical application of principle has been discussed in connection with Wechsler's discussion of *Brown*. It is a requirement, like the others, addressed to the judge's integrity. Having derived and defined the principle to be applied, he must apply it consistently and without regard to his sympathy or lack of sympathy with the parties before him. This does not mean that the judge will never change the principle he has derived and defined. Anybody who has dealt extensively with law knows that a new case may seem to fall within a principle as stated and yet not fall within the rationale underlying it. As new cases present new patterns, the principle will often be restated and redefined. There is nothing wrong with that; it is, in fact,

highly desirable. But the judge must be clarifying his own reasoning and verbal formulations and not trimming to arrive at results desired on grounds extraneous to the Constitution. This requires a fair degree of sophistication and self-consciousness on the part of the judge. The only external discipline to which the judge is subject is the scrutiny of professional observers who will be able to tell over a period of time whether or not he is displaying intellectual integrity.

THE STRUCTURE OF GOVERNMENT THE Founders of this nation intended most certainly did not give courts a political role. The debates surrounding the Constitution focused much more upon theories of representation than upon the judiciary, which was thought to be a comparatively insignificant branch. There were, however, repeated attempts at the Constitutional Convention in Philadelphia to give judges a policy-making role. The plan of the Virginia delegation, which, amended and expanded, ultimately became the Constitution of the United States, included a proposal that the new national legislature be controlled by placing a veto power in a Council of Revision consisting of the executive and "a convenient number of the National Judiciary." That proposal was raised four times and defeated each time. Among the reasons, as reported in James Madison's notes, was the objection raised by Elbridge Gerry of Massachusetts that it "was quite foreign from the nature of ye office to make them judges of policy of public measures." Rufus King, also of Massachusetts, added that judges should "expound the law as it should come before them, free from the bias of having participated in its formation." Judges who create new constitutional rights are judges of the policy of public measures and are biased by having participated in the policy's formation.

The intention of the Convention was accurately described by Alexander Hamilton in *The Federalist* No. 78: "[T]he judiciary, from the nature of its functions, will always be the least dangerous to the political rights of the Constitution; because it will be least in a capacity to annoy or injure them." The political rights of the Constitution are, of course, the rights that make up democratic self-government. Hamilton obviously did not anticipate a judiciary that would injure those rights by adding to the list of subjects that were removed from democratic control. Thus, he could say that the courts were "beyond comparison the weakest of the three departments of power," and he appended a quotation from the "celebrated Montesquieu": "Of the three powers above mentioned [the others being the legislative and the executive], the JUDICIARY is next to nothing." This was true because judges were, as Rufus King said, merely to "expound" the law.

Even if evidence of what the Founders thought about the judicial role were unavailable, we would have to adopt the rule that judges must stick to the original meaning of the Constitution's words. If that method of interpretation were not common in the law, if James Madison and Justice Joseph Story had never endorsed it, if Chief Justice John Marshall had rejected it, we would have to invent the approach of original understanding in order to save the constitutional design. No other method of constitutional adjudication can confine courts to a defined sphere of authority and thus prevent them from assuming powers whose exercise alters, perhaps radically, the design of the American Republic. The philoso-

phy of original understanding is thus a necessary inference from the structure of government apparent on the face of the U.S. Constitution.

WE COME NOW TO THE QUESTION OF PRE-cedent. It is particularly important because, as Professor Henry Monaghan of Columbia University Law School notes, "much of the existing constitutional order is at variance with what we know of the original understanding." Some commentators have argued from this obvious truth that the approach of original understanding is impossible or fatally compromised, since they suppose it would require the Court to declare paper money unconstitutional and overturn the centralization accomplished by abandoning restrictions on congressional powers during the New Deal. But to say that prior courts have allowed, or initiated, deformations of the Constitution is not enough to create a warrant for present and future courts to do the same thing.

All serious constitutional theory centers upon the duties of judges, and that comes down to the question: What should the judge decide in the case now before him? Obviously, an originalist judge should not deform the Constitution further. Just as obviously, he should not attempt to undo all mistakes made in the past. At the center of the philosophy of original understanding, therefore, must stand some idea of when the judge is bound by prior decisions and when he is not.

Is judicial precedent an ironclad rule? It is not, and never has been. As Felix Frankfurter once explained, "*stare decisis* is a principle of policy and not a mechanical formula of adherence to the latest decision, however recent and questionable, when such adherence involves collision with a prior doctrine more embracing in its scope, intrinsically sounder, and verified by experience." Thus, in Justice Powell's words, "[i]t is . . . not only [the Court's] prerogative but also [its] duty to re-examine a precedent where its reasoning or understanding of the Constitution is fairly called into question." The Supreme Court frequently overrules its own precedents. *Plessy v. Ferguson*, and the rule of separate-but-equal in racial matters, lasted 58 years before it was dispatched in *Brown v. Board of Education*. In a period of 16 years the Court took three different positions with respect to the constitutionality of federal power to impose wage and price regulations on states and localities as employers. Indeed, Justice Blackmun explained in the last of these decisions that prior cases, even of fairly recent vintage, should be reconsidered if they "disserve principles of democratic self-governance." Every year the Court overrules a number of its own precedents.

The practice of overruling precedent is particularly common in constitutional law, the rationale being that it is extremely difficult for an incorrect constitutional ruling to be corrected through the amendment process. Almost all Justices have agreed with Felix Frankfurter's observation that "the ultimate touchstone of constitutionality is the Constitution itself and not what we have said about it." But that, of course, is only a partial truth. It is clear, first, that Frankfurter was talking about the Supreme Court's obligations with respect to its own prior decisions. Lower courts are not free to ignore what the Supreme Court has said about the Constitution, for that would introduce chaos into the legal system as courts of appeal refused to follow Supreme Court rulings and district courts

disobeyed their appellate courts' orders. Second, what "the Constitution itself" says may, as in the case of paper money, be irretrievable, not simply because of "what [the Justices] have said about it," but because of what the nation has done or become on the strength of what the Court said.

To say that a decision is so thoroughly embedded in our national life that it should not be overruled, even though clearly wrong, is not necessarily to say that its principle should be followed in the future. Thus, the expansion of Congress's commerce, taxing, and spending powers has reached a point where it is not possible to state that, as a matter of articulated doctrine, there are any limits left. That does not mean, however, that the Court must necessarily repeat its mistake as congressional legislation attempts to reach new subject areas. Cases now on the books would seem to mean that Congress could, for example, displace state law on such subjects as marriage and divorce, thus ending such federalism as remains. But the Court could refuse to extend the commerce power so far, without overruling its prior decisions, thus leaving existing legislation in place but not giving generative power to the faulty principle by which that legislation was originally upheld. It will be said that this is a lawless approach, but that is not at all clear. The past decisions are beyond reach, but there remains a constitutional principle of federalism that should be regarded as law more profound than the implications of the past decisions. They cannot be overruled, but they can be confined to the subject areas they concern. When we cannot recover the transgressions of the past, then the best we can do is say to the Court, "Go and sin no more."

Finally, it should be said that those who adhere to a philosophy of original understanding are more likely to respect precedent than those who do not. As Justice Scalia has said, if revisionists can ignore "the most solemnly and democratically adopted text of the Constitution and its Amendments . . . on the basis of current values, what possible basis could there be for enforced adherence to a legal decision of the Supreme Court?" If you do not care about stability, if today's result is all-important, there is no occasion to respect either the constitutional text or the decisions of your predecessors.

NO

Leonard W. Levy

THE FRAMERS AND ORIGINAL INTENT

James Madison, Father of the Constitution and of the Bill of Rights, rejected the doctrine that the original intent of those who framed the Constitution should be accepted as an authoritative guide to its meaning. "As a guide in expounding and applying the provisions of the Constitution," he wrote in a well-considered and consistent judgment, "the debates and incidental decisions of the Convention can have no authoritative character." The fact that Madison, the quintessential Founder, discredited original intent is probably the main reason that he refused throughout his life to publish his "Notes of Debates in the Federal Convention," incomparably our foremost source for the secret discussions of that hot summer in Philadelphia in 1787.

We tend to forget the astounding fact that Madison's Notes were first published in 1840, fifty-three years after the Constitutional Convention had met. That period included the beginnings of the Supreme Court plus five years beyond the entire tenure of John Marshall as Chief Justice. Thus, throughout the formative period of our national history, the High Court, presidents, and Congress construed the Constitution without benefit of a record of the Convention's deliberations. Indeed, even the skeletal Journal of the Convention was not published until 1819. Congress could have authorized its publication anytime after President George Washington, who had presided at the 1787 Convention, deposited it at the State Department in 1796. Although the Journal merely revealed motions and votes, it would have assisted public understanding of the secret proceedings of the Convention, no records of which existed, other than the few spotty and jaundiced accounts by Convention members who opposed ratification. The Convention had, after all, been an assembly in which "America," as George Mason of Virginia said, had "drawn forth her first characters," and even Patrick Henry conceded that the Convention consisted of "the greatest, the best, and most enlightened of our citizens." Thomas Jefferson, in Paris, referred to the "assembly of demigods." The failure of the Framers to have officially preserved and published their proceedings seems inexplicable, especially in a nation that promptly turned matters of state into questions of constitu-

Excerpted with permission of Macmillan Publishing Company, a division of Macmillan, Inc., from *Original Intent and the Framers' Constitution*, by Leonard W. Levy. Copyright © 1988 by Macmillan Publishing Company. Notes omitted.

tional law; but then, the Framers seem to have thought that "the original understanding at Philadelphia," which Chief Justice William H. Rehnquist has alleged to be of prime importance, did not greatly matter. What mattered to them was the text of the Constitution, construed in light of conventional rules of interpretation, the ratification debates, and other contemporary expositions.

If the Framers, who met in executive sessions every day of their nearly four months of work, had wanted their country and posterity to construe the Constitution in the light of their deliberations, they would have had a stenographer present to keep an official record, and they would have published it. They would not have left the task of preserving their debates to the initiative of one of their members who retained control of his work and a proprietary interest in it. "Nearly a half century" after the convention, Madison wrote a preface to his Notes in which he explained why he had made the record. He had determined to preserve to the best of his ability "an exact account of what might pass in the Convention," because the record would be of value "for the History of a Constitution on which would be staked the happiness of a young people great even in its infancy, and possibly the cause of Liberty throughout the world." That seems to have been a compelling reason for publication as soon as possible, not posthumously—and Madison outlived all the members of the Convention. . . .

A constitutional jurisprudence of original intent is insupportable for reasons other than the fact that the records of the framing and ratification of both the Constitution and the Bill of Rights are inadequate because they are incomplete and inaccurate. Original intent also fails as a

concept that can decide real cases. Original intent is an unreliable concept because it assumes the existence of one intent on a particular issue such as the meaning of executive powers or of the necessary and proper clause, the scope of the commerce clause, or the definition of the obligation of contracts. The entity we call "the Framers" did not have a collective mind, think in one groove, or possess the same convictions.

In fact, they disagreed on many crucial matters, such as the question whether they meant Congress to have the power to charter a bank. In 1789 Hamilton and Washington thought Congress had that power, but Madison and Randolph believed that it did not. Although the Journal of the Convention, except as read by Hamilton, supports Madison's view, all senators who had been at the Convention upheld the power, and Madison later changed his mind about the constitutionality of a bank. Clearly the Convention's "intent" on this matter lacks clarity; revelation is hard to come by when the Framers squabbled about what they meant. They often did, as political controversies during the first score of years under the Constitution revealed.

Sometimes Framers who voted the same way held contradictory opinions on the meaning of a particular clause. Each believed that his understanding constituted the truth of the matter. James Wilson, for example, believed that the ex post facto clause extended to civil matters, while John Dickinson held the view that it applied only to criminal cases, and both voted for the clause. George Mason opposed the same clause because he wanted the states to be free to enact ex post facto laws in civil cases, and he believed that the clause was not clearly confined to criminal cases; but Elbridge

Gerry, who wanted to impose on the states a prohibition against retroactive civil legislation, opposed the clause because he thought it seemed limited to criminal cases. William Paterson changed his mind about the scope of the ex post facto clause. Seeking original intent in the opinions of the Framers is seeking a unanimity that did not exist on complex and divisive issues contested by strong-minded men. Madison was right when he spoke of the difficulty of verifying the intention of the Convention.

A serious problem even exists as to the identity of the Framers and as to the question whether the opinions of all are of equal importance in the determination of original intent. Who, indeed, were the Framers? Were they the fifty-five who were delegates at Philadelphia or only the thirty-nine who signed? If fathoming original intent is the objective, should we not also be concerned about the opinions of those who ratified the Constitution, giving it legitimacy? About 1,600 men attended the various state ratifying conventions, for which the surviving records are so inadequate. No way exists to determine their intent as a guide for judicial decisions; we surely cannot fathom the intent of the members of eight states for which no state convention records exist. The deficiencies of the records of the other five permit few confident conclusions and no basis for believing that a group mind can be located. Understanding ratifier intent is impossible except on the broadest kind of question: Did the people of the states favor scrapping the Articles of Confederation and favor, instead, the stronger Union proposed by the Constitution? Even as to that question, the evidence, which does not exist for a majority of the states, is unsatisfactorily incomplete, and it allows only rough estimates of the answers to questions concerning popular understanding of the meaning of specific clauses of the Constitution. . . .

A CONSTITUTIONAL JURISPRUDENCE OF ORIGINAL INTENT?

A constitutional jurisprudence of original intent would be as viable and sound as Mr. Dooley's understanding of it. Mr. Dooley, Finley Peter Dunne's philosophical Irish bartender, believed that original intent was "what some dead Englishman thought Thomas Jefferson was goin' to mean whin he wrote th' Constitution." Acceptance of original intent as the foundation of constitutional interpretation is unrealistic beyond belief. It obligates us, even if we could grasp that intent, to interpret the Constitution in the way the Framers did in the context of conditions that existed in their time. Those conditions for the most part no longer exist and cannot be recalled with the historical arts and limited time available to the Supreme Court. Anyway, the Court resorts to history for a quick fix, a substantiation, a confirmation, an illustration, or a grace note; it does not really look for the historical conditions and meanings of a time long gone in order to determine the evidence that will persuade it to decide a case in one way rather than another. The Court, moreover, cannot engage in the sort of sustained historical analysis that takes professional historians some years to accomplish. In any case, for many reasons already described, concerning the inadequacies of the historical record and the fact that we cannot in most instances find a collective mind of the Framers, original intent analysis is not really possible, however desirable.

We must keep reminding ourselves that the most outspoken Framers disagreed with each other and did not necessarily reflect the opinions of the many who did not enter the debates. A point that Justice Rufus Peckham made for the Court in an 1897 case about legislative intent carries force with respect to the original intent of the Constitutional Convention. In reference to the difficulty of understanding an act by analyzing the speeches of the members of the body that passed it, Peckham remarked: "Those who did not speak may not have agreed with those who did; and those who spoke might differ from each other; the result being that the only proper way to construe a legislative act is from the language used in the act, and, upon occasion, by a resort to the history of the times when it was passed." We must keep reminding ourselves, too, that the country was deeply divided during the ratification controversy. And we must keep reminding ourselves that the Framers who remained active in national politics divided intensely on one constitutional issue after another—the removal power, the power to charter a corporation, the power to declare neutrality, the executive power, the power to enact excise and use taxes without apportioning them on population, the power of a treaty to obligate the House of Representatives, the power of judicial review, the power to deport aliens, the power to pass an act against seditious libel, the power of the federal courts to decide on federal common law grounds, the power to abolish judicial offices of life tenure, and the jurisdiction of the Supreme Court to decide suits against states without their consent or to issue writs of mandamus

against executive officers. This list is not exhaustive; it is a point of departure. The Framers, who did not agree on their own constitutional issues, would not likely speak to us about ours with a single loud, clear voice. . . .

CONCLUSIONS

Fifty years ago, in his fine study of how the Supreme Court used original intent (not what the Framers and ratifiers believed), Jacobus tenBroek asserted, rightly, that "the intent theory," as he called it, "inverts the judicial process." It described decisions of the Court as having been reached as a result of a judicial search for Framers' intent, "whereas, in fact, the intent discovered by the Court is most likely to be determined by the conclusion that the Court wishes to reach." Original intent analysis involves what tenBroek called "fundamental misconceptions of the nature of the judicial process." It makes the judge "a mindless robot whose task is the utterly mechanical function" of using original intent as a measure of constitutionality. In the entire history of the Supreme Court, as tenBroek should have added, no Justice employing the intent theory has ever written a convincing and reliable study. Lawyers making a historical point will cite a Court opinion as proof, but no competent historian would do that. He knows that judges cannot do their own research or do the right kind of research and that they turn to history to prove some point they have in mind. To paraphrase tenBroek, Justices mistakenly use original intent theory to depict a nearly fixed Constitution, to give the misleading impression that they have decided an issue of constitutionality by finding original intent, and to make a constitutional issue merely a historical question. The entire theory, tenBroek asserted, "falsely describes what the Court actually does," and it "hypothesizes a mathematically exact technique of discovery and a practically inescapable conclusion." That all added up, said tenBroek, to "judicial hokum."

If we could ascertain original intent, one may add, cases would not arise concerning that intent. They arise because the intent is and likely will remain uncertain; they arise because the Framers either had no discernible intent to govern the issue or their intent cannot control it because the problem before the Court would have been so alien to the Framers that only the spirit of some principle implied by them can be of assistance. The Framers were certainly vaguer on powers than on structure and vaguer still on rights.

If, as Robert H. Bork noticed, people rarely raise questions about original intent on issues involving powers or structure, the reason is likely that the Constitution provides the answer, or it has been settled conclusively by the Court, making inquiry futile or unnecessary. For example, the question of constitutional powers to regulate the economy has overwhelmingly been put beyond question by the 1937 "constitutional revolution, limited," in Edward S. Corwin's phrase. Not even the most conservative Justices on today's Court question the constitutionality of government controls. Congress has the constitutional authority under Court decisions to initiate a socialist economy; political restraints, not constitutional ones, prevent that. There are no longer any serious limits on the commerce powers of Congress. The government can take apart the greatest corporations, like Ma Bell; if it does not

proceed against them, the reason is to be found in national defense needs and in politics, not in the Constitution.

The states are supplicants before the United States government, beneficiaries of its largesse like so many welfare recipients, unable to control their own policies, serving instead as administrative agencies of federal policies. Those federal policies extend to realms not remotely within the federal power to govern under the Constitution, except for the fact that the spending power, so called, the power to spend for national defense and general welfare can be exercised through programs of grants-in-aid to states and to over 75,000 substate governmental entities; they take federal tax money and obediently enforce the conditions laid down by Congress and by federal agencies for control of the expenditures. Federalism as we knew it has been replaced by a new federalism that even conservative Republican administrations enforce. The government today makes the New Deal look like a backer of Adam Smith's legendary free enterprise and a respecter of John C. Calhoun's state sovereignty.

Even conservative Justices on the Supreme Court accept the new order of things. William H. Rehnquist spoke for the Court in *PruneYard*, Sandra Day O'Connor in *Hawaii Housing Authority*, and the Court was unanimous in both. In the first of these cases, decided in 1980, the Court held that a state does not violate the property rights of a shopping center owner by authorizing the solicitation of petitions in places of business open to the public. Rehnquist, finding a reasonable police power regulation of private property, asserted that the public right to regulate the use of property is as fundamental as the right to property itself. One might have thought that as a matter of constitutional theory and of original intent, the property right was fundamental and the regulatory power was an exception to it that had to be justified. Rehnquist did not explain why the regulation was justifiable or reasonable; under its rational basis test the Court has no obligation to explain anything. It need merely believe that the legislature had some rational basis for its regulation. . . .

' The Constitution of the United States is our national covenant, and the Supreme Court is its special keeper. The Constitution's power of survival derives in part from the fact that it incorporates and symbolizes the political values of a free people. It creates a representative, responsible government empowered to serve the great objectives specified in the Preamble, while at the same time it keeps government bitted and bridled. Through the Bill of Rights and the great Reconstruction amendments, the Constitution requires that the government respect the freedom of its citizens, whom it must treat fairly. Courts supervise the process, and the Supreme Court is the final tribunal. "The great ideals of liberty and equality," wrote Justice Benjamin N. Cardozo, "are preserved against the assaults of opportunism, the expediency of the passing hour, the scorn and derision of those who have no patience with general principles, by enshrining them in constitutions, and consecrating to the task of their protection a body of defenders." Similarly, Justice Hugo L. Black once wrote for the Court, "Under our constitutional system, courts stand against any winds that blow, as havens of refuge for those who might otherwise suffer because they are helpless, weak, outnumbered, or because they are nonconforming victims of prejudice and public excitement."

The Court should have no choice but to err on the side of the constitutional liberty and equality of the individual, whenever doubt exists as to which side requires endorsement. Ours is so secure a system, precisely because it is free and dedicated to principles of justice, that it can afford to prefer the individual over the state. To interpose original intent against an individual's claim defeats the purpose of having systematic and regularized restraints on power; limitations exist for the minority against the majority, as Madison said. Original intent analysis becomes a treacherous pursuit when it turns the Constitution and the Court away from assisting the development of a still freer and more just society.

The history of Magna Carta throws dazzling light on a jurisprudence of original intent. Magna Carta approaches its 800th anniversary. It was originally "reactionary as hell," to quote the chief justice of West Virginia. But the feudal barons who framed it could not control its evolution. It eventually came to signify many things that are not in it and were not intended. Magna Carta is not remotely important for what it intended but for what it has become. It stands now for government by contract of the people, for fundamental law, for the rule of law, for no taxation without representation, for due process of law, for habeaus corpus, for equality before the law, for representative government, and for a cluster of the rights of the criminally accused. No one cares, or should, that the original document signifies none of this. The Constitution is comparably dynamic.

The Court has the responsibility of helping regenerate and fulfill the noblest aspirations for which this nation stands. It must keep constitutional law constantly rooted in the great ideals of the past yet in a state of evolution in order to realize them. Something should happen to a person who dons the black robe of a Justice of the Supreme Court of the United States. He or she comes under an obligation to strive for as much objectivity as is humanly attainable by putting aside personal opinions and preferences. Yet even the best and most impartial of Justices, those in whom the judicial temperament is most finely cultivated, cannot escape the influences that have tugged at them all their lives and inescapably color their judgment. Personality, the beliefs that make the person, has always made a difference in the Court's constitutional adjudication. There never has been a constitutional case before the Court in which there was no room for personal discretion to express itself.

We may not want judges who start with the answer rather than the problem, but so long as mere mortals sit on the Court and construe its majestic but murky words, we will not likely get any other kind. Not that the Justices knowingly or deliberately read their presuppositions into law. There probably has never been a member of the Court who consciously decided against the Constitution or was unable in his own mind to square his opinions with it. Most judges convince themselves that they respond to the words on parchment, illuminated, of course, by historical and social imperatives. The illusion may be good for their psyches or the public's need to know that the nine who sit on the nation's highest tribunal really become Olympians, untainted by considerations that move lesser beings into political office.

Even those Justices who start with the problem rather than the result cannot transcend themselves or transmogrify the obscure or inexact into impersonal truth. At bottom, constitutional law reflects great public policies enshrined in the form of supreme and fundamental commands. It is truer of constitutional law than of any other branch that "what the courts declare to have always been the law," as Holmes put it, "is in fact new. It is legislative in its grounds. The very considerations which judges most rarely mention, and always with an apology, are the secret root from which the law draws all the juices of life. I mean, of course, consideration of what is expedient for the community concerned." Result-oriented jurisprudence or, at the least, judicial activism is nearly inevitable—not praiseworthy, or desirable, but inescapable when the Constitution must be construed. Robert H. Bork correctly said that the best way to cope with the problem "is the selection of intellectually honest judges." One dimension of such honesty is capacity to recognize at the propitious moment a need for constitutional evolution, rather than keep the Constitution in a deepfreeze.

POSTSCRIPT

Should the Federal Courts Be Bound by the "Original Intent" of the Framers?

Bork's view of the limits of judicial power is often characterized as judicial self-restraint. It tends to be conservative and opposed to policies that alter the historical boundaries of the separation of powers, the federal division of power between the nation and the states, or long-observed standards regarding the extent of constitutional liberties and rights. A fuller statement of his position can be found in his book *The Tempting of America: The Political Seduction of the Law* (Free Press, 1990).

By contrast, Levy's position is usually defined as judicial activism, because it permits elected officials to undertake, and judges to endorse, policies that extend the powers of government and the rights of persons beyond those contemplated by the authors of the Constitution and its amendments.

An interesting and intimate account of how the Supreme Court works can be found in William H. Rehnquist's book *The Supreme Court: How It Is* (William Morrow, 1987), the first interpretation of the highest court by a sitting chief justice. A short history and defense of judicial review, *The Court and the Constitution* (Houghton Mifflin, 1987), has been written by Alexander Cox, law professor, solicitor general, and original Watergate prosecutor. Cox is unsympathetic to the doctrine of original intent as embodying a too narrow interpretation of judicial power.

Several essays on opposing sides of original intent can be found in Steven Anzovin and Janet Podell's book *The United States Constitution and the Supreme Court* (H. W. Wilson, 1988).

In recent years, the Supreme Court has been narrowly divided in choosing between opposed standards in the controversial issues that come before it, including cases involving affirmative action, flag-burning, abortion rights, and school prayer. As noted in the introduction to this issue, Alexis de Tocqueville observed that "scarcely any political question arises in the United States today that is not resolved, sooner or later, into a judicial question." It does not seem like an overstatement today. However, a Supreme Court that applies controversial constitutional standards to bitterly divisive issues cannot escape becoming the subject of political controversy itself.

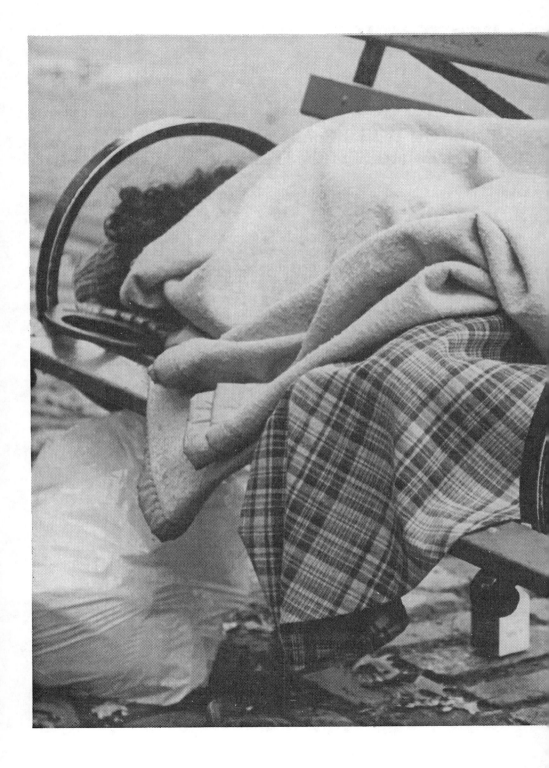

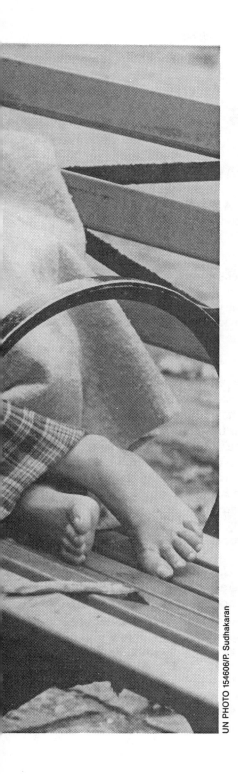

PART 3

Social Change and Public Policy

It is difficult to imagine any topic more emotional and divisive than one that involves social morality. Whatever consensus once existed on such issues as public school prayer, abortion, and equality of opportunity, that consensus has been shattered in recent years as Americans have lined up very clearly on opposing sides—and what is more important, they have taken those competing views into Congress, state legislatures, and the courts.

The issues in this section generate intense emotions because they ask us to clarify our values on a number of very personal concerns.

Will Tougher Sentencing Reduce Crime?

Is Capital Punishment Justified?

Is Affirmative Action Reverse Discrimination?

Should "Hate Speech" Be Protected?

Should Drugs Be Legalized?

Are the Poor Being Harmed by Welfare?

Is the National Debt a National Liability?

Does the United States Need Socialized Medicine?

Was *Roe v. Wade* a Mistake?

Should There Be a "Wall of Separation" Between Church and State?

ISSUE 9

Will Tougher Sentencing Reduce Crime?

YES: Stanley C. Brubaker, from "In Praise of Punishment," *The Public Interest* (Fall 1989)

NO: Linda Rocawich, from "Lock 'Em Up: America's All-Purpose Cure for Crime," *The Progressive* (August 1987)

ISSUE SUMMARY

YES: Political scientist Stanley C. Brubaker argues that punishment for crime, whether or not it deters crime or rehabilitates criminals, is important because it helps to underscore the community's sense of right and wrong.
NO: Editor Linda Rocawich contends that locking people up is inhumane, is often applied in a racially discriminatory manner, and does not deter crime.

Crime is a major social problem in America, and most Americans suspect that it is growing worse. Everyone, except perhaps criminals themselves, wants to eliminate crime. The question is: how?

The problem is serious and complex. In fact, even the federal crime index does not give a precise idea of the incidence of major crime. (Major crimes are identified by the Federal Bureau of Investigation as criminal homicide, rape, robbery, aggravated assault, burglary, larceny over $50, and auto theft.) It is even uncertain whether the crime rate has been growing because the incidence of major crimes has increased strikingly in recent decades or whether it is because more crimes are being reported by victims (perhaps because of the increase in personal, automobile, and home insurance) and more accurately recorded by police.

However, some aspects of crime in the United States are indisputable. Crime is widespread, but is more concentrated in urban areas. It is disproportionately committed by the young, the poor, and members of minority groups. The commission of some crimes (those that require public knowledge of the activity, such as prostitution, drug selling, and gambling) involve the corruption of law-enforcement officials. The rates for some crimes, particularly violent crimes, are much higher in the United States than in many other countries. For example, there are more criminal homicides in New York City (where the rate of homicide is lower than that of a number of other American cities) than in all of Great Britain or Japan, which have, respectively, 9 and 15 times the population of New York.

There is little dispute about the increased public awareness of the problem and the widespread fear that people—particularly parents and older people—feel in high-crime areas. Something needs to be done; but what? Reform society? Reform criminals? Some would deal with crime's "root causes," but as yet we do not know what those root causes are. Others think the solution lies in the severity of punishment, as in the slogan "Lock them up and throw away the keys!"

Practical, moral, and constitutional questions have been raised about imprisonment. Who should be imprisoned? Only 7 percent of new prisoners in federal prisons in 1987 were convicted of violent crimes. More than 40 percent were convicted of drug-related crimes, but prisons do not offer drug abuse programs. For how long should criminals be sentenced? Harsher sentencing has contributed to a prison population that doubled between 1980 and 1990. Incarceration rates in the United States are about the highest in the world.

How much are we willing to pay? A 30-year sentence is equivalent to a $1 million investment. The cost of prisons at all levels amounted to $20 billion in 1988. The federal system alone is expected to spend more than $70 billion to build new prisons between 1990 and 1995.

Should white-collar offenders be treated differently from street criminals? Does punishment deter people from breaking the law? If it does, is it the severity of the punishment, or its swiftness, or its certainty—or some combination of these— that deters? Are there better, perhaps more enlightened, ways of reducing crime in America? Among the alternatives that are proposed are community service, restitution or compensation to the victim, supervised probation, and psychological and physical treatment. Would any of these work better to reduce crime?

These are some of the questions touched upon by Stanley C. Brubaker and Linda Rocawich in the selections that follow. Like so many thoughtful observers of crime in America, they have come to opposed conclusions.

YES

Stanley C. Brubaker

IN PRAISE OF PUNISHMENT

In American political life, no one deserves praise more than Abraham Lincoln. And perhaps no one could express more clearly the character of Lincoln's political nobility than Frederick Douglass; having experienced the degradation of slavery, Douglas apprehended more fully the peaks of civic virtue. Thus, at the unveiling of the Freedmen's Monument in memory of Lincoln, Douglass delivered one of the most moving statements of praise in American oratory. The statement was devoid of illusions. Lincoln was, said Douglass, "pre-eminently the white man's President"; white Americans were his children, black Americans "at best only his step-children; children by adoption, children by force of circumstances and necessity." Yet the speech was replete with the sentiments of "gratitude and appreciation."

Douglass spoke with gratitude, for "though the Union was more to him than our freedom or our future, under his wise and beneficent rule we saw ourselves gradually lifted from the depths of slavery to the heights of liberty and manhood." And he spoke with appreciation, for

> taking him for all in all, measuring the tremendous magnitude of the work before him, considering the necessary means to ends, and surveying the end from the beginning, infinite wisdom has seldom sent any man into the world better fitted for his mission than Abraham Lincoln. His birth, his training, and his natural endowments, both mental and physical, were strongly in his favor. Born and reared among the lowly, a stranger to wealth and luxury, compelled to grapple single-handed with the flintiest hardships of life, from tender youth to sturdy manhood, he grew strong in the manly and heroic qualities demanded by the great mission to which he was called by the votes of his countrymen.

No less striking than Douglass's praise of Lincoln as the epitome of American virtue is his understanding of praise itself, and its role in the polity's civil religion:

> The sentiment that brings us here today is one of the noblest that can stir and thrill the human heart. It has crowned and made glorious the high places of all civilized nations with the grandest and most enduring works of art, designed

From Stanley C. Brubaker, "In Praise of Punishment," *The Public Interest*, no. 97 (Fall 1989), pp. 44–55. Copyright © 1989 by National Affairs, Inc. Reprinted by permission.

to illustrate the characters and perpetuate the memories of great public men. It is the sentiment which from year to year adorns with fragrant and beautiful flowers the graves of our loyal, brave, and patriotic soldiers who fell in defence of the Union and liberty.

And for his mostly black audience, the new freedmen, to "join in this high worship, and march conspicuously in the line of this time-honored custom" was an occasion for "manly pride." For by this expression they were affirming their citizenship as well as their humanity. Thus Douglas both began and concluded his oration with congratulations to the new "fellow citizens":

> In doing honor to the memory of our friend and liberator, we have been doing highest honors to ourselves and those who come after us; we have been fastening ourselves to a name and fame imperishable and immortal; we have also been defending ourselves from blighting scandal. When now it shall be said that the colored man is soulless, that he has no appreciation of benefits or benefactors; when the foul reproach of ingratitude is hurled at us, and it is attempted to scourge us beyond the range of human brotherhood, we may calmly point to the monument we have this day erected to the memory of Abraham Lincoln.

In praising praise, Douglass echoed the ancient wisdom that a political community is constituted not simply as an alliance for property rights or for the sake of mere life—if it were, fragrant and beautiful flowers would not adorn patriots' graves, for there would be no patriots—but by a way of life and by the qualities of character that inform it. With story and stone, we celebrate noble deeds and noble people; we thereby make more manifest and enduring those qualities of soul that make for a political community. And we affirm that we are members of this community, for what we praise in others we must by implication esteem in ourselves. Through these rituals of praise we may more fully apprehend, appreciate, and affirm the beauty of soul that best expresses our community's way of life.

PUNISHMENT

We should understand punishment as a kind of mirror image of praise. If praise expresses gratitude and approbation, punishment expresses resentment and reprobation. If praise expresses what the political community admires and what unites it, punishment expresses what the community condemns and what threatens it. Punishment, like praise, publicly expresses our determinations of what people deserve.

There is no great novelty in this view of punishment. Much that I have said and will say is drawn from Aristotle. Similarly, Emile Durkheim wrote that "[punishment's] real function is to maintain inviolate the cohesion of society by sustaining the common consciousness in all its vigor." Among contemporary philosophers, Joel Feinberg has identified punishment with the "expression of attitudes of resentment and indignation, and of judgments of disapproval and reprobation." In this view, what punishment expresses is retribution, giving the criminal what he deserves. Retribution then defines as well as justifies punishment. Although such a view of punishment is not novel, it is unpopular among today's intellectuals, many of whom would proclaim with the psychiatrist Karl Menninger that "punishment" is itself a crime. Even more would agree with Justice Thurgood Marshall's seemingly enlightened judgment that "retribution has been condemned by scholars for centuries," and they would follow him further in thinking that "punishment for the sake of retribution [is] not permissible under the Eighth Amendment."

But if punishment is not "for the sake of retribution," can it still be punishment? I think not. We should distinguish punishment from related phenomena, such as *taxes, reparations, rehabilitation,* and *deterrents*. We should ask whether these latter phenomena can account for what we wish to say with our criminal sanctions, or whether the sanctions must instead be rooted in retribution. Perfectly sharp distinctions are not to be expected, for the phenomena blur and blend at the margins. Yet their central and distinguishing features are quite clear. Taxes and licenses, like punishments and penalties, may discourage activities, but they do not usually prohibit them. Laws that require licenses for or that impose taxes upon a course of conduct say that those who wish to engage in it must pay a fee or pass an examination; laws concerning punishments and penalties say that the conduct is impermissible. Here the distinction might blur; taxes may be prohibitive and penalties trivial, in which cases the messages are reversed. Usually, however, penalties and punishments are easily distinguishable from taxes.

Deterrent penalties, of course, lie closer than taxes to punishment, but they are still distinguishable from it. They announce that certain courses of conduct are frowned upon. But typically, as in ticketing drivers who marginally exceed the speed limit, the disapproval is less serious than it is when real punishment is meted out; less hardship is imposed, less shame is attached, we are held less

rigorously to the mark, and violators are pursued less forcefully. Not uncommonly, the penalty is accompanied by other implicit messages that cushion its impact, assuring people that though they broke the law, they are not really bad: they are told that anyone might have done what they did, or that the penalty is a risk that they run for engaging in a certain line of conduct, and that for public benefit they must be held accountable. As these messages suggest, in framing penalties lawmakers often consider it reasonable to apply strict liability; whether someone did the action is the only question, not whether he was justified or made a mistake. But where punishment is involved, justification and excuse must be considered, and strict liability is virtually unthinkable.

This distinction points to the difference between deterrents and punishments. Deterrence works better when would-be violators know that they cannot slip through the system by faking an excuse or justification. Because the offender may in fact have had good reason or excuse, strict liability is occasionally unfair. But exactly because the offense in question is not thought "serious" (because it does not seriously reflect on the offender's character), the gain in deterrence outweighs the loss in fairness.

Rehabilitation, like deterrence, finds its justification in the future. It need have no essential tie to what was done or why; it concerns these things only insofar as they help rehabilitators assess what is required to prevent future criminal behavior. Because it has no essential tie to the crime, rehabilitation itself has no necessary proportion to the offense. If a criminal proves unresponsive to the methods of rehabilitation, he may, in consequence of a relatively minor offense, spend the rest of his life in a "rehabilitation center"; if he needs no rehabilitation or responds quickly to treatment, he may go free soon after committing a serious offense.

If penalties and rehabilitation focus on the future, punishment focuses on the past. In looking back, punishment resembles reparation. But reparation looks back in order to make the victim whole, and it does this typically as a matter of private law; reparation is not essentially a public concern. If punishment makes the victim whole, it does so metaphorically and incidentally; its essential concern is public.

Punishment, then, is distinct from a tax, a license, rehabilitation, reparation, or a deterrent penalty. What distinguishes punishment is the expression of resentment and reprobation, the expression of our deeply held conviction that criminals should get what they deserve: in a word, *retribution*.

RESPONSIBILITY AND JUDGMENT

Retribution in punishment, like gratitude and approbation in praise, pays tribute to man's distinctive capacity for moral responsibility; it declares that man is moved not simply by mechanical force or biological instinct, but by deliberate choice. If the "hero," like Woody Allen playing Boris in *Love and Death*, performs all his deeds inadvertently, we are unlikely to celebrate his character—even if his actions significantly benefit us. Similarly, if the accused has a satisfactory excuse (e.g., he made a good-faith mistake) or a justification (e.g., he acted out of self-defense), anger is inappropriate. Only if the person is responsible do we feel anger and seek revenge. As Walter Berns points out, "We can become angry with an inanimate object (the door we

run into and kick in return) only by foolishly attributing responsibility to it, and we cannot do that for long, which is why we do not think of returning later to revenge ourselves on the door." Nor, we might add, can an offending animal hold our interest for long. (Here Captain Ahab would have to be excepted; but he was mad in a different sense.) Anger, like gratitude, presupposes essentially human attributes in its object, and directing it in an enduring way toward nonhumans can be done only ironically or insanely.

Anger, according to Aristotle, is "an impulse, accompanied by pain, to a conspicuous revenge for a conspicuous slight directed without justification towards what concerns oneself or towards what concerns one's friends." It is also, he noted, accompanied by a "certain pleasure" arising from the anticipation of revenge. While anger may stem from a conspicuous slight to oneself, the anger that underlies legal punishment concerns oneself and one's "friends" in a broader sense. It displays a caring for people and for principles that transcends narrow self-interest. It does not simply affix to the harm a person or a principle suffers; it also relates to how that harm was caused by a responsible human being, and to the attitude that he displayed toward the people and principles we care about. Punishment both expresses and satisfies our longing for vindication.

The criminal law, wrote James Fitzjames Stephen, gives "shape to moral indignation, and hatred of the criminal. . . . The sentence of the law is to the moral sentiment of the public what a seal is to hot wax." It gives proper form to anger, measuring it according to reprobation, to the judgment that the deed is shameful and deserves hard treatment in proportion to the gravity of the crime. This stern, measured judgment makes punishment what it is. As George Gardner observed, "The essence of punishment lies in the criminal conviction itself. One may lose more money on the stock market than in the courtroom; a prisoner-of-war camp may well provide a harsher environment than a state prison; death on the field of battle has the same physical characteristics as death by sentence of law." It is the condemnatory judgment alone, expressing the ideas of desert and righteous vindication, that renders "mere" hardship a punishment.

Similarly, it is the favorable judgment alone that differentiates benefiting someone from praising him. We praise and reward people to express our appreciation of their deeds and our admiration of the noble character that their deeds bespeak; in doing so, we elevate, display, preserve, and render more secure the things that we care about. We punish and blame people to express our resentment and disapproval of their deeds and our detestation of the ugliness of character that their crimes bespeak. Both in praising and in blaming we intend the deserved treatment to hit home and to sink in deep, *to mark our judgments of the person in virtue of the deed*. In this way rewards differ from compensation and incentives, and punishments differ from reparations and disincentives. Compensation and incentives, like reparation and disincentives, do not and are specifically intended not to reflect deeply on the person; they are largely external to the self. Though contemporary liberalism, as we shall see, has gone far to diminish the range of the self that can be publicly recognized, most citizens (for whom the self is more expansive) wish to mark its dimensions; they wish to erect monu-ments of gratitude to reward the greatest of heroes with lasting fame and to punish the vilest of criminals with death. *Praise and punishment thus reflect a vision of the moral order in which the virtuous flourish and the wicked suffer.*

THE JOHN MACK CASE

A recent case nicely illustrates the inability of deterrence, incapacitation, or rehabilitation—the commonly invoked "enlightened" justifications for criminal sanctions—to explain our fundamental sentiments about crime and punishment. In 1973 Pamela Small, then a college student in search of furnishings for her first apartment, entered a store in Arlington, Virginia, shortly before it was to close. When she discovered a flaw in the window blinds that she was about to purchase, the clerk, who was alone with her in the store, told her that there were other blinds in the storeroom and invited her to follow him to make her selection. Once there, the clean-cut and seemingly innocent clerk, John Mack, closed the door behind them and told her to lie down. When she refused, he snatched a hammer and smashed her skull with five blows, any one of which, doctors later reported, might have killed her. Mack then grabbed a steak knife, plunged it into her chest five times, and slit her throat repeatedly. After leaving Small for dead in her car, Mack went to the movies.

Mack was sentenced to fifteen years in the Virginia State Penitentiary; but he served less than twenty-seven months in the more commodious Fairfax County Jail. The brevity and leniency of the incarceration was due in part to Mack's previously clean record and in part to the intercession of Congressman Jim Wright, whose son-in-law was Mack's brother. Even before Mack's sentencing, Wright had offered him a job on Capitol Hill. Following his release, Mack rose to become top aide of then-Speaker of the House Wright, serving as executive director of the Steering and Policy Committee—perhaps the most powerful staff position in the House, with a salary equal to that of congressmen and federal district judges.

Miraculously, Pamela Small recovered; as many readers know, she recently agreed to be interviewed by the *Washington Post* for an extensive article that coincided with the ethics investigation of Speaker Wright. The public reacted to this whole affair, understandably, with outrage. And its outrage was inexplicable except in terms of retribution, bespeaking the belief that neither his punishment nor his present position had given Mack what he deserved. No doubt the judicial system was correct in saying that Mack had been "rehabilitated"—though he never expressed remorse to Small or offered her restitution. Indeed, by the criterion of rehabilitation he could probably have been released much sooner; perhaps he could have served no time at all. Nobody doubted that he was now a hardworking, talented, and trusted aide on Capitol Hill. Nor was the outrage explicable in terms of deterrence. In the extensive commentary following the exposé, one searches in vain for the contention that the lenient sentence given to Mack would make brutal attacks more likely.

Mack himself and his allies on Capitol Hill spoke of his act and sentence in terms appropriate to mere "penalties"; the very inadequacy of that vocabulary only swelled the public's outrage. At his sentencing hearing, Mack told the judge that "I just blew my cool for a second." A year after the attack, Mack explained to a court-appointed psychiatrist that he had "reacted in a way in which any man would perhaps react under similar circumstances." Mack suggested that he had made a "mistake," and that perhaps he should have been penalized for it to help discourage others (though he did not admit quite this much); nevertheless, it was a mistake that any normal human being could have made. He still characterized his crime in this way sixteen years later; he made virtually the same statement to the *Post* reporter and in his resignation statement a week later in the face of the public outcry: "When I was nineteen, I made a terrible, tragic mistake." Speaker Wright explained his hiring and promotion of Mack along similar lines: "I have never regretted giving John an opportunity all these years. I don't suppose anybody is immune from mistakes."

The disproportion between the deed and its punishment, and between the deed and its characterization, were rendered all the more vivid by Mack's position on Capitol Hill. For Douglass's oration on Lincoln, Capitol Hill provided a perfect setting: "We are here in the place where the ablest and best men of the country are sent to devise the policy, enact the laws, and shape the destiny of the Republic; we are here, with the stately pillars and majestic dome of the Capitol of the nation looking down upon us." It was the right place to praise Lincoln, and a mark of their own honor that Douglass and the freedmen stood there. Though Capitol Hill seldom inspires such comments today, the expectation remains that its highest positions should go to men and women of honor. John Mack did not fit his office, just as his punishment did not fit his crime.

WILLIE HORTON AND CONTEMPORARY LIBERALISM

Many who were adamant in calling for John Mack's resignation and in denouncing the injustice of his lenient sentence and his rapid rise to power on Capitol Hill were no doubt among those who saw only "racism" in the Willie Horton story. This centerpiece of the 1988 presidential campaign featured the Massachusetts policy, supported by Governor Michael Dukakis, of giving furloughs to convicts—including those who, like Willie Horton, were serving life sentences for murder and were ineligible for parole. While on furlough, Horton, who is black, raped a woman and tortured her husband, both white. I do not know what role racism may have played in the minds of the strategists who decided to make Willie Horton a campaign issue, or whether racism helped make him a forceful symbol. But I think it a mistake of the first magnitude to underestimate the effectiveness of the ad's surface message: that contemporary liberals, though they may be horrified by "systemic" injustices, do not take personal crime and punishment seriously enough.

Indeed if contemporary liberal theorists, such as John Rawls in *A Theory of Justice*, articulate the self-understanding of today's activists, they cannot take crime seriously, for their theory prevents them from either praising or punishing. Rawls's work, which has gained nearly canonical status among liberal academics, maintains that the basic principles of justice are those that free, equal, and rational actors would adopt in what he calls the "original position." In that position, we abstract ourselves from everything alleged to be morally arbitrary—positions in society, conceptions of the good, the distribution of genetic endowments, psychological propensities, talents and traits—and choose behind a "veil of ignorance" the principles of justice for our society, knowing only that we will have some conception of the good and some combination of these other morally arbitrary features without knowing what they will be. In such a position, according to Rawls, rational actors would be "risk averse"; they would seek to avoid the worst situation that might befall them. Accordingly, they would choose two fundamental principles: first, that "each person is to have an equal right to the most extensive basic liberty compatible with a similar liberty for others," and second, that "social and economic inequalities are to be arranged so that they are both a) to the greatest benefit of the least advantaged [the so-called 'difference principle'] and b) attached to offices and positions open to all under conditions of fair equality of opportunity."

Such a theory can account for incentives and disincentives, for penalties and rewards of a sort, but not for praise and punishment. It cannot account for these because the very structure of the original position assumes that virtually all features of human pesonality that one might praise or condemn—the good that one chooses, one's talents, even one's character—are morally arbitrary.

In the original position you would authorize incentives or "rewards" not because you think an individual might really *deserve* these or higher honors, nor even because you might want them yourself, but because you might end up in the class of the least advantaged; thus you would want incentives leading individuals to develop talents that might bring you benefits that you would not otherwise enjoy. No one really deserves the products of his natural endowments, for "no one deserves his place in the distribution of natural endowments." Nor does one gain credit for the superior character by which he develops those talents, for one does not even deserve his own character: "[One's] character depends in large part upon fortunate family and social circumstances for which he can claim no credit. The notion of desert seems not to apply to these cases."

If Frederick Douglass had studied with John Rawls, he might have restated his praise as follows:

Fellow citizens: We, the new freedmen, have been and will remain for some time the least advantaged class in America. In affirming principles of justice, others merely hypothesize that they will be in our position; but we are actually in that position and for that reason can speak forthrightly of our interest. We are gathered beneath the nation's Capitol, whose very edifice bespeaks the sentiment that draws us here today. We stand across from Arlington, where that self-same sentiment adorns patriots' graves with fragrant flowers. I speak, of course, neither of gratitude, nor of honor, nor of praise, nobility, and heroism, but of self-interest. Just as taxpayers have erected majestic domes to lure clever men to enact laws for their advantage, just as parents, lovers, and children have set flowers on patriots' graves to get others to die for them, so do we, by erecting this monument to Abraham Lincoln, hope to encourage others to bring us things that we cannot get for ourselves.

Favored in the toss of the cosmic dice with useful traits, encouraged to develop these by fortunate social and family circumstances, Lincoln cannot be said in any sense to have deserved his character. But then nobody else deserves it either. So for those benefits that came to us by virtue of those traits that came to him, we wish to give proper recognition. We should not be sentimental about this. Our recognition implies neither gratitude nor approbation. We cannot really be grateful, for Lincoln responded as would any rational actor to the incentive structure in his life. Nor can we express approbation, for whatever one thinks of his character, the notion of desert seems not to apply to his case. Still, so that others so favored in the distribution of useful talents will be encouraged to favor us, and so that other Americans will realize that we are as self-interested as they, we erect this monument.

Rawls is more concerned with denying praise for superior character and noble deeds than he is with denying blame for deficient character and crimes. He styles his theory an "ideal" one that develops and elaborates principles of justice under conditions of "strict compliance"; only secondarily is he concerned with violations of these principles. Nevertheless, his account of "noncompliance" is revealing. "Penalties," he tells us, are necessary in this theory to enable social cooperation and to deal with the "free rider" problem: if you cannot safely assume that others will abide by the social contract or by other implicit and explicit agreements, your own fidelity might set you at a disadvantage. Thus, to give effect to the principles you would choose in the original position and later agreements, you would affirm the use of sanctions against those who fail to abide by their agreements. But as Rawls emphasizes, this criminal sanction is not "primarily retributive"; instead it is a scheme of "penalities that stabilize a scheme of cooperation." Without these disincentives, any normal fellow whom you might meet behind the veil of ignorance (even if he did not "blow his cool" for a second) might rationally choose to break the law for his own advantage.

In this vision of today's liberal activists, atrocity as well as nobility of character and deed both emerge from things "arbitrary from a moral point of view." The voice behind this vision is reassuring and generous. It tells you that nobody—regardless of talent, character, or beauty of mind and soul—is more deserving than you. And generosity undoubtedly draws many to it. But *sotto voce* we hear the more revealing words: nobody deserves anything. The hero will get his pension, but no praise; the villain will get his penalty, but no punishment; both will get what they are "entitled" to and neither will get what he deserves, for "the notion of desert seems not to apply to these cases." Whether you are to become a hero or a villain is shrouded by the veil of ignorance. This casual blurring of heroes and villains, this utter denial of responsibility for the characters we become, recalls a comment by Nietzsche:

> There is a point in the history of society when it becomes so pathologically soft and tender that among other things it sides even with those who harm it, criminals, and does this quite seriously and honestly. Punishing somehow seems unfair to it, and it is certain that imagining "punishment" and "being supposed to punish" hurts it, arouses fear in it. "Is it not enough to render him *undangerous?* Why still punish? Punishing itself is terrible."

IN PRAISE OF PUNISHMENT

Why still punish? In part, because punishment *is* terrible, or more precisely, because it is awful. Punishment and praise should indeed fill us with awe, for through these institutions we pay tribute to the awesome range of human responsibility, from the depths of depravity to the heights of nobility. And they bespeak a deeper sense of awe. Human responsibility makes dignity possible; to accept responsibility is to recognize that our understanding of depravity and nobility is not self-willed, or "arbitrary from a moral point of view." It is not simply the result of human conventions or hypothetical contracts among rational actors; it is more a matter of discovery than one of choice. We do, of course, "choose" our criminal laws and sanctions, our honors and prizes, but we do so with the sense that we choose them because we think them right, not that we think them right because we choose them.

Similarly, we abstain from crime—at least most of us still do—not simply because it is disadvantageous but because it is wrong. Criminal sanctions must express that conviction. They cannot simply say that crime is against your interest; they must also express, reinforce, and sustain the sentiment that crime is wrong. To be sure, ours would be a better world were there no crime, and hence no need for punishment; but given the world as it is, we should give punishment its due, for it reminds us of human responsibility as well as the limits of human choice. Without these, in the words of Lincoln, no nation can long endure.

NO

Linda Rocawich

LOCK 'EM UP

In 1790, when Philadelphia Quakers opened the Walnut Street Jail, the first prison in the world to use confinement as punishment for crime, they were following the lead of Cesare Beccaria, the Italian criminologist who advocated imprisonment as an alternative to execution. Their experiment, now copied everywhere in the world, will shortly be 200 years old, but don't expect that bicentennial to be commemorated on your cereal boxes.

America's prisons are an overcrowded mess. Our society officially expects these mean, gloomy, brutal places somehow to turn criminals into pillars of the community. They have a better chance of doing the reverse—and probably do, on the rare occasions when they get a shot at a pillar of the community.

But we keep building them, and then we fill them up faster than we can build still more.

Now, in 1987, we lock up so many people every week that, at the end of seven days, our state and Federal prisons hold a thousand more than they did the week before. Fifty thousand *more* prisoners every year.

Fifteen years ago, the population of our prisons was about 200,000. Ten years ago it was near 300,000. On December 31, 1986, the population was 546,659 and growing.

Ten years ago, critics of our criminal-justice system often said that only the Soviet Union and South Africa, among industrialized nations, imprisoned a larger proportion of their people than the United States. This may no longer be true. The U.S. incarceration rate—the number of prisoners per 100,000 in the general population—was seventy-nine in 1925. In 1980, it was 179; in 1985, it was 201. That is about double the incarceration rate in most Western European nations.

White Americans are incarcerated at a rate of 114 per 100,000. But for black Americans, the story is much different: The rate is well over 700. On this front, we definitely are Number One, according to Steven Whitman of Northwestern University's Center for Urban Affairs and Policy Research. "Incredibly," Whitman says, "blacks in the United States go to prison more often than blacks in South Africa. In fact, the United States' black imprisonment rate is the highest in the world."

What is going on here? The crime rate explains nothing, and no one has a tidy answer. But those who study the prison-population explosion blame the extremely conservative ideology that permeates our society, an individualistic, every-man-for-himself ideology. When it comes to crime, this is manifested in a vicious punitive streak—lock 'em up and throw away the key.

Research into the nature of the prison population bears this out. Judges are handing down longer sentences than before because they perceive a public demand for them. For the same reason, they are sending people to prison for crimes that formerly did not merit incarceration.

The strength of the punitive impulse is demonstrated by what it costs. At a time of extreme fiscal conservatism, Americans spend $9 billion a year just to operate the state prisons. Billions more go to the Federal system and to capital outlays and construction costs for new prisons.

As public policy, this is insane.

The libraries are full of exposés of prison conditions, descriptions of what is wrong with them, why they achieve none of their "purposes" but punishment, which many corrections professionals won't even admit is a purpose.

Periodically, the prisons explode with riots and waves of violence. These are often followed by the appointment of Presidential commissions to look into the crisis. The commissions always come to the same conclusion: The prisons are a mess and we should not be using them to warehouse people. The National Advisory Commission on Criminal Justice Standards and Goals advised the nation in 1973, for example, that prisons should be society's *last resort* for dealing with its problems. The Commission said prisons fail to reduce crime, succeed in punishing but not deterring criminals, provide only temporary protection to the community, and change the offender (but mostly for the worse).

Obviously, the nation wasn't listening.

CRIME RATES HAVE NOTHING TO DO WITH incarceration rates. Of the ten states with the highest rates of violent crime, only Nevada, South Carolina, Maryland, and Arizona also rank in the top ten on incarceration. Incarceration rates for other states with the highest crime rates are way down the list—New York is twentieth; California is twenty-first; Illinois is twenty-sixth.

Racism, however, explains a great deal. Nine of the eleven states of the Old Confederacy are in the top sixteen on incarceration rate. The top twenty also include the former slave states of Delaware, Maryland, Oklahoma, and Missouri. Social scientist William Nagel studied the phenomenon in the 1970s and found that states with large non-white populations, even those with low crime rates, have large prison populations. "There is no significant correlation between a state's racial composition and its crime rate," he wrote, "but there is a very great positive relationship between its racial composition and its incarceration rate."

Steven Whitman, the researcher who calculated the incarceration rate of blacks at more than 700, recently wrote about "The Crime of Black Imprisonment" for the *Chicago Tribune*. About one of every four black men, he says, will go to prison in his lifetime. A reader later objected to Whitman's conclusion that blacks go to prison because they are black. "The reason more blacks go to prison," said this letter, "is that they commit more crimes."

The letter writer is wrong.

Blacks commit crimes and whites commit crimes. After that, they aren't treated the same. Criminologist Donald Taft studied the subject more than thirty years ago. In a 1956 criminology text, he summarized what he found: "Negroes are more likely to be suspected of crime than are whites. They are also more likely to be arrested. If the perpetrator of a crime is known to be a Negro, the police may arrest all Negroes who were near the scene—a procedure they would rarely dare to follow with whites. After arrest, Negroes are less likely to secure bail, and so are more liable to be counted in jail statistics. They are more liable than whites to be indicted and less likely to have their cases *nol prossed* or otherwise dismissed. If tried, Negroes are more likely to be convicted. If convicted, they are less likely to be given probation. For this reason they are more likely to be included in the count of prisoners. Negroes are also more liable than whites to be kept in prison for the full terms of their commitments and correspondingly less like to be paroled."

No one who has seriously studied the subject since then disputes Taft's findings.

THE STATUS OF WOMEN IN THE PRISON system *is* changing, however, and the new punitive streak is at work. For about fifty years after incarceration rates were first computed in 1925, the rate for women varied between six and nine per 100,000. It hit ten in 1977 and has been climbing steadily ever since, to its current rate of seventeen-plus. The female prison population has grown at a faster rate than the male population every year since 1981. About 27,000 women were in Federal or state custody in 1986, an increase of about 15 percent over the year before.

While several recent studies show a jump in the number of violent crimes committed by women since the women's movement came to prominence, what is more noticeable is a tendency to sentence women to prison for crimes for which they used to get probation—thus making them more equal to men.

The fast growth in the female prison population is "the result of harsher sentencing" says Nicole Hahn Rafter, author of a history of the women's prison system called *Partial Justice*. She recently told *The Christian Science Monitor* that the nature of the crimes committed by most women convicts and the backgrounds of the women do not warrant their being in prison. "Most of them don't belong there," she said.

What is "the nature of their crimes"? Typically, according to *The Monitor*'s report, women serve time for relatively minor crimes such as larceny, welfare fraud, prostitution, receiving stolen property, and shoplifting. Drug or alcohol abuse is often a complicating factor. The violent crimes for which women most often go to prison are murder or manslaughter of men who have abused them over a period of years, according to the American Correctional Association (ACA).

"Battered Women and Criminal Justice" is the report of New York State researchers who looked into the cases of twelve women whose physical abuse led them to kill their husbands. Three are under life sentence; the others average a maximum term of fifteen years. "The nature of their crimes and the existence of a very low recidivism rate for those who have committed murder and manslaughter provide substantial evidence that these women and others like them are not a danger to society," the study finds. "The wisdom of imprisoning them at all is certainly questionable."

If the wisdom of imprisoning women who have killed is in question, what about the vast majority who haven't lifted a violent finger? The ACA—which, as an association of professionals who work, for the most part, within the system, has never been known as a gang of raving reformers—has just put out a new handbook on public policy for corrections. Attorney Edwin Meese III has even endorsed it.

The ACA handbook, noting that most women in the prison system's net were arrested for property crimes, says that few pose a risk to society. "Community placement," it says, "can provide the level of structure and support needed by many female offenders. At the same time, community placement considerably reduces the cost burden to taxpayers."

To take this story one step further: If the wisdom of imprisoning all these women is in question, what about imprisoning all those men? The people who know them best, the prison administrators, don't believe very many of their boarders belong behind bars.

Arnold Pontesso has been among the more vocal. A retired Federal warden who began his career as a guard almost fifty years ago, Pontesso has also been director of Oklahoma's correctional system, running not only the prisons but also the state's parole and probation department. He has often testified as an expert witness for the inmates in lawsuits complaining of unconstitutional or unlawful prison conditions, and he is always careful to insist that there are some offenders whom society must lock up. When pressed for a number—how many ought to be in prison, how many would we do better to handle some other way—Pontesso usually says no more than about 5 per cent of prisoners belong inside. Certainly, he adds, no one whose offense was nonviolent should be imprisoned.

As much as Pontesso's former colleagues hate to see him take the stand when the inmates are suing them, his opinion is not much different from theirs. When Jessica Mitford was writing *Kind and Usual Punishment*, her book on the prison business, she discovered, "Even the toughest wardens of the roughest prisons will quote some such figure off the record. Somewhere between 10 per cent and 25 per cent of 'hard-core' criminals are 'too dangerous' to be loosed on society." Ronald Goldfarb and Linda Singer reached a similar conclusion in their study *After Conviction*. "We have asked every experienced, practicing prison official we know," they said, "how many of the inmates currently held in confinement really need to be incarcerated in order to protect the public from personal injury. All agree that only a small minority of all the present inmates in American prisons—most estimated between 10 and 15 per cent—could be considered to be so dangerous."

Why are the prisons bursting at their seams if the professionals believe what they say they believe?

Their stock answer is that they don't control the number of prisoners. An official of the Texas Department of Corrections once patiently explained to me that not he but judges and juries sentence convicted offenders to serve time in his prisons, and then they stay there until they're paroled or their sentences are up or they die.

That's true as far as it goes. But prison officials could exercise their credibility as law-and-order types by telling legislatures and judges and every public forum they can find what they seem to tell only inquiring journalists and social scientists.

Moreover, correctional policies do affect the size of the population. The administration of discipline and the classification of inmates affect both the amount of "good time" prisoners earn (extra credit toward time served) and their parole eligibility. And, in the case of the Texas system, officials (including the one who lectured me) often used to testify in favor of legislation, such as bills affecting parole policy, which had the direct effect of increasing the number of inmates.

WHAT TO DO WITH CRIMINAL OFFENDERS, if not lock them up? This has been a major preoccupation of reformers. A task force of the American Friends Service Committee charged with studying crime and punishment in America pointed out with some exasperation in 1971 that ever since Alexis de Tocqueville and Charles Dickens separately expressed their condemnations of America's prisons, the experts' prescriptions for change had made no significant progress. "The apparent novelty," the group said, "is merely a manifestation of the public's ignorance of the history of penal and legal reform."

Aside from more extensive use of probation and parole, "community-based corrections" have been the reform of choice for the past twenty years. These are billed as "alternatives to incarceration" because they are supposed to be sentences meted out to people who otherwise would be sent to prison. The President's Crime Commission in 1967 and the National Advisory Commission in 1973 both advocated sentencing based on the principle of the "least restrictive alternative" appropriate to the individual offender.

There are new wrinkles, of course. A popular experiment is intensive-supervision probation—a program in which probation officers have small caseloads and a probationer has a team of supervisors instead of just one. In the age of Reagan, it was inevitable that economic programs would also enter the field; in one such, the states offer local jurisdictions financial incentives not to sentence offenders to the state prison but, instead, to figure out something to do with them at home.

Both these ideas show some promise. But so did many of the old kinds of "alternatives to incarceration."

The difficulty arises as the new programs become institutionalized. Instead of being a less restrictive alternative to prison, as intended, they become ways to "help" those offenders the system had no way to "help" in the past.

Say a man commits a minor crime, a nonviolent misdemeanor, his first offense. He has a stable home and job. Say the judge and court workers who make presentence recommendations must choose between sending him to jail and a fine or restitution. So the judge lectures him, fines him, and sends him on his way. If the court has a probation department, however, the judge chooses probation—the *more* restrictive alternative.

Halfway houses for parolees, designed to let people out of prison sooner than parole boards would have released them to society at large, became halfway houses for troublesome probationers: halfway in instead of halfway out.

When a program is new, it often operates as intended: to keep some offenders out of prison. But when the judges and prosecutors and pre-sentence investigators get used to having the program around, they start using it to slap more restrictions on the people who clearly shouldn't be jailed.

This pattern has been repeated time and again, with program after program. And it will happen again with the new "alternatives to incarceration."

The surprise would be if this system functioned other than it does. Most judges are people who enjoy exercising power and authority over other people—it's why they wanted to be judges. And most criminal-court personnel—the probation department caseworkers who do the pre-sentence investigations and supervise probationers—are social workers who think the "clients" are better off not left alone.

The proof is in the prison-population explosion. Almost twenty years ago, Congress passed the Omnibus Crime Control and Safe Streets Act, in the wake of the reformist prescriptions of the President's Crime Commission. Among many other things, the Safe Streets Act created the Law Enforcement Assistance Administration. Best known for its aid to police departments across the land—gifts of helicopter gunships for crowd control and SWAT teams for terrorist control—LEAA also gave the states millions of dollars in the 1970s and early 1980s to experiment with community-based correctional programs: alternatives to incarcertion. Some of the programs died quiet deaths after a few years; others live on as regular components of the system.

And now, after all that, the prison population has tripled. So has the number of people on parole. The number of probationers is eight times what it was twenty years ago. In fact, one in every thirty-five adult males in the United States is under correctional supervision. And *no one* knows how many people regularly get sucked into the informal pretrial programs that "divert" offenders, without benefit of conviction, into "voluntary" supervision and treatment programs.

Meanwhile, nothing much has happened to the crime rate.

IT WAS A PRETTY FALL SUNDAY IN NASHville, but threatening rain. A group of people—twenty, maybe a few more—gathered just outside the walls of the Tennessee State Prison around the perimeter of a grassy circular mound of earth with a flagpole in its middle. It was still too early for flags to be flying.

The people carried pots and pans, spoons and spatulas to bang on the pans, and other improvised tools for raising a racket. They sang hymns, held hands, walked around the circle, listened to a preacher, and prayed, but mostly they made noise. They took their text from Joshua at the Battle of Jericho; they were trying to make the walls come tumbling down.

"Bunch of religious yippies," muttered a man standing near me. He was keeping his distance, just outside the circle, snapping pictures. But the spirit was infectious, and his resistance was breaking down.

Then an inmate, a trustee, walked out the prison door, broke through our circle, and raised the flags. He was trying not to stare but couldn't help himself. He seemed to think we were out of our minds. Soon after going back inside, he reappeared along with a few other men. They watched from a distance. Some of us called to them to join us in the noise-making, but they wouldn't. Who would risk his trustee status to join a bunch of nuts who think they can make prisons disappear?

None of us expected the walls to crumble, of course, but we did really want to make prisons disappear. Some in the crowd, in fact, worked full-time toward that end. Not everyone thought all prisons should be abolished, but many did.

That was 1979. The demonstration was the closing event of an annual meeting of the Southern Coalition on Jails and Prisons. Coalition staff and sympathizers could be found in the forefront of the opposition any time a Southern state announced plans to build a new prison. There were like-minded activists in many other places and an umbrella group—the National Moratorium on Prison Construction, a project since the mid-1970s of the Unitarian Universalist Service Committee.

The people trying to stop prison construction didn't always win the individual battles, but sometimes they did. They also kept the issue alive and in the public eye.

No more. The National Moratorium closed its doors this spring. The Southern Coalition folks—many of them the same people who gathered eight years ago at the Tennessee prison—are still a bright spot of activism and still opposed to prison construction. But most of them have found it necessary to turn their attention to saving the lives of the thousand of Southerners languishing on Death Rows. Other prison deconstructionists burned out or decided other issues were more important.

It's been a long time since I heard about a demonstration like the one in Nashville, or even a concerted effort to stop a new prison.

Yet the problem, of course, is more overwhelming than ever—the states are building spaces to lock up an additional 100,000 people, and the Federal Bureau of Prisons figures it must be able to accommodate about 100,000 inmates by the turn of the century, almost 60,000 more than today.

ARE PRISONS APPROPRIATE PLACES EVEN for that 5 or 10 or 15 per cent of the prison population that the professionals think belong there?

Certainly for as long as our society is as unjust as it is, some people will react in dangerously violent ways to their environment. Probably a few would be that way even in a just society. And the rest of us need protection from them. Prisons as we know them, however, are not the answer, they only brutalize the violent among their inmates. Something different will be needed.

Who should decide, and on what grounds, which individuals should be incarcerated? Our present criminal-justice system certainly inspires little confidence in its ability to handle the task fairly—or even rationally. Can we devise a system that protects the individual "offender" as well as the rest of us?

In a long tradition of abolitionist thinking, no one has satisfactorily answered these questions, but they do not have to be answered before we begin undoing a great deal, if not all, of the evils of the present system. We can, today, start to let go of the first 90 per cent of the prison population, and figure out what to do with the rest when we have freed up all the mental and financial resources now used to lock the first half-million away.

There is something absurd, something not really believable, about a society with our wealth and talent that can find no solution but warehouses to its social problems. We have had 200 years to try to make the prison idea work. It doesn't and it won't. It will never be "reformed" into a system we can point to with pride. The time is long since past when we should abandon the idea and tear down the walls.

POSTSCRIPT

Will Tougher Sentencing Reduce Crime?

It may be said of crime—as Mark Twain said of the weather—that everyone talks about it but nobody does anything about it. Perhaps that is because the easy solutions only sound easy. If authorities are to "lock 'em all up," where are they going to put them? The public applauds tough talk but seems unwilling to pay for new prison space. On the other hand, getting at the so-called root causes of crime—which supposedly include poverty and discrimination—is no easier. This approach assumes that these phenomena *are* the basic causes of crime. Yet the rate of violent crime was much lower during the poverty-ridden, racist decade of the 1930s than it was during the affluent and enlightened 1960s. Unfortunately, crime is a problem that will not yield to slogans, whether those slogans are liberal or conservative in origin.

Dramatic increases in prison population and the rising cost of imprisonment have been accompanied by revelations of appalling conditions that cannot contribute to rehabilitation. Larry E. Sullivan, in *The Prison Reform Movement: Forlorn Hope* (Twayne, 1990), explores the possibilities of reforming prisons.

Much recent writing about crime and punishment examines the possibility of alternatives to prison, particularly for people guilty of so-called victimless crimes, such as marijuana smoking, curfew violations, or public drunkenness. Restitution, community work service, monitored home confinement, and other sanctions are considered in Andrew R. Klein's *Alternative Sentencing: A Practitioner's Guide* (Anderson, 1988).

In addition to sentencing reform, Michael Tonry and Franklin E. Zimring, the editors of *Reform and Punishment: Essays on Criminal Sentencing* (University of Chicago Press, 1983), look at how the criminal justice system deals with the mentally ill, and they examine sentencing in European countries. In *Criminal Violence, Criminal Justice* (Random House, 1978), Charles Silberman concludes that police action cannot do much to control crime if the community's morale and spirit of self-control have disintegrated.

No matter what solutions are attempted, Rocawich and Brubaker have helped to set the terms of the debate. Rocawich considers crime to be a reaction to people oppressed by our unjust society. Brubaker sees crime as a grievous threat to the community for which no excuse should be offered. For Rocawich, the solution is to rely less on prison and more on social reform. For Brubaker, such seemingly rational solutions miss the essential point: that people must understand the moral evil of crime. Both are adept at finding the weakness in the positions they reject. If together they fail to inspire fresh answers to the crime problem, they at least show us that the old answers, whether grounded upon "toughness" or "compassion," need considerable rethinking.

ISSUE 10

Is Capital Punishment Justified?

YES: Walter Berns, from *For Capital Punishment: Crime and the Morality of the Death Penalty* (Basic Books, 1979)

NO: Mary Meehan, from "The Death Penalty in the United States: Ten Reasons to Oppose It," *America* (November 20, 1982)

ISSUE SUMMARY

YES: Professor of government Walter Berns is convinced that the death penalty has a place in modern society and that it serves a need now, as it did when the Constitution was framed.
NO: Social writer Mary Meehan gives a variety of reasons, from the danger of killing the innocent to the immorality of killing even the guilty, why she thinks the death penalty is wrong.

Although capital punishment (the death penalty) is ancient, both the definition of a capital crime and the methods used to put convicted persons to death have changed. In eighteenth-century Massachusetts, capital crimes included blasphemy and the worship of false gods. Slave states often imposed the death penalty upon blacks for crimes that were punished by only two or three years' imprisonment when committed by whites. It has been estimated that in this century approximately 10 percent of all legal executions have been for the crime of rape, 1 percent for all other crimes except murder (robbery, burglary, attempted murder, etc.), and nearly 90 percent for the commission of murder.

Long before the Supreme Court severely limited the use of the death penalty, executions in the United States were becoming increasingly rare. In the 1930s there were 1,667; the total for the 1950s was 717. In the 1960s, the numbers fell even more dramatically. For example, seven persons were executed in 1965, one in 1966, and two in 1967. Put another way, in the 1930s and 1940s, there was 1 execution for every 60 or 70 homicides committed in states that had the death penalty; in the first half of the 1960s, there was 1 execution for every 200 homicides; and by 1966 and 1967, there were only 3 executions for approximately 20,000 homicides.

Then came the case of *Furman v. Georgia* (1972), which many thought—mistakenly—"abolished" capital punishment in America. Actually, only two members of the *Furman* majority thought that capital punishment *per se* violates the Eighth Amendment's injunction against "cruel and unusual punishment." The other three members of the majority took the view that capital punishment is unconstitutional only when applied in an arbitrary or a racially discriminatory manner, as they believed it was in this case. There were four dissenters in the *Furman* case, who were prepared to uphold capital punishment both in general and in this particular instance. Not surprisingly, then, with a slight change of Court personnel—and with a different case before the Court—a few years later, the majority vote went the other way.

In the latter case, *Gregg v. Georgia* (1976), the majority upheld capital punishment under certain circumstances. In his majority opinion in the case, Justice Potter Stewart noted that the law in question (a new Georgia capital punishment statute) went to some lengths to avoid arbitrary procedures in capital cases. For example, Georgia courts were not given complete discretion in handing out death sentences to convicted murderers, but had to consult a series of guidelines spelling out "aggravating circumstances," such as if the murder had been committed by someone already convicted of murder, if the murder endangered the lives of bystanders, and if the murder was committed in the course of a major felony. These guidelines, Stewart said, together with other safeguards against arbitrariness included in the new statute, preserved it against Eighth Amendment challenges.

Although the Court has upheld the constitutionality of the death penalty, it can always be abolished by state legislatures. However, that seems unlikely to happen in many states. If anything, the opposite is occurring. Almost immediately after the *Furman* decision of 1972, state legislatures began enacting new death penalty statutes designed to meet the objections raised in the case. By the time of the *Gregg* decision, 35 new death penalty statutes had been enacted.

In the readings that follow, Walter Berns focuses his defense upon the moral right of retribution and its compatibility with the American Constitution, while Mary Meehan sums up a number of widely used arguments against the death penalty.

YES
Walter Berns

CRIME AND THE MORALITY
OF THE DEATH PENALTY

It must be one of the oldest jokes in circulation. In the dark of a wild night a ship strikes a rock and sinks, but one of its sailors clings desperately to a piece of wreckage and is eventually cast up exhausted on an unknown and deserted beach. In the morning, he struggles to his feet and, rubbing his salt-encrusted eyes, looks around to learn where he is. The only human thing he sees is a gallows. "Thank God," he exclaims, "civilization." There cannot be many of us who have not heard this story or, when we first heard it, laughed at it. The sailor's reaction was, we think, absurd. Yet, however old the story, the fact is that the gallows has not been abolished in the United States even yet, and we count ourselves among the civilized peoples of the world. Moreover, the attempt to have it abolished by the U.S. Supreme Court may only have succeeded in strengthening its structure. . . .

Perhaps the Court began to doubt its premise that a "maturing society" is an ever more gentle society; the evidence on this is surely not reassuring. The steady moderating of the criminal law has not been accompanied by a parallel moderating of the ways of criminals or by a steadily evolving decency in the conditions under which men around the world must live their lives. . . .

An institution that lacks strength or purpose will readily be what its most committed constituents want it to be. Those who maintain our criminal justice institutions do not speak of deferring to public opinion but of the need to "rehabilitate criminals"—another pious sentiment. The effect, how-ever, is the same. They impose punishments only as a last resort and with the greatest reluctance, as if they were embarrassed or ashamed, and they avoid executing even our Charles Mansons. It would appear that Albert Camus was right when he said that "our civilization has lost the only values that, in a certain way, can justify [the death] penalty." It is beyond doubt that our intellectuals are of this opinion. The idea that the presence of a gallows could indicate the presence of a civilized people is, as I indicated at the outset, a joke. I certainly thought so the first time I heard the story; it was only a few years ago that I began to suspect that that sailor may have been right. What led me to change my mind was the phenomenon of Simon Wiesenthal.

Like most Americans, my business did not require me to think about criminals or, more precisely, the punishment of criminals. In a vague way, I was aware that there was some disagreement concerning the purpose of punishment—deterrence, rehabilitation, or retribution—but I had no reason then to decide which was right or to what extent they may all have been right. I did know that retribution was held in ill repute among criminologists. Then I began to reflect on the work of Simon Wiesenthal, who, from a tiny, one-man office in Vienna, has devoted himself since 1945 exclusively to the task of hunting down the Nazis who survived the war and escaped into the world. Why did he hunt them, and what did he hope to accomplish by finding them? And why did I respect him for devoting his life to this singular task? He says that his conscience forces him "to bring the guilty ones to trial." And if they are convicted, then what? Punish them, of course. But why? To rehabilitate them? The very idea is absurd. To incapacitate them? But they represent no present danger. To deter others from doing what they did? That is a hope too extravagant to be indulged. The answer—to me and, I suspect, everyone else who agrees that they should be punished—was clear: *to pay them back.* And how do you pay back SS Obersturmführer Franz Stangl, SS Untersturmführer Wilhelm Rosenbaum, SS Obersturmbannführer Adolf Eichmann, or someday—who knows?—Reichsleiter Martin Bormann? As the world knows, Eichmann was executed, and I suspect that most of the decent, *civilized* world agrees that this was the only way he could be paid back. . . .

The argument . . . does not turn on the answer to the utilitarian question of whether the death penalty is a deterrent . . . The evidence on this is unclear and, besides, as it is usually understood, deterrence is irrelevant. The real issue is whether justice permits or even requires the death penalty. I am aware that it is a terrible punishment, but there are terrible crimes and terrible criminals. . . .

Anger is expressed or manifested on those occasions when someone has acted in a manner that is thought to be unjust, and one of its bases is the opinion that men are responsible, and should be held responsible, for what they do. Thus, anger is accompanied not only by the pain caused by him who is the object of anger, but by the pleasure arising from the expectation of exacting revenge on someone who is thought to deserve it. We can become very angry with an inanimate object (the door we run into and then kick in return) only foolishly attributing responsibility to it, and we cannot do that for long, which is why we do not think of returning later to revenge ourselves on the door. For the same reason, we cannot be more than momentarily angry with an animate creature other than man: only a fool or worse would dream of taking revenge on a dog. And, finally, we tend to pity rather than to be angry with men who—because they are insane, for example—are not responsible for their acts. Anger, then, is a very human passion not only because only a human being can be angry, but also because it acknowledges the humanity of its objects: it holds them accountable for what they do. It is an expression of that element of the soul that is connected with the view that there is responsibility in the world; and in holding particular men responsible, it pays them that respect which is due them as men. Anger recognizes that only men have the capacity to be moral beings and, in so doing, acknowledges the dignity of human beings. Anger is somehow connected with justice, and it is this that modern penology has not understood; it tends, on the whole, to regard anger as merely a selfish passion. . . .

Criminals are properly the objects of anger, and the perpetrators of terrible crimes—for example, Lee Harvey Oswald and James Earl Ray—are properly the objects of great anger. They have done more than inflict an injury on an isolated individual; they have violated the foundations of trust and friendship, the necessary elements of a moral community, the only community worth living in. A moral community, unlike a hive of bees or a hill of ants, is one whose members are expected freely to obey the laws and, unlike a tyranny, are trusted to obey the laws. The criminal has violated that trust, and in so doing has injured not merely his immediate victim but the community as such. He has called into question the very possibility of that community by suggesting that men cannot be trusted freely to respect the property, the person, and the dignity of those with whom they are associated. If, then, men are not angry when someone else is robbed, raped, or murdered, the implication is that there is no moral community because those men do not care for anyone other than themselves. Anger is an expression of that caring, and society needs men who care for each other, who share their pleasures and their pains, and do so for the sake of the others. It is the passion that can cause us to act for reasons having nothing to do with selfish or mean calculation; indeed, when educated, it can become a generous passion, the passion that protects the community or country by demanding punishment for its enemies. It is the stuff from which heroes are made. . . .

THE CONSTITUTIONAL ARGUMENT

We Americans have debated the morality and necessity of the death penalty throughout almost the entire period of our experience as a nation, and, until 1976 when the Supreme Court ruled in favor of its constitutionality, it had been debated among us in constitutional terms, which is not true elsewhere. The Eighth Amendment clearly and expressly forbids the imposition of "cruel and unusual punishments," a prohibition that applies now to the states as well as to the national government; it was argued that the death penalty was such a punishment.

It is, of course, incontestable that the death penalty was not regarded as cruel and unusual by the men who wrote and ratified the amendment. They may have forbidden cruel and unusual punishments but they acknowledged the legitimacy of capital punishment when, in the Fifth Amendment, they provided that no person "shall be held to answer for a capital . . . crime, unless on a presentment or indictment of a Grand Jury," and when in the same amendment they provided that no one shall, for the same offense, "be twice put in jeopardy of life or limb," and when, in the Fifth as well as in the Fourteenth Amendment, they forbade, not the taking of life, but the taking of life "without due process of law." We also know that the same Congress which proposed the Eighth

Amendment also provided for the death penalty for murder and treason, and George Washington, despite powerful entreaties, could not be persuaded to commute the death sentence imposed on Major John Andre, the British officer and spy involved in Benedict Arnold's treachery. So the death penalty can be held to be cruel and unusual in the constitutional sense only if it has somehow become so in the passage of time. . . .

In 1958 the Supreme Court . . . said that the meaning of cruel and unusual depends on "the evolving standards of decency that mark the progress of a maturing society." Surely, it is argued, hanging or electrocution or gassing is, in our day, regarded as equally cruel as expatriation, if not more cruel. Is it not relevant that the American people have insisted that executions be carried out by more humane methods, that they not be carried out in public, and that the penalty be imposed for fewer and fewer crimes; and is it not significant that juries have shown a tendency to refuse to convict for capital crimes? In these ways the people are merely demonstrating what has been true for centuries, namely, that when given the opportunity to act, the average man (as opposed to judges and vindictive politicians) will refuse to be a party to legal murder. . . . The fact of the matter, or so it is alleged, is that American juries have shown an increasing tendency to avoid imposing the death penalty except on certain offenders who are distinguished not by their criminality but by their race or class. Justice Douglas emphasized this in his opinion in the 1972 capital punishment cases. "One searches our chronicles in vain for the execution of any members of the affluent strata of this society," he said. "The Leopolds and Loebs are given prison terms, not sentenced to death." . . . Death sentences are imposed not out of a hatred of the crimes committed, it is said, but out of a hatred of blacks. Of the 3,859 persons executed in the United States in the period 1930–1967, 2,066 or 54 percent, were black. More than half of the prisoners now under sentence of death are black. In short, the death penalty, we have been told, "may have served" to keep blacks, especially southern blacks, "in a position of subjugation and subservience." That in itself is unconstitutional.

In the 1972 cases only two of the nine justices of the Supreme Court argued that the death penalty as such is a violation of the Eighth Amendment, regardless of the manner of its imposition. Justice Brennan was persuaded by what he saw as the public's growing reluctance to impose it that the rejection of the death penalty "could hardly be more complete without becoming absolute." Yet, on the basis of his own evidence it is clear that the American people have not been persuaded by the arguments against the death penalty and that they continue to support it for *some* criminals—so long as it is carried out privately and as painlessly as possible. At the very time he was writing there were more than 600 persons on whom Americans had imposed the sentence of death. He drew the conclusion that the American people had decided that capital punishment does not comport with human dignity, and is therefore unconstitutional, but the facts do not support this conclusion. This may explain why his colleague, Justice Marshall, felt obliged to take up the argument.

Marshall acknowledged that the public opinion polls show that, on the whole, capital punishment is supported by a majority of the American people, but he denied the validity—or the "utililty"—of ascertaining opinion on this subject by simply polling the people. The polls ask the wrong question. It is not a question of whether the public accepts the death penalty, but whether the public when "fully informed as to the purposes of the penalty and its liabilities would find [it] shocking, unjust, and unacceptable."

> In other words, the question with which we must deal is not whether a substantial proportion of American citizens would today, if polled, opine that capital punishment is barbarously cruel, but whether they would find it to be so in the light of all information presently available.

This information, he said, "would almost surely convince the average citizen that the death penalty was unwise." He conceded that this citizen might nevertheless support it as a way of exacting retribution, but, in his view, the Eighth Amendment forbids "punishment for the sake of retribution"; besides, he said, no one has ever seriously defended capital punishment on retributive grounds. It has been defended only with "deterrent or similar theories." From here he reached his conclusion that "the great mass of citizens" would decide that the death penalty is not merely unwise but also "immoral and therefore unconstitutional." They would do so if they knew what he knew, and what he knew was that retribution is illegitimate and unconstitutional and that the death penalty is excessive and unnecessary, being no more capable than life imprisonment of deterring the crimes for which it is imposed. He conceded that the evidence on the deterrence issue is not "convincing beyond all doubt, but it is persuasive." Thus, the death penalty *is* cruel and un-

usual punishment because the American people *ought* to think so. Shortly after this decision thirty-five states enacted new statutes authorizing the death penalty for certain crimes.

This public support for capital punishment is a puzzling fact, especially in our time. It is a policy that has almost no articulate supporters in the intellectual community. The subject has been vigorously debated and intensively investigated by state after state and country after country—California and Connecticut, Texas and Wisconsin; Britain and Canada, Ceylon and "Europe"; even the United Nations; and, of course, various committees of the U.S. Congress. Among those willing to testify and publish their views, the abolitionists outweigh the "retentionists" both in number and, with significant exceptions, in the kind of authority that is recognized in the worlds of science and letters. Yet the Harris poll reports 59 percent of the general population to be in favor of capital punishment, and that proportion is increasing—at this time, at least. . . .

It is sometimes argued that the opinion polls are deceptive insofar as the question is posed abstractly—and can only be posed abstractly—and that the responses of these publics would be different if they had to decide whether particular persons should be executed. This is entirely possible, or even probable; nevertheless, there is no gainsaying the fact that juries, for whom the issue is very concrete indeed, continue to impose death sentences on a significant number of criminals. Ordinary men and women seem to be unpersuaded by the social science argument against deterrence, or they regard it as irrelevant: they seem to be oblivious to the possibility that innocent people might be executed; they know nothing about the natural public law disagreement between Beccaria and Kant; they surely do not share the opinion that executions are contrary to God's commands; indeed, they seem to display the passions of many a biblical character in their insistence that, quite apart from all these considerations, murderers should be paid back. In fact, the essential difference between the public and the abolitionists is almost never discussed in our time; it has to do with retribution: the public insists on it without using the word and the abolitionists condemn it whenever they mention it.

The abolitionists condemn it because it springs from revenge, they say, and revenge is the ugliest passion in the human soul. They condemn it because it justifies punishment for the sake of punishment alone, and they are opposed to punishment that serves no purpose beyond inflicting pain on its victims. Strictly speaking, they are opposed to punishment. They may, like Beccaria, sometimes speak of life imprisonment as the alternative to executions, but they are not in fact advocates of life imprisonment and will not accept it. . . .

They condemn retribution because they see it, rightly or wrongly, as the only basis on which the death penalty can be supported. To kill an offender is not only unnecessary but precludes the possibility of reforming him, and reformation, they say, is the only civilized response to the criminal. Even murderers—indeed, especially murderers—are capable of being redeemed or of repenting their crimes. . . .

The goal of the abolitionists is not merely the elimination of capital punishment but the reform or rehabilitation of the criminal, *even*, if he is a murderer. The public that favors capital punishment is of the opinion that the murderer deserves to be punished, and does not deserve to be treated, even if by treatment he *could* be rehabilitated. . . .

When abolitionists speak of the barbarity of capital punishment and when Supreme Court justices denounce expatriation in almost identical language, they ought to be reminded that men whose moral sensitivity they would not question have supported both punishments. Lincoln, for example, albeit with a befitting reluctance, authorized the execution of 267 persons during his presidency, and ordered the "Copperhead" Clement L. Vallandigham banished; and it was Shakespeare's sensitivity to the moral issue that required him to have Macbeth killed. They should also be given some pause by the knowledge that the man who originated the opposition to both capital and exilic punishment, Cesare Beccaria, was a man who argued that there is no morality outside the positive law and that it is reasonable to love one's property more than one's country. There is nothing exalted in these opinions, and there is nothing exalted in the versions of them that appear in today's judicial opinions. Capital punishment was said by Justice Brennan to be a denial of human dignity, but in order to reach this conclusion he had to reduce human dignity to the point where it became something possessed by "the vilest criminal." Expatriation is said by the Court to be unconstitutional because it deprives a man of his right to have rights, which *is* his citizenship, and no one, no matter what he does, can be dispossessed of the right to have rights. (Why not a right to the right to have rights?) Any notion of what Justice Frankfurter in dissent referred to as "the communion of our citizens," of a community that can be violated by murderers or traitors, is wholly absent from these opinions; so too is any notion that it is one function of the law to protect that community.

But, contrary to abolitionist hopes and expectations, the Court did not invalidate the death penalty. It upheld it. It upheld it on retributive grounds. In doing so, it recognized, at least implicitly, that the American people are entitled *as a people* to demand that criminals be paid back, and that the worst of them be made to pay back with their lives. In doing this, it gave them the means by which they might strengthen the law that makes them a people, and not a mere aggregation of selfish individuals.

NO

Mary Meehan

THE DEATH PENALTY IN THE UNITED STATES: TEN REASONS TO OPPOSE IT

Over 1,000 state prisoners are on death row in America today. A Justice Department official recently said that many of them are exhausting their appeals and that we may soon "witness executions at a rate approaching the more than three per week that prevailed during the 1930's."

On Capitol Hill, meanwhile, there is an effort to restore the death penalty as a punishment for certain Federal crimes. A bill to accomplish this was approved by the Judiciary Committee in a 13-to-6 vote last year when conservatives lined up for the death penalty and liberals declaimed in vain against it. [Despite committee approval the measure failed to pass Congress. But in 1988 a new drug law was passed, which permitted the death penalty for major drug traffickers who commit or counsel murder.—Eds.] Yet one need not be a certified liberal in order to oppose the death penalty. Richard Viguerie, premier fund-raiser of the New Right, is a firm opponent of capital punishment.

Some of the arguments against the death penalty are essentially conservative, and many others transcend ideology. No one has to agree with all of the arguments in order to reach a decision. As President Reagan has said in another context, doubt should always be resolved on the side of life.

Nor need one be "soft on crime" in order to oppose the death penalty. Albert Camus, an opponent of capital punishment, said: "We know enough to say that this or that major criminal deserves hard labor for life. But we don't know enough to decree that he be shorn of his future—in other words, of the chance we all have of making amends."

But many liberals in our country, by their naïve ideas about quick rehabilitation and by their support for judicial discretion in sentencing, have done much to create demand for the death penalty they abhor. People are right to be alarmed when judges give light sentences for murder and other violent crimes. It is reasonable for them to ask: "Suppose some crazy judge lets him out, and members of my family are his next victims?" The inconsistency of the judicial system leads many to support the death penalty.

There are signs that some liberals now understand the problem. Senators Patrick Leahy (D., Vt.) and Edward Kennedy (D., Mass.), in opposing the death-penalty bill approved by the Senate Judiciary Committee, are suggesting as an alternative "a real life sentence" for murder and "heinous crimes." By this they mean a mandatory life sentence without possibility of parole. And if we adopt [former] Chief Justice Warren Burger's proposal about making prisons into "factories with fences," perhaps murderers can pay for their prison room and board and also make financial restitution to families they have deprived of breadwinners.

With these alternatives in mind, let us consider 10 good reasons to oppose the death penalty.

1. *There is no way to remedy the occasional mistake.* One of the witnesses against the death penalty before the Senate committee last year was Earl Charles, a man who spent over three years on a Georgia death row for murders he did not commit. Another witness remarked that, had Mr. Charles faced a system "where the legal apparatus was speedier and the death penalty had been carried out more expeditiously, we would now be talking about the late Mr. Charles and bemoaning our error."

What happens when the mistake is discovered *after* a man has been executed for a crime he did not commit? What do we say to his widow and children? Do we erect an apologetic tombstone over his grave?

These are not idle questions. A number of persons executed in the United States were later cleared by confessions of those who had actually committed the crimes. In other cases, while no one else confessed, there was great doubt that the condemned were guilty. Watt Espy, an Alabamian who has done intensive research on American executions, says that he has "every reason to believe" that 10 innocent men were executed in Alabama alone. Mr. Espy cites names, dates and other specifics of the cases. He adds that there are similar cases in virtually every state.

We might consider Charles Péguy's words about the turn-of-the-century French case in which Capt. Alfred Dreyfus was wrongly convicted of treason: "We said that a single injustice, a single crime, a single illegality, particularly if it is officially recorded, confirmed . . . that a single crime shatters and is sufficient to shatter the whole social pact, the whole social contract, that a single legal crime, a single dishonorable act will bring about the loss of one's honor, the dishonor of a whole people."

2. *There is racial and economic discrimination in application of the death penalty.* This is an old complaint, but one that many believe has been remedied by court-mandated safeguards. All five of the prisoners executed since 1977—one shot, one gassed and three electrocuted—were white. This looks like a morbid kind of affirmative action plan, making up for past discrimination against blacks. But the five were not representative of the death-row population, except in being male. About 99 percent of the death-row inmates are men.

Of the 1,058 prisoners on death row by Aug. 20, 1982, 42 percent were black, whereas about 12 percent of the United States population is black. Those who receive the death penalty still tend to be poor, poorly educated and represented by public defenders or court-appointed lawyers. They are not the wealthy murderers of Perry Mason or Agatha Christie fame.

Discriminatory application of the death penalty, besides being unjust to the condemned, suggests that some victims' lives are worth more than others. A study published in Crime & Delinquency (October 1980) found that, of black persons in Florida who commit murder, "those who kill whites are nearly 40 times more likely to be sentenced to death than those who kill blacks."

Even Walter Berns, an articulate proponent of the death penalty, told the Senate Judiciary Committee last year that capital punishment "has traditionally been imposed in this country in a grossly discriminatory fashion" and said that "it remains to be seen whether this country can impose the death penalty without regard to race or class." If it cannot, he declared, then capital punishment "will have to be invalidated on equal-protection grounds."

It is quite possible to be for the death penalty in theory ("If this were a just world, I'd be for it"), but against it in practice ("It's an unjust, crazy, mixed-up world, so I'm against it").

3. *Application of the death penalty tends to be arbitrary and capricious; for similar crimes, some are sentenced to death while others are not.* Initially two men were charged with the killing for which John Spenkelink was electrocuted in Florida in 1979. The second man turned state's evidence and was freed; he remarked: "I didn't intend for John to take the rap. It just worked out that way."

Soon after the Spenkelink execution, former San Francisco official Dan White received a prison sentence of seven years and eight months in prison for killing two people—the Mayor of San Francisco and another city official.

Anyone who follows the news can point to similar disparities. Would the outcome be much different if we decided for life or death by rolling dice or spinning a roulette wheel?

4. *The death penalty gives some of the worst offenders publicity that they do not deserve.* Gary Gilmore and Steven Judy received reams of publicity as they neared their dates with the grim reaper. They had a chance to expound before a national audience their ideas about crime and punishment, God and country, and anything else that happened to cross their minds. It is hard to imagine two men less deserving of a wide audience.

It can be argued, of course, that if executions become as widespread and frequent as proponents of the death penalty hope, the publicity for each murderer will decline. That may be so, but each may still be a media celebrity on a statewide basis.

While the death penalty undoubtedly deters some would-be murderers, there is evidence that it encourages others—especially the unstable who are attracted to media immortality like moths to a flame. If instead of facing heady weeks before television cameras, they faced a lifetime of obscurity in prison, the path of violence might seem less glamorous to them.

5. *The death penalty involves medical doctors, who are sworn to preserve life, in the act of killing.* This issue has been much discussed in recent years because several states have provided for execution by lethal injection. In 1980 the American Medical Association, responding to this innovation, declared that a doctor should not participate in an execution. But it added that a doctor may determine or certify death in any situation.

The A.M.A. evaded a major part of the ethical problem. When doctors use their stethoscopes to indicate whether the electric chair has done its job, they are assisting the executioner.

6. *Executions have a corrupting effect on the public.* Thomas Macaulay said of the Puritans that they "hated bear-baiting, not because it gave pain to the bear, but because it gave pleasure to the spectators." While wrong on the first point, they were right on the second. There is something indecent in the rituals that surround executions and the excitement— even the entertainment—that they provide to the public. There is the cat-and-mouse ritual of the appeals process, with prisoners sometimes led right up to the execution chamber and then given a stay of execution. There are the last visits from family, the last dinner, the last walk, the last words. Television cameras, which have fought their way into courtrooms and nearly everywhere else, may some day push their way right up to the execution chamber and give us all, in living color, the very last moments.

7. *The death penalty cannot be limited to the worst cases.* Many people who oppose capital punishment have second thoughts whenever a particularly brutal murder occurs. When a Richard Speck or Charles Manson or Steven Judy emerges, there is a tendency to say, "That one *really* deserves to die." Disgust, anger and genuine fear support the second thoughts.

But it is impossible to write a death penalty law in such a way that it will apply only to the Specks and Mansons and Judys of this world. And, given the ingenuity of the best lawyers money can buy, there is probably no way to apply it to the worst murderers who happen to be wealthy.

The death penalty, like every other form of violence, is extremely difficult to limit once the "hard cases" persuade society to let down the bars in order to solve a few specific problems. A sentence intended for Charles Manson is passed instead on J. D. Gleaton, a semiliterate on South Carolina's death row who had difficulty understanding his trial. Later he said: "I don't know anything about the law that much and when they are up there speaking those big words, I don't even know what they are saying." Or Thomas Hays, under sentence of death in Oklahoma and described by a fellow inmate as "nutty as a fruit cake." Before his crime, Mr. Hays was committed to mental hospitals several times; afterwards, he was diagnosed as a paranoid schizophrenic.

8. *The death penalty is an expression of the absolute power of the state; abolition of that penalty is a much-needed limit on government power.* What makes the state so pure that it has the right to take life? Look at the record of governments throughout history—so often operating with deception, cruelty and greed, so often becoming masters of the citizens they are supposed to serve. "Forbidding a man's execution," Camus said, "would amount to proclaiming publicly that society and the state are not absolute values." It would amount to saying that there are some things even the state may not do.

There is also the problem of the state's involving innocent people in a premeditated killing. "I'm personally opposed to killing and violence," said the prison warden who had to arrange Gary Gilmore's execution, "and having to do that is a difficult responsibility." Too often, in killing and violence, the state compels people to act against their consciences.

And there is the point that government should not give bad examples— especially not to children. Earl Charles, a veteran of several years on death row for crimes he did not commit, tried to explain this last year: "Well, it is difficult for me to sit down and talk to my son about 'thou shalt not kill,' when the state itself . . . is saying, 'Well, yes, we can kill under certain circumstances.' " With great understatement, Mr. Charles added, "That is difficult. I mean, that is confusing to him."

9. *There are strong religious reasons for many to oppose the death penalty.* Some find compelling the thought that Cain, the first murderer, was not executed but was marked with a special sign and made a wanderer upon the face of the earth.

Richard Viguerie developed his position on capital punishment by asking what Christ would say and do about it. "I believe that a strong case can be made," Mr. Viguerie wrote in a recent book, "that Christ would oppose the killing of a human being as punishment for a crime." This view is supported by the New Testament story about the woman who faced execution by stoning (John 8:7, "He that is without sin among you, let him cast the first stone").

Former Senator Harold Hughes (D., Iowa), arguing against the death penalty in 1974, declared: " 'Thou shalt not kill' is the shortest of the Ten Commandments, uncomplicated by qualification or exception. . . . It is as clear and awesomely commanding as the powerful thrust of chain lightning out of a dark summer sky."

10. *Even the guilty have a right to life.* Leszek Syski is a Maryland antiabortion activist who says that he "became convinced that the question of whether or not murderers deserve to die is the wrong one. The real question is whether other humans have a right to kill them." He concluded that they do not after conversations with an opponent of capital punishment who asked, "Why don't we torture prisoners? Torturing them is less than killing them." Mr. Syski believes that "torture is dehumanizing, but capital punishment is the essence of dehumanization."

Richard Viguerie reached his positions on abortion and capital punishment independently, but does see a connection between the two issues: "To me, life is sacred," Mr. Viguerie says. "And I don't believe I have a right to terminate someone else's life either way—by abortion or capital punishment." Many others in the prolife movement have come to the same conclusion. They don't think they have a right to play God and they don't believe that the state encourages respect for life when it engages in premeditated killing.

Camus was right: We know enough to say that some crimes require severe punishment. We do not know enough to say when anyone should die.

POSTSCRIPT

Is Capital Punishment Justified?

Opinion on the death penalty has always been sharply divided in the United States. While Massachusetts in 1785 defined 9 capital crimes (that is, crimes punishable by death) and North Carolina as late as 1837 had more than 20, other states rejected the death sentence entirely at an early date. American sentiment has been so divided that at least 11 states have abolished the death penalty only to restore it some years later.

In the readings in this issue, Mary Meehan employs a variety of arguments to make her case against the death penalty. Berns takes a different approach. He narrows in on one of the more controversial justifications for punishment—retribution, "paying back" the criminal—and tries to show that it speaks to something decent and humane in our nature. Neither of these closely reasoned arguments is likely to be upset by further statistical or historical data. Facts, even inconvenient ones, can usually be incorporated into a wide variety of viewpoints. Nevertheless, the debate can only be enriched by empirical study, and the student will find a trove of it in William J. Bowers's *Executions in America* (Lexington Books, 1974). The movement that led to the abolition of the death penalty in Great Britain prompted the publication of several books, the most stimulating of which is Arthur Koestler and C. H. Rolph's *Hanged by the Neck* (Penguin Books, 1961). Probably the most reflective, and almost certainly the most engrossing, literature on the subject is to be found in the many books dealing with the executions of Sacco and Vanzetti (plays and films have also dealt with their case), the Rosenbergs, and Caryl Chessman. In each of these cases, deep feelings favoring and opposing their execution were aroused by political issues and questions regarding their guilt, as well as by divided sentiments on the exercise of capital punishment.

Apart from the constitutional issues, the debate is more narrowly drawn than in earlier times. Although the death penalty is sometimes urged as punishment for such acts as treason or skyjacking, it is principally considered in connection with the crime of murder. There is little dispute over the proposition that the manner of execution should be as painless as possible (no one is drawn and quartered in civilized society), although there is no unanimity of opinion about whether death by electrocution, gas, or hanging best meets that test. Some states, such as Texas and New Jersey, have adopted the method of fatal injections, though the experience with its use in Texas has raised doubts about its painlessness. It may well be that the firing squad, perhaps the most violent means of execution permitted in the United States, could also be the quickest and most painless. However, how or how often to impose capital punishment is not the question society must examine, but whether we should take a life for a life.

ISSUE 11

Is Affirmative Action Reverse Discrimination?

YES: Stephen L. Carter, from *Reflections of an Affirmative Action Baby* (Basic Books, 1991)

NO: Herbert Hill, from "Race, Affirmative Action, and the Constitution," Rosenberg/Humphrey Lecture at City College of New York (April 27, 1988)

ISSUE SUMMARY

YES: Law professor Stephen L. Carter expresses his concern that affirmative action programs may lower standards and deprive African Americans of the incentive necessary to achieve excellence.

NO: Professor of African American studies Herbert Hill argues that affirmative action is necessary to reverse America's long history of racist practices.

"We didn't land on Plymouth Rock, my brothers and sisters—Plymouth Rock landed on *us!*" Malcolm X's observation is borne out by the facts of American history. Snatched from their native land, transported thousands of miles—in a nightmare of disease and death—and sold into slavery, blacks were reduced to the legal status of farm animals. Even after emancipation, blacks were segregated from whites—in some states by law, and by social practice almost everywhere. American apartheid continued for another century.

In 1954 the Supreme Court declared state-compelled segregation in schools unconstitutional, and it followed up that decision with others that struck down many forms of official segregation. Still, discrimination survived, and in most southern states blacks were either discouraged or prohibited from exercising their right to vote. Not until the 1960s was compulsory segregation finally and effectively challenged. Between 1964 and 1968 Congress passed the most sweeping civil rights legislation since the end of the Civil War. It banned discrimination in employment, public accommodations (hotels, motels, restaurants, etc.), and housing; it also guaranteed voting rights for blacks and even authorized federal officials to take over the job of voter registration in areas suspected of disenfranchising blacks. Today, several agencies in the federal government exercise sweeping powers to enforce these civil rights measures.

But is that enough? Equality of condition between blacks and whites seems as elusive as ever. The black unemployment rate is double that of whites, and the percentage of black families living in poverty is nearly four times that of whites. Only a small percentage of blacks ever make it into medical school or law school.

Advocates of affirmative action have focused upon these *de facto* differences to bolster their argument that it is no longer enough just to stop discrimination. The damage done by three centuries of racism now has to be remedied, they argue, and effective remediation requires a policy of "affirmative action." At the heart of affirmative action is the use of "numerical goals." Opponents call them "racial quotas." Whatever the name, what they imply is the setting aside of a certain number of jobs or positions for blacks or other historically oppressed groups. Opponents charge that affirmative action really amounts to reverse discrimination, that it penalizes innocent people simply because they are white, that it often results in unqualified appointments, and that it ends up harming blacks instead of helping them.

Affirmative action has had an uneven history in U.S. federal courts. In *Regents of the University of California v. Bakke* (1978), which marked the first time the Supreme Court directly dealt with the merits of affirmative action, a 5–4 majority ruled that a white applicant to a medical school had been wrongly excluded due to the school's affirmative action policy; yet the majority also agreed that "race-conscious" policies may be used in admitting candidates—as long as they do not amount to fixed quotas. The ambivalence of *Bakke* has run through the Court's treatment of the issue since 1978. Decisions have gone one way or the other depending on the precise circumstances of the case (such as whether it was a federal or state policy, whether or not it was mandated by a congressional statute, and whether quotas were required or simply permitted). In recent years, however, most of the Court's decisions seem to have run against affirmative action programs.

In the following selections, Stephen L. Carter and Herbert Hill debate the merits of affirmative action. Carter worries that such programs may lower standards and rob African Americans of the incentive to achieve excellence, while Hill, who is a former labor director of the National Association for the Advancement of Colored People, maintains that they are essential if America is ever to undo the effects of racism.

YES

Stephen L. Carter

SPECIAL BUT EQUAL

I have no illusion that we can (and, I think, no desire that we should) move toward a world in which nobody notices that anybody is different from anybody else, for that would be a world made dull and (literally) colorless, a world in which no subculture could celebrate itself or call upon the larger culture to share, even for a moment, its ethnic pride. I do not even want to insist that the ideal government would at all times and at all places be entirely blind to color, because that stance would make it impossible for the state to play a role in celebrating those same achievements. What is needed, rather, is the development of a better grammar of race, a way through which we can at once take account of it and not punish it.

And a sensible way to start, so it seems to me, is to say that with all the various instances in which race might be relevant, either to the government or to individuals, it will not be used as an indicator of merit—no one will be more valued than anyone else because of skin color. The corollary is that everyone's merit would therefore be judged by the same tests, and if the tests in question are unfair . . . then they will be swept away *and replaced with something else.*

It is that last step, I think, that is often missed in debates over qualifications for admission or employment. No matter how bad one might think current standards are, some standard will be used, either explicitly or implicitly. My argument is that the standard should be explicit, and that once it is selected, everyone should be required to meet it.

And yet, in a nation with the turbulent racial history of this one, one must wonder: Somewhere along the way, has there been an error of analysis? Were the nationalists right—is this path to the profession simply a lure to get us to give up on true freedom? Mario Baeza, a member of New York's legal elite who also happens to be black, has put the dilemma this way: "You go to law school, you study like crazy, *and* you have to continually wonder, Am I adopting a way of thinking that could be used to enslave me?" This possibility lies very near the core of the diversity movement, which counsels

From Stephen L. Carter, *Reflections of an Affirmative Action Baby* (Basic Books, 1991). Copyright © 1991 by Basic Books, Inc. Reprinted by permission of Basic Books, a division of HarperCollins Publishers. Notes omitted.

people of color against what is usually termed surrender of their identity in the cause of success. The same possibility, albeit put in far less sophisticated terms, motivates those black children who tell other kids that studying and even going to class is acting white. Why else, the nationalists demanded back in the 1960s, would whitey have made the opportunity of higher education available? Clearly, the power structure has something in mind, and whatever it is . . . cannot possibly be good for people who are black.

All of which returns us to the matter of academic and professional standards. There, too, it is whispered (and sometimes shouted) that people of color are victims of a plan—of the centuries of affirmative action favoring white males, for example, or at least of the virulent societal racism that has held us in a subordinate status. When one challenges racial preferences on the ground that they sometimes result in the admission or employment of people not as good (as well prepared, as professionally capable) as some who are turned away, or even on the ground that preferences call into question the legitimate achievements of very smart and very capable people of color, the modern vision of affirmative action quickly turns the challenge back on itself: the standards by which these judgments are made, the standards that black people are often less able than white people to meet, are said to lack objectivity, to import cultural bias, or simply to be racist. The idea that even if all of this is true, we should aim to meet and beat them anyway—that we should put ourselves beyond criticism on this ground, as well as on the ground of our leaders' conduct—is quickly dismissed as irrelevant, or as a smokescreen, or as naive, or even as thinking white.

But what it really is, is thinking like a professional. To rise to the pinnacle of professional success, a black person must function in an integrated world, but to do so is no more a betrayal of one's birthright than it is for white people to do the same thing. As Mario Baeza has put it, resolving his own dilemma, "I'm integrated, but I've never tried to be white. That's not what I aspire to in life."

The professional world is competitive, now more than ever, and has little time or space for argument over what should count as standards of achievement. In the professions, unlike the campuses, there is a market test: one either performs well enough to justify one's compensation or one does not. And it is because successful professionals know this, I think, that many of them have grown impatient with the argument over affirmative action for hiring and advancement in their fields. "I've made it because I'm good," said [one black] corporate executive, . . . and that, at bottom, is what all professionals, black or white, must believe in order to succeed.

Making it because one is good is not a conceit that we develop in order to live in white America. It is, rather, the outcome of a deliberate decision to try to live in a world that encourages and rewards excellence. In "The Duty of the Intellectual," the thought-provoking essay that opens his fine book *Pathos of Power,* the renowned psychologist Kenneth Clark makes the following observation:

An unfinished task of our society— probably one that must be clearly identified, defined, and justified by intellectuals—is to learn to differentiate between democratic philosophy, goals, and methods and stable standards of excellence. Literalistic egalitarianism, appropriate and relevant to problems of political and social life, cannot be permitted to invade and dominate the crucial areas of the intellect, aesthetics, and ethics.

Clark's is straightforward and sensible: a commitment to an inclusionary politics bears no necessary relation to a judgment about what is good and right and what is bad and wrong. Affirmative action, diversity, cultural pluralism, and the like are all simply words or, too often, slogans; what matters is the understanding of society that they signify. For whatever one might want to call the effort to broaden opportunities for groups that have been kept out of the mainstream of American life, it seems to me quite clear—indeed, it seems to be common rhetorical ground among all sides in the affirmative action dispute, but bears repeating—that progress should never come at the price of pretending that nobody is ever better than anybody else at anything.

One must be very careful about the leveling that is implicit in the conversational habit that affirmative action has become. Elite educational institutions, after all, owe their existence in part to a belief that some people are smarter and more likely to achieve. This, I take it, is just the reason that people of color are beating so hard on the doors to get in. So I wince when I hear supporters of preferences talk blithely of tossing out the window standards of excellence—for college entry, grading, hiring, or promotion—that might actually be rational. Sometimes the argument is that the standards are the playthings of white males, manipulated by this amorphous set for their own advantage. Sometimes the argument is that standards are not possible. Sometimes the argument is that meritocracy is itself a bad idea.

My own view is that the traditional justification for accepting a concept of merit is correct: standards of excellence are a requisite of civilization. To say instead that excellence cannot be judged is to say that excellence is not possible. To say that excellence is not possible is to say, really, that nothing is better than anything else. And if nothing is better than anything else, then the entire project of human progress is a joke. But it isn't a joke. There is such a thing as excellence; there is such a thing as civilization. We live in a world of brilliant scientific discoveries, remarkable acts of moral and spiritual courage, profound literary achievements, and outstanding professional performances. We live in a world that cares about excellence, needs it, and should not be afraid to judge it. . . .

TO THINK ABOUT THE FUTURE IS ALSO TO reflect on the past. If we as a people were not defeated by slavery and Jim Crow, we will not be beaten by the demise of affirmative action. Before there were any racial preferences, before there was a federal antidiscrimination law with any teeth, our achievements were already on the rise: our middle class was growing, as was our rate of college matriculation—both of them at higher rates than in the years since. Black professionals, in short, should not do much worse without affirmative action than we are doing with it, and thrown on our own resources and knowing that we have no choice but to meet the same tests as everybody else, we may do better.

We must be about the business of defining a future in which we can be fair to ourselves and demand opportunities without falling into the trap of letting others tell us that our horizons are limited, that we cannot make it without assistance. I recall the historian Vincent Harding's discussion of black reaction to the Emancipation Proclamation and the prospect of a constitutional amendment banning slavery. These were fine as far as they went, says Harding, but "white definitions of black people's freedom had never been sufficient." Therefore, "the black community was not idly waiting for answers and clarifications from others." Instead, black people were "working toward their own answers, attempting in their own wisdom, through their own vision and prayer, to come to terms with this new stage of the struggle."

The likely demise, or severe restriction, of racial preferences will also present for us a new stage of struggle, and we should treat it as an opportunity, not a burden. It is our chance to make ourselves free of the assumptions that too often underlie affirmative action, assumptions about our intellectual incapacity and other competitive deficiencies. It is our chance to prove to a doubting, indifferent world that our future as a people is in our hands.

My own faith is that we can, and will, survive in a world free of preferences. They are a convenience, true, but in their current form, as I have explained, they can also be an insult or, worse, counterproductive. Besides, the battle to preserve affirmative action will be won, if at all, only at an enormous cost—and after all of our political capital has been spent, the fight may well be lost anyway. Moreover, for all that it has assisted the black middle class, affirmative action has done nothing at all for the true victims of racism. We can talk all we want about diversity, about the need to bring into the corridors of power the excluded viewpoint of the oppressed, but that is not the same as bringing into the corridors of power the oppressed themselves.

To continue to make affirmative action the centerpiece of our strategy for the future will also have another cost, however: the continuing collapse of solidarity in our community. When white people criticize affirmative action, the response is anger. When black people criticize it, the response is bewilderment, pain, and, in the end, open hostility. In the difficult years ahead, we cannot afford the luxury of letting our squabble over preferences, which help mostly those who can best survive without them, interfere with the needed dialogue on what to do next. And the cost in solidarity might be greater than some would imagine, for it is my sense (admittedly anecdotal) that among successful black professionals, there is a growing uneasiness with any forms of affirmative action that allow black people to meet different standards than other people. As one black director of an investment banking firm put it, "I feel that if we're all on a level playing field, we'll be stronger."

NO

Herbert Hill

RACE, AFFIRMATIVE ACTION, AND THE CONSTITUTION

1988 begins the third century of the United States Constitution and having survived the ritual celebration of the 1987 bicentennial, it is appropriate that we take a fresh critical look at that document and its legacy. As we examine the historical circumstances in which the Constitution emerged, we must acknowledge the continuing centrality of race in the evolution of the Constitution and of this nation.

Under the original Constitution, a system of slavery based on race existed for many generations, a system that legally defined black people as property and declared them to be less than human. Under its authority an extensive web of racist statutes and judicial decisions emerged over a long period. The Naturalization Law of 1790 explicitly limited citizenship to "white persons," the Fugitive Slave Acts of 1793 and 1850 made a travesty of law and dehumanized the nation, and the Dred Scott Decision of 1857, where Chief Justice Taney declared that blacks were not people but "articles of merchandise," are but a few of the legal monuments grounded on the assumption that this was meant to be a white man's country and that all others had no rights in the law.

With the ratification of the 13th, 14th, and 15th Amendments in 1865, 1868 and 1870 respectively and the adoption of the Civil Rights Acts of 1866, 1870 and 1875, a profoundly different set of values was asserted. This new body of law affirmed that justice and equal treatment were not for white persons exclusively, and that black people, now citizens of the nation, also were entitled to "the equal protection of the laws."

The Civil Rights Amendments and the three related Acts proclaim a very different concept of the social order than that implicit in the "three-fifths" clause contained in Section 2 of Article 1 of the Constitution. A concept that required the reconstruction of American society so that it could be free of slavery, free of a racism that was to have such terrible long-term consequences for the entire society.

From Herbert Hill, "Race, Affirmative Action, and the Constitution." Copyright © 1988 by Herbert Hill. Reprinted by permission. This article was given as the Third Annual Hubert Humphrey Memorial Lecture, City College of New York, April 27, 1988.

The struggle to realize the great potential of the Reconstruction amendments to the Constitution, the struggle to create a just, decent and compassionate society free of racist oppression, is a continuing struggle that has taken many different forms in each era since the Reconstruction Period and one that continues today. In our own time the old conflict between those interests intent on perpetuating racist patterns rooted in the past and the forces that struggle for a society free of racism and its legacy continues in the raging battle for and against affirmative action.

During the late 1950's and early 1960's, as a result of direct confrontation with the system of state imposed segregation, together with the emergence of a new body of constitutional law on race, a hope was born that the legacy of centuries of slavery and racism would finally come to an end. But that hope was not yet to be realized. The high moral indignation of the 1960's was evidently but a passing spasm which was quickly forgotten.

A major manifestation of the sharp turning away from the goals of justice and equality is to be found in the shrill and paranoid attacks against affirmative action. The effort to eliminate the present effects of past discrimination, to correct the wrongs of many generations was barely underway when it came under powerful attack. And now, even the very modest gains made by racial minorities through affirmative action are being erased, as powerful institutions try to turn the clock of history back to the dark and dismal days of a separate and unequal status for black Americans.

Judging by the vast outcry, it might be assumed that the remedy of affirmative action to eliminate racist and sexist patterns has become as widespread and destructive as discrimination itself. And once again, the defenders of the racial *status quo* have succeeded in confusing the remedy with the original evil. The term "reverse discrimination," for example, has become another code word for resisting the elimination of prevailing patterns of discrimination.

The historic dissent of Justice John Marshall Harlan in the 1883 decision of the Supreme Court in the Civil Rights Cases defines the constitutional principle requiring the obligation of the government to remove all the "badges and incidents" of slavery. Although initially rejected, the rationale of Harlan's position was of course vindicated in later Supreme Court decisions, as in *Brown v. Board of Education* in 1954 and *Jones v. Mayer* in 1968, among others.

The adoption by Congress of the Civil Rights Act of 1964 further confirmed this constitutional perception of the equal protection clause of the 14th Amendment and reinforced the legal principle that for every right there is a remedy. I believe that what Justice Harlan called the "badges and incidents" of slavery include every manifestation of racial discrimination, not against black people alone, but also against other people of color who were engulfed by the heritage of racism that developed out of slavery.

In this respect, I believe that an interpretation of the law consistent with the meaning of the 13th and 14th Amendments to the Constitution holds that affirmative action programs carry forth the contemporary legal obligation to eradicate the consequences of slavery and racism. In order to do that, it is necessary to confront the present effects of past discrimination and the most effective remedy to achieve that goal is affirmative action. Mr. Justice Blackmun in his opinion in *Bakke* wrote, " . . . in order to get beyond racism, we must first take account of race. There is no other way."

By now it should be very clear, that the opposition to affirmative action is based on perceived group interest rather than on abstract philosophical differences about "quotas," "reverse discrimination," "preferential treatment" and the other catchphrases commonly raised in public debate. After all the pious rhetoric equating affirmative action with "reverse discrimination" is stripped away, it is evident that the opposition to affirmative action is in fact the effort to perpetuate the privileged position of white males in American society.

In his dissent in *Bakke*, Justice Thurgood Marshall wrote, "The experience of Negroes in America has been different in kind, not just in degree, from that of other ethnic groups. It is not merely the history of slavery alone but also that a whole people were marked as inferior by the law. And that mark has endured. The dream of America as the great melting pot has not been realized for the Negro; because of his skin color he never even made it into the pot."

I propose to examine some important aspects of the historical process so aptly described by Mr. Justice Marshall. A major recomposition of the labor force occurred in the decades after the Civil War. By the end of the 19th century the American working class was an immigrant working class and European immigrants held power and exercised great influence within organized labor. For example, in 1900, Irish immigrants or their descendants held the presidencies of over fifty of the 110 national unions in the American Federation of Labor. Many of the other unions were also led by immi-

grants or their sons, with Germans following the Irish in number and prominence, while the president of the AFL was a Jewish immigrant. Records of labor organizations confirm the dominant role of immigrants and their descendants in many individual unions and city and state labor bodies throughout the country at the turn of the century and for decades later.

For the immigrant worker loyalty was to the ethnic collective, and it was understood that advancement of the individual was dependent upon communal advancement. Participation in organized labor was a significant part of that process, and many of the dramatic labor conflicts of the 19th and 20th centuries were in fact ethnic group struggles. For blacks, both before and after emancipation, the historical experience was completely different. For them, systematic racial oppression was the basic and inescapable characteristic of the society, north and south, and it was the decisive fact of their lives. The problems of the white immigrant did not compare with the oppression of racism, an oppression that was of a different magnitude, of a different order.

Initially isolated from the social and economic mainstream, white immigrants rapidly came to understand that race and ethnic identity was decisive in providing access to employment and in the eventual establishment of stable communities. For white immigrant workers assimilation was achieved through group mobility and collective ethnic advancement that was directly linked to the work place. The occupational frame of reference was decisive.

Wages, and the status derived from steady work could only be obtained by entering the permanent labor force and labor unions were most important in providing access to the job market for many groups of immigrant workers. In contrast to the white ethnics, generations of black workers were systematically barred from employment in the primary sectors of the labor market, thereby denied the economic base that made possible the celebrated achievements and social mobility of white immigrant communities.

An examination of briefs *amicus curiae* filed in the Supreme Court cases involving affirmative action reveal the active role these two historically interrelated groups, white ethnics and labor unions have played in the repeated attacks against affirmative action. With some few exceptions, this has been the pattern from *De Funis* in 1974 and *Bakke* in 1978 to the most recent cases.[1] Given the context in which this issue evolved, the historical sources of the opposition to affirmative action are not surprising.

The nineteenth-century European migrations to the United States took place during the long age of blatant white supremacy, legal and extralegal, formal and informal, and as the patterns of segregation and discrimination emerged north and south, the doors of opportunity were opened to white immigrants but closed to blacks and other non-whites. European immigrants and their descendants explain their success as the result of their devotion to the work ethic, and ignore a variety of other factors such as the systematic exclusion of non-Caucasians from competition for employment. As white immigrants moved up in the social order, black workers and those of other non-white races could fill only the least desirable places in a marginal secondary labor market, the only places open to them.

The elimination of traditional patterns of discrimination required by the Civil Rights Act of 1964 adversely affected the expectations of whites, since it compelled competition with black workers and other minority group members where none previously existed. White worker expectations had become the norm and any alteration of the norm was considered "reverse discrimination." When racial practices that have historically placed blacks at a disadvantage are removed to eliminate the present effects of past discrimination, whites believe that preferential treatment is given to blacks. But it is *the removal of the preferential treatment traditionally enjoyed by white workers at the expense of blacks as a class* that is at issue in the affirmative action controversy.

In many different occupations, including a variety of jobs in the public sector such as in police and fire departments, white workers were able to begin their climb on the seniority ladder precisely because non-whites were systematically excluded from the competition for jobs. Various union seniority systems were established at a time when racial minorities were banned from employment and union membership. Obviously blacks as a group, not just as individuals, constituted a class of victims who could not develop seniority status. A seniority system launched under these conditions inevitably becomes the institutionalized mechanism whereby whites as a group are granted racial privileges.

After long delay and much conflict, a new comprehensive body of law is emerging that has a significant potential and gives hope to women and racial minorities in the labor force.

On March 25, 1987, in *Johnson v. Transportation Agency,* the Supreme Court issued its fifth affirmative action ruling within an eleven month period. In *Johnson,* the Court upheld a voluntary affirmative action plan for hiring and promoting women and minorities adopted by the Transportation Agency of Santa Clara County, California. *Johnson* firmly supports the conclusion that affirmative action is a valid remedy to eliminate discrimination in public sector employment.

In *United States v. Paradise*, the Court upheld a lower court's decision requiring the Alabama Department of Public Safety to promote one black state trooper for each white promoted until either 25 percent of the job category was black or until an acceptable alternative promotion plan was put into place.

Wygant v. Jackson Board of Education, in which the Court struck down a provision in a collective bargaining agreement which provided that, in the event of teacher layoffs, the percentage of minority personnel laid off would be no greater than the percentage of minority personnel employed by the Jackson, Michigan, school system at the time of the layoffs. However, a majority of the Court agreed that voluntary affirmative action plans by public employers are constitutional in some instances.

Local 28 of the Sheet Metal Workers International Association v. EEOC, in which the Court upheld a lower court's order requiring a New York construction union to adopt an affirmative action plan, including a special fund to recruit and train minority workers and a 29 percent minority membership goal. This decision was the culmination of almost forty years of struggle in state and federal courts to end the racist practices of this AFL-CIO affiliate. Other cases involving unions in the building trades have a similar history and after years of litigation are still pending in Federal courts. (See for example, *Commonwealth of Pennsylvania and Williams v. Operating Engineers, Local 542*, 347 F. Supp. 268, E. D. PA. 1979.)

Local No. 93, International Association of Firefighters v. City of Cleveland, in which the Court upheld a consent decree which contained promotion goals for minorities and other affirmative action provisions in settlement of a job discrimination suit by minority firefighters.

The adverse decision in *Wygant* notwithstanding, these decisions of the Supreme Court in conjunction with the Court's 1979 decision in *Steelworkers v. Weber* make it very clear that the principle of affirmative action applied in several different contexts is well established in the law and recognized as an effective and valid remedy to eliminate traditional discriminatory employment practices. But the opponents of affirmative action continue their attacks. Powerful forces, through a well-orchestrated propaganda campaign, based upon misrepresentation and the manipulation of racial fears among whites continue their efforts to perpetuate discriminatory practices. In this, they have been aided and abetted again and again by the Reagan Administration, the most reactionary administration on civil rights in the 20th century.

In reviewing the attacks upon affirmative action, it is necessary to note the disingenuous argument of those who state that they are not against affirmative action, but only against "quotas." Affirmative action without numbers, whether in the form of quotas, goals, or timetables, is meaningless; there must be some benchmark, some tangible measure of change. Statistical evidence to measure performance is essential. Not to use numbers is to revert to the era of symbolic gesture or, at best, "tokenism."

White ethnic groups and many labor unions frequently argue that affirmative action programs will penalize innocent whites who are not responsible for past discriminatory practices. This argument turns on the notion of individual rights and sounds very moral and highminded. But it ignores social reality. It ignores the fact that white workers benefited from the systematic exclusion of blacks in many trades and industries. As has been repeatedly demonstrated in lawsuits, non-whites and women have been denied jobs, training and advancement not as individuals but as a class, no matter what their personal merit and qualification. Wherever discriminatory employment patterns exist, hiring and promotion without affirmative action perpetuate the old injustice.

Before the emergence of affirmative action remedies, the legal prohibitions against job discrimination were for the most part declarations of abstract morality that rarely resulted in any change. Pronouncements of public policy such as state and municipal fair employment practice laws were mainly symbolic, and the patterns of job discrimination remained intact. Because affirmative action programs go beyond individual relief to attack long-established patterns of discrimination and, if vigorously enforced by government agencies over a sustained period can become a major instrument for social change, they have come under powerful and repeated attack.

As long as Title VII litigation was concerned largely with procedural and conceptual issues, only limited attention was given to the consequences of remedies. However, once affirmative action was widely applied and the focus of litigation shifted to the adoption of affirmative action plans, entrenched interests were threatened. And as the gains of the 1960's are eroded, the nation becomes even more mean-spirited and self-deceiving.

Racism in the history of the United States has not been an aberration. It has been systematized and structured into the functioning of the society's most important institutions. In the present as in the past, it is widely accepted as a basis for promoting the interests of whites. For many generations the assumptions of white supremacy were codified in the law, imposed by custom and often enforced by violence. While the forms have changed, the legacy of white supremacy is expressed in the continuing patterns of racial discrimination, and for the vast majority of black and other non-white people, race and racism remain the decisive factors in their lives.

The current conflict over affirmative action is not simply an argument about abstract rights or ethnic bigotry. In the final analysis it is an argument between those who insist upon the substance of a long-postponed break with the traditions of American racism, and those groups that insist upon maintaining the valuable privileges and benefits they now enjoy as a consequence of that dismal history.

NOTE

1. In *De Funis*, briefs attacking affirmative action came from the Anti-Defamation League of B'nai B'rith, the American Jewish Committee, the American Jewish Congress and the Jewish Rights Council. The National Organization of Jewish Women filed a brief in support of affirmative action which was endorsed by the Commission on Social Action of the Union of American Hebrew Congregations. The AFL-CIO filed a brief against affirmative action, as did the National Association of Manufacturers. The United Auto Workers, United Farm Workers, American Federation of State, County, and Municipal Employees filed briefs in support, as did the United Mine Workers. In *Bakke*, among the groups which filed *amici* briefs against affirmative action were the American Jewish Committee, American Jewish Congress, Anti-Defamation League of B'nai B'rith, Jewish Labor Committee, National Jewish

Commission on Law and Public Affairs, UNICO National (the largest Italian American organization in the U.S.), Italian-American Foundation, Chicago Division of UNICO, Hellenic Bar Association of Illinois, Ukrainian Congress Committee of America, Polish American Affairs Council, and Polish American Educators Association. All seven Jewish organizations filed briefs opposing affirmative action, the two Jewish groups that had supported affirmative action in the *De Funis* case did not file in *Bakke*. The American Federation of Teachers, an affiliate of the AFL-CIO, filed against affirmative action, while some other unions submitted a joint brief in support. In *Weber* (1979), five *amici* briefs urged the Supreme Court to decide against affirmative action; these were from the Anti-Defamation League of B'nai B'rith, the National Jewish Commission on Law and Public Affairs, the Ukrainian Congress Committee of America, and UNICO National. Several unions with large black memberships filed in support. In *Fullilove* (1980), the Anti-Defamation

League of B'nai B'rith joined with employer groups and the Pacific League Foundation to argue against affirmative action. The Anti-Defamation League filed briefs in opposition to affirmative action in several lower court cases and has been among the most active of all groups in attacking affirmative action in the Courts. In 1982, the ADL filed a brief against minority interests in the Boston Firefighters case (*Boston Firefighters Union, Local 718 v. Boston Branch, NAACP*) with the Supreme Court as did the AFL-CIO and the U.S. Department of Justice. One June 12, 1984, the Supreme Court in the Memphis firefighters case (*Firefighters Local Union No. 1784 v. Stotts*) held that layoffs must be made on the basis of applicable union seniority rules even if advances in minority employment as a result of court ordered affirmative action are destroyed in the process. In this case, many labor unions and ethnic organizations again joined with the Justice Department in urging the Court to rule against affirmative action.

POSTSCRIPT

Is Affirmative Action Reverse Discrimination?

Much of the argument between Carter and Hill turns on the question of "color blindness." To what extent should our laws be color-blind? During the 1950s and early 1960s, civil rights leaders were virtually unanimous on this point. Said Martin Luther King, Jr., "I have a dream my four little children will one day live in a nation where they will not be judged by the color of their skin but by the content of their character." This was the consensus view in 1963, but today Hill seems to be suggesting that the statement needs to be qualified. In order to *bring about* color blindness, it may be necessary to become temporarily color-conscious. But for how long? And is there a danger that this temporary color consciousness may become a permanent policy?

Robert M. O'Neil, in *Discriminating Against Discrimination* (Indiana University Press, 1975), studied preferential admissions to universities and supports preferential treatment without racial quotas. Lino A. Graglia's *Disaster by Decree: The Supreme Court Decisions on Race and the Schools* (Cornell University Press, 1976) is highly critical of busing. The focus of Allan P. Sindler's *Bakke, DeFunis, and Minority Admissions* (Longman, 1978) is on affirmative action in higher education, as is Nicholas Capaldi's *Out of Order: Affirmative Action and the Crisis of Doctrinaire Liberalism* (Prometheus Books, 1985). A more general discussion is found in Thomas Sowell's *Civil Rights: Rhetoric or Reality?* (William Morrow, 1984). Chapter 13 of *The Constitution: That Delicate Balance* (Random House, 1984) by Fred W. Friendly and Martha J. H. Elliott, provides an account of the events leading to the landmark *Bakke* case on affirmative action.

Affirmative action is one of those issues, like abortion, in which the opposing sides seem utterly intransigent. It is hard to imagine any compromise acceptable to both sides of the controversy. But there may be a large middle sector of opinion that is simply weary of the whole controversy and may be willing to support any expedient solution worked out by pragmatists in the executive and legislative branches.

ISSUE 12

Should "Hate Speech" Be Protected?

YES: Nat Hentoff, from " 'Speech Codes' on the Campus: And Problems of Free Speech," *Dissent* (Fall 1991)

NO: Stanley Fish, from "There's No Such Thing as Free Speech and It's a Good Thing Too," *Boston Review* (February 1992)

ISSUE SUMMARY

YES: Columnist Nat Hentoff is worried that political orthodoxy and "politically correct" speech codes on American college campuses will inhibit discussion of important issues.
NO: Professor of law Stanley Fish argues that speech in and of itself has no value, and when its only aim is to humiliate people, it does not deserve protection.

In 1942, on a busy public street in Rochester, New Hampshire, a man named Walter Chaplinsky was passing out literature promoting the Jehova's Witnesses, which would have been all right except that the literature denounced all other religions as "rackets." As might be expected, Chaplinsky's activities caused a stir. The city marshall warned Chaplinsky that he was on the verge of creating a riot and told him that he ought to leave, whereupon Chaplinsky answered him in these words: "You are a Goddamned racketeer . . . a damned Fascist, and the whole government of Rochester are Fascists or agents of Fascists." Chaplinsky was arrested for disturbing the peace and he appealed on the grounds that his First Amendment right to free speech had been violated. The Supreme Court of the United States ruled unanimously against him. In *Chaplinsky v. New Hampshire* (1942) the Court said that his words were "fighting words," not deserving of First Amendment protection because they were "likely to provoke the average person to retaliation."

In 1984 a Texan named Gregory Lee Johnson stood in front of Dallas City Hall, doused an American flag in kerosene, and set it on fire while chanting, "Red, white, and blue, we spit on you." When he was arrested for flag desecration, he appealed to the Supreme Court on grounds of free speech—and won. In *Texas v. Johnson* (1989) the Court ruled that flag-burning was a form of "symbolic speech" protected by the First Amendment.

So Chaplinsky used his mouth and was punished for it, and Johnson burned a flag and was not. How do we square these decisions, or should we? What about cases today? If flag-burning is symbolic speech, what about cross-burning? If a state can punish a person for calling someone a "God-damned racketeer," can it also punish someone for shouting racial epithets?

On many college campuses today, so-called speech codes have been promulgated that punish people for denigrating others because of race, religion, gender, or sexual orientation. Some municipalities have also enacted laws that punish "hate speech" directed at women and minorities. The intention of these codes and laws is to ensure at least a minimum of civility in places where people of very diverse backgrounds must live and work together. But do they infringe upon essential freedoms?

In 1992 the Supreme Court confronted this issue in a case testing the constitutionality of a St. Paul, Minnesota, statute punishing anyone who displays symbols attacking people because of their "race, color, creed, religion, or gender." A group of St. Paul teenagers had burned a cross in the yard of a black family. Prosecutors used this newly enacted law, which raised the essential issues in the case: Did the statute violate freedoms guaranteed by the First Amendment? If so, why? In its decision of *R. A. V. v. St. Paul* (1992), the Court gave a unanimous answer to the first question. All nine justices agreed that the statute was indeed a violation of the First Amendment. But on the second question—*why* was it a violation?—the Court was deeply divided. Four members thought that it was unconstitutional because it was "overbroad," that is, worded in such general language that it would reach beyond the narrow bounds of speech activities that the Court has deemed punishable. But the majority, in an opinion by Justice Antonin Scalia, struck down the statute for a very different reason: because it contained "content discrimination." By punishing speech that attacks people because of their "race, color, creed, religion, or gender," it was prohibiting speech "solely on the basis of the subjects the speech addresses." A statute punishing speech may not single out specific categories like race or creed for protection, for to do so is to involve the state in deciding which sorts of people deserve protection against "hate speech."

A related controversy that has inflamed American college campuses in recent years also involves questions of "content discrimination." The term *politically correct* (p.c.) is a sarcastic term used by opponents of the new campus speech codes and other efforts to punish verbal attacks on minorities. It implies that the codes discriminate according to speech content because they punish mainly the kinds of speech whose contents offend people on the Left, but seldom punish speech that particularly offends conservatives. The net effect, they charge, is to smother dissent in favor of left-wing orthodoxy (political correctness).

Although Nat Hentoff is himself a liberal, in the following selection he protests against what he perceives as an atmosphere of left-wing orthodoxy on American campuses and worries that campus speech codes may further chill free speech. Stanley Fish responds that "speech in and of itself cannot be a value" and if it produces results that no decent person could want—such as the denigration of minorities—then it is not worth defending.

YES Nat Hentoff

"SPEECH CODES" ON THE CAMPUS

During three years of reporting on anti–free-speech tendencies in higher education, I've been at more than twenty colleges and universities—from Washington and Lee and Columbia to Mesa State in Colorado and Stanford.

On this voyage of initially reverse expectations—with liberals fiercely advocating censorship of "offensive" speech and conservatives merrily taking the moral high ground as champions of free expression—the most dismaying moment of revelation took place at Stanford.

In the course of a two-year debate on whether Stanford, like many other universities, should have a speech code punishing language that might wound minorities, women, and gays, a letter appeared in the *Stanford Daily*. Signed by the African-American Law Students Association, the Asian-American Law Students Association, and the Jewish Law Students Association, the letter called for a harsh code. It reflected the letter and the spirit of an earlier declaration by Canetta Ivy, a black leader of student government at Stanford during the period of the grand debate. "We don't put as many restrictions on freedom of speech," she said, "as we should."

Reading the letter by this rare ecumenical body of law students (so pressing was the situation that even Jews were allowed in), I thought of twenty, thirty years from now. From so bright a cadre of graduates, from so prestigious a law school would come some of the law professors, civic leaders, college presidents, and maybe even a Supreme Court Justice of the future. And many of them would have learned—like so many other university students in the land—that censorship is okay provided your motives are okay.

The debate at Stanford ended when the president, Donald Kennedy, following the prevailing winds, surrendered his previous position that once you start telling people what they can't say, you will end up telling them what they can't think. Stanford now has a speech code.

This is not to say that these gags on speech—every one of them so overboard and vague that a student can violate a code without knowing he or she has done so—are invariably imposed by student demand. At most

From Nat Hentoff, " 'Speech Codes' on the Campus: And Problems of Free Speech," *Dissent* (Fall 1991), pp. 546–549. Copyright © 1991 by *Dissent*. Reprinted by permission.

colleges, it is the administration that sets up the code. Because there have been racist or sexist or homophobic taunts, anonymous notes or graffiti, the administration feels it must *do something*. The cheapest, quickest way to demonstrate that it cares is to appear to suppress racist, sexist, homophobic speech.

Usually, the leading opposition among the faculty consists of conservatives—when there is opposition. An exception at Stanford was law professor Gerald Gunther, arguably the nation's leading authority on constitutional law. But Gunther did not have much support among other faculty members, conservative or liberal.

At the University of Buffalo Law School, which has a code restricting speech, I could find just one faculty member who was against it. A liberal, he spoke only on condition that I not use his name. He did not want to be categorized as a racist.

On another campus, a political science professor for whom I had great respect after meeting and talking with him years ago has been silent—students told me—on what Justice William Brennan once called "the pall of orthodoxy" that has fallen on his campus.

When I talked to him, the professor said, "It doesn't happen in my class. There's no 'politically correct' orthodoxy here. It may happen in other places at this university, but I don't know about that." He said no more.

One of the myths about the rise of p.c. (political correctness) is that, coming from the left, it is primarily intimidating conservatives on campus. Quite the contrary. At almost every college I've been to, conservative students have their own newspaper, usually quite lively and fired by a muckraking glee at exposing "politically correct" follies on campus.

By and large, those most intimidated—not so much by the speech codes themselves but by the Madame Defarge-like spirit behind them—are liberal students and those who can be called politically moderate.

I've talked to many of them, and they no longer get involved in class discussions where their views would go against the grain of p.c. righteousness. Many, for instance, have questions about certain kinds of affirmative action. They are not partisans of Jesse Helms or David Duke, but they wonder whether progeny of middle-class black families should get scholarship preference. Others have a question about abortion. Most are not pro-life, but they believe that fathers should have a say in whether the fetus should be sent off into eternity.

Jeff Shesol, a recent graduate of Brown, and now a Rhodes scholar at Oxford, became nationally known while at Brown because of his comic strip, "Thatch," which, not too kindly, parodied p.c. students. At a forum on free speech at Brown before he left, Shesol said he wished he could tell the new students at Brown to have no fear of speaking freely. But he couldn't tell them that, he said, advising the new students to stay clear of talking critically about affirmative action or abortion, among other things, in public.

At that forum, Shesol told me, he said that those members of the left who regard dissent from their views as racist and sexist should realize that they are discrediting their goals. "They're honorable goals," said Shesol, "and I agree with them. I'm against racism and sexism. But these people's tactics are obscuring the goals. And they've resulted in

Brown no longer being an open-minded place." There were hisses from the audience.

Students at New York University Law School have also told me that they censor themselves in class. The kind of chilling atmosphere they describe was exemplified last year as a case assigned for a moot court competition became subject to denunciation when a sizable number of law students said it was too "offensive" and would hurt the feelings of gay and lesbian students. The case concerned a divorced father's attempt to gain custody of his children on the grounds that their mother had become a lesbian. It was against p.c. to represent the father.

Although some of the faculty responded by insisting that you learn to be a lawyer by dealing with all kinds of cases, including those you personally find offensive, other faculty members supported the rebellious students, praising them for their sensitivity. There was little public opposition from the other students to the attempt to suppress the case. A leading dissenter was a member of the conservative Federalist Society.

What is p.c. to white students is not necessarily p.c. to black students. Most of the latter did not get involved in the N.Y.U. protest, but throughout the country many black students do support speech codes. A vigorous exception was a black Harvard Law School student who spoke during a debate on whether the law school should start punishing speech. A white student got up and said that the codes are necessary because, without them, black students would be driven away from colleges and thereby deprived of the equal opportunity to get an education.

The black student rose and said that the white student had a hell of a nerve to assume that he—in the face of racist speech—would pack up his books and go home. He'd been familiar with that kind of speech all his life, and he had never felt the need to run away from it. He'd handled it before and he could again.

The black student then looked at his white colleague and said that it was condescending to say that blacks have to be "protected" from racist speech. "It is more racist and insulting," he emphasized, "to say that to me than to call me a nigger."

But that would appear to be a minority view among black students. Most are convinced they do need to be protected from wounding language. On the other hand, a good many black student organizations on campus do not feel that Jews have to be protected from wounding language.

THOUGH IT'S NOT MUCH WRITTEN ABOUT in reports of the language wars on campuses, there is a strong strain of anti-Semitism among some—not all, by any means—black students. They invite such speakers as Louis Farrakhan, the former Stokely Carmichael (now Kwame Touré), and such lesser but still burning bushes as Steve Cokely, the Chicago commentator who has declared that Jewish doctors inject the AIDS virus into black babies. That distinguished leader was invited to speak at the University of Michigan.

The black student organization at Columbia University brought to the campus Dr. Khallid Abdul Muhammad. He began his address by saying: "My leader, my teacher, my guide is the honorable Louis Farrakhan. I thought that should be said at Columbia Jewniversity."

Many Jewish students have not censored themselves in reacting to this form of political correctness among some blacks. A Columbia student, Rachel Stoll, wrote a letter to the *Columbia Spectator*: "I have an idea. As a white Jewish American, I'll just stand in the middle of a circle comprising . . . Khallid Abdul Muhammad and assorted members of the Black Students Organization and let them all hurl large stones at me. From recent events and statements made on this campus, I gather this will be a good cheap method of making these people feel good."

At UCLA, a black student magazine printed an article indicating there is considerable truth to the *Protocols of the Elders of Zion*. For months, the black faculty, when asked their reactions, preferred not to comment. One of them did say that the black students already considered the black faculty to be insufficiently militant, and the professors didn't want to make the gap any wider. Like white liberal faculty members on other campuses, they want to be liked—or at least not too disliked.

Along with quiet white liberal faculty members, most black professors have not opposed the speech codes. But unlike the white liberals, many honestly do believe that minority students have to be insulated from barbed language. They do not believe—as I have found out in a number of conversations—that an essential part of an education is to learn to demystify language, to strip it of its ability to demonize and stigmatize you. They do not believe that the way to deal with bigoted language is to answer it with more and better language of your own. This seems very elementary to me, but not to the defenders, black and white, of the speech codes.

Consider University of California president David Gardner. He has imposed a speech code on all campuses in his university system. Students are to be punished—and this is characteristic of the other codes around the country—if they use "fighting words"—derogatory references to "race, sex, sexual orientation or disability."

The term "fighting words" comes from a 1942 Supreme Court decision, *Chaplinsky v. New Hampshire*, which ruled that "fighting words" are not protected by the First Amendment. That decision, however, has been in disuse at the High Court for many years. But it is thriving on college campuses.

In the California code, a word becomes "fighting" if it is directly addressed to "any ordinary person" (presumably, extraordinary people are above all this). These are the kinds of words that are "inherently likely to provoke a violent reaction, *whether or not they actually do.*" (Emphasis added.)

Moreover, he or she who fires a fighting word at any ordinary person can be reprimanded or dismissed from the university because the perpetrator should "reasonably know" that what he or she has said will interfere with the "victim's ability to pursue effectively his or her education or otherwise participate fully in university programs and activities."

Asked Gary Murikami, chairman of the Gay and Lesbian Association at the University of California, Berkeley: "What does it mean?"

Among those—faculty, law professors, college administrators—who insist such codes are essential to the university's purpose of making *all* students feel at home and thereby able to concentrate on their work, there has been a celebratory resort to the Fourteenth Amendment.

That amendment guarantees "equal protection of the laws" to all, and that means to all students on campus. Accordingly, when the First Amendment rights of those engaging in offensive speech clash with the equality rights of their targets under the Fourteenth Amendment, the First Amendment must give way.

This is the thesis, by the way, of John Powell, legal director of the ACLU (American Civil Liberties Union), even though that organization has now formally opposed all college speech codes—after a considerable civil war among and within its affiliates.

The battle of the amendments continues, and when harsher codes are called for at some campuses, you can expect the Fourteenth Amendment—which was not intended to censor *speech*—will rise again.

A precedent has been set at, of all places, colleges and universities, that the principle of free speech is merely situational. As college administrators change, so will the extent of free speech on campus. And invariably, permissible speech will become more and more narrowly defined. Once speech can be limited in such subjective ways, more and more expression will be included in what is forbidden.

One of the exceedingly few college presidents who speaks out on the consequences of the anti–free-speech movement is Yale University's Benno Schmidt [President Schmidt retired from Yale in 1992—Eds.]:

> Freedom of thought must be Yale's central commitment. It is not easy to embrace. It is, indeed, the effort of a lifetime. . . . Much expression that is free may deserve our contempt. We may well be moved to exercise our own freedom to counter it or to ignore it. But universities cannot censor or suppress speech, no matter how obnoxious in

content, without violating their justification for existence. . . .

> On some other campuses in this country, values of civility and community have been offered by some as paramount values of the university, even to the extent of superseding freedom of expression.

> Such a view is wrong in principle and, if extended, is disastrous to freedom of thought. . . . The chilling effects on speech of the vagueness and open-ended nature of many universities' prohibitions . . . are compounded by the fact that these codes are typically enforced by faculty and students who commonly assert that vague notions of community are more important to the academy than freedom of thought and expression. . . .

> This is a flabby and uncertain time for freedom in the United States.

On the Public Broadcasting System in June, I was part of a Fred Friendly panel at Stanford University in a debate on speech codes versus freedom of expression. The three black panelists, including a Stanford student; strongly supported the codes. So did the one Asian-American on the panel. But then so did Stanford law professor Thomas Grey, who wrote the Stanford code, and Stanford president Donald Kennedy, who first opposed and then embraced the code. We have a new ecumenicism of those who would control speech for the greater good. It is hardly a new idea, but the mix of advocates is rather new.

But there are other voices. In the national board debate at the ACLU on college speech codes, the first speaker—and I think she had a lot to do with making the final vote against codes unanimous—was Gwen Thomas. A black community college administrator from Colorado, she is a fiercely persistent exposer of racial discrimination.

She started by saying, "I have always felt as a minority person that we have to protect the rights of all because if we infringe on the rights of any persons, we'll be next.

"As for providing a nonintimidating educational environment, our young people have to learn to grow up on college campuses. We have to teach them how to deal with adversarial situations. They have to learn how to survive offensive speech they find wounding and hurtful."

Gwen Thomas is an educator—an endangered species in higher education.

NO

Stanley Fish

THERE'S NO SUCH THING AS FREE SPEECH AND IT'S A GOOD THING TOO

Lately many on the liberal and progressive left have been disconcerted to find that words, phrases and concepts thought to be their property and generative of their politics have been appropriated by the forces of neoconservatism. This is particularly true of the concept of free speech, for in recent years First Amendment rhetoric has been used to justify policies and actions the left finds problematical if not abhorrent: pornography, sexist language, campus hate-speech. How has this happened? The answer I shall give in this essay is that abstract concepts like free speech do not have any "natural" content but are filled with whatever content and direction one can manage to give them. Free speech, in short, is not an independent value but a political prize, and if that prize has been captured by a politics opposed to yours, it can no longer be invoked in ways that further your purposes for it is now an obstacle to those purposes. This is something that the liberal left has yet to understand and what follows is an attempt to pry its members loose from a vocabulary that may now be a disservice to them.

Not far from the end of his *Aereopagitica,* and after having celebrated the virtues of toleration and unregulated publication in passages that find their way into every discussion of free speech and the First Amendment, John Milton catches himself up short and says, of course I didn't mean Catholics, *them* we exterminate:

> I mean not tolerated popery, and open superstition, which as it extirpates all religious and civil supremacies, so itself should be extirpate . . . that also which is impious or evil absolutely against faith or manners no law can possibly permit that intends not to unlaw itself.

Notice that Milton is not simply stipulating a single exception to a rule generally in place; the kinds of utterance that might be regulated and even prohibited on pain of trial and punishment comprise an open set; popery is named only as a particularly perspicuous instance of the advocacy that cannot be tolerated. No doubt there are other forms of speech and action that might be categorized as "open superstitions" or as subversive of piety, faith, and manners, and presumably these too would be candidates for "extirpation." Nor would Milton think himself culpable for having failed to provide a list of unprotected utterances. The list will fill itself out as utterances are put to the test implied by his formulation: would this form of speech or advocacy, if permitted to flourish, tend to undermine the very purposes for which our society is constituted? One cannot answer this question with respect to a particular utterance in advance of its emergence on the world's stage; rather one must wait and ask the question in the full context of its production and (possible) dissemination. It might appear that the result would be ad hoc and unprincipled, but for Milton the principle inheres in the core values in whose name men of like mind came together in the first place. Those values, which include the search for truth and the promotion of virtue, are capacious enough to accommodate a diversity of views. But at some point—again impossible of advance specification—capaciousness will threaten to become shapelessness, and at that point fidelity to the original values will demand acts of extirpation.

I want to say that all affirmations of freedom of expression are like Milton's, dependent for their force on an exception that literally carves out the space in which expression can then emerge. I do not mean that expression (saying something) is a realm whose integrity is sometimes compromised by certain restrictions, but that restriction, in the form of an underlying articulation of the world that necessarily (if silently) negates alternatively possible articulations, is constitutive of expression. Without restriction,

without an in-built sense of what it would be meaningless to say or wrong to say, there could be no assertion and no reason for asserting it. The exception to unregulated expression is not a negative restriction, but a positive hollowing out of value—we are for *this*, which means we are against *that*—in relation to which meaningful assertion can then occur. It is in reference to that value—constituted as all values are by an act of exclusion—that some forms of speech will be heard as (quite literally) intolerable. Speech, in short, is never a value in and of itself, but is always produced within the precincts of some assumed conception of the good to which it must yield in the event of conflict. When the pinch comes (and sooner or later it will always come) and the institution (be it church, state, or university) is confronted by behavior subversive of its core rationale, it will respond by declaring "of course we mean not tolerated _____, that we extirpate"; not because an exception to a general freedom has suddenly and contradictorily been announced, but because the freedom has never been general and has always been understood against the background of an originary exclusion that gives it meaning. . . .

Despite the apparent absoluteness of the First Amendment, there are any number of ways of getting around it, ways that are known to every student of the law. In general, the preferred strategy is to manipulate the distinction, essential to First Amendment jurisprudence, between speech and action. The distinction is essential because no one would think to frame a First Amendment that began "Congress shall make no law abridging freedom of action;" for that would amount to saying "Congress shall make no law," which would amount to saying

"There shall be no law," only actions uninhibited and unregulated. If the First Amendment is to make any sense, have any bite, speech must be declared not to be a species of action, or to be a special form of action lacking the aspects of action that cause it to be the object of regulation. The latter strategy is the favored one and usually involves the separation of speech from consequences. This is what Archibald Cox does when he assigns to the First Amendment the job of protecting "expressions separable from conduct harmful to other individuals and the community." The difficulty of managing this segregation is well known: speech always seems to be crossing the line into action where it becomes, at least potentially, consequential. In the face of this categorical instability, First Amendment theorists and jurists fashion a distinction within the distinction: some forms of speech are not really speech because they have a tendency to incite violence; they are, as the court declares in *Chaplinsky v. New Hampshire* (1942), "fighting words," words "likely to provoke the average person to retaliation, and thereby cause a breach of the peace."

The trouble with this definition is that it distinguishes not between fighting words and words that remain safely and merely expressive, but between words that are provocative to one group (the group that falls under the rubric "average person") and words that might be provocative to other groups, groups of persons not now considered average. And if you ask what words are likely to be provocative to those non-average groups, what are likely to be *their* fighting words, the answer is anything and everything, for as Justice Holmes said long ago (in *Gitlow v. New York*), every idea is an incitement to somebody, and

since ideas come packaged in sentences, in words, every sentence is potentially, in some situation that might occur tomorrow, a fighting word and therefore a candidate for regulation. That may be why the doctrine of "fighting words" has been more invoked than honored since 1942. If the category is not a formal one, but one that varies with the varying sensitivities of different groups, there is no utterance that it does not include, and we are led to the conclusion that there is nothing for the First Amendment to protect, no such thing as "speech alone" or speech separable from harmful conduct, no such thing as "mere speech" or the simple non-consequential expression of ideas. It would follow from this conclusion that when a court rules in the name of these non-existent things, it is really doing something else; it is deciding to permit certain harms done by words because it believes that by permitting them it upholds a value greater than the value of preventing them. That value will not, however, be the value of speech, per se, but of whatever set of concerns is judged by the court to override the concerns of those who find a particular form of speech harmful.

At this point a First Amendment purist might ask, "Why couldn't that overriding concern be the protection of speech? Why couldn't freedom of speech be the greater value to which other values must yield in the event of a clash?" The answer is that freedom of expression would only be a primary value if it didn't matter what was said; didn't matter in the sense that no one gave a damn, but just liked to hear talk. There are contexts like that, a Hyde Park corner or a call-in talk show where people get to sound off for the sheer fun of it. These, however, are special contexts, artificially bounded spaces designed to assure that talking is not taken seriously. In ordinary contexts, talk is produced with the goal of trying to move the world in one direction rather than another. In these contexts—the contexts of everyday life—you go to the trouble of asserting that x is y only because you suspect that some people are wrongly asserting that x is z or that x doesn't exist. You assert, in short, because you give a damn, not about assertion—as if it were a value in and of itself—but about what your assertion is about. It may seem paradoxical, but free expression could only be a primary value if what you are valuing is the right to make noise; but if you are engaged in some purposive activity in the course of which speech happens to be produced, sooner or later you will come to a point when you decide that some forms of speech do not further but endanger that purpose.

Take the case of universities and colleges. Could it be the purpose of such places to encourage free expression? If the answer were "yes" it would be hard to say why there would be any need for classes, or examinations, or departments, or disciplines, or libraries, since freedom of expression requires nothing but a soapbox or an open telephone line. The very fact of the university's machinery—of the events, rituals, and procedures that fill its calendar—argues for some other, more substantive, purpose. In relation to that purpose (which will be realized differently in different kinds of institutions), the flourishing of free expression will in almost all circumstances be an obvious good; but in some circumstances, freedom of expression may pose a threat to that purpose, and at that point, it may be necessary to discipline or regulate speech, lest, to paraphrase

Milton, the institution sacrifice itself to one of its *accidental* features. . . .

The objection to this line of reasoning is well known and has recently been reformulated by Benno Schmidt, [former] president of Yale University. According to Schmidt, speech-codes on campuses constitute "well-intentioned but misguided efforts to give values of community and harmony a higher place than freedom" (*Wall Street Journal*, May 6, 1991). "When the goals of harmony collide with freedom of expression," he continues, "freedom must be the paramount obligation of an academic community." The flaw in this logic is on display in the phrase "academic community"; for the phrase recognizes what Schmidt would deny, that expression only occurs in communities; if not in an academic community, then in a shopping mall community or a dinner-party community or an airplane-ride community or an office community. Arguments like Schmidt's only get their purchase by imagining expression occurring in *no* community, in an environment without the pervasive pressures and pressurings that come along with any socially organizing activity. The same (impossibly) quarantined and pristine space is the location of his preferred value, freedom, which in his conception is not freedom *for* anything, but just "freedom," an urge without direction, as expression is for him an emission without assertive content. Of course the speech to which campus codes are a response is full of content and productive of injury; but Schmidt is able to skirt this difficulty by reducing the content to a matter of style and the injury to an offense against sensibility. This is the work done by the word "obnoxious" when Schmidt urges us to protect speech "no matter how obnoxious in content." In this formulation, obnoxiousness becomes the content of the speech and the deeper affront that might provoke efforts to curtail it is pushed into the background. "Obnoxious" suggests that the injury or offense is a surface one that a large-minded ("liberated and humane") person should be able to tolerate if not embrace. The idea that the effects of speech can penetrate to the core—either for good or for ill—is never entertained; everything is kept on the level of weightless verbal exchange; there is no sense of the lacerating harms that speech of certain kinds can inflict.

To this Schmidt would no doubt reply, as he does in his essay, that harmful speech should be answered not by regulation, but by more speech; but that would make sense only if the effects of speech could be canceled out by additional speech, only if the pain and humiliation caused by racial or religious epithets could be ameliorated by saying something like "So's your old man." What Schmidt fails to realize at every level of his argument is that expression is more than a matter of proffering and receiving propositions, that words do work in the world of a kind that cannot be confined to a purely cognitive realm of "mere" ideas.

It could be said, however, that I myself mistake the nature of the work done by freely tolerated speech because I am too focused on short-run outcomes and fail to understand that the good effects of speech will be realized not in the present, but in a future whose emergence regulation could only inhibit. This line of reasoning would also weaken one of my key points, that speech in and of itself cannot be a value and is only worth worrying about if it is in the service of something with which it cannot be identical. My mistake, one could argue, is to equate the "something" in whose service speech is with some locally espoused value (e.g., the end of racism, the empowerment of disadvantaged minorities), whereas in fact we should think of that "something" as a now inchoate shape that will be given firm lines only by time's pencil. That is why the shape now receives such indeterminate characterizations (e.g., true self-fulfillment, a more perfect polity, a more capable citizenry, a less partial truth); we cannot now know it, and therefore we must not prematurely fix it in ways that will bind successive generations to error.

This forward-looking view of what the First Amendment protects has a great appeal, in part because it continues in a secular form the Puritan celebration of millenarian hopes, but it imposes a requirement so severe that one would expect more justification than is usually provided. The requirement is that we endure whatever pain racist and hate speech inflicts for the sake of a future whose emergence we can only take on faith. In a specifically religious vision like Milton's this makes perfect sense (it is indeed the whole of Christianity), but in the context of a politics that puts its trust in the world and not in the Holy Spirit, it raises more questions than it answers and could be seen as the other prong of a strategy designed to de-legitimize the complaints of victimized groups. The first strategy, as I have noted, is to define speech in such a way as to render it inconsequential (on the model of "sticks and stones will break my bones but . . ."); the second strategy is to acknowledge the (often grievous) consequences of speech, but declare that we must suffer them in the name of something that cannot be named. The two strategies are denials from slightly different directions of the *present* effects of racist speech; one confines those effects to a closed and safe realm of pure mental activity; the other imagines the effects of speech spilling over into the world, but only in an ever-receding future for whose sake we must forever defer taking action.

I find both strategies unpersuasive, but my own skepticism concerning them is less important than the fact that in general they seem to have worked; in the parlance of the marketplace (a parlance First Amendment commentators love), many in the society seemed to have bought them. Why? The answer, I think, is that people cling to First Amendment pieties because they do not wish to face what they correctly take to be the alternative. That alternative is *politics*, the realization (at which I have already hinted) that decisions about what is and is not protected in the realm of expression will rest not on principle or firm doctrine, but on the ability of some persons to interpret—recharacterize or re-write—principle and doctrine in ways that lead to the protection of speech they want heard and the regulation of speech they want silenced. (That is how George Bush can argue *for* flag-burning statutes and *against* campus hate-speech codes.) When the First Amendment is successfully invoked the result is not a victory for free speech in the face of a challenge from politics, but a *political victory* won by the party that has managed to wrap its agenda in the mantle of free speech. It is from just such a conclusion—a conclusion that would put politics *inside* the First Amendment—that commentators recoil, saying things like "this could render the First Amendment a dead letter," or "this would leave us with no normative guidance in deter-

mining when and what speech to protect," or "this effaces the distinction between speech and action," or "this is incompatible with any viable notion of freedom of expression." To these statements (culled more or less at random from recent law review pieces) I would reply that the First Amendment has always been a dead letter if one understood its "liveness" to depend on the identification and protection of a realm of "mere" expression or discussion distinct from the realm of regulatable conduct; the distinction between speech and action has always been effaced in principle, although in practice it can take whatever form the prevailing political conditions mandate; we have never had any normative guidance for marking off protected from unprotected speech; rather the guidance we have has been fashioned (and refashioned) in the very political struggles over which it then (for a time) presides. In short, the name of the game has always been politics, even when (indeed, especially when) it is played by stigmatizing politics as the area to be avoided.

It is important to be clear as to what this means. It does *not* mean that in the absence of normative guidelines we should throw up our hands and either regulate everything or allow everything. Rather it means that the question of whether or not to regulate will always be a local one and that we can not rely on abstractions that are either empty of content or filled with the content of some partisan agenda to generate a "principled" answer. Instead we must consider in every case what is at stake and what are the risks and gains of alternative courses of action. In the course of this consideration many things will be of help, but among them will not be phrases like "freedom of speech" or "the right of individual expression," because as they are used now, these phrases tend to obscure rather than clarify our dilemmas. Once they are deprived of their talismanic force, once it is no longer strategically effective simply to invoke them in the act of walking away from a problem, the conversation could continue in directions that are now blocked by a First Amendment absolutism that has only been honored in the breach anyway. To the student reporter who complains that in the wake of the promulgation of a speech code at the University of Wisconsin there is now something in the back of his mind as he writes, one could reply, "There was always something in the back of your mind and perhaps it might be better to have this code in the back of your mind than whatever was in there before." And when someone warns about the slippery slope and predicts mournfully that if you restrict one form of speech, you never know what will be restricted next, one could reply, "some form of speech is always being restricted; else there could be no meaningful assertion; we have always and already slid down the slippery slope; someone is always going to be restricted next, and it is your job to make sure that the someone is not you." And when someone observes, as someone surely will, that anti-harassment codes chill speech, one could reply that since speech only becomes intelligible against the background of what isn't being said, the background of what has already been silenced, the only question is the political one of which speech is going to be chilled, and, all things considered, it seems a good thing to chill speech like "nigger," . . . "kike," and "faggot." And if someone then says, "But what happened to free speech prin-

ciples?" one could say what I have now said a dozen times, free speech principles don't exist except as a component in a bad argument in which such principles are invoked to mask motives that would not withstand close scrutiny.

An example of a wolf wrapped in First Amendment clothing is an advertisement that ran recently in the Duke University student newspaper, *The Chronicle*. Signed by Bradley R. Smith, well-known as a purveyor of anti-Semitic neo-Nazi propaganda, the ad is packaged as a scholarly treatise: four densely packed columns complete with "learned" references, undocumented statistics, and an array of so-called authorities. The message of the ad is that the Holocaust never occurred and that the German state never "had a policy to exterminate the Jewish people (or anyone else) by putting them to death in gas chambers." In a spectacular instance of the increasingly popular "blame the victim" strategy, the Holocaust "story" or "myth" is said to have been fabricated in order "to drum up world sympathy for Jewish causes." The "evidence" supporting these assertions is a slick blend of supposedly probative facts—"not a single autopsied body has been shown to be gassed"— and sly insinuations of a kind familiar to readers of *Mein Kampf* and *The Protocols of the Elders of Zion*.

The slickest thing of all, however, is the presentation of the argument as an exercise in free speech—the ad is subtitled *The Case for Open Debate*—that could be objected to only by "thought police" and censors. This strategy bore immediate fruit in the decision of the newspaper staff to accept the ad despite a longstanding (and historically honored) policy of refusing materials that contain ethnic and racial slurs or are otherwise offensive. The reasoning of the staff (explained by the editor in a special column) was that under the First Amendment advertisers have the "right" to be published. "American newspapers are built on the principles of free speech and free press, so how can a newspaper deny these rights to anyone?" The answer to this question is that an advertiser is not denied his rights simply because a single media organ declines his copy, so long as other avenues of publication are available and there has been no state suppression of his views. This is not to say that there could not be a case for printing the ad; only that the case cannot rest on a supposed First Amendment obligation. One might argue for example that printing the ad would foster healthy debate or that lies are more likely to be shown up for what they are if they are brought to the light of day, but these are precisely the arguments the editor *disclaims* in her eagerness to take a "principled" free speech stand. By running the First Amendment up the nearest flagpole and rushing to salute it, the editor and her staff short-circuited their thought processes and threw away the opportunity to take the serious measure of a complicated issue. They allowed First Amendment slogans to blur the distinction between the positive effects of the exchange of ideas and the harm done—a harm to which they contribute—when flat-out lies are able to merchandise themselves as ideas. They rented the dignity of their publication to a hatemonger masquerading as a scholar because they were bamboozled by the invocation of a doctrine that did not really apply and was certainly not dispositive. In this case, at least, the First Amendment did bad work, first in the mouth (or pen) of Mr. Smith and then in the collective brain of the student editors.

Let me be clear. I am not saying that First Amendment principles are inherently bad (they are *inherently* nothing), only that independent of some particular partisan vision, they have no necessary content; and if the vision by which they have been appropriated is hostile to your interests, you would be well advised not to rely on them. This does not mean that you would be better off if they were not available; like any other formulas embedded in the process by which decisions are made, free speech principles function to protect society against over-hasty outcomes; they serve as channels through which an argument must pass on its way to ratification. But the channels are not, as they are sometimes said to be, merely and reassuringly procedural. They have as much content as the contents they "filter," and therefore one must be alert to the content they presently bear and not look to them for a deliverance from politics, for it is politics, either your own or someone else's, that is responsible for the form free speech principles now have. My counsel is therefore pragmatic rather than draconian: so long as so-called "free speech principles" have been fashioned by your enemies, contest their relevance to the issue at hand; but if you manage to refashion them in line with your purposes, urge them with a vengeance.

POSTSCRIPT

Should "Hate Speech" Be Protected?

In a public debate with Hentoff at the City College of New York, Fish corrected the moderator's misquotation of famed American jurist Oliver Wendell Holmes, Jr. The moderater quoted Holmes as saying we should protect freedom for the "opinions that we hate." What Holmes actually said, Fish pointed out, was that we should protect freedom for the "opinions that we loathe." We use the term "loathe," Fish said, to denote mere taste, as in "I loathe your necktie," which does not mean that we have any intention of ripping it off the wearer, for it does not really bother us that much. This is one of Fish's main points: Toleration makes sense only when we do not care a lot about the subject matter. The point is certainly arguable, but it is doubtful that Holmes would agree. A closer look at the Holmes quote shows that he said that we should protect freedom for "the expression of opinions that we loathe *and believe to be fraught with death*" (emphasis added). We do not usually say that about people's neckties.

Hentoff's *The First Freedom: The Tumultuous History of Free Speech in America* (Delacorte Press, 1980) is a lively study of major free speech battles. Franklyn C. Haiman's *Speech and Law in a Free Society* (University of Chicago Press, 1981) surveys various meanings given to the clauses in the First Amendment. Richard Polenberg's *Fighting Faiths* (Alfred A. Knopf, 1987) is a study of political dissent and American reactions to it. *A Critique of Pure Tolerance* (Beacon Press, 1965), a collection of essays written in the 1960s by Robert Paul Wolff, Barrington Moore, and Herbert Marcuse, contains some arguments that support Fish's views, while former American Civil Liberties Union director Aryeh Neier strikes a Holmsean note in the title of his book about the ACLU's defense of American Nazis' right to march, *Defending My Enemy* (E. P. Dutton, 1979).

It is hard to predict what the future of legislation and codes aimed at protecting minorities against verbal abuses will be. All nine justices of the Supreme Court struck down the St. Paul ordinance, but five of them may uphold a law abridging speech, provided that it does not single out any particular group for protection. Apparently the Court majority still considers "fighting words" outside the realm of First Amendment protection.

ISSUE 13

Should Drugs Be Legalized?

YES: Ethan A. Nadelmann, from "The Case for Legalization," *The Public Interest* (Summer 1988)

NO: James Q. Wilson, from "Against the Legalization of Drugs," *Commentary* (February 1990)

ISSUE SUMMARY

YES: Assistant professor of politics and public affairs Ethan A. Nadelmann contends that drug legalization would help put the criminal drug dealers out of business while protecting the rights of adults to make their own choices, free of criminal sanctions.

NO: Political scientist James Q. Wilson argues that drug legalization would vastly increase dangerous drug use and the social ills created by such usage.

A century ago, drugs of every kind were freely available to Americans. Laudanum, a mixture of opium and alcohol, was popularly used as a painkiller. One drug company even claimed that it was a very useful substance for calming hyperactive children, and they called it Mother's Helper. Morphine came into common use during the Civil War. Heroin, developed as a supposedly less addictive substitute for morphine, began to be marketed at the end of the nineteenth century. By that time, drug paraphernalia could be ordered through Sears and Roebuck catalogues, and Coca-Cola, which contained small quantities of cocaine, had become a popular drink.

Public concerns about addiction and dangerous patent medicines and an active campaign for drug laws waged by Dr. Harvey Wiley, a chemist in the U.S. Department of Agriculture, led Congress to pass the first national drug regulation act in 1906. The Pure Food and Drug Act required that medicines containing certain drugs, such as opium, must say so on their labels. Later amendments to the Act required that the labels must also state the quantity of each drug and affirm that the drug met official standards of purity. The Harrison Narcotic Act of 1914 went much further and cut off completely the supply of legal opiates to addicts. Since then, ever-stricter drug laws have been passed by Congress and by state legislatures.

Drug abuse in America again came to the forefront of public discourse during the 1960s, when heroin addiction started growing rapidly in inner-city neighborhoods. Also, by the end of the decade, drug experimentation had spread to the middle-class, affluent Baby Boomers who were then attending college. (The name "Baby Boom" generation has been given to Americans born during the late 1940s through 1960, whose cohort history has been widely analyzed and widely publicized because they are far more numerous than were older generations.) Indeed, certain types of drugs began to be celebrated by some of the leaders of the counterculture. Heroin was still taboo, but other drugs, notably marijuana and LSD (a psychedelic drug), were regarded as harmless and even spiritually transforming. At music festivals, like Woodstock in 1969, marijuana and LSD were used openly and associated with love, peace, and heightened sensitivity. Much of this enthusiasm cooled over the next 20 years as Baby Boomers entered the work force full-time and began their careers. But even among the careerists, certain types of drugs enjoyed high status. Cocaine, noted for its highly stimulating effects, became the drug of choice for many hard-driving young lawyers, TV writers, and Wall Street bond traders.

The high price of cocaine put it out of reach for many people, but by the early 1980s, cheap substitutes began to appear on the streets and to overtake poor urban communities. Crack cocaine, a potent, highly addictive, smokable form of cocaine, came into widespread use. More recently a new drug known as "ice," or as it is called on the West Coast, "L.A. glass," a smokable form of amphetamine, hit the streets. These stimulants tend to produce very violent, disorderly behavior. Moreover, the street gangs who sell it are frequently at war with one another and are well-armed. Not only gang members but also many innocent people have become victims of contract killings, street battles, and drive-by shootings.

This new drug epidemic prompted President Bush to declare a "war on drugs." He appointed former education secretary William Bennett to the Cabinet-level post of "drug czar," and he asked Congress to appropriate $10.6 billion for the fight. Reaction has been mixed. Some support it in its entirety; others think that more money is needed or that spending priorities should be shifted more toward treatment than law enforcement. Still, the vast majority of Americans seem ready to support some version of a major national campaign to fight drugs. Others, however, see the whole effort as doomed to failure, and they argue that the best solution to the drug problem would be to legalize, tax, and control drugs, as has been done with alcohol.

These contrasting views are presented in the readings that follow, with Ethan A. Nadelmann arguing for legalization and James Q. Wilson arguing against it.

YES

Ethan A. Nadelmann

THE CASE FOR LEGALIZATION

What can be done about the "drug problem"? Despite frequent proclamations of war and dramatic increases in government funding and resources in recent years, there are many indications that the problem is not going away and may even be growing worse. During the past year alone, more than thirty million Americans violated the drug laws on literally billions of occasions. Drug-treatment programs in many cities are turning people away for lack of space and funding. In Washington, D.C., drug-related killings, largely of one drug dealer by another, are held responsible for a doubling in the homicide rate over the past year. In New York and elsewhere, courts and prisons are clogged with a virtually limitless supply of drug-law violators. In large cities and small towns alike, corruption of policemen and other criminal-justice officials by drug traffickers is rampant. . . .

If there were a serious public debate on this issue, far more attention would be given to one policy option that has just begun to be seriously considered, but which may well prove more successful than anything currently being implemented or proposed: legalization. Politicians and public officials remain hesitant even to mention the word, except to dismiss it contemptuously as a capitulation to the drug traffickers. Most Americans perceive drug legalization as an invitation to drug-infested anarchy. Even the civil-liberties groups shy away from this issue, limiting their input primarily to the drug-testing debate. The minority communities in the ghetto, for whom repealing the drug laws would promise the greatest benefits, fail to recognize the costs of our drug-prohibition policies. And the typical middle-class American, who hopes only that his children will not succumb to drug abuse, tends to favor any measures that he believes will make illegal drugs less accessible to them. Yet when one seriously compares the advantages and disadvantages of the legalization strategy with those of current and planned policies, abundant evidence suggests that legalization may well be the optimal strategy for tackling the drug problem. . . .

There is, of course, no single legalization strategy. At one extreme is the libertarian vision of virtually no government restraints on the production

From Ethan A. Nadelmann, "The Case for Legalization," *The Public Interest*, vol. 92, no. 3 (1988). Copyright © 1988 by Ethan A. Nadelmann. Reprinted by permission of the author. Notes omitted.

and sale of drugs or any psychoactive substances, except perhaps around the fringes, such as prohibiting sales to children. At the other extreme is total government control over the production and sale of these goods. In between lies a strategy that may prove more successful than anything yet tried in stemming the problems of drug abuse and drug-related violence, corruption, sickness, and suffering. It is one in which government makes most of the substances that are now banned legally available to competent adults, exercises strong regulatory powers over all large-scale production and sale of drugs, makes drug-treatment programs available to all who need them, and offers honest drug-education programs to children. This strategy, it is worth noting, would also result in a net benefit to public treasuries of at least ten billion dollars a year, and perhaps much more.

There are three reasons why it is important to think about legalization scenarios, even though most Americans remain hostile to the idea. First, current drug-control policies have failed, are failing, and will continue to fail, in good part because they are fundamentally flawed. Second, many drug-control efforts are not only failing, but also proving highly costly and counter-productive; indeed, many of the drug-related evils that Americans identify as part and parcel of the "drug problem" are in fact caused by our drug-prohibition policies. Third, there is good reason to believe that repealing many of the drug laws would not lead, as many people fear, to a dramatic rise in drug abuse. . . .

By most accounts, the dramatic increase in drug-enforcement efforts over the past few years has had little effect on the illicit drug market in the United States. The mere existence of drug-prohibition laws, combined with a minimal level of law-enforcement resources, is sufficient to maintain the price of illicit drugs at a level significantly higher than it would be if there were no such laws. Drug laws and enforcement also reduce the availability of illicit drugs, most notably in parts of the United States where demand is relatively limited to begin with. Theoretically, increases in drug-enforcement efforts should result in reduced availability, higher prices, and lower purity of illegal drugs. That is, in fact, what has happened to the domestic marijuana market (in at least the first two respects). But in general the illegal drug market has not responded as intended to the substantial increases in federal, state, and local drug-enforcement efforts.

Cocaine has sold for about a hundred dollars a gram at the retail level since the beginning of the 1980s. The average purity of that gram, however, has increased from 12 to 60 percent. Moreover, a growing number of users are turning to "crack," a potent derivative of cocaine that can be smoked; it is widely sold in ghetto neighborhoods now for five to ten dollars per vial. Needless to say, both crack and the 60 percent pure cocaine pose much greater threats to users than did the relatively benign powder available eight years ago. Similarly, the retail price of heroin has remained relatively constant even as the average purity has risen from 3.9 percent in 1983 to 6.1 percent in 1986. Throughout the southwestern part of the United States, a particularly potent form of heroin known as "black tar" has become increasingly prevalent. And in many cities, a powerful synthetic opiate, Dilaudid, is beginning to compete with heroin as the preferred opiate. The growing number of heroin-related hospital emergencies and deaths is directly related to these developments.

All of these trends suggest that drug-enforcement efforts are not succeeding and may even be backfiring. There are numerous indications, for instance, that a growing number of marijuana dealers in both the producer countries and the United States are switching to cocaine dealing, motivated both by the promise of greater profits and by government drug-enforcement efforts that place a premium on minimizing the bulk of the illicit product (in order to avoid detection). It is possible, of course, that some of these trends would be even more severe in the absence of drug laws and enforcement. At the same time, it is worth observing that the increases in the potency of illegal drugs have coincided with decreases in the potency of legal substances. Motivated in good part by health concerns, cigarette smokers are turning increasingly to lower-tar and nicotine tobacco products, alcohol drinkers from hard liquor to wine and beer, and even coffee drinkers from regular to decaffeinated coffee. This trend may well have less to do with the nature of the substances than with their legal status. It is quite possible, for instance, that the subculture of illicit-drug use creates a bias or incentive in favor of riskier behavior and more powerful psychoactive effects. If this is the case, legalization might well succeed in reversing today's trend toward more potent drugs and more dangerous methods of consumption.

The most "successful" drug-enforcement operations are those that succeed in identifying and destroying an entire drug-trafficking organization. Such operations can send dozens of people to jail and earn the government millions of dollars in asset forfeitures. Yet these op-

erations have virtually no effect on the availability or price of illegal drugs throughout much of the United States. During the past few years, some urban police departments have devoted significant manpower and financial resources to intensive crackdowns on street-level drug dealing in particular neighborhoods. Code-named Operation Pressure Point, Operation Clean Sweep, and so on, these massive police efforts have led to hundreds, even thousands, of arrests of low-level drug dealers and drug users, and have helped improve the quality of life in the targeted neighborhoods. In most cases, however, drug dealers have adapted relatively easily by moving their operations to nearby neighborhoods. In the final analysis, the principal accomplishment of most domestic drug-enforcement efforts is not to reduce the supply or availability of illegal drugs, or even to raise their price; it is to punish the drug dealers who are apprehended, and cause minor disruptions in established drug markets. . . .

THE COSTS OF PROHIBITION

The fact that drug-prohibition laws and policies cannot eradicate or even significantly reduce drug abuse is not necessarily a reason to repeal them. They do, after all, succeed in deterring many people from trying drugs, and they clearly reduce the availability and significantly increase the price of illegal drugs. These accomplishments alone might warrant retaining the drug laws, were it not for the fact that these same laws are also responsible for much of what Americans identify as the "drug problem." Here the analogies to alcohol and tobacco are worth noting. There is little question that we could reduce the health costs associated with use and abuse of alcohol and tobacco if we were to criminalize their production, sale, and possession. But no one believes that we could eliminate their use and abuse, that we could create an "alcohol-free" or "tobacco-free" country. Nor do most Americans believe that criminalizing the alcohol and tobacco markets would be a good idea. Their opposition stems largely from two beliefs: that adult Americans have the right to choose what substances they will consume and what risks they will take; and that the costs of trying to coerce so many Americans to abstain from those substances would be enormous. It was the strength of these two beliefs that ultimately led to the repeal of Prohibition, and it is partly due to memories of that experience that criminalizing either alcohol or tobacco has little support today. . . .

COSTS TO THE TAXPAYER

Since 1981, federal expenditures on drug enforcement have more than tripled—from less than one billion dollars a year to about three billion. According to the National Drug Enforcement Policy Board, the annual budgets of the Drug Enforcement Administration (DEA) and the Coast Guard have each risen during the past seven years from about $220 million to roughly $500 million. During the same period, FBI resources devoted to drug enforcement have increased from $8 million a year to over $100 million; U.S. Marshals resources from $26 million to about $80 million; U.S. Attorney resources from $20 million to about $100 million; State Department resources from $35 million to $100 million; U.S. Customs resources from $180 million to over $400 million; and Bureau of Prison resources from $77 million to about $300

million. Expenditures on drug control by the military and the intelligence agencies are more difficult to calculate, although by all accounts they have increased by at least the same magnitude, and now total hundreds of millions of dollars per year. Even greater are the expenditures at lower levels of government. In a 1987 study for the U.S. Customs Service by Wharton Econometrics, state and local police were estimated to have devoted 18 percent of their total investigative resources, or close to five billion dollars, to drug-enforcement activities in 1986. This represented a 19 percent increase over the previous year's expenditures. All told, 1987 expenditures on all aspects of drug enforcement, from drug eradication in foreign countries to imprisonment of drug users and dealers in the United States, totalled at least ten billion dollars.

Of course, even ten billion dollars a year pales in comparison with expenditures on military defense. Of greater concern than the actual expenditures, however, has been the diversion of limited resources—including the time and energy of judges, prosecutors, and law-enforcement agents, as well as scarce prison space—from the prosecution and punishment of criminal activities that harm far more innocent victims than do violations of the drug laws. . . .

DRUGS AND CRIME

The drug/crime connection is one that continues to resist coherent analysis, both because cause and effect are so difficult to distinguish and because the role of the drug-prohibition laws in causing and labelling "drug-related crime" is so often ignored. There are four possible connections between drugs and crime, at least three of which would be much diminished if the drug-prohibition laws were repealed. First, producing, selling, buying, and consuming strictly controlled and banned substances is itself a crime that occurs billions of times each year in the United States alone. In the absence of drug-prohibition laws, these activities would obviously cease to be crimes. Selling drugs to children would, of course, continue to be criminal, and other evasions of government regulation of a legal market would continue to be prosecuted; but by and large the drug/crime connection that now accounts for all of the criminal-justice costs noted above would be severed.

Second, many illicit-drug users commit crimes such as robbery and burglary, as well as drug dealing, prostitution, and numbers running, to earn enough money to purchase the relatively high-priced illicit drugs. Unlike the millions of alcoholics who can support their habits for relatively modest amounts, many cocaine and heroin addicts spend hundreds and even thousands of dollars a week. If the drugs to which they are addicted were significantly cheaper—which would be the case if they were legalized—the number of crimes committed by drug addicts to pay for their habits would, in all likelihood, decline dramatically. Even if a legal-drug policy included the imposition of relatively high consumption taxes in order to discourage consumption, drug prices would probably still be lower than they are today.

The third drug/crime connection is the commission of crimes—violent crimes in particular—by people under the influence of illicit drugs. This connection seems to have the greatest impact upon the popular imagination. Clearly, some drugs do "cause" some people to commit crimes by reducing normal inhibitions,

unleashing aggressive and other antisocial tendencies, and lessening the sense of responsibility. Cocaine, particularly in the form of crack, has gained such a reputation in recent years, just as heroin did in the 1960s and 1970s, and marijuana did in the years before that. Crack's reputation for inspiring violent behavior may or may not be more deserved than those of marijuana and heroin; reliable evidence is not yet available. No illicit drug, however, is as widely associated with violent behavior as alcohol. According to Justice Department statistics, 54 percent of all jail inmates convicted of violent crimes in 1983 reported having used alcohol just prior to committing their offense. The impact of drug legalization on this drug/crime connection is the most difficult to predict. Much would depend on overall rates of drug abuse and changes in the nature of consumption, both of which are impossible to predict. It is worth noting, however, that a shift in consumption from alcohol to marijuana would almost certainly contribute to a decline in violent behavior.

The fourth drug/crime link is the violent, intimidating, and corrupting behavior of the drug traffickers. Illegal markets tend to breed violence—not only because they attract criminally-minded individuals, but also because participants in the market have no resort to legal institutions to resolve their disputes. . . .

The conspicuous failure of law-enforcement agencies to deal with this drug/crime connection is probably most responsible for the demoralization of neighborhoods and police departments alike. Intensive police crackdowns in urban neighborhoods do little more than chase the menace a short distance away to infect new areas. By contrast, legalization of the drug market would drive the drug-dealing business off the streets and out of the apartment buildings, and into legal, government-regulated, tax-paying stores. It would also force many of the gun-toting dealers out of business, and would convert others into legitimate businessmen. Some, of course, would turn to other types of criminal activities, just as some of the bootleggers did following Prohibition's repeal. Gone, however, would be the unparalleled financial temptations that lure so many people from all sectors of society into the drug-dealing business.

THE COSTS OF CORRUPTION

All vice-control efforts are particularly susceptible to corruption, but none so much as drug enforcement. When police accept bribes from drug dealers, no victim exists to complain to the authorities. Even when police extort money and drugs from traffickers and dealers, the latter are in no position to report the corrupt officers. What makes drug enforcement especially vulnerable to corruption are the tremendous amounts of money involved in the business. Today, many law-enforcement officials believe that police corruption is more pervasive than at any time since Prohibition. In Miami, dozens of law-enforcement officials have been charged with accepting bribes, stealing from drug dealers, and even dealing drugs themselves. Throughout many small towns and rural communities in Georgia, where drug smugglers en route from Mexico, the Caribbean, and Latin America drop their loads of cocaine and marijuana, dozens of sheriffs have been implicated in drug-related corruption. In New York, drug-related corruption in one Brooklyn police precinct has generated the city's most far-reaching police-corruption scandal since the 1960s. More than a hundred cases of drug-related corruption are now prosecuted each year in state and federal courts. Every one of the federal law-enforcement agencies charged with drug-enforcement responsibilities has seen an agent implicated in drug-related corruption.

It is not difficult to explain the growing pervasiveness of drug-related corruption. The financial temptations are enormous relative to other opportunities, legitimate or illegitimate. Little effort is required. Many police officers are demoralized by the scope of the drug traffic, their sense that many citizens are indifferent, and the fact that many sectors of society do not even appreciate their efforts—as well as the fact that many of the drug dealers who are arrested do not remain in prison. Some police also recognize that enforcing the drug laws does not protect victims from predators so much as it regulates an illicit market that cannot be suppressed, but can be kept underground. In every respect, the analogy to Prohibition is apt. Repealing the drug-prohibition laws would dramatically reduce police corruption. By contrast, the measures currently being proposed to deal with the growing problem, including better funded and more aggressive internal investigations, offer relatively little promise.

Among the most difficult costs to evaluate are those that relate to the widespread defiance of the drug-prohibition laws: the effects of labelling as criminals the tens of millions of people who use drugs illicitly, subjecting them to the risks of criminal sanction, and obliging many of these same people to enter into relationships with drug dealers (who may be criminals in many more senses of the word) in order to purchase their drugs; the cynicism that such laws generate toward other laws and the law in general; and the sense of hostility and suspicion that many otherwise law-abiding individuals feel toward law-enforcement officials. It was costs such as these that strongly influenced many of Prohibition's more conservative opponents.

PHYSICAL AND MORAL COSTS

Perhaps the most paradoxical consequence of the drug laws is the tremendous harm they cause to the millions of drug users who have not been deterred from using illicit drugs in the first place. Nothing resembling an underground Food and Drug Administration has arisen to impose quality control on the illegal-drug market and provide users with accurate information on the drugs they consume. Imagine that Americans could not tell whether a bottle of wine contained 6 percent, 30 percent, or 90 percent alcohol, or whether an aspirin tablet contained 5 or 500 grams of aspirin. Imagine, too, that no controls existed to prevent winemakers from diluting their product with methanol and other dangerous impurities, and that vineyards and tobacco fields were fertilized with harmful substances by ignorant growers and sprayed with poisonous herbicides by government agents. Fewer people would use such substances, but more of those who did would get sick. Some would die.

The above scenario describes, of course, the current state of the illicit drug market. Many marijuana smokers are worse off for having smoked cannabis that was grown with dangerous fertilizers, sprayed with the herbicide paraquat, or mixed with more dangerous substances. Consumers of heroin and the various synthetic substances sold on the street face even severer consequences, including fatal overdoses and poisonings from unexpectedly potent or impure drug supplies. More often than not, the quality of a drug addict's life depends greatly upon his or her access to reliable supplies. Drug-enforcement operations that succeed in temporarily disrupting supply networks are thus a double-edged sword: they encourage some addicts to seek admission into drug-treatment programs, but they oblige others to seek out new and hence less reliable suppliers; the result is that more, not fewer, drug-related emergencies and deaths occur.

Today, over 50 percent of all people with AIDS in New York City, New Jersey, and many other parts of the country, as well as the vast majority of AIDS-infected heterosexuals throughout the country, have contracted the disease directly or indirectly through illegal intravenous drug use. Reports have emerged of drug dealers beginning to provide clean syringes together with their illegal drugs. But even as other governments around the world actively attempt to limit the spread of AIDS by and among drug users by instituting free syringe-exchange programs, state and municipal governments in the United States resist following suit, arguing that to do so would "encourage" or "condone" the use of illegal drugs. Only in January 1988 did New York City approve such a program on a very limited and experimental basis. At the same time, drug-treatment programs remain notoriously underfunded, turning away tens of thousands of addicts seeking help, even as billions of dollars more are spent to arrest, prosecute, and imprison illegal drug sellers and users. In what may represent a sign of shifting priorities, the President's

Commission on AIDS, in its March 1988 report, emphasized the importance of making drug-treatment programs available to all in need of them. In all likelihood, however, the criminal-justice agencies will continue to receive the greatest share of drug-control funds.

Most Americans perceive the drug problem as a moral issue and draw a moral distinction between use of the illicit drugs and use of alcohol and tobacco. Yet when one subjects this distinction to reasoned analysis, it quickly disintegrates. The most consistent moral perspective of those who favor drug laws is that of the Mormons and the Puritans, who regard as immoral any intake of substances to alter one's state of consciousness or otherwise cause pleasure: they forbid not only the illicit drugs and alcohol, but also tobacco, caffeine, and even chocolate. The vast majority of Americans are hardly so consistent with respect to the propriety of their pleasures. Yet once one acknowledges that there is nothing immoral about drinking alcohol or smoking tobacco for non-medicinal purposes, it becomes difficult to condemn the consumption of marijuana, cocaine, and other substances on moral grounds. The "moral" condemnation of some substances and not others proves to be little more than a prejudice in favor of some drugs and against others.

The same false distinction is drawn with respect to those who provide the psychoactive substances to users and abusers alike. If degrees of immorality were measured by the levels of harm caused by one's products, the "traffickers" in tobacco and alcohol would be vilified as the most evil of all substance purveyors. That they are perceived instead as respected members of our community, while providers of the no more

dangerous illicit substances are punished with long prison sentences, says much about the prejudices of most Americans with respect to psychoactive substances, but little about the morality or immorality of their activities. . . .

THE BENEFITS OF LEGALIZATION

Repealing the drug-prohibition laws promises tremendous advantages. Between reduced government expenditures on enforcing drug laws and new tax revenue from legal drug production and sales, public treasuries would enjoy a net benefit of at least ten billion dollars a year, and possibly much more. The quality of urban life would rise significantly. Homicide rates would decline. So would robbery and burglary rates. Organized criminal groups, particularly the newer ones that have yet to diversify out of drugs, would be dealt a devastating setback. The police, prosecutors, and courts would focus their resources on combatting the types of crimes that people cannot walk away from. More ghetto residents would turn their backs on criminal careers and seek out legitimate opportunities instead. And the health and quality of life of many drug users—and even drug abusers—would improve significantly.

All the benefits of legalization would be for naught, however, if millions more Americans were to become drug abusers. Our experience with alcohol and tobacco provides ample warnings. Today, alcohol is consumed by 140 million Americans and tobacco by 50 million. All of the health costs associated with abuse of the illicit drugs pale in comparison with those resulting from tobacco and alcohol abuse. In 1986, for example, alcohol was identified as a contributing factor in 10 percent of work-related injuries, 40 percent of suicide attempts, and about 40 percent of the approximately 46,000 annual traffic deaths in 1983. An estimated eighteen million Americans are reported to be either alcoholics or alcohol abusers. The total cost of alcohol abuse to American society is estimated at over 100 billion dollars annually. Alcohol has been identified as the direct cause of 80,000 to 100,000 deaths annually, and as a contributing factor in an additional 100,000 deaths. The health costs of tobacco use are of similar magnitude. In the United States alone, an estimated 320,000 people die prematurely each year as a consequence of their consumption of tobacco. By comparison, the National Council on Alcoholism reported that only 3,562 people were known to have died in 1985 from use of all illegal drugs combined. Even if we assume that thousands more deaths were related in one way or another to illicit drug abuse but not reported as such, we are still left with the conclusion that all of the health costs of marijuana, cocaine, and heroin combined amount to only a small fraction of those caused by tobacco and alcohol. . . .

CAN LEGALIZATION WORK?

It is impossible to predict whether legalization would lead to much greater levels of drug abuse, and exact costs comparable to those of alcohol and tobacco abuse. The lessons that can be drawn from other societies are mixed. China's experience with the British opium pushers of the nineteenth century, when millions became addicted to the drug, offers one worst-case scenario. The devastation of many native American tribes by alcohol presents another. On the other hand, the legal availability of opium and cannabis in many Asian societies did not result in large addict populations until recently. Indeed, in many countries U.S.-inspired opium bans imposed during the past few decades have paradoxically contributed to dramatic increases in heroin consumption among Asian youth. Within the United States, the decriminalization of marijuana by about a dozen states during the 1970s did not lead to increases in marijuana consumption. In the Netherlands, which went even further in decriminalizing cannabis during the 1970s, consumption has actually declined significantly. The policy has succeeded, as the government intended, in making drug use boring. Finally, late nineteenth-century America was a society in which there were almost no drug laws or even drug regulations—but levels of drug use then were about what they are today. Drug abuse was considered a serious problem, but the criminal-justice system was not regarded as part of the solution.

There are, however, reasons to believe that none of the currently illicit substances would become as popular as alcohol or tobacco, even if they were legalized. Alcohol has long been the principal intoxicant in most societies, including many in which other substances have been legally available. Presumably, its diverse properties account for its popularity—it quenches thirst, goes well with food, and promotes appetite as well as sociability. The popularity of tobacco probably stems not just from its powerful addictive qualities, but from the fact that its psychoactive effects are sufficiently subtle that cigarettes can be integrated with most other human activities. The illicit substances do not share these qualities to the same extent, nor is it likely that they would acquire them if they were legalized. Moreover, none of the illicit substances can compete with alcohol's special place in American culture and history.

An additional advantage of the illicit drugs is that none of them appears to be as insidious as either alcohol or tobacco. Consumed in their more benign forms, few of the illicit substances are as damaging to the human body over the long term as alcohol and tobacco, and none is as strongly linked with violent behavior as alcohol. On the other hand, much of the damage caused today by illegal drugs stems from their consumption in particularly dangerous ways. There is good reason to doubt that many Americans would inject cocaine or heroin into their veins even if given the chance to do so legally. And just as the dramatic growth in the heroin-consuming population during the 1960s leveled off for reasons apparently having little to do with law enforcement, so we can expect a levelling-off—which may already have begun—in the number of people smoking crack. The logic of legalization thus depends upon two assumptions: that most illegal drugs are not so dangerous as is commonly believed; and that the drugs and methods of consumption that are most risky are unlikely to prove appealing to many people, precisely because they are so obviously dangerous.

Perhaps the most reassuring reason for believing that repeal of the drug-prohibition laws will not lead to tremendous increases in drug-abuse levels is the fact that we have learned something from our past experiences with alcohol and tobacco abuse. We now know, for instance, that consumption taxes are an effective method of limiting consumption rates. We also know that restrictions and bans on advertising, as well as a campaign of negative advertising, can make a difference. The same is true of other government measures, including restrictions on time and place of sale, prohibition of consumption in public places, packaging requirements, mandated adjustments in insurance policies, crackdowns on driving while under the influence, and laws holding bartenders and hosts responsible for the drinking of customers and guests. There is even some evidence that government-sponsored education programs about the dangers of cigarette smoking have deterred many children from beginning to smoke.

Clearly it is possible to avoid repeating the mistakes of the past in designing an effective plan for legalization. We know more about the illegal drugs now than we knew about alcohol when Prohibition was repealed, or about tobacco when the anti-tobacco laws were repealed by many states in the early years of this century. Moreover, we can and must avoid having effective drug-control policies undermined by powerful lobbies like those that now protect the interests of alcohol and tobacco producers. We are also in a far better position than we were sixty years ago to prevent organized criminals from finding and creating new opportunities when their most lucrative source of income dries up.

It is important to stress what legalization is not. It is not a capitulation to the drug dealers—but rather a means to put them out of business. It is not an endorsement of drug use—but rather a recognition of the rights of adult Americans to make their own choices free of the fear of criminal sanctions. It is not a repudiation of the "just say no" approach—but rather an appeal to government to provide assistance and positive inducements, not criminal penalties and more repressive measures, in support of that approach. It is not even a call for the elimination of the criminal-justice system from drug regulation—but rather a proposal for the redirection of its efforts and attention.

There is no question that legalization is a risky policy, since it may lead to an increase in the number of people who abuse drugs. But that is a risk—not a certainty. At the same time, current drug-control policies are failing, and new proposals promise only to be more costly and more repressive. We know that repealing the drug-prohibition laws would eliminate or greatly reduce many of the ills that people commonly identify as part and parcel of the "drug problem." Yet legalization is repeatedly and vociferously dismissed, without any attempt to evaluate it openly and objectively. The past twenty years have demonstrated that a drug policy shaped by exaggerated rhetoric designed to arouse fear has only led to our current disaster. Unless we are willing to honestly evaluate our options, including various legalization strategies, we will run a still greater risk: we may never find the best solution for our drug problems.

NO

James Q. Wilson

AGAINST THE LEGALIZATION OF DRUGS

In 1972, the President appointed me chairman of the National Advisory Council for Drug Abuse Prevention. Created by Congress, the Council was charged with providing guidance on how best to coordinate the national war on drugs. (Yes, we called it a war then, too.) In those days, the drug we were chiefly concerned with was heroin. When I took office, heroin use had been increasing dramatically. Everybody was worried that this increase would continue. Such phrases as "heroin epidemic" were commonplace.

That same year, the eminent economist Milton Friedman published an essay in *Newsweek* in which he called for legalizing heroin. His argument was on two grounds: as a matter of ethics, the government has no right to tell people not to use heroin (or to drink or to commit suicide); as a matter of economics, the prohibition of drug use imposes costs on society that far exceed the benefits. Others, such as the psychoanalyst Thomas Szasz, made the same argument.

We did not take Friedman's advice. (Government commissions rarely do.) I do not recall that we even discussed legalizing heroin, though we did discuss (but did not take action on) legalizing a drug, cocaine, that many people then argued was benign. Our marching orders were to figure out how to win the war on heroin, not to run up the white flag of surrender.

That was 1972. Today, we have the same number of heroin addicts that we had then—half a million, give or take a few thousand. Having that many heroin addicts is no trivial matter; these people deserve our attention. But not having had an increase in that number for over fifteen years is also something that deserves our attention. What happened to the "heroin epidemic" that many people once thought would overwhelm us?

The facts are clear: a more or less stable pool of heroin addicts has been getting older, with relatively few new recruits. In 1976 the average age of heroin users who appeared in hospital emergency rooms was about twenty-seven; ten years later it was thirty-two. More than two-thirds of all heroin users appearing in emergency rooms are now over the age of thirty. Back in the early 1970's, when heroin got onto the national political agenda, the

From James Q. Wilson, "Against the Legalization of Drugs," *Commentary* (February 1990). Reprinted by permission of *Commentary* and the author. All rights reserved. Note omitted.

typical heroin addict was much younger, often a teenager. Household surveys show the same thing—the rate of opiate use (which includes heroin) has been flat for the better part of two decades. More fine-grained studies of inner-city neighborhoods confirm this. John Boyle and Ann Brunswick found that the percentage of young blacks in Harlem who used heroin fell from 8 percent in 1970–71 to about 3 percent in 1975–76.

Why did heroin lose its appeal for young people? When the young blacks in Harlem were asked why they stopped, more than half mentioned "trouble with the law" or "high cost" (and high cost is, of course, directly the result of law enforcement). Two-thirds said that heroin hurt their health; nearly all said they had had a bad experience with it. We need not rely, however, simply on what they said. In New York City in 1973–75, the street price of heroin rose dramatically and its purity sharply declined, probably as a result of the heroin shortage caused by the success of the Turkish government in reducing the supply of opium base and of the French government in closing down heroin-processing laboratories located in and around Marseilles. These were short-lived gains for, just as Friedman predicted, alternative sources of supply—mostly in Mexico—quickly emerged. But the three-year heroin shortage interrupted the easy recruitment of new users.

Health and related problems were no doubt part of the reason for the reduced flow of recruits. Over the preceding years, Harlem youth had watched as more and more heroin users died of overdoses, were poisoned by adulterated doses, or acquired hepatitis from dirty needles. The word got around: heroin can kill you. By 1974 new hepatitis cases and drug-overdose deaths had dropped to a fraction of what they had been in 1970.

Alas, treatment did not seem to explain much of the cessation in drug use. Treatment programs can and do help heroin addicts, but treatment did not explain the drop in the number of *new* users (who by definition had never been in treatment) nor even much of the reduction in the number of experienced users.

No one knows how much of the decline to attribute to personal observation as opposed to high prices or reduced supply. But other evidence suggests strongly that price and supply played a large role. In 1972 the National Advisory Council was especially worried by the prospect that U.S. servicemen returning to this country from Vietnam would bring their heroin habits with them. Fortunately, a brilliant study by Lee Robins of Washington University in St. Louis put that fear to rest. She measured drug use of Vietnam veterans shortly after they had returned home. Though many had used heroin regularly while in Southeast Asia, most gave up the habit when back in the United States. The reason: here, heroin was less available and sanctions on its use were more pronounced. . . .

RELIVING THE PAST

Suppose we had taken Friedman's advice in 1972. What would have happened? We cannot be entirely certain, but at a minimum we would have placed the young heroin addicts (and, above all, the prospective addicts) in a very different position from the one in which they actually found themselves. Heroin would have been legal. Its price would have been reduced by 95 percent (minus whatever we chose to recover in taxes). Now that it could be sold by the same people who make aspirin, its quality would have been assured—no poisons, no adulterants. Sterile hypodermic needles would have been readily available at the neighborhood drugstore, probably at the same counter where the heroin was sold. No need to travel to big cities or unfamiliar neighborhoods—heroin could have been purchased anywhere, perhaps by mail order.

There would no longer have been any financial or medical reason to avoid heroin use. Anybody could have afforded it. We might have tried to prevent children from buying it, but as we have learned from our efforts to prevent minors from buying alcohol and tobacco, young people have a way of penetrating markets theoretically reserved for adults. . . .

Under these circumstances, can we doubt for a moment that heroin use would have grown exponentially? Or that a vastly larger supply of new users would have been recruited? Professor Friedman is a Nobel Prize-winning economist whose understanding of market forces is profound. What did he think would happen to consumption under his legalized regime? Here are his words: "Legalizing drugs might increase the number of addicts, but it is not clear that it would. Forbidden fruit is attractive, particularly to the young."

Really? I suppose that we should expect no increase in Porsche sales if we cut the price by 95 percent, no increase in whiskey sales if we cut the price by a comparable amount—because young people only want fast cars and strong liquor when they are "forbidden." Perhaps Friedman's uncharacteristic lapse from the obvious implications of price theory can be explained by a misunderstanding of how drug users are recruited. In his 1972 essay he said that "drug addicts are deliberately made by pushers, who give likely prospects their first few doses free." If drugs were legal it would not pay anybody to produce addicts, because everybody would buy from the cheapest source. But as every drug expert knows, pushers do not produce addicts. Friends or acquaintances do. In fact, pushers are usually reluctant to deal with non-users because a non-user could be an undercover cop. Drug use spreads in the same way any fad or fashion spreads: somebody who is already a user urges his friends to try, or simply shows already-eager friends how to do it.

But we need not rely on speculation, however plausible, that lowered prices and more abundant supplies would have increased heroin usage. Great Britain once followed such a policy and with almost exactly those results. Until the mid-1960's, British physicians were allowed to prescribe heroin to certain classes of addicts. (Possessing these drugs without a doctor's prescription remained a criminal offense.) For many years this policy worked well enough because the addict patients were typically middle-class people who had become dependent on opiate painkillers while undergoing hospital treatment. There was no drug culture. The British system worked for many years, not because it prevented drug abuse, but because there was no problem of drug abuse that would test the system.

All that changed in the 1960's. A few unscrupulous doctors began passing out heroin in wholesale amounts. One doctor prescribed almost 600,000 heroin tablets—that is, over thirteen pounds—in just one year. A youthful drug culture emerged with a demand for drugs far different from that of the older addicts.

As a result, the British government required doctors to refer users to government-run clinics to receive their heroin.

But the shift to clinics did not curtail the growth in heroin use. Throughout the 1960's the number of addicts increased—the late John Kaplan of Stanford estimated by fivefold—in part as a result of the diversion of heroin from clinic patients to new users on the streets. An addict would bargain with the clinic doctor over how big a dose he would receive. The patient wanted as much as he could get, the doctor wanted to give as little as was needed. The patient had an advantage in this conflict because the doctor could not be certain how much was really needed. Many patients would use some of their "maintenance" dose and sell the remaining part to friends, thereby recruiting new addicts. As the clinics learned of this, they began to shift their treatment away from heroin and toward methadone, an addictive drug that, when taken orally, does not produce a "high" but will block the withdrawal pains associated with heroin abstinence.

Whether what happened in England in the 1960's was a mini-epidemic or an epidemic depends on whether one looks at numbers or at rates of change. Compared to the United States, the numbers were small. In 1960 there were 68 heroin addicts known to the British government; by 1968 there were 2,000 in treatment and many more who refused treatment. (They would refuse in part because they did not want to get methadone at a clinic if they could get heroin on the street.) Richard Hartnoll estimates that the actual number of addicts in England is five times the number officially registered. At a minimum, the number of British addicts increased by thirtyfold in

ten years; the actual increase may have been much larger.

In the early 1980's the numbers began to rise again, and this time nobody doubted that a real epidemic was at hand. The increase was estimated to be 40 percent a year. By 1982 there were thought to be 20,000 heroin users in London alone. Geoffrey Pearson reports that many cities—Glasgow, Liverpool, Manchester, and Sheffield among them—were now experiencing a drug problem that once had been largely confined to London. The problem, again, was supply. The country was being flooded with cheap, high-quality heroin, first from Iran and then from Southeast Asia. . . .

BACK TO THE FUTURE

Now cocaine, especially in its potent form, crack, is the focus of attention. Now as in 1972 the government is trying to reduce its use. Now as then some people are advocating legalization. Is there any more reason to yield to those arguments today than there was almost two decades ago?

I think not. If we had yielded in 1972 we almost certainly would have had today a permanent population of several million, not several hundred thousand, heroin addicts. If we yield now we will have a far more serious problem with cocaine.

Crack is worse than heroin by almost any measure. Heroin produces a pleasant drowsiness and, if hygienically administered, has only the physical side effects of constipation and sexual impotence. Regular heroin use incapacitates many users, especially poor ones, for any productive work or social responsibility. They will sit nodding on a street corner, helpless but at least harmless. By contrast, regular cocaine use leaves the user neither helpless nor harmless. When smoked (as with crack) or injected, cocaine produces instant, intense, and short-lived euphoria. The experience generates a powerful desire to repeat it. If the drug is readily available, repeat use will occur. Those people who progress to "bingeing" on cocaine become devoted to the drug and its effects to the exclusion of almost all other considerations—job, family, children, sleep, food, even sex. Dr. Frank Gawin at Yale and Dr. Everett Ellinwood at Duke report that a substantial percentage of all high-dose, binge users become uninhibited, impulsive, hypersexual, compulsive, irritable, and hyperactive. Their moods vacillate dramatically, leading at times to violence and homicide.

Women are much more likely to use crack than heroin, and if they are pregnant, the effects on their babies are tragic. Douglas Besharov, who has been following the effects of drugs on infants for twenty years, writes that nothing he learned about heroin prepared him for the devastation of cocaine. Cocaine harms the fetus and can lead to physical deformities or neurological damage. Some crack babies have for all practical purposes suffered a disabling stroke while still in the womb. The long-term consequences of this brain damage are lowered cognitive ability and the onset of mood disorders. Besharov estimates that about 30,000 to 50,000 such babies are born every year, about 7,000 in New York City alone. There may be ways to treat such infants, but from everything we now know the treatment will be long, difficult, and expensive. Worse, the mothers who

are most likely to produce crack babies are precisely the ones who, because of poverty or temperament, are least able and willing to obtain such treatment. In fact, anecdotal evidence suggests that crack mothers are likely to abuse their infants.

The notion that abusing drugs such as cocaine is a "victimless crime" is not only absurd but dangerous. Even ignoring the fetal drug syndrome, crack-dependent people are, like heroin addicts, individuals who regularly victimize their children by neglect, their spouses by improvidence, their employers by lethargy, and their co-workers by carelessness. Society is not and could never be a collection of autonomous individuals. We all have a stake in ensuring that each of us displays a minimal level of dignity, responsibility, and empathy. We cannot, of course, coerce people into goodness, but we can and should insist that some standards must be met if society itself—on which the very existence of the human personality depends—is to persist. Drawing the line that defines those standards is difficult and contentious, but if crack and heroin use do not fall below it, what does?

The advocates of legalization will respond by suggesting that my picture is overdrawn. Ethan Nadelmann of Princeton argues that the risk of legalization is less than most people suppose. Over 20 million Americans between the ages of eighteen and twenty-five have tried cocaine (according to a government survey), but only a quarter million use it daily. From this Nadelmann concludes that at most 3 percent of all young people who try cocaine develop a problem with it. The implication is clear: make the drug legal and we only have to worry about 3 percent of our youth.

The implication rests on a logical fallacy and a factual error. The fallacy is this: the percentage of occasional cocaine users who become binge users *when the drug is illegal* (and thus expensive and hard to find) tells us nothing about the percentage who will become dependent when the drug is legal (and thus cheap and abundant). Drs. Gawin and Ellinwood report, in common with several other researchers, that controlled or occasional use of cocaine changes to compulsive and frequent use "when access to the drug increases" or when the user switches from snorting to smoking. More cocaine more potently administered alters, perhaps sharply, the proportion of "controlled" users who become heavy users.

The factual error is this: the federal survey Nadelmann quotes was done in 1985, *before* crack had become common. Thus the probability of becoming dependent on cocaine was derived from the responses of users who snorted the drug. The speed and potency of cocaine's action increases dramatically when it is smoked. We do not yet know how greatly the advent of crack increases the risk of dependency, but all the clinical evidence suggests that the increase is likely to be large.

It is possible that some people will not become heavy users even when the drug is readily available in its most potent form. So far there are no scientific grounds for predicting who will and who will not become dependent. Neither socioeconomic background nor personality traits differentiate between casual and intensive users. Thus, the only way to settle the question of who is correct about the effect of easy availability on drug use, Nadelmann or Gawin and Ellinwood, is to try it and see. But that

social experiment is so risky as to be no experiment at all, for if cocaine is legalized and if the rate of its abusive use increases dramatically, there is no way to put the genie back in the bottle, and it is not a kindly genie.

HAVE WE LOST?

Many people who agree that there are risks in legalizing cocaine or heroin still favor it because, they think, we have lost the war on drugs. "Nothing we have done has worked" and the current federal policy is just "more of the same." Whatever the costs of greater drug use, surely they would be less than the costs of our present, failed efforts.

That is exactly what I was told in 1972—and heroin is not quite as bad a drug as cocaine. We did not surrender and we did not lose. We did not win, either. What the nation accomplished then was what most efforts to save people from themselves accomplish: the problem was contained and the number of victims minimized, all at a considerable cost in law enforcement and increased crime. Was the cost worth it? I think so, but others may disagree. What are the lives of would-be addicts worth? I recall some people saying to me then, "Let them kill themselves." I was appalled. Happily, such views did not prevail.

Have we lost today? Not at all. High-rate cocaine use is not commonplace. The National Institute of Drug Abuse (NIDA) reports that less than 5 percent of high-school seniors used cocaine within the last thirty days. Of course this survey misses young people who have dropped out of school and miscounts those who lie on the questionnaire, but even if we inflate the NIDA estimate by some plausible percentage, it is still not much above 5 percent. Medical examiners reported in 1987 that about 1,500 died from cocaine use; hospital emergency rooms reported about 30,000 admissions related to cocaine abuse.

These are not small numbers, but neither are they evidence of a nationwide plague that threatens to engulf us all. Moreover, cities vary greatly in the proportion of people who are involved with cocaine. To get city-level data we need to turn to drug tests carried out on arrested persons, who obviously are more likely to be drug users than the average citizen. The National Institute of Justice, through its Drug Use Forecasting (DUF) project, collects urinalysis data on arrestees in 22 cities. As we have already seen, opiate (chiefly heroin) use has been flat or declining in most of these cities over the last decade. Cocaine use has gone up sharply, but with great variation among cities. New York, Philadelphia, and Washington, D.C., all report that two-thirds or more of their arrestees tested positive for cocaine, but in Portland, San Antonio, and Indianapolis the percentage was one-third or less.

In some neighborhoods, of course, matters have reached crisis proportions. Gangs control the streets, shootings terrorize residents, and drug-dealing occurs in plain view. The police seem barely able to contain matters. But in these neighborhoods—unlike at Palo Alto cocktail parties—the people are not calling for legalization, they are calling for help. And often not much help has come. Many cities are willing to do almost anything about the drug problem except spend more money on it. The federal government cannot change that; only local voters and politicians can. It is not clear that they will.

It took about ten years to contain heroin. We have had experience with crack for only about three or four years. Each year we spend perhaps $11 billion on law enforcement (and some of that goes to deal with marijuana) and perhaps $2 billion on treatment. Large sums, but not sums that should lead anyone to say, "We just can't afford this any more."

The illegality of drugs increases crime, partly because some users turn to crime to pay for their habits, partly because some users are stimulated by certain drugs (such as crack or PCP) to act more violently or ruthlessly than they otherwise would, and partly because criminal organizations seeking to control drug supplies use force to manage their markets. These also are serious costs, but no one knows how much they would be reduced if drugs were legalized. Addicts would no longer steal to pay black-market prices for drugs, a real gain. But some, perhaps a great deal, of that gain would be offset by the great increase in the number of addicts. These people, nodding on heroin or living in the delusion-ridden high of cocaine, would hardly be ideal employees. Many would steal simply to support themselves, since snatch-and-grab, opportunistic crime can be managed even by people unable to hold a regular job or plan an elaborate crime. Those British addicts who get their supplies from government clinics are not models of law-abiding decency. Most are in crime, and though their per-capita rate of criminality may be lower thanks to the cheapness of their drugs, the total volume of crime they produce may be quite large. Of course, society could decide to support all unemployable addicts on welfare, but that would mean that gains from lowered rates of crime would have to be offset by large increases in welfare budgets.

Proponents of legalization claim that the costs of having more addicts around would be largely if not entirely offset by having more money available with which to treat and care for them. The money would come from taxes levied on the sale of heroin and cocaine.

To obtain this fiscal dividend, however, legalization's supporters must first solve an economic dilemma. If they want to raise a lot of money to pay for welfare and treatment, the tax rate on the drugs will have to be quite high. Even if they themselves do not want a high rate, the politicians' love of "sin taxes" would probably guarantee that it would be high anyway. But the higher the tax, the higher the price of the drug, and the higher the price the greater the likelihood that addicts will turn to crime to find the money for it and that criminal organizations will be formed to sell tax-free drugs at below-market rates. If we managed to keep taxes (and thus prices) low, we would get much less money to pay for welfare and treatment and more people could afford to become addicts. There may be an optimal tax rate for drugs that maximizes revenue while minimizing crime, bootlegging, and the recruitment of new addicts, but our experience with alcohol does not suggest that we know how to find it.

THE BENEFITS OF ILLEGALITY

The advocates of legalization find nothing to be said in favor of the current system except, possibly, that it keeps the number of addicts smaller than it would otherwise be. In fact, the benefits are more substantial than that.

First, treatment. All the talk about providing "treatment on demand" implies that there is a demand for treatment. That is not quite right. There are some drug-dependent people who genuinely want treatment and will remain in it if offered; they should receive it. But there are far more who want only short-term help after a bad crash; once stabilized and bathed, they are back on the street again, hustling. And even many of the addicts who enroll in a program honestly wanting help drop out after a short while when they discover that help takes time and commitment. Drug-dependent people have very short time horizons and a weak capacity for commitment. These two groups—those looking for a quick fix and those unable to stick with a long-term fix—are not easily helped. Even if we increase the number of treatment slots—as we should—we would have to do something to make treatment more effective.

One thing that can often make it more effective is compulsion. Douglas Anglin of UCLA, in common with many other researchers, has found that the longer one stays in a treatment program, the better the chances of a reduction in drug dependency. But he, again like most other researchers, has found that dropout rates are high. He has also found, however, that patients who enter treatment under legal compulsion stay in the program longer than those not subject to such pressure. His research on the California civil-commitment program, for example, found that heroin users involved with its required drug-testing program had over the long term a lower rate of heroin use than similar addicts who were free of such constraints. If for many addicts compulsion is a useful component of treatment, it is not clear how compulsion could be achieved in a society in which purchasing, possessing, and using the drug were legal. It could be managed, I suppose, but I would not want to have to answer the challenge from the American Civil Liberties Union that it is wrong to compel a person to undergo treatment for consuming a legal commodity.

Next, education. We are now investing substantially in drug-education programs in the schools. Though we do not yet know for certain what will work, there are some promising leads. But I wonder how credible such programs would be if they were aimed at dissuading children from doing something perfectly legal. We could, of course, treat drug education like smoking education: inhaling crack and inhaling tobacco are both legal, but you should not do it because it is bad for you. That tobacco is bad for you is easily shown; the Surgeon General has seen to that. But what do we say about crack? It is pleasurable, but devoting yourself to so much pleasure is not a good idea (though perfectly legal)? Unlike tobacco, cocaine will not give you cancer or emphysema, but it will lead you to neglect your duties to family, job, and neighborhood? Everybody is doing cocaine, but you should not?

Again, it might be possible under a legalized regime to have effective drug-prevention programs, but their effectiveness would depend heavily, I think, on first having decided that cocaine use, like tobacco use, is purely a matter of practical consequences; no fundamental moral significance attaches to either. But if we believe—as I do—that dependency on certain mind-altering drugs *is* a moral issue and that their illegality rests in part on their immorality, then legalizing them undercuts, if it does not eliminate altogether, the moral message.

That message is at the root of the distinction we now make between nico-

tine and cocaine. Both are highly addictive; both have harmful physical effects. But we treat the two drugs differently, not simply because nicotine is so widely used as to be beyond the reach of effective prohibition, but because its use does not destroy the user's essential humanity. Tobacco shortens one's life, cocaine debases it. Nicotine alters one's habits, cocaine alters one's soul. The heavy use of crack, unlike the heavy use of tobacco, corrodes those natural sentiments of sympathy and duty that constitute our human nature and make possible our social life. To say, as does Nadelmann, that distinguishing morally between tobacco and cocaine is "little more than a transient prejudice" is close to saying that morality itself is but a prejudice.

THE ALCOHOL PROBLEM

Now we have arrived where many arguments about legalizing drugs begin: is there any reason to treat heroin and cocaine differently from the way we treat alcohol?

There is no easy answer to that question because, as with so many human problems, one cannot decide simply on the basis either of moral principles or of individual consequences; one has to temper any policy by a common-sense judgment of what is possible. Alcohol, like heroin, cocaine, PCP, and marijuana, is a drug—that is, a mood-altering substance—and consumed to excess it certainly has harmful consequences: auto accidents, barroom fights, bedroom shootings. It is also, for some people, addictive. We cannot confidently compare the addictive powers of these drugs, but the best evidence suggests that crack and heroin are much more addictive than alcohol.

Many people, Nadelmann included, argue that since the health and financial costs of alcohol abuse are so much higher than those of cocaine or heroin abuse, it is hypocritical folly to devote our efforts to preventing cocaine or drug use. But as Mark Kleiman of Harvard has pointed out, this comparison is quite misleading. What Nadelmann is doing is showing that a *legalized* drug (alcohol) produces greater social harm than *illegal* ones (cocaine and heroin). But of course. Suppose that in the 1920's we had made heroin and cocaine legal and alcohol illegal. Can anyone doubt that Nadelmann would now be writing that it is folly to continue our ban on alcohol because cocaine and heroin are so much more harmful?

And let there be no doubt about it—widespread heroin and cocaine use are associated with all manner of ills. Thomas Bewley found that the mortality rate of British heroin addicts in 1968 was 28 times as high as the death rate of the same age group of non-addicts, even though in England at the time an addict could obtain free or low-cost heroin and clean needles from British clinics. Perform the following mental experiment: suppose we legalized heroin and cocaine in this country. In what proportion of auto fatalities would the state police report that the driver was nodding off on heroin or recklessly driving on a coke high? In what proportion of spouse-assault and child-abuse cases would the local police report that crack was involved? In what proportion of industrial accidents would safety investigators report that the forklift or drill-press operator was in a drug-induced stupor or frenzy? We do not know exactly what the proportion would be, but anyone who asserts that it would not be much higher than it is now would have to believe that these drugs have little appeal except when they are illegal. And that is nonsense. . . .

IF I AM WRONG . . .

No one can know what our society would be like if we changed the law to make access to cocaine, heroin, and PCP easier. I believe, for reasons given, that the result would be a sharp increase in use, a more widespread degradation of the human personality, and a greater rate of accidents and violence.

I may be wrong. If I am, then we will needlessly have incurred heavy costs in law enforcement and some forms of criminality. But if I am right, and the legalizers prevail anyway, then we will have consigned millions of people, hundreds of thousands of infants, and hundreds of neighborhoods to a life of oblivion and disease. To the lives and families destroyed by alcohol we will have added countless more destroyed by cocaine, heroin, PCP, and whatever else a basement scientist can invent.

Human character is formed by society; indeed, human character is inconceivable without society, and good character is less likely in a bad society. Will we, in the name of an abstract doctrine of radical individualism, and with the false comfort of suspect predictions, decide to take the chance that somehow individual decency can survive amid a more general level of degradation?

I think not. The American people are too wise for that, whatever the academic essayists and cocktail-party pundits may say. But if Americans today are less wise than I suppose, then Americans at some future time will look back on us now and wonder, what kind of people were they that they could have done such a thing?

POSTSCRIPT

Should Drugs Be Legalized?

The analogy often cited by proponents of drug legalization is the ill-fated attempt to ban the sale of liquor in the United States, which lasted from 1919 to 1933. Prohibition has been called "an experiment noble in purpose," but it was an experiment that greatly contributed to the rise of organized crime. The repeal of Prohibition brought about an increase in liquor consumption and alcoholism, but it also deprived organized crime of an important source of income. Would drug decriminalization similarly strike a blow at the drug dealers? Possibly, and such a prospect is obviously appealing. But would drug decriminalization also exacerbate some of the ills associated with drugs? Would there be more violence, more severe addiction, more crack babies born to addicted mothers?

David F. Musto's *The American Disease* (Yale University Press, 1973) is a classic discussion of the drug problem in America. H. Wayne Morgan's *Drugs in America: A Social History, 1800–1980* (Syracuse University Press, 1981) is also useful for anyone seeking a historical background on the drug problem. James A. Inciardi's book *The War on Drugs: Heroin, Cocaine, Crime and Public Policy* (Mayfield, 1986) gives a close-up look at the cocaine and crime scene. Numerous periodicals are devoted to discussions of drugs in America. For example, *The Drug Policy Letter,* published every two months by the Drug Policy Foundation in Washington, D.C., considers issues relating to the legal status of drugs. *The Drug Educator,* published quarterly by the American Council for Drug Education of Rockville, Maryland, stresses the health hazards associated even with so-called soft drugs like marijuana.

Erich Goode, *Drugs in American Society* (McGraw-Hill, 1988), provides a sociological perspective on drugs. Larry Sloman's book *Reefer Madness: The History of Marijuana in America* (Grove Press, 1983) describes changing attitudes and laws regarding marijuana, while Lester Brinspoon and James B. Bakalar do the same for cocaine in *Cocaine: A Drug and Its Social Evolution* (Basic Books, 1985). Thomas S. Szasz, *Ceremonial Chemistry: The Ritual Persecution of Drugs, Addicts, and Pushers,* rev. ed. (Learning Publications, 1985), criticizes the current antidrug crusades.

Whatever the future of drug abuse in America, the present situation is grim. The use of hard drugs has been linked to the staggering increases in crime, violence, and AIDS over the past decade. All sides agree that something must be done. The question is what: What will work without causing undue restrictions on personal freedoms? The debate, partly pragmatic and partly an argument over the value and place of liberty in America, will continue for as long as drugs continue to plague the nation.

ISSUE 14

Are the Poor Being Harmed by Welfare?

YES: Robert Rector, from "Requiem for the War on Poverty: Rethinking Welfare After the L.A. Riots," *Policy Review* (Summer 1992)

NO: Barbara Ehrenreich, from "The New Right Attack on Social Welfare," in Fred Block et al., eds., *The Mean Season: The Attack on the Welfare State* (Pantheon Books, 1987)

ISSUE SUMMARY

YES: Social policy analyst Robert Rector argues that the welfare system undermines the work ethic and discourages the formation of two-parent families. He feels that true welfare reform would encourage personal responsibility and effort.

NO: Journalist Barbara Ehrenreich believes that social welfare should not be blamed for the ills of the poor, and she argues that unfettered free enterprise and the consumer culture are responsible for the permissiveness and perceived moral decline of modern America.

The Great Depression that began with the stock market crash of 1929 and continued through the 1930s led to the adoption of far-reaching government policies designed to put people to work. These in turn led to the Social Security Act in 1935, to provide some measure of economic protection for retired workers and their survivors, disabled workers, and the unemployed.

Social Security insured only working people, and neither it nor Aid to Families with Dependent Children nor public housing programs met the needs of the poorest people. President Franklin D. Roosevelt called attention in 1937 to the plight of "one-third of a nation, ill-housed, ill-clad, ill-nourished," and, a generation later, President Lyndon B. Johnson proposed a War on Poverty "to lift this forgotten fifth of our nation above the poverty line." Almost surely the proportion was less than it had been, but it was clear that poverty remained widespread and deeply rooted in American society.

It was during Johnson's presidency that the federal government initiated food stamps, Medicaid for the poor, Medicare for the elderly, Head Start educational programs for underprivileged children, and the Job Corps. Still later came Supplemental Security Income for the blind, disabled, and low-income aged.

The election of Ronald Reagan in 1980 and his reelection in 1984 brought to the presidency an opponent of welfare policies who succeeded in securing sharp cuts in the growth rate of such welfare programs as food stamps and Aid to Families with Dependent Children. Although he spoke of a "safety net" to ensure that those who genuinely required governmental assistance would be able to secure it, his critics maintained that the so-called net was full of holes.

Reagan's vice president and successor as president, George Bush, spoke of a "kinder, gentler nation," but shared Reagan's economic philosophy. He stressed reliance on the stimulation of business activity rather than on welfare. Bush urged reduction in taxes on investment income as a spur to business investment, which could create jobs—thus helping everyone, including the poor. "A rising tide lifts all boats," a motto used in the early 1960s by officials in the Kennedy administration to justify tax cuts, was revived, at least in spirit, during the Reagan and Bush administrations. The problem is that a rising tide will not raise shipwrecks from the bottom of the sea. People too long unemployed become unemployable because they lack both the skills they would need in the workplace and the will to find employment.

The least controversial American welfare programs have probably been Social Security, Medicare, college grants and loans, and unemployment insurance. These programs are universal or nearly so in bestowing benefits, as distinguished from programs that involve a means test in order to make them available only to the poor.

During the last decade there has been an increasing public perception of the growing number of homeless people. How many people in America are homeless is disputed, with 1990 figures ranging from 300,000 to 3 million. There is even less agreement on the causes of homelessness. Among the most frequently cited reasons are the unprofitability of low-cost housing and the decline of government subsidies, soaring rents, and the fact that many mentally ill people have been released from institutions without being provided shelter and economic support. Here, as with other welfare issues, conservatives are skeptical of the value of throwing money at the problem.

Can poverty be eliminated or sharply reduced, or must there always be poor people? Has government intervention failed because it sought to do too much, didn't do enough, or didn't do the right things? Why does the poverty level remain high in a nation in which so many enjoy a high standard of living? Why is the disparity between poor and rich Americans wider than in other prosperous industrial nations?

Both Robert Rector and Barbara Ehrenreich take a glum view of our economic policy and its impact on the poor. Rector blames the lost War on Poverty on the increase in single-parent families and long-term dependency on welfare, both of which are the direct result of federal welfare programs. Ehrenreich rejects these conclusions of welfare critics. She indicts the economic greed and consumerism of what she calls "capitalist culture" as the enemies of democracy.

YES

Robert Rector

REQUIEM FOR THE WAR ON POVERTY: RETHINKING WELFARE AFTER THE L.A. RIOTS

The War on Poverty has failed. Twenty-five years after the riots under Lyndon Johnson led to a massive expansion of urban welfare programs, the riots in Los Angeles show that the problems of the inner city have not been solved and have actually gotten worse.

This failure is not due to a lack of spending. In 1990 federal, state, and local governments spent $215 billion on assistance programs for low-income persons and communities. This figure includes only spending on programs for the poor and excludes middle-class entitlements such as Social Security and Medicare. Adjusting for inflation, total welfare spending in 1990 was five times the level of welfare spending in the mid-1960s when the War on Poverty began. Total welfare spending in the War on Poverty since its inception in 1964 has been $3.5 trillion (in constant 1990 dollars); an amount that exceeds the entire cost of World War II after adjusting for inflation.

The problem with the welfare state is not the level of spending, it is that nearly all of this expenditure actively promotes self-destructive behavior among the poor. Current welfare may best be conceptualized as a system that offers each single mother a "paycheck" as long as she fulfills two conditions: 1) she does not work; and 2) she does not marry an employed male. I call this the incentive system made in hell.

MATERIAL VS. BEHAVIORAL POVERTY

All too often policy-makers fail to recognize that there are two separate kinds of poverty: "material poverty" and "behavioral poverty." Material poverty means, in the simplest sense, having a family income below the official poverty income threshold, which was $12,675 for a family of four in 1991.

To the average American, however, to say someone is poor implies that he or she is malnourished, inadequately clothed, and lives in inadequate housing. There is little material poverty in the United States in this sense generally understood by the public. Today, the fifth of the population with the lowest incomes has a level of economic consumption higher than that of the median American family in 1955.

For instance, there is little or no poverty-induced malnutrition in the United States. People defined by the U.S. government as "poor" have almost the same average level of consumption of protein, vitamins, and other nutrients as people in the upper middle class. Children living in "poverty" today, far from being malnourished, actually grow up to be one inch taller and 10 pounds heavier than the average child of the same age in the general population in the late 1950s. The principal nutrition-related problem facing poor people in the United States today is obesity, not hunger.

Similarly, a "poor" American has more housing space and is less likely to be overcrowded than is the *average* citizen in Western Europe. Nearly all of the American poor live in decent housing that is well-maintained. In fact, nearly 40 percent of the households defined as poor by the government own their homes.

"Behavioral poverty," by contrast, refers to a breakdown in the values and conduct that lead to the formation of healthy families, stable personalities, and self-sufficiency. Behavioral poverty is a cluster of social pathologies including: dependency and eroded work ethic, lack of educational aspiration and achievement, inability or unwillingness to control one's children, increased single parenthood and illegitimacy, criminal activity, and drug and alcohol abuse. While there may be little material poverty in the United States, behavioral poverty is abundant and growing.

LIBERALISM'S DASHED ASSUMPTIONS

There are three distinct approaches to dealing with the interrelated problems of material poverty and behavioral poverty. The first approach, which could be called "liberal," maintains that decreasing material poverty leads to decreasing behavioral poverty. Thus raising the incomes of the poor through cash, food aid, and housing assistance will increase emotional stability, educational success, and so forth.

The second approach, which could be called "redistributionist," posits no clear link between raising incomes and reducing behavioral problems. This theory promotes welfare expansion to raise the incomes of the less affluent for its own sake. While this approach focuses initially on dealing with vital needs such as eliminating malnutrition, its aims are open-ended. Thus, although welfare spending is already more than twice the amount needed to eliminate all poverty in the United States, demands for more spending are as vociferous as ever. Most advocates of this position believe strongly that income redistribution is a positive goal in and of itself, and seek to use welfare policy as a means of attaining that goal. The more income redistributed the better.

The third approach might be termed "conservative." It rests on the belief that spending on most welfare programs actually has increased behavioral poverty. In particular, this approach holds that welfare has led to an increase in prolonged dependency and has undermined family structure, thereby contributing to increases in other dysfunctional behaviors.

The assumptions behind the first, or liberal, approach to welfare policy are decisively refuted by historical experience. Throughout most of the 20th century the incomes of Americans of all social classes have increased dramatically. As noted, after adjusting for inflation, the per capita economic consumption of the least affluent 20 percent of households today exceeds the per-capita income of the median-income U.S. family in 1955. . . . According to the axioms of liberal welfare policy, as incomes in all social classes rose dramatically throughout the century, we should have seen increases in cognitive ability, emotional stability, and marital stability, and decreases in crime. Instead we have seen the opposite.

Most people alive today had at least one parent or grandparent who was "poor" by the current government definition adjusted for inflation. But most of these individuals were not poor in spirit or behavior. Although their incomes were low, their values, disciplines, and behavior were middle-class—as were the values they passed on to their children. Merely raising someone's income does not inculcate middle-class values and behavior; in fact, most welfare programs do exactly the opposite.

COMMUNITY DEVASTATION

Following the liberal and redistributionist approaches to welfare, the present welfare system is designed almost exclusively to raise the material living standards of less-affluent Americans. The federal government provides cash, food, housing and medical assistance, and other benefits through more than 75 separate welfare programs. As noted, total federal, state, and local welfare spending reached $215 billion in 1990, excluding all middle-class entitlement programs such as Social Security and Medicare. This figure was more than twice the amount needed to raise the income of every American above the current poverty income thresholds.

But for the general public the real problem with welfare is not the rapidly expanding cost, which now absorbs over 4 percent of the entire national economy—but the sense that welfare actually harms rather than helps the poor. The key dilemma of the welfare state is that the prolific spending intended to alleviate material poverty has led to a dramatic increase in behavioral poverty. The War on Poverty may have raised the material standard of living of poor Americans, but at a cost of creating whole communities where traditional two-parent families have vanished, work is rare or nonexistent, and multiple generations have grown up dependent on government transfers. . . .

Welfare's effectiveness in undermining the work ethic is readily apparent. In the mid-1950s nearly one-third of poor households were headed by an adult who worked full time throughout the year. Today, with greater welfare benefits available, only 16.4 percent of poor families are headed by a full-time working adult.

HUSBAND AS HANDICAP

Another devastating legacy of the past 25 years has been the dramatic reduction in family formation. The current welfare system has made marriage economically irrational for most low-income parents by converting the low-income working husband from a necessary breadwinner into a net financial handicap. It has transformed marriage from a legal institution designed to protect and nurture children into one that financially penalizes nearly all low-income parents who enter into it.

Across the nation, the current welfare system has all but destroyed family structure in the inner city by establishing strong financial disincentives to marriage. Suppose a young man fathers a child out of wedlock. If this young father abandons his responsibilities to the mother and child, government will step in and support them with welfare. If the mother has a second child out of wedlock, average combined benefits will reach around $13,000 per year.

If, on the other hand, the young man does what society believes is morally correct (that is, marries the mother and takes a job to support the family), government policy takes the opposite course. Welfare benefits would be almost completely eliminated. If the young father makes more than $4.50 per hour, the federal government actually begins taking away his income through taxes. (The federal welfare reform act of 1988 permits the young father to marry the mother and join the family to receive welfare, but only as long as he does not work. Once he takes a full-time job to support his family, the welfare benefits are quickly eliminated and the father's earnings are subject to taxation.) . . .

CRIPPLING FAMILY BREAKDOWN

The collapse of family structure has crippling effects on the health, emotional stability, educational achievements, and life prospects of low-income children. Children raised in single-parent families, when compared with those in intact families, are one-third more likely to exhibit behavioral problems such as hyperactivity, antisocial behavior, and anxiety.

Children deprived of a two-parent home are two to three times more likely to need psychiatric care than those in two-parent families. And as teen-agers they are more likely to commit suicide. Absence of a father increases the probability that a child will use drugs and engage in criminal activity.

. . . In all respects, the differences between children raised in single-parent homes and those raised in intact homes are profound, and such differences persist even if single-parent homes are compared with two-parent homes of exactly the same income level and educational standing.

But the greatest tragedy is that family instability and its attendant problems are passed on to future generations. Children from single-parent homes are far less likely to establish a stable married life when they in turn become adults. White women raised in single-parent families are 164 percent more likely to bear children out of wedlock themselves; they are 111 percent more likely to have children as teen-agers. If these women do marry, their marriages are 92 percent more likely to end in divorce than are the marriages of women raised in two-parent families. Similar trends are found among black women.

Long-term dependency on welfare also appears to be passed down from one generation to another. Of the over four million families currently receiving assistance through Aid to Families with Dependent Children (AFDC), well over half will remain dependent for over 10 years, many for 15 years or longer. Children raised in families that receive welfare assistance are themselves three times more likely than other children to be on welfare when they become adults. This inter-generational dependency is a clear indication that the welfare system is failing in its goal to lift the poor from poverty to self-sufficiency.

WELFARE'S CRUEL LOGIC

By nature, Americans are optimists and believe that all problems have solutions. Therefore, American politicians and the public have difficulty believing that there are no easy solutions to the anti-marriage, anti-work incentives provided by the current welfare system. But no easy solutions exist.

In the current public debate there are a number of quick fixes to welfare that fall short of true reform. The most common of these is the current liberal drive to encourage work and reduce dependency by "making work pay." Under these proposals, the key to welfare reform is to ensure that all single mothers will be financially better off in the job market than on welfare.

While a step in the right direction, there are two problems with this idea. First, the average welfare mother receives around $11,000 per year in welfare benefits plus Medicaid. Thus the mother must obtain a job with medical coverage paying more than $11,000 per year (or $5.50 per hour) in order to be even slightly better off with a job than on welfare. Second, even if every mother could be guaranteed a job with medical coverage paying say $7.00 per hour, the financial incentives for taking a job would remain slight. For example, if a mother gives up welfare benefits worth $11,000 per year plus Medicaid and takes a full-time job with medical coverage paying $14,000 per year (or $7.00 per hour), she obtains an annual post-tax income increase of about $2,500 in exchange for working 2,000 hours during the course of the year. This is an effective pay rate of $1.25 per hour. The AFDC mother is expected to make a very large increase in labor for very little, if any, financial reward.

A similar recommendation is to reduce the disincentives to marriage by raising the earnings capacity of low-income fathers. While this would be another step in the right direction, it would not eliminate the anti-marriage effects of conventional welfare. Even if the earnings capacity of all low-income fathers were raised to the point where *every* working father could provide a standard of living for his family higher than the standard of living welfare provides to single mothers—low-income mothers and fathers would still be better off financially if they avoided marriage.

The economic logic of welfare is simple and cruel. If a mother and father do not marry, their joint income is the value of welfare benefits for the mother plus the father's earnings. If they do marry their joint income equals the father's earnings alone.

SEVEN REFORMS

Many current liberal proposals fall short because they add small new rewards for constructive behavior while ignoring the huge rewards for idleness and single parenthood already embedded in the present welfare system. Serious welfare reform must not only provide new incentives for positive behavior, it must also reduce the huge rewards for destructive behavior that exist in the current system.

What is needed is a comprehensive welfare reform strategy that would balance these two key elements. Not only must it increase the rewards for work and marriage among low-income families, it must reduce the incentives currently provided by welfare for non-work and single parenthood.

Although many elements of comprehensive reform can be implemented at the state level, state actions should be complemented by tax relief and an overhaul of the U.S. medical system at the federal level. While tax policy and medical reform are formally outside the welfare system, reforms in these areas would have a significant impact on the opportunities and behavior of low-income families, and therefore are an important part of any welfare reform strategy.

A comprehensive welfare reform package would include seven important policy innovations:

1) Require work in return for benefits. States should require some but not all welfare recipients to work in exchange for benefits received. Recipients of food stamps and general assistance who are not elderly and not disabled and who are not directly caring for small children should be required to obtain a job or if a job is not available to perform community service for at least 20 hours per week. Within the AFDC program, mothers who do not have children under age five or who have received AFDC for over five years should be required to find private-sector employment. If such employment is not available, they should be required to perform community service for at least 35 hours per week in exchange for benefits. In all two-parent families receiving AFDC, one parent should be required to work. For all programs the work requirement should be permanent, lasting as long as the individual or family receives benefits.

This policy specifically exempts most mothers with pre-school children from the work requirement. . . . However, a second rule requiring work from mothers who received AFDC payments for over five years, either continuously or in separate periods, is needed to discourage mothers from intentionally having additional children to avoid their work obligation. . . .

Of the seven reforms of the welfare incentive system presented here, the work requirement is the most important. Under the current welfare system a non-working single mother receives an income from the government for free; if she becomes employed she must give up all or part of this free income. However, if the welfare recipient is required to work in exchange for benefits, a new cost is attached to welfare dependence and the attractiveness of welfare relative to employment is greatly reduced. . . .

Surprisingly, a work requirement also eliminates the anti-marriage incentives of the current welfare system. Under the current welfare system, when a single mother marries a fully employed male she loses most of her welfare benefits. Under a welfare system with a work requirement, a single mother still would lose her benefits upon marrying—but she would not be losing benefits that she had to earn rather than a free income, so the loss would be far less significant. As long as the mother could obtain a private-sector job that paid roughly as much as welfare, then marriage would no longer impose a significant financial or personal cost on the mother or her prospective spouse. . . .

2) Reduce benefits. Welfare benefits for families on AFDC should be reduced. This is particularly true in states with high benefits levels. AFDC recipients are eligible for benefits from nearly one dozen major welfare programs. In all but five states, the combined value of benefits received by the average AFDC family exceeds the federal poverty income threshold. Moreover, there is considerable inequality in welfare benefit levels within each state. Because some families receive aid from many programs, they will have overall benefits much greater than other welfare families of the same size and characteristics within the state. AFDC families who also receive housing aid will have overall benefits some $4,000 to $5,000 higher than other AFDC families within the state. In almost every state such families will have combined welfare benefits well above the poverty threshold. States should reduce AFDC payments to families who also receive housing aid.

3) Require responsible behavior. States should require responsible behavior as a condition of receiving welfare benefits. This would include policies such as insisting that unmarried minor mothers reside with their parents or in some other adult-supervised setting, and reducing payments to mothers who fail to provide their children with free immunizations. Most important, mothers who bear additional children while they are already receiving welfare should not receive an increase in welfare benefits.

4) Establish paternity and enforce child-support payments. Single mothers should not be eligible for welfare unless they are willing to identify the father of their children. Contrary to popular perception, most unwed mothers are not promiscuous; the father of the child is well known to them. In cases where more than one male may be the father, modern scientific methods permit the determination of the true biological parent with nearly absolute certainty.

All single mothers prospectively enrolling in the AFDC program should be required to have the paternity of their child legally established as a condition of receiving benefits. The absent fathers should then be required to pay child support to offset at least some of the costs of providing welfare to their children. If an absent father claims he cannot pay child support because he cannot find work, he should be required to perform community service to pay off his child-support obligations.

Establishing a rigorous paternity and child-support system will greatly reduce the incentives for young males to enhance their macho image by siring children out of wedlock whom they have no intention of supporting. Another benefit of the proposed system is that it increases the rewards to responsible couples who marry relative to those who do not and thus, over time, will encourage marriage. However, a warning is needed: the government should avoid aggressively pursuing child support payments among young, low-skilled males without the firm backup of required community service for absent fathers who report they are unemployed. Aggressive child-support activities among this group without an accompanying community service requirement will counterproductively induce many young men to leave the labor force or work "off the books" to evade their child-support obligations.

5) Enforce education requirements. States presently fail to enforce the current federal law requiring all AFDC mothers under age 18 who have not completed high school or passed a GED to attend school. This provision should be enforced. To avoid the negative effects of separating infants from their mothers, however, mothers with infant children should not be required to participate for more than 20 hours per week.

6) Provide tax credits or vouchers for medical coverage to all working families. The current welfare system provides free medical coverage to single parents and non-working two-parent families on AFDC, but does not provide medical assistance to low-income working families. This discourages work because a welfare mother considering a low-income job in a small firm—which typically will not include a health benefits plan—faces the loss of thousands of dollars' worth of medical benefits if she accepts employment. It also discourages marriage because a welfare mother marrying a man in a low-wage job in a firm without family medical benefits will again lose medical coverage.

The federal government could reduce the anti-work/anti-marriage effects of welfare by enacting the comprehensive medical reform proposed by The Heritage Foundation in *A National Health System for America*. This plan would, among other reforms, provide federal tax credits and vouchers for the purchase of medical insurance to low-income working families not eligible for Medicaid. . . .

7) Provide tax relief to all families with children. The federal government currently imposes heavy taxes on low-income working families with children. A family of four making $20,000 a year currently pays $3,780 in federal taxes. This heavy taxation promotes welfare dependence by reducing the rewards of work and marriage relative to welfare. A crucial step in welfare reform is broad family tax relief along the lines proposed in The Heritage Foundation's *A Prosperity Plan for America: How to Strengthen Family Finances, Revive the Economy, and Balance the Budget*. This plan would provide a $1,000 tax credit for each school-age child and a $1,500 tax credit for each preschool child; the tax credits could be used to reduce the family's income-tax liability and both the employee and employer share of the Social Security payroll tax. The plan would eliminate all federal taxes on working families with children with incomes below 120 percent of the poverty threshold. The revenue loss of these tax credits would be offset by corresponding spending constraints through capping the growth of total federal domestic spending at 5 percent per annum. Thus the plan would not add to the federal deficit.

RESPONSIBILITY AND INCENTIVES

Reform of the welfare system must ultimately be based on two principles. The first is personal responsibility. Society should provide aid to those in need. But aid that is merely a one-way handout is harmful to both society and the recipient. Such aid undermines the individual's ability to take responsibility for his or her own life. If the habit of dependence becomes entrenched, it destroys the individual's capability to become a fully functioning member of mainstream society. Currently, welfare is a check in the mail with no obligations. Reformed welfare should be based on reciprocal responsibility; society will provide assistance, but able-bodied recipients must be expected to behave responsibly and to contribute back to society in exchange for the benefits they receive.

The second principle is that incentives matter. Any attempt to reform the current structure of public welfare must begin with the realization that most programs designed to alleviate material poverty have led to an increase in behavioral poverty. The rule in welfare, as in other government programs, is simple: you get what you pay for. For over 40 years the welfare system has been paying for non-work and single parenthood and has obtained dramatic increases in both. But welfare that discourages work and penalizes marriage ultimately harms its intended beneficiaries.

The incentives provided by welfare must be reversed. But balance is crucial: comprehensive welfare reform must combine toughness and refusal to reward negative behavior with positive rewards for constructive behavior. Reforms that fail to include both sides of the equation will not succeed.

NO
Barbara Ehrenreich

THE NEW RIGHT ATTACK ON SOCIAL WELFARE

"PERMISSIVENESS" AND SOCIAL WELFARE

The oldest conservative argument against social welfare is that it undermines the work ethic. The contemporary right has gone well beyond this, arguing that social welfare not only frees people from the discipline of the market but is an indulgence on a par with sexual libertinism, drug abuse, and uncontrolled consumerism. Most often the argument is made by a process of linguistic association, the key link being the notion of "permissiveness." To the right, permissiveness is the fundamental crime of liberalism, and is responsible for every perceived form of decadence and moral breakdown. Thus political analyst Kevin Phillips (a conservative but not a New Rightist) finds that liberalism is responsible for "permissiveness of various economic, diplomatic, sociological and sexual hues," which turn out to include homosexuality and abortion, "judicial permissiveness" toward criminals, and "welfarism."

The effect, and no doubt the intent, of the right's emphasis on permissiveness and its moral consequences is to take social welfare out of the realm of economic issues and into the realm of what the New Right identifies as "social issues." The genius of the New Right has lain in recognizing that while middle Americans tend to be liberal on economic issues, many are conservative on social issues. By transmuting social welfare into a social or moral issue, an appeal could be made to people who were loyal to Democratic social welfare initiatives but disturbed about a perceived "moral breakdown" of American society.

"Permissiveness," like many contemporary right-wing notions, entered the political discourse in the 1960s, when it was used principally to castigate student radicals. In the argument popularized by Agnew and repeated by Nixon, the student left and the youthful counterculture were both products of permissive child-raising practices. In the seventies, neoconservatives expanded the notion of permissiveness to include the sexual revolution and sundry other manifestations of what they perceived as a breakdown of traditional sources of authority. Today the term has almost automatic connotations of sexual laxity and, at the same time, has become almost indispensable in conservative attacks on social welfare. In a recent short op-ed piece by conservative social scientist Lawrence Mead, for example, the word "permissive" appears four times, and is as tightly linked to the words "welfare programs" as the elements of a Homeric epithet. . . .

"Permissiveness" is a complex metaphor and derives an insidious power from the wealth of associations it calls up. In the first place, if welfare programs are permissive and analogous to certain child-raising practices, then the poor are analogous to children. The image of the poor as childlike and undisciplined is a very old one; in the "culture of poverty" theories of the sixties, which many liberals subscribed to, the poor were described as intrinsically hedonistic, incapable of deferred gratification, and having little sense of time. (In fact, it is interesting that the War on Poverty grew out of earlier programs focused on juvenile delinquency.) In the New Right's view, the childlike traits of the poor have been imposed from the outside, through the new class's indulgent social policies. [Social researcher Charles] Murray is insistent on this point. The poor did not change; they did not become more vicious, more dependent, on their own. Only "the rules changed" with the expansion of social welfare programs in the sixties. The poor did not participate in changing the rules—that was the work of the "intelligentsia"; they merely responded to the new, more indulgent expectations. They are a tabula rasa, awaiting the imprint of sterner, character-building policies. . . .

To reject the image of the poor as children is not to deny that individuals in poverty are more likely to suffer from personal dislocation and a disordered life-style than are middle-class people. One of the goals of the War on Poverty, in fact, was to help overcome the disorganization of ghetto life by providing channels for leadership and decision-making in community-based services. But in the right-wing view that obliterates the poor as conscious participants in history, no such community involvement is possible, or perhaps even thinkable. Worse, if the poor are not innocents awaiting opportunities for citizenly involvement (as liberals, paternalistically, saw them), if they are already spoiled children, then the only course of action is to discipline them with punitive right-wing policies.

Implicit in the assumption that the poor are a temperamentally homogeneous group, and beyond that, that they bear the marks of a shared historical experience (having been spoiled by the briefly more generous social welfare programs of the sixties and early seventies), is the idea that the poor are a constant, self-reproducing subpopulation—the "underclass" of conservative theory. In reality . . . there is considerable turnover within the poverty population, which is likely to include, at any give time, many recent recruits from the middle class—divorced mothers, laid-off industrial workers, dispossessed farmers. Such individuals surely bring with them into poverty the traditional values of hard work that conservatives find so admirable, and none of them could have been spoiled by prior shifts in social welfare policy. To imagine the poor as children, and particularly as a single cohort of children, is to deny the heterogeneity of the poverty population, and hence to deny the widespread vulnerability to poverty that so many Americans share.

The metaphor of social welfare permissiveness, like the notion that social welfare is the self-serving program of an elite, effectively undercuts the moral foundations of the welfare state. If social welfare programs are actually an avenue of contagion by which personal decadence spreads from liberal members of the middle class to the poor, then surely these programs should be abandoned in toto, as Charles Murray suggests. If, to state it less dramatically, social welfare programs are the means by which the poor have been misguided, exposed to the wrong "rules," and so forth, liberal social welfare advocates should at least feel remorse. And in some cases, they seem to do so. In a 1985 article presenting him as a "defender of 'the Welfare System,' " liberal social-policy analyst Sar Levitan is quoted as confessing, "We went too far. Permissiveness is the key word. We gave up on old-fashioned standards."

THE SOURCES OF "PERMISSIVENESS"

The success of the metaphor of permissiveness has depended on a widespread sense that there has indeed been a moral breakdown within American society. Many factors have contributed to the perception that such a breakdown, or as the neoconservatives often put it, a "crisis of authority," occurred in the 1960s and 1970s. There was the emergence of a youth-oriented counterculture that did indeed uphold an ethic of self-indulgence and immediate gratification. There was a precipitous rise in the divorce rate, beginning in the early sixties and still under way. There were the various manifestations of a sexual revolution, including a proliferation of commercial pornography, increasingly explicit sexual references in the mass media, and the emergence of a visible gay-rights movement. Finally, there was the emergence of a feminist movement that explicitly challenged male authority within the family as well as in public life. All of these changes, magnified at times by the media and superimposed on a massive black insurgency, have been as threatening to some as they have been liberating to others.

But the "crisis of authority," as seen by the right, can hardly be blamed on elite "social engineering" or government permissiveness. In some cases government did take liberal social initiatives (though often only to liberalize previously punitive and authoritarian laws): abortion was decriminalized, divorce laws liberalized, and the voting age lowered. However, the public sector played only a small role in encouraging the *demand* for such reforms. The right's ideological link between moral breakdown, as evidenced by pornography and greater sexual freedom, on the one hand, and government policies undertaken by a liberal "elite," on the other, is a highly imaginative construction.

To the extent that America has become in any way a permissive society, the source of permissiveness lies outside the public sector, and the machinations of government bureaucrats: in the private sector, and particularly in the consumer culture. Take the problem of sexual laxity, which so alarms conservatives. No new-class elite decreed the various manifestations of sexual revolution (though individuals of different social classes, including what could be construed as the new class, worked to achieve a liberalization of American sexual mores). Rather, it is the media, including the advertising and entertainment industries, that have "sexualized" our culture with images intended to command attention and ultimately to sell products.

Or take the "youth rebellion" and the perceived youthful disrespect for authority. Certainly social welfare policy had little to do with the emergence of the "youth culture" in the sixties (though the argument is often made that AFDC enables young women to flout parental authority and indulge their sexuality). In fact, the consumer culture played a major role in encouraging the sense of youth identity that underlay the emergence of a youth culture. Teenagers as teenagers became a major marketing target in the 1950s and 1960s; and marketing strategies that focused on teenagers recognized the importance of heightening young people's self-awareness as a legitimate social group, different from both children and young adults. Advertising to teenagers necessarily encourages the assertion of youthful needs in the face of parental restraint, while the emergence of distinctly teen products such as music and fashions creates an area of youth expertise impenetrable to many adults. Whether these are positive or negative developments is open to debate, but there can be no question about the role of the consumer culture in promoting them.

Or consider the "breakdown of the family," which is of so much concern to the New Right. The right uniformly attributes the rise of single-parent families among the poor to the disruptive effects of welfare. When they take into account

similar trends among the middle class, they are likely to blame "women's liberation" or even male irresponsibility. Arguably, both of these factors have contributed to the rising divorce rate: women's increased work-force participation (which hardly represents "liberation," I might add) makes it easier for women to leave unhappy marriages, just as changed attitudes toward men's responsibility as breadwinners has made it easier for them to leave their families or never to marry in the first place. Both of these changes, however, can be related to the mounting demands of the consumer culture. As Barbara Bergmann and others have argued, women's influx into the work force represented not just the triumph of feminist ideology, or even the pressure of economic necessity (the great influx took place among women who were already middle class, not among the poor), but the need to keep up with a rising standard of living, as defined by the mass media and, to a certain extent, required by suburban living.

Similarly, the decline in male "responsibility," or long-term financial commitment to the family, can be linked, as I have argued elsewhere, to the rise of a marketing strategy directed toward men as consumers in their own right. In general, there has been a shift since the 1950s away from a marketing focus on the family as the unit of consumption to a focus on the individual. Products for individual consumption by males have proliferated to include increasingly differentiated styles of clothing (not just for "work" and for "good" but for a range of leisure options), housewares (for the bachelor apartment), and most recently, cosmetics. At the same time, media vehicles responsible for targeting the male market, such as *Playboy* and *GQ* magazines, glamorize the single male and, sometimes explictly, criticize traditionalist assumptions about men's responsibility as breadwinners.

In general, the consumer culture has little stake in the family as traditionally defined: working husband, homemaker wife, and children. For one thing, such a family does not earn or spend enough compared to a family with a wife who holds a job. For another thing, a family of any composition by its nature underconsumes key items like household appliances, at least relative to the amount that can be consumed by the same number of people occupying individual households. It is better for the consumergoods market if the consumers (or at least the affluent ones) remain single or, if they marry, get divorced at some point and duplicate many of their possessions.

But more generally, we know from everyday experience that the "ethic of self-indulgence" does not come from an overly generous government, but from a consumer culture that is endlessly inventive in producing new temptations and new rationales for yielding to them. Advertising's ubiquitous message is that every whim is a genuine need; every passing inclination, an imperative to consume. Nor is this message the adventitious result of a concentration of newclass operatives within the advertising and marketing industries. American capitalism, with its heavy reliance on individual consumer products, *requires* a mass disposition to self-indulgence, and would be severely threatened by a genuine resurgence of the traditional values of self-denial and deferred gratification attributed by the right to middle Americans. . . .

Just as the Protestant work ethic was appropriate to the earlier, accumulative stage of industrial capitalism, the "hedonistic approach" became an economic necessity as affluence created a vast domestic market for consumer goods. Actually, both are demanded of us: traditional values at the workplace and often in the family, and hedonism in the realm of consumption. As Daniel Bell has written, capitalist society is torn by a fundamental contradiction between the traditional values appropriate to stable community and family life and the hedonistic imperative of the consumer culture. . . .

It would hardly be in character for the right—old or new—to concur in pinpointing capitalism as a major source of permissiveness and moral breakdown. Shifting the blame to government, and particularly to social welfare programs, represents a remarkable, and on the face of it, almost nonsensical displacement. No government on earth is ideologically or practically permissive in the way that the capitalist consumer culture is; and those governments that are most intrusive and most controlling are also the least permissive. Yet the right continues to berate government for permissiveness and to uphold the free market as the natural inculcator of traditional values of discipline and self-denial.

There are hints that the leadership of the New Right may be ready to acknowledge the dominant role of capitalism in promoting moral breakdown. A recent column by Paul Weyrich, one of the four men credited with creating the New Right, points to "direct tension between cultural conservatives and some economic conservatives." If cultural conservatism, or an emphasis on the "social issues," was initially an opportunistic way of advancing economic conservatism, the cart may now be dragging the horse. In what is almost a direct criticism of modern capitalist culture, Weyrich quotes William Lind:

> In a "free market" of values, the limits, restraints and self-discipline traditional ways of living require cannot compete with aggressively promoted self-gratification, sensual pleasures, and materialism. . . .

While traditional conservatism sought only to limit government, Weyrich's new "cultural conservatism" would use government to enforce the traditional values of family stability, hard work, and sexual puritanism. Such a variety of conservatism, which would enlarge government in order to enforce certain styles of individual behavior, is inescapably reminiscent of fascism. . . .

CONCLUSION

Perhaps the most surprising feature of the New Right's rise to national power and prominence is the degree to which its ideological assumptions have been absorbed or accepted within the moderate-to-liberal political mainstream. One of these assumptions is that liberalism is, if not elitist, at least inherently incapable of being populist. Thus, even as polls have repeatedly shown substantial and growing public support for social welfare, erstwhile liberal politicians have persisted in the belief, inspired by the New Right, that social welfare advocacy is unwise or even suicidal. Even more pervasive is the New Right's assumption that *the* problem of American society is permissiveness, and that liberalism is inherently incapable of curbing it.

The New Right has been able to seize the moral initiative from liberalism, above all, because it has dared to advance a strong *qualitative* critique of capitalist society. Liberalism too once had the moral initiative, pressing for measures to bring the poor and racial minorities into the mainstream of American life. But liberalism offered no alternative vision of—or for—that mainstream. Just as business unionism has demanded "more" (Samuel Gompers's emphatic vision) for its constituents, the crusading liberalism of two decades ago offered "more" for the excluded, but without questioning the content or limits of such a demand. Morally speaking, liberalism was made vulnerable to ideological attack because it failed to address the meaning of "more" in a consumer culture that advertises unlimited acquisition and pointlessly commodified hedonism. It is not that the old quantitative, redistributive demands of liberalism are any less urgent than they were twenty years ago. But they have been upstaged, so to speak, by a right-wing ideology that insists we do not need simply more of what there is to have, but a profoundly different way of living.

Like other right-wing movements of this century, the American New Right *does* offer an alternative vision to the endless disruptions and aimless individualism of bourgeois society. It is a vision of the future in which people will live in stable families within stable communities and will work hard and be sober and chaste. Authority will be firmly vested in adults over children, in men over women, and in ancient sources of wisdom, such as the Bible, over modern science and "humanism." If there is still poverty after such a moral reformation of society, it will be dealt with through individual or local charity rather than impersonal government mechanisms. In short, this is the traditional nostalgic vision of *Gemeinschaft*—of the organic community associated with small-scale agriculture restored, only in the midst of a technologically modern capitalist society.

Lacking an alternative vision, today's liberals have simply appropriated the most evocative themes and language of the right: family, hard work, the importance of replacing permissiveness with sterner values. While criticizing the excesses of the New Right, they have implicitly accepted its cultural polarity: permissiveness versus traditional values, hedonism versus repression. . . . As a result, liberalism itself has come to seem vacuous and yielding, not so much a coherent ideological vision as a surrender to the moral breakdown that the right proposes to address. It offers no new ideas other than the old notion of gradually amending the status quo, while the right offers a future—even if it is, manifestly, only the past, or a distorted version of it.

An effective response to the New Right would have to begin with an unambiguous rejection of its pastoral vision of the future. So far, feminists and civil libertarians have been in the forefront of the effort to counter the New Right's social vision, and they have done so on the grounds that it is a threat to individual rights—the rights of women and young people, and potentially the freedom of expression of all citizens. This kind of response is valuable and essential, for surely individual liberty ought to be one of the traditional values we hold most dear. But it is also a limited and inadequate response. First, it only reiterates the libertarian ideology which the New Right has effectively learned to associate with the "permissive," cosmopolitan interests of the new class. A response that focuses only on individual rights cannot allay either the anxieties or the class resentments which the right seeks to exploit. In fact, to counter the New Right with arguments that rest ultimately only on a liberal conception of individualism is to miss what is most powerful and appealing about the current ideology of the right: that it *does* dare to challenge the unrewarding individualism (coded as "hedonism" or "permissiveness") cultivated by the consumer society.

A more effective response to the New Right must emphasize not only what is distasteful about the right's vision—for example, from a libertarian perspective—but what is fundamentally duplicitous about that vision. As we have observed throughout this chapter, there is an inescapable contradiction between the New Right's stance on social issues and the (old or new) right's championship of unfettered free enterprise. The New Right's nostalgic vision of *Gemeinschaft* (or, some might say, a patriarchal version of fascism) cannot be achieved within the context of unregulated capitalism. It is not the new class that uproots communities and engenders pervasive anxiety even among the stably employed, but, in the most direct sense, corporations in search of lower labor costs and higher profits. And it is not the new class that foments the addictive materialism and self-indulgence of our society, but the consumer culture with its dynamic of endless expansion and ceaseless cultivation of "needs."

Ultimately, an effective response to the right must rest on a genuine critique of capitalist culture and on a genuinely radical alternative vision. This requires, first, that we transcend the right's false polarity of "traditional values" versus "permissiveness." The choices, as the basis either for society or for our lives as individuals, do not have to be self-denial or self-indulgence, repressiveness or what [social philosopher Herbert] Marcuse termed the "repressive desublimation" offered by the consumer culture. There are alternative values that are, at least in American culture, every bit as traditional as, say, hard work and self-denial. And these are the old small-R republican values of active citizenship, democratic participation, and the challenge and conviviality of the democratic process.

POSTSCRIPT

Are the Poor Being Harmed by Welfare?

Confronted with the poverty, homelessness, single-parent households, and permanent unemployment that are all too common in America, no one is likely to argue that America has dealt adequately with its welfare problem, let alone solved it. Is it insoluble? As Jacqueline Jones, *The Dispossessed: America's Underclass from the Civil War to the Present* (Basic Books, 1992) makes clear, there have always been many poor people in the United States. However, Americans want to believe that abject poverty is not a necessary condition in a society that extols liberty and equality.

The fault does lie with the welfare system, according to Charles Murray, *Losing Ground: American Social Policy, 1950–1980* (Basic Books, 1984), and the essayists in Paul M. Weyrich and Connaught Marshner, eds., *Future 21: Directions for America in the 21st Century* (Devon-Adair, 1984). Lawrence M. Mead, an early advocate of workfare, a policy that would penalize nonhandicapped people who refuse employment, states, in *The New Politics of Poverty: The Nonworking Poor in America* (Basic Books, 1992), that the issue is not whether or not there are enough jobs for the poor but why so many poor people will not work at jobs that are available.

The failure of our welfare system lies not with the system or the poor themselves, according to Lisbeth B. Schoor, *Within Our Reach: Breaking the Cycle of Disadvantage* (Anchor Press, 1988). She concludes that social programs for poor children work and, if pursued on a larger scale, they can lead to a decline in poverty. William Julius Wilson, *The Truly Disadvantaged: The Inner City, the Underclass, and Public Policy* (University of Chicago Press, 1987), believes that social changes leading to a sharp rise in black male unemployment, not welfare policy, have contributed to the economic decline of the poor.

In a series of books, Jonathan Kozol has sought to demonstrate that inequality in access to good schools leads to poverty for those deprived of genuine educational opportunity. Surveying the worst schools in *Savage Inequalities* (Crown, 1991), Kozol wrote: "We want the game to be unfair and we have made it so." Essays by many authors in Christopher Jencks and Paul E. Peterson, eds., *The Urban Underclass* (Brookings Institution, 1991), examine the impact on poverty of such factors as race, class, environment, years of schooling, marriage, and pregnancy.

America faces tough questions: Is there a permanent class of dependent people who lack both the skills and aspirations to support themselves? How do we break the cycle of poverty for teenage single mothers and their children? What should be the role of government in ensuring educational and employment opportunities? What are the long-term consequences of social and economic inequality?

ISSUE 15

Is the National Debt a National Liability?

YES: Benjamin M. Friedman, from *Day of Reckoning: The Consequences of American Economic Policy Under Reagan and After* (Random House, 1988)

NO: Robert L. Bartley, from *Seven Fat Years and How to Do It Again* (Free Press, 1992)

ISSUE SUMMARY

YES: Professor of political economics Benjamin M. Friedman believes that the steeply rising national debt of the 1980s led to a sharp decline in the economy, the reversal of which requires radical economic remedies.
NO: *Wall Street Journal* editor Robert L. Bartley holds that the significance of the deficit is exaggerated and that it takes attention away from fiscal policies that will enhance our economic growth.

Many people find it easy and relevant to talk about economics when the topic is employment and income, and it is clear that American elections have often turned on these issues. But when the focus turns to the balance of payments, budget deficits, and the national debt, voters seem decidedly less sure of what the issues are and where they stand.

To put it simply, the balance of payments refers to whether a country is selling or spending more (in dollar value) in foreign countries. The consequence is that the nation has a surplus or deficit in its trade. For most of the modern history of the United States, it was a creditor nation, and as the world's leading industrial power, it sold far more abroad than it bought in foreign markets. This created jobs and prosperity for millions of Americans. All this has turned around in recent years.

Each year's deficit must be added to the remaining total of indebtedness, and this constitutes the national debt. What may make this onerous is exactly the same as for an individual who borrows money for major purchases or spends money not at hand through the use of a credit card. Each month the money owed increases by the amount owed in new interest. Allow a debt to accumulate for a long period, and a large part of each month's payment will be interest charges that do not discharge the original debt or result in any new purchases.

The total national debt of the United States in 1980 was $900 billion—under $1 trillion. By 1992, it had grown to over $4 trillion, more than four times as much, and that year's probable deficit would be approximately $400 billion. In other words, a current single year's deficit can be nearly half as much as the total national debt was for the first 190 years of the nation's history.

The obvious result is that nearly 15 cents of every dollar the national government collects in taxes goes to pay interest on that debt. Other economic results, however, are less obvious. For example, debtor countries tend to be less competitive than creditor countries; their currency decreases in value in international trade; and more of their industrial and other assets are bought by foreign investors, thus removing corporate and other profits from the native country. All of these consequences have occurred in the United States, and they have contributed to economic decline.

In the 1990s adult Americans, perhaps for the first time in the nation's history, do not anticipate that their children's generation will be better off economically than theirs. Many critics of recent economic policy blame the deficit and debt for this increased pessimism about the nation's future.

Yet some economists believe that the dangers of the deficit and debt are greatly exaggerated. This is not a novel idea. Alexander Hamilton, the nation's first secretary of the treasury, wrote in 1781: "A national debt, if it is not excessive, will be a national blessing."

Hamilton's position raises two questions. First: Is the debt excessive? The present national debt is not a greater percentage of the nation's gross national product than it was 50 years ago, and not more than that of many other industrial countries. Second: Is it a blessing? The relevant question is, Why do we borrow? The debt is desirable and should be encouraged if the borrowed money is used to invest in the research and development of new products, buy new machinery, open new factories, and rebuild the roads, rails, and other resources that move goods to market. The American economy would suffer disastrously if people stopped taking on the personal debt incurred in buying a home, making major purchases, or starting up a new business.

In the following selections, Benjamin M. Friedman analyzes why, in his judgment, the taxing and spending policies America pursued in the 1980s have had disastrous results, and he suggests ways in which we can reverse economic decline. Robert L. Bartley maintains that the deficit and debt are often misunderstood, and that, in fact, the debt can be a national blessing if we wisely use the money we borrow in order to improve our productivity and competitiveness.

YES

Benjamin M. Friedman

BROKEN FAITH

A good man leaveth an inheritance to his children's children.
—PROVERBS, XIII:22

What can you say to a man on a binge who asks why it matters? Flush with cash from liquidating his modest investment portfolio and from taking out a second mortgage on the inflated value of his house, he can spend seemingly without limit. The vacation cruise his family has dreamed about for years, the foreign sports car he has always wanted, new designer clothes for his wife and even his children, meals in all the most expensive restaurants—life is wonderful. What difference does it make if he has to pay some interest? If necessary, next year he can sell his house for enough to pay off both mortgages and have enough left over to buy an even faster car. What difference does it make whether he owns a house at all? For the price of the extra sports car, he can afford the first year's rent in the fanciest apartment building in town. Why worry?

Americans have traditionally confronted such questions in the context of certain values, values that arise from the obligation that one generation owes to the next. Generations of Americans have opened up frontiers, fought in wars at home and abroad, and made countless personal economic sacrifices because they knew that the world did not end with themselves and because they cared about what came afterward. The American experiment, from the very beginning, has been forward looking—economically as well as politically and socially. The earliest Americans saw this experiment as an explicit break with the past and devoted their energies to constructing the kind of future they valued both individually and collectively. The generations that followed accepted their debt to the past by attempting to repay it to the future.

. . . [T]he radical course upon which United States economic policy was launched in the 1980s violated the basic moral principle that had bound each generation of Americans to the next since the founding of the republic: that men and women should work and eat, earn and spend, both privately and

From Benjamin M. Friedman, *Day of Reckoning: The Consequences of American Economic Policy Under Reagan and After* (Random House, 1988). Copyright © 1988 by Benjamin M. Friedman. Reprinted by permission of Random House, Inc. Notes omitted.

collectively, so that their children and their children's children would inherit a better world. Since 1980 we have broken with that tradition by pursuing a policy that amounts to living not just in, but for, the present. We are living well by running up our debt and selling off our assets. America has thrown itself a party and billed the tab to the future. The costs, which are only beginning to come due, will include a lower standard of living for individual Americans and reduced American influence and importance in world affairs. . . .

In short, our prosperity was a false prosperity, built on borrowing from the future. The trouble with an economic policy that artificially boosts consumption at the expense of investment, dissipates assets, and runs up debt is simply that each of these outcomes violates the essential trust that has always linked each generation to those that follow. We have enjoyed what appears to be a higher and more stable standard of living by selling our and our children's economic birthright. With no common agreement or even much public discussion, we are determining as a nation that today should be the high point of American economic advancement compared not just to the past but to the future as well.

The decision to mortgage America's economic future has not been a matter of individual choice but of legislated public policy. Popular talk of the "me generation" to the contrary, most individual Americans are working just as hard, and saving nearly as much, as their parents and grandparents did. What is different is economic policy. The tax and spending policies that the U.S. government has pursued throughout Ronald Reagan's presidency have rendered every citizen a borrower and every industry a liquidator

of assets. The reason that the average American has enjoyed such a high standard of living lately is that since January 1981 our government has simply borrowed more than $20,000 on behalf of each family of four.

Worse still, we owe nearly half of this new debt to foreign lenders. At the beginning of the 1980s, foreigners owed Americans far more than we owed foreigners. The balance in our favor, amounting to some $2,500 per family, made the United States the world's leading creditor country, enjoying the advantages of international influence and power that have always accompanied such a position. Today, after a half dozen years in which our government has borrowed record sums on our behalf, we owe foreigners far more than they owe us. The balance against us, already amounting to more than $7,000 per family, now makes the United States the world's largest debtor. Foreigners have already begun to settle these debts by taking possession of office buildings in American cities, houses in American suburbs, farm land in the heartland, and even whole companies. We are selling off America, and living on the proceeds.

Our unprecedented splurge of consumption financed by borrowing has broken faith with the future in two ways, each of which carries profound implications not just for our standard of living but for the character of our society more generally. Whether we continue or reverse our current economic policy will determine how Americans in the future will think of themselves and their society, whether the free ideals and democratic institutions at the core of the American experiment will continue to prosper, and whether America as a nation will be in a position to advance these ideals and institutions beyond our own borders.

THE COST OF THE ECONOMIC POLICY WE have pursued in the 1980s is no more than what any society pays for eating its seed corn rather than planting it. With the federal deficit averaging 4.2 percent of our total income since the beginning of the decade, compared to a net private saving rate of just 5.7 percent, our rate of investment in business plant and equipment has fallen beneath that of any previous sustained period since World War II. So has our investment in roads, bridges, airports, harbors, and other kinds of government-owned infrastructure. Our investment in education has also shrunk compared to our total income despite the urgent need to train a work force whose opportunities will arise more than ever before from industries oriented to technologically advanced production and the processing of information.

With so little investment in the basic structure of a strong economy, our ability to produce the goods and services that people want has been disappointing in the 1980s despite a marked improvement in some of the other factors that affect business performance. Workers on average are older and more experienced, business is spending more on research and development, and most of the investment needed to meet environmental regulations is already in place. But these favorable developments have been swamped by the weakness of business investment, so that there has been no significant increase in the amount of capital at the disposal of the average American worker. Since 1979, the last year of full employment before the pair of business recessions that began this decade, our overall productivity growth has averaged just 1.1 percent per annum. If productivity growth continues at this pace, we shall, at best, be able to do no more than pay the interest on our mounting foreign debt. On our current trajectory, there will be no margin to provide for increases over time in our standard of living.

To persist in our present policy is therefore to risk the material basis for the progress that has marked Americans' perceptions of themselves and their society since its very beginnings. Forging a great nation from a raw continent within just a few centuries provided the momentum, the spirit of progress, the dynamic, that by de Tocqueville's day had already come to characterize the American outlook. This sense of America as a dynamic and progressive society has always had an economic basis. Economic incentives motivated the first explorers to seek out what were then unknown lands, and economic incentives also led many of the earliest settlers to establish themselves here. Subsequent waves of immigration swelled the population with men and women led here by aspirations for political freedoms and for economic opportunities, often opportunities that only their children would be able to exploit fully. The conquest of the frontier, the building of a nation that was at first mostly rural and agricultural, and the subsequent development of that nation into a largely urban and industrial power, all required tangible and visible economic progress.

The idea of progress for the nation as a whole both reflected and demanded continual economic betterment for the individual citizen. As Americans' standard of living doubled roughly once every thirty years—not as a one-time phenomenon but as an ongoing process that compounded itself from one generation to the next—the assumption of a better life as time passed became a basic element in the outlook of Americans who lived out their lives here, no less than of those who came from elsewhere. The idea that each generation of Americans would enjoy a noticeably greater level of material well-being was a fact, not just a hope.

And over time, the fact of continual economic progress shaped the character of American society more broadly. A rising standard of living is worth having not only on its own account but even more so because it provides the material basis for a free and democratic society. The nature of the choices any society has to make is different when its citizens' incomes are regularly doubling every generation than when incomes stagnate. The openness, the social mobility, the breadth of individual opportunity, and the tolerance of diversity that have given American society its unique flavor are inseparable from a continually rising overall living standard. So is the ability to make crucial choices, which in the end determine the shares that individuals and groups can claim from what the nation produces, without destructive social conflict.

But all this depends on progress and continuity. In the simplest terms, that means adequate saving, investment in productive assets and housing for a growing population, and in general, sufficient attention to creating new wealth rather than living off the endowments left by prior generations. There is no evidence of a breakdown of the deep-rooted inhibitions against abandoning these obligations to the future on the part of individual Americans. As we shall see, Americans have not suffered an attack of laziness in the 1980s or a sudden urge to burn up

their savings or even a failure of foresight. Yet as a nation, we are consuming more than we earn, investing less than we used to, and all the while borrowing from abroad and selling off our property. . . .

THE CHALLENGE TO AMERICAN ECONOMIC policymaking is twofold. We must first set a new fiscal policy that commits most if not all our saving to investment in productive capital rather than to funding the government deficit. That means paying more taxes or cutting back on government spending or both. Second, we must adjust our economic policy in the broadest sense to confront the debt left by the Reagan era. Even a complete reversal of our current fiscal policy beginning immediately will not magically wipe away the legacy of almost a decade of overconsumption and excessive borrowing. But it will be a start, and the sooner we start the smaller the sacrifices we shall eventually be forced to make.

Neither of these tasks will be accomplished simply. The agonizing bipartisan negotiations that finally delivered a $30 billion grab bag of small tax hikes, small spending cuts, and assorted accounting gimmicks in the wake of the October 1987 stock market crash showed once again that there are no easy solutions to our current problem. But then why should there be? Nobody enjoys consuming less. Nobody likes doing without the services or the benefit payments that our government provides. And nobody wants to pay more taxes. Our new fiscal policy abandoned the long-standing American commitment to paying our government's way, and the excess consumption that resulted sacrificed our future prospects, but few Americans found the experience unpleasant along the way. To correct course will now require a retrenchment from the combined levels of private consumption and government services to which we have become accustomed. . . .

HOW HAVE WE GOTTEN INTO SUCH A MESS? It is tempting, of course, simply to blame what has happened on shortsightedness, or greed, or even sheer folly on the part of the American public. Or to suppose that there is some inherent flaw in the American system of representative government. But claims of public irrationality or of shortcomings of the democratic process fail to explain this decade's sudden departure from America's prior fiscal conduct.

If Americans as a political body are somehow incapable of following an economic course that pays adequate attention to their and their children's future, why did our fiscal posture remain as stable as it did for so many years until the 1980s? If the American system of government is inherently faulty, why did federal revenues sufficiently cover spending over two centuries, so that until the 1980s our national debt never rose faster than the country's income except in wartime and at the bottom of the Great Depression? If the entire system is prone to overconsumption and dissipation, why did Americans throughout this century steadily build their net international asset position, rather than spend it away? The sharpness of the discontinuity that has occurred in the 1980s calls for more than vague laments about the inadequacy of the American character or the failure of our form of self-government.

The place to begin to understand what happened is to remember that Americans chose the fiscal policy their nation has followed in the 1980s, at least in part because its architects had assured them that it would lead to a better future, not mortgage that future or squander it. It is safe to say that few Americans who welcomed Ronald Reagan's election victory over Jimmy Carter in 1980 or applauded his string of legislative victories in 1981 foresaw fully what his fiscal policy would bring. The persistent argument used to sell this policy to the public—and at the same time to market the candidates who proposed it—was that it would revive America's economy and provide what Reagan billed as a "New Beginning for the Economy" after the harsh experience of the mid- and late seventies.

No one asked Americans to vote for doubling our national debt or diverting our saving away from productive investment or making our industry uncompetitive or turning our country into the world's largest debtor, all within less than a decade. Yet the policy that Americans were asked to endorse and that they did endorse has had just that effect.

Above all, Reagan was explicit and emphatic, both as a candidate and then as President, that his policy would deliver a balanced budget. Throughout the campaign he held forth the prospect of balancing the budget by 1983. This was a central objective that his fiscal policy, in contrast to Carter's, would achieve. In the very first minute of his first televised address to the nation after taking office in January 1981, he pointed to that year's "runaway deficit of nearly $80 billion" as evidence that "the federal budget is out of control." And two weeks later in his first address to Congress, he echoed the same warning in a different way. "Can we, who man the ship of state, deny that it is somewhat out of control?" he asked. "Our national debt is approaching one trillion dollars." . . .

The essence of the "supply-side" argument that Reagan advanced in 1980 (and to which he has resolutely clung ever since) is that the incentive effects of across-the-board cuts in personal tax rates would so stimulate individuals' work efforts and business initiatives that lower tax *rates* would deliver higher tax *revenues*. Lower tax rates, according to this notion, would help balance the federal budget, despite sharp increases in military spending, without requiring cuts in the nondefense programs that people genuinely valued. Americans could therefore enjoy both continued government spending and lower tax rates too. There was no need to worry about what deficits meant for the nation's future, because under this policy the government would run no deficits.

The idea that lower tax *rates* meant higher tax *revenues* neatly severed the link between the inherent attraction of easier taxes and the economic consequences of tax cuts without spending cuts—which Americans had traditionally regarded as irresponsible—because the theory promised that lower tax rates would *prevent* deficits and that the government would therefore borrow less, not more. The investment needed to renew America's productivity growth and restore competitiveness abroad would not wither but flourish. The costs of Reagan's new fiscal policy were not an issue, because it would bring only benefits, both immediately and in the future. . . .

IT WOULD BE SIMPLISTIC TO PRETEND THAT the deficit has been responsible for all our economic disappointments in the 1980s. We have also faced forces that are beyond our control, like the spread of advanced technologies to countries where labor is cheaper than we would ever want ours to be, or the steady shift of our economic activity from the production of goods to the provision of services, or the ongoing agricultural revolution which has already rendered countries like India and Bangladesh self-sufficient in food. Other major impediments to our productivity and competitiveness may stem more directly from our own decisions but still have little to do with the deficit. No doubt much of our difficulty has reflected such factors as poor product design, lack of innovation, an inadequately trained and motivated work force, and short-sighted management. We can and we should address each of these problems.

But it is fair to say that the deficit has been the greatest single force underlying the most severe failures of our economic performance in the 1980s, especially those with the most troubling implications for the future. The realization that our fiscal policy is a failure is now spreading rapidly. So is the desire, at some abstract level, to change it. Yet even in the aftermath of the stock market crash, which brought these concerns to the top of the public policy agenda, we did not do so to any meaningful extent.

Ironically, because of how our crisis-activated political machinery works, it might be better if our fiscal policy produced some highly visible cataclysm sufficient to rivet attention and demand an immediate response, something even more arresting than the stock market crash. Instead, the damage that this policy inflicts is subtle, intangible, and corrosive. Its full impact, as seen from any moment, always lies in the future. Because most of its consequences will occur only gradually—indeed they are already occurring, but only gradually—they are likely to remain mostly imperceptible from day to day or even year to year. And because this gradual decay preserves the illusion of prosperity today at the expense of the generation that is too young to vote, not to mention the generation that is not yet born, it is harder still for the nation's political system to address. . . .

As we shall see, fixing the problem will mean making genuine sacrifices, not just gestures. Because of the accumulated damage that our binge of overconsumption has already done, those sacrifices must now be greater than they need have been if we had corrected course by the middle of the decade. What is economically necessary will therefore be politically possible only if Americans fully comprehend what is at stake.

NO

Robert L. Bartley

THE DREAD DEFICIT

The deficit is not a meaningless figure, only a grossly overrated one. It measures something, but it does not measure the impulse of the economy— either pushing it up as the Keynesians believe or dragging it down as the flow-of-funds school holds. In particular, the deficit has no detectable effect on interest rates; if it tends to raise interest rates, its effect is swamped by other more important variables. And if it doesn't affect interest rates, it can scarcely affect the sectors of the economy thought to depend on interest rates, investment, for example. Nor is what we call "the deficit" an appropriate or particularly meaningful measure of the "burden we are leaving our grandchildren"; the federal government has many other ways of imposing future burdens, which may or may not move in tandem with its direct borrowing.

The fiscal health of the federal government certainly does matter, but the government's impact on the economy is far too large and diffuse to measure by any one number. A decent measure of the federal fisc would have to be something like the change in the net worth of the government; we have no such figure and, given its complications, are not likely to. But it will not help to pretend "the deficit" is some other figure we do not have, and then to invoke it in place of judgment. The deficit as we measure it is no sort of bottom line.

Yet we having increasingly made "the deficit" the centerpiece of economic policy, even writing it into law. Both the Gramm-Rudman Act and the 1990 budget deal pretend to control the deficit, or some convoluted version of it. Unable to do the right things on their own, our politicians have conjured the deficit into a bogeyman with which to scare themselves. In symbolizing the bankruptcy of our political process, the deficit has become a great national myth with enormous power. But behind this political symbol, we need to understand the economic reality, or lack of it. Otherwise the symbol may lead us to do dumb things, like trying to fight recessions by increasing taxes.

In the advanced economic literature, the big debate is over whether deficits matter *at all*. Professional economists have noticed that the much-publicized

From Robert L. Bartley, *Seven Fat Years and How to Do it Again* (Free Press, 1992). Copyright © 1992 by The Free Press. Reprinted by permission of The Free Press, a division of Macmillan, Inc. Notes omitted.

deficits of the 1980s somehow didn't spell the end of the world, or even the end of the economic boom. They understand that the prime rate was 20 to 21.5 percent in 1981, when the deficit ran 2.6 percent of GNP [gross national product] and 7.25 to 8 percent in 1986, when the deficit was 5.3 percent of GNP. Unlike politicians or the articulate public, they have tried to adjust their thinking to this empirical reality. . . .

THE LACK OF A CORRELATION BETWEEN deficits and interest rates is less surprising if you understand that the deficit is a curious figure from the standpoint of accounting. I remember sharing garden-party cocktails with Paul Volcker one summer night when he was approached by the CEO of a highly successful regional retailer, demanding how the government could go deeper and deeper into debt everywhere. He was quite right in looking to Volcker for support of his view, but Paul mischievously turned to me and said, "You answer that, Bob," then grinned and ambled away leaving me with a worked-up CEO. Well, I asked, doesn't your company add to its debt every year. I guess it does, he responded, but that's different.

It sure is. Corporations have Generally Accepted Accounting Principles. The government has the National Income Accounts. If you are going to speculate about the economic impact of "the deficit," you have to have some sense of the differences among accrual accounting, cash accounting and government accounting.

If a corporation borrows $200 million to build a shopping center, this will be reflected in its balance sheet. It will have $200 million in liabilities for the debt, and $200 million in assets for the shopping center. But in its annual income accounts,

it will not charge the entire $200 million as an expense. Instead of "expensing" the sum in the first year, it will "depreciate" it. That is, it will charge some portion of it as an expense against income each year over the assumed useful life of the shopping center.

Similarly, if a family takes out a $400,000 mortgage to buy a home, it recognizes that it has gone $400,000 in debt. But in trying to match income with outgo, it does not consider the $400,000 but the monthly or yearly payment to amortize the mortgage. Both corporations and households consider it entirely appropriate to borrow to buy capital items, and pay off the loan as the asset is used. As former Citicorp Chairman Walter Wriston put it, "The familiar refrain that every family must balance its budget, so why can't the federal government, has a nice ring to it, but no family I know of expenses its home." In the federal budget, he added, "All in all, capital expenditures totaled 13.2% of total outlays, a not inconsiderable amount to expense, and if funded in a capital budget would produce near balance in the operating budget.

So too with state and local governments. Typically they are required by law to "balance" their operating budgets, but this does not include bond issues for capital items, which usually must be approved by voters at referendum. Most foreign governments also have distinct capital budgets, if only for help in deciding how much yearly deficit may be sustainable. Not so the U.S. federal budget; indeed, Treasury Secretary Donald Regan was nearly laughed out of Washington for suggesting the government needs a capital budget.

So "the deficit" may be borrowing to pay welfare benefits or farm subsidies, or it may be borrowing to pay for a highway or an airplane. We have constructed our accounts to make it impossible to tell the difference. Partly this is because we don't trust our politicians to be honest in designating capital projects. Some state and local governments, New York City in particular, got into financial trouble by cheating on their capital budgets—by designating more and more operating expenses as capital expenses for which it was legitimate to borrow. . . .

THAT THE DEFICIT DOES NOT ACCOUNT FOR capital spending is the good news, however. The bad news is that it also does not account for the government's future liabilities. One night in 1980, Congress increased federal deposit insurance to $100,000 an account from $40,000. This one act increased the liabilities of the U.S. government by some $150 billion, half the cost of bailing out the savings and loan [S&L] accounts insured by the government. But it did not change the 1980 deficit a penny. The recorded 1980 deficit was $73.8 billion; the unrecorded liability of the deposit insurance boost amounted to twice the borrowing for all the government's on-the-book activities.

That's an example of why "the deficit" does not measure anything that could realistically be called "the burden we are leaving our grandchildren." What the federal debt represents is government bonds outstanding, or to put it plainly, that portion of future liabilities on which the government has chosen to pay interest.

The actual liabilities are far larger, so much so that changes in them can swamp changes in the official deficit; the deficit numbers can go up while the burden to our grandchildren goes down, or vice versa. In terms of the burden for our grandchildren, the elephant in the room is the social society system. At the end of fiscal 1981, in the midst of Ronald Reagan's first year in office, federal debt held by the public amounted to $785 billion. The unfunded liabilities of the social security system, however, came in at $5.9 *trillion*. The pension liabilities for federal personnel, at $842 billion, were themselves larger than the cumulative "deficits" over two centuries.

In the National Income Accounts these numbers do not count, of course; they are not relevant to the current year's aggregate demand. They are highly relevant, though, to the burden on our grandchildren. Is the government any more likely to default on a social security payment than it is on a Treasury bond? The danger to the latter is that its value will be inflated away, but under current law social security payments are indexed to inflation, while future benefits are linked to future wage levels, increasing with both inflation and real advances in the standard of living.

It is somehow not surprising that an administration that cuts taxes would also compile a better record on the government's off-budget liabilities. Also, slower inflation and more real growth make the fiscal climate easier, since figures like social security liabilities depend on estimates of future economic performance. The 1983 Greenspan Commission dealt with the social security deficit, in no small way by advancing previously scheduled increases in the payroll tax. With the economy performing better than expected during that reform, social security looks healthier, at least in the short term.

Thomas E. Daxon, a certified public accountant and former state auditor in Oklahoma, calculated the burden to future taxpayers in a 1989 article in *Policy Review*. His calculation included interest-bearing debt, social security, personal pensions and a variety of other liabilities and offsetting assets. He concluded that the burden to future taxpayers was $7.185 trillion at the end of fiscal 1981, and $7.952 trillion at the end of fiscal 1987. As a percentage of GNP, it declined from 241 percent to 180 percent.

Such calculations need to be taken with a grain of salt, of course. We do not know which contingent liabilities may explode the way deposit insurance did with the S&Ls. Government has assumed much of the liability for medical care for the elderly, for example, and seems poised to assume more. The Greenspan Commission fix of social security really only pushed the problem into the future; if we want to reduce the burden on our grandchildren, the first thing we should do is reduce the incomes we expect to claim when we retire.

At the same time, government accounting takes no notice of the government's asset position. We know that federal debt held by the public is now some $2.7 trillion. But how does this liability compare with the asset of, say, federal land holdings—nearly all of Alaska and Nevada, for example, and much of California?

The deficit is not much of a measure of any of these issues. It seems likely that during the 1980s even as the deficit grew, other burdens on our grandchildren declined. Deposit insurance of course clouds the picture, and it's not easy to assess responsibility for these enormous costs. . . . Even so, it's possible that during the 1980s the net worth of the government, if we could measure it, may have gone up rather than down. This is perhaps a hidden secret of the Seven Fat Years [1983–1989]. . . .

THE ISSUE, IN SHORT, IS WHETHER CONgress is more afraid of a deficit or of having to levy taxes; which will cause more restraint in congressional spending? This is of course not an economic question but a political and psychological one. For the record, . . . spending rose sharply in the early 1980s, plateaued and started to decline as a percent of GNP after 1983, then started to soar again in 1990. Of course, this measurement depends not only on federal spending but on GNP, which grew nicely during the Seven Fat Years.

Congress, it seems, is not much deterred by either fear of taxes or fear of a deficit. Under the current institutional arrangements, an administration does well merely to insure that federal spending grows no more rapidly than GNP. This was accomplished in the 1983–90 period, in part because the Gramm-Rudman sequester gave the executive a bit more say in the process. It also no doubt helped that James Miller, OMB [Office of Management and Budget] chief during these years, never became a household word, unlike his predecessor or his successor. For some reason, presidents seem to assign scatbacks to a post that requires an interior lineman.

The broader issue, though, concerns the institutional arrangements themselves. . . . [I]n 1974, the Budget Control and Impoundment Act of 1974 [was enacted]. Congress won a fight with a Watergate-weakened president over the previous practice of presidential "impoundment" of congressionally appropriated funds. Henceforth the president would be obligated to spend expeditiously whatever Congress appropriated. And ever since 1974, Congress has been trying one expedient after another to try to prove it can behave itself in spending money. The obvious truth is that establishing and enforcing a budget requires someone to take responsibility, and Congress is a committee of 535 members. Even with good will, not to be taken for granted, it is not humanly possible.

Congress has further eroded executive powers by the practice of wrapping all its spending into a last-minute "omnibus appropriation" or "continuing resolution." A presidential veto, or even a Gramm-Rudman sequester, would be a drastic act closing down the government. Nor does the president have time to deliberate, or even to adequately read the legislation.

In his 1988 State of the Union Address, President Reagan displayed the continuing resolution passed the previous December, some 1,194 pages and weighing nearly 30 pounds. As provisions of this bill were digested, it was found to contain a stealth provision increasing congressional staff salaries by 20 percent. The conference report supposedly explaining the legislation had no mention of this provision, and no one ever discovered where the law originated.

The same resolution also turned out to contain a provision putting Rupert Murdoch out of the newspaper business in Boston and New York. This time there was no mystery; Sen. Ted Kennedy inserted the provision to close down an unfriendly newspaper. Since the papers in question were financially strained, the Federal Communications Commission had exercised its discretion to give Murdoch waivers of the rule against owning papers and television stations in the same town; the continuing resolution provision said no funds should be expended to extend waivers "currently in effect." This applied only to Murdoch; the D.C. Court of Appeals struck down

the provision as a violation of the constitutional provisions against bills of attainder, legislation intended to punish specific persons.

The obvious institutional change to correct such practices is of course the item veto, giving the president power to veto some items in a bill without vetoing the whole bill. In the states, 43 governors have item vetos, and it has been repeatedly called for by presidents of both parties. It is an injection of executive power and responsibility that would put some discipline in the budget process, which of course is why Congress has opposed it.

Before 1974 presidents asserted the impoundment power, if less sweepingly than President Nixon did. Whether through the loss of impoundment, the creation of the CBO, the institution of the "current services budget," some balance-wheel on spending went out of kilter in 1974 and needs to be set right if "the deficit" is ever to be brought under control.

Intriguingly, the 1975 Supreme Court decision on the Nixon water impoundments never reached constitutional issues. Stephen Glazier, a securities lawyer, started a constitutional debate by observing that the veto provision has two separate clauses. One requires that "every bill" be presented to the president for a veto, and the other requires the same for "every order, resolution, or vote" requiring action by both Houses. This means, he asserted, that the framers intended all along to give the president an item veto, a right exercised by impoundment until 1974 and overthrown by the Impoundment Act. Constitutional historian Forrest McDonald lent his support to this interpretation, but others disagreed. There is also the issue of whether a thousand-page last-minute resolution is properly "presented" for the veto.

The control of spending, the government's unrecognized future liabilities, the capital investment in the nation's infrastructure—all these are serious issues. They have been obscured rather than clarified by preoccupation with a number called "the deficit."

By fiscal 1990 and 1991, for example, government spending was soaring to new heights. Some of this, of course, is for the Savings and Loan bailout, and there is a debate whether this spending "counts" as part of the deficit. Many economists view it as merely a shuffling of funds, without imposing new demands on the savings "pool." For that matter, some entirely respectable economists concentrate on the "primary deficit," excluding all interest payments as merely fund-shuffling with no effect in the real sector.

In terms of the government's net worth, some incalculable part of the S&L spending clearly should be netted out as acquisition of assets. The early years of the budget agreement do set high ceilings for program spending, and the apparent intention is to fund spending in later years by selling S&L assets. Good luck, but the immediate return on the 1990 budget agreement was that the deficit soared.

As a political matter, the most interesting observation is that just as the deficit soared in 1991, public rhetoric about it almost vanished. Partly this was recession and partly it was confusion over the increasingly convoluted numbers; economists disagreed on whether the S&L bailout numbers really counted. But mostly it was something else. Concern about the deficit vanished on June 26, 1990, when President Bush revoked his no-tax pledge.

The Congress and its boosters got what they wanted, and stopped stoking the fires of "the deficit." We are now back to the formula of spend, tax, and elect. To the extent conservative boosters of "the deficit" and "balancing the budget" hoped to restrain the government, their formula has proved a two-edged sword. The no-tax pledge was a crude instrument, but on the record reasonably effective in an unsatisfactory environment.

If we want a fiscal policy that speeds economic growth, we know what needs to be done with or without a deficit number: hold government spending to essentials, keep marginal tax rates as low as possible, keep the dollar sound, let the price mechanism work, avoid imposing unnecessary regulation and unnecessary costs. Preoccupation with "the deficit" was a hindrance the Reagan administration had to overcome in implementing the program that produced the Seven Fat Years, and in the 1990s the danger is that the same preoccupation will lead us away from these fundamentals.

POSTSCRIPT

Is the National Debt a National Liability?

The federal government has three economic choices. One is to cut costs. There is always much sentiment to do so, as well as much opposition in any area where specific interests feel threatened. A second choice is to raise taxes. This is seldom popular, least of all with those who fear that their taxes specifically will be raised. The third alternative is to go deeper into debt.

It is easier to understand debt in terms of private economic behavior. If we spend beyond our means to pay, we incur debts, pay high interest charges, and, as our indebtedness rises, suffer bad credit ratings (and the unwillingness of banks to extend loans), canceled credit cards, repossession of purchases, and forfeited mortgages.

American state governments are obliged to balance their budgets, which means that each year they must strive to bring their expenditures (outgo) in line with their receipts (income). But the federal government does not operate under such constraints, although in recent years President Bush and others have urged adoption of a balanced budget amendment that would require Congress and the president not to incur further debt. Critics of a balanced budget amendment argue that Congress and the president would find ways of avoiding compliance. Besides, critics argue, no recent president has proposed anything close to a balanced budget to Congress.

Friedman's conclusion that the growing national debt damages America's economic well-being is supported by Lawrence Malkin, *The National Debt* (Henry Holt, 1987). Malkin believes that one consequence of the growing debt is that America's economic destiny is being increasingly determined by foreigners. David P. Calleo, *The Bankrupting of America: How the Federal Budget Is Impoverishing the Nation* (William Morrow, 1992) explains what the deficit is and what its short- and long-term consequences are.

In *The Deficit and the Public Interest: The Search for Responsible Budgeting in the 1980s* (University of California Press, 1989), Joseph White and Aaron Wildavsky reject the view that balancing the budget is more important than the losses in government and public activity that would result. Besides, they say, "The short-term economic evils ascribed to the deficit keep failing to appear." Other arguments sympathetic to Bartley can be found in Robert Heilbroner and Peter Bernstein, *The Debt and the Deficit: False Alarms/Real Possibilities* (W. W. Norton, 1989).

Perhaps the debt can be both harmful and helpful to an economy. Susan George, *A Fate Worse Than Debt: The World Financial Crisis and the Poor* (Grove Press, 1988), argues that on the one hand, national debts result in trade deficits, unemployment, and economic stagnation; but on the other hand, "Debt could be used to promote democracy and real development."

ISSUE 16

Does the United States Need Socialized Medicine?

YES: Nancy Watzman, from "Socialized Medicine Now—Without the Wait," *The Washington Monthly* (October 1991)

NO: John C. Goodman, from "An Expensive Way to Die," *National Review* (April 16, 1990)

ISSUE SUMMARY

YES: Policy analyst Nancy Watzman argues that the Canadian model of universal medical insurance can be adapted and improved in order to provide superior and less expensive care for all Americans.
NO: John C. Goodman, president of the National Center for Policy Analysis, maintains that Americans get more and better health care more promptly than do individuals in countries with compulsory schemes of national health insurance.

Since World War II, more Nobel Prizes in physiology and medicine have been awarded to physicians and medical scientists working in the United States than in the rest of the world. It is widely acknowledged that the training and education of medical personnel in the United States is the best in the world. The latest medical technology is more widely available in the United States than anywhere else. It is no surprise that when wealthy people in other countries have a disease that is difficult to treat, they often seek treatment in one of the renowned medical clinics or research hospitals in the United States.

By contrast, it is estimated that more than 30 million Americans have no medical coverage and another 100 million are underinsured. This is true despite the fact that roughly $750 billion a year is currently spent on health care in the United States. One-third of this amount is spent directly by the federal government. In 1991, the total expenditure for health care amounted to more than 14 percent of the gross national product, nearly 10 times the amount spent in the United States 40 years ago, and every year the total grows higher.

There are two overriding political issues involved in health care reform: coverage and cost. In 1965, the national government recognized and tried to remedy the problems of coverage and the availability of medical care by establishing Medicare, which provides some government-sponsored medical care for older people, and Medicaid, which provides some medical coverage for the poor. Nevertheless, the rising cost of private medical care increasingly puts it beyond the means of millions of Americans.

Although there is widespread conviction that something should be done, it is more difficult to decide what and how. Should we improve the present mix of private payments, employer-sponsored medical programs, Medicaid, and Medicare? Should public policy encourage the creation of health maintenance organizations so that administrative costs can be reduced? Should the government help to ensure that employers and employees establish such programs? Should the federal government adopt universal health insurance for all employed persons, all citizens, or all persons?

Critics argue that medical costs in the United States are higher per capita than in other advanced countries, but too many people receive inadequate or no medical service. They point out that other industrial nations have some form of comprehensive national health insurance that prevents these problems. Opponents of a national scheme counter that experience indicates that a government bureaucracy would do a poor job of administering such a program, that it would deny individuals the right to choose their own physicians, and that additional costs would add to the national debt.

The government has at least three possible choices in confronting this issue. The first is to rely largely on the free market. This could be compatible with such reforms as requiring insurance companies to accept all potential buyers or providing tax credits for taxpayers and vouchers for poor people to make certain that everyone has the financial ability to obtain medical insurance. A second approach would require employers to provide medical coverage or contribute to a fund that would pay for coverage for those not otherwise insured. The most sweeping change in medical care would be brought about by the adoption of national health insurance, where the national government would be the single paying agent. Such a system could allow, as it does in Great Britain, for a parallel system of private-fee medical services.

Nancy Watzman, who works for Public Citizen, a liberal political action group, urges the adoption of a national health system similar to Canada's, which she claims is fairer, better, and cheaper than what America now has. John C. Goodman, president of the National Center for Policy Analysis, concludes that any examination of national health insurance in Canada and elsewhere shows that these systems result in less medical care at higher costs.

YES

Nancy Watzman

SOCIALIZED MEDICINE NOW—
WITHOUT THE WAIT

By now, you've seen a million stories on the Canadian health care system, and perhaps even read a few. If so, you've discovered that they all apply the same formula. First, like a slap in the face, comes the horror story: In Orange County, California, a woman goes into business for herself, giving up her health insurance—and discovers she has breast cancer. She takes to selling flowers from her garden in a desperate effort to keep up with her bills. Next come the terrifying statistics: Americans spend more than $750 billion—or nearly 14 percent of the GNP—on health care each year. If costs continue to rise at current rates, they'll eat up 37 percent of the GNP by 2030. Yet 28 percent of U.S. citizens lack basic health care; 35 million are uninsured—and nearly two thirds of them have jobs.

Now the emergency is clear, and the stage is set for a hero. But as he comes into focus, our savior looks a lot less like a chiseled Mountie on a galloping steed than a . . . "Worthwhile Canadian Initiative," to borrow the inspirational title for a Most Boring Headline contest in *The New Republic* a few years back. The stories, you see, are carefully "balanced." On the plus side, they point out that "our neighbors to the north" spend only 9 percent of their GNP on a tax-financed national health program, yet everybody is covered, from the wealthiest businesswoman to the poorest, unemployed IV-drug user. Then comes the downside: Canadians must wait longer than Americans do for high-tech treatments such as coronary bypasses, MRIs, CAT scans, and even cancer treatments. It appears to be a trade-off, conclude *The Washington Post*, *The New York Times*, *The Miami Herald*, and Walter Cronkite. Who can say, they shrug, which system is better? Will America ever reform its health care system, and will Canada be the model? One thing is certain: Only time will tell.

Hey! How about a little American initiative? If our system's broke—as everyone from Physicians for a National Health Program to the Heritage Foundation agrees—let's fix it. That means choosing the best model we've

From Nancy Watzman, "Socialized Medicine Now—Without the Wait," *The Washington Monthly*, vol. 23, no. 10 (October 1991). Copyright © 1991 by The Washington Monthly Company, 1611 Connecticut Avenue, NW, Washington, DC 20009; (202) 462-0128. Reprinted by permission of *The Washington Monthly*.

got—the Canadian system—and eliminating the bugs. After all, the Canadians don't have to give us a blueprint, just a beginning.

Despite the utopian claims of universal health care advocates, the problems with the Canadian system are real. Making it right for us will take hard work and, above all, brutal honesty about its flaws. But the end result will be advanced, humane medical care for all Americans. That it will also be billions of dollars cheaper than the jury-rigged, inequitable system we've got now—well, that's just added incentive to do the right thing.

WEALTH CARE

On New York City's Park Avenue, doctors understand the subtleties of putting together a practice. The artwork is understated but expensive, the *New Yorkers* uncreased and up-to-date. The nurse is as gentle as a Swedish masseuse, the gown as ample as your backside. And the doctor, one of the best in his field, gives you his undivided attention for an hour.

At $200 a visit, this is American medicine at its best. For the worst, walk 30 blocks uptown, to the "Medicaid mills" of Harlem. These "doctors' offices," which actually boast no doctors except on the requisite city licenses, serve thousands of New York's poorest people. A recent *Washington Post* story described the care provided at one such institution: A clerk collects a patient's Medicaid card, scribbles out an Rx, and sends him on his way. Given this sham service, why do dozens of people pass through these revolving doors every day? Because many doctors in the city refuse to accept patients on Medicaid.

Now head northwest to the village of Tofino in the Pacific Rim region of Canada's Vancouver Island—one of the few places on earth that harbors more eagles than people. It also harbors the only hospital in 100 miles: a low-slung green building with one doctor, one nurse, one ambulance, one helipad, and nine clean yellow rooms. Inside tonight are an elder of the Ucluelets, an impoverished fishing tribe located several miles away; two injured loggers; and one affluent, 30-year-old ecotourist who escaped from Vancouver to hike the coast and promptly broke his leg. His starchy wife sits, reading Barry Lopez's *Arctic Dreams*, by the bed.

Universal access like this is the chief rationale for the Canadian system: Instead of some Americans receiving miserable treatment or none at all while others enjoy the best in the world, all would be taken care of. The rub is that universal access also means *equal* access—that all Americans will meet somewhere in the medical middle, sharing the same waiting room, the same doctor, the same equipment, the same quality of care. That leveling effect is wonderful if you're among the millions of Americans without insurance. It may not be so wonderful if you are accustomed to the Park Avenue touch.

But if you are, you're in a class virtually by yourself. Only 10 percent of Americans approve of their health care system. Meanwhile, according to a recent Harvard study, *56 percent* of Canadians approve of theirs. That shouldn't be surprising, since all Canadians enjoy not just access to health care but choice about whom they're going to see to get it.

Opponents of "socialized medicine" always trot out the British system as the prime example of how state control can lead to consumer misery. And they're right—but only because the Brits made the mistake of depriving patients of any say over who peers in their ears, prods their stomachs, or cuts them open. Canadians can make an appointment with any doctor they choose. And what those doctors do for them is clearly working. Canadians are much healthier than Americans. They're less likely to die as babies or from surgical complications, and they live longer.

Mary Lou and Robert Dunn of Brampton, Ontario, have alternated medical crises through the years. Twenty years ago, she was in a car accident that left "the windshield with an imprint of my face." She had nine operations to fix multiple fractures and rebuild her nose, lips, and eyes. Robert's medical history includes one operation for hemorrhoids and several for his back. He's about to go in for an operation on his shoulder. Quality of care? The Dunns' praise is unqualified. Waiting time for an appointment? Just the other day, when they both woke up sick, "I called our doctor at about 9:30 a.m. and she said 'Come right on in, I have an opening in 15 minutes,'" says Mary Lou.

Even by south-of-the-border standards, that's good service. But it gets better. In all those operations, through vaccines and infections and a dozen bouts of flu, the Dunns have never seen a hospital bill. The only money they ever hand over for health care is what goes to the government in taxes—and, believe it or not, it's less than what it costs to supply the average American with health care. According to *Consumer Reports,* a Canadian who earns the equivalent of $26,000 pays about $1,300 for health care. People in the U.S.—or their employers, who pass the costs along as lower wages or higher prices—pay about $2,500.

The Canadian system is actually several different systems, as each province administers its own health plan using federal and local funds. What's constant is the way the system is structured to keep costs down. First, hospitals and clinics receive fixed amounts of money to cover day-to-day expenses, such as Q-tips and syringes. If administrators want more money to make capital investments—for a new CAT scanner, for example—they must apply to the province. Second, the provinces negotiate with medical associations to establish how much doctors are allowed to charge for certain services. This is not too different from the established reimbursement rates used by U.S. health insurers and government programs, except that U.S. doctors can always charge their patients more than what insurers are willing to pay. Canadian doctors are simply not allowed to do that.

The government-issued health plan cards that the Dunns carry in their pockets entitle them to care in every province in Canada and every country in the world. Their province will pick up the bill. That generosity ensures they won't end up stranded without coverage in some medical hellhole . . . like Washington, D.C., where their niece, 24-year-old Mamie Stobie, has been turned down for coverage by over 30 health insurance companies.

The reason? Mamie's diabetic. In health insurance jargon, that's a "pre-existing condition," a term that roughly translates to: Because Mamie needs health care, she can't have any insurance to help pay for it. That's the American way.

HOME OF THE FEE

One reason we'll be able to afford Mamie's insurance under a Canadian-style plan is that such a system would put an end to several perversions and inefficiencies in the U.S. medical market. Critics of the Canadian approach may rail about creeping socialism, but right now, American medicine turns the laws of supply and demand on their head.

Let's say, for example, you've had a heart attack. To dissolve the clots forming in your blood, you need to start taking one of two equally effective drugs. One costs $76 to $300 a dose, the other $2,200. So you take the cheaper one, right? Wrong. *Because* one of the drugs costs more, your doctor would probably prescribe it to you. As Andrew Pollack showed in *The New York Times* last summer, Genentech, the company behind the more expensive drug, pumps enormous amounts of money into studies and aggressive marketing (performed by 278 salespeople) to push its product. The other drug has been around for decades, is unprotected by patents—and so is too cheap to make marketing worthwhile. That's how the free market functions in American medicine: The development of more expensive, high-tech treatments creates the demand for more expensive, high-tech treatments; likewise, more doctors means higher fees, and that means—you guessed it—more doctors. And even higher fees.

Estimates vary among surveys, but there is no doubt that each year huge numbers of Americans undergo treatments they don't need. A 1988 *New England Journal of Medicine* study, for example, concluded that two thirds of patients who receive heart surgery do so for either "equivocal" or "inappropriate" reasons. Perhaps this is because the American medical establishment helps them decide that they want it. . . .

WE NEED OUR HIPS

Under the Canadian system, the government doesn't step in just to iron out inefficiencies in the health care market. It actually takes control of supply, and therefore of demand, through rationing, a notion Canadians accept but Americans shudder to consider. Of course, some rationing decisions are fairly easy (like which of the two equally effective heart drugs doctors should be allowed to offer). In vitro fertilization, cosmetic surgery, and sex change operations are among the services for which Canadians most often have to dip into their own pockets. But the calls quickly get tougher. It's much easier to turn away than to confront hard rationing decisions, to trust in the invisible hand and our tattered patchwork of support programs rather than in some new government bureaucracy—a federal Department For Whether We Feel Like Saving Your Life.

Trouble is, the invisible hand isn't known for its compassion. As a result of the laissez-faire approach to medical care, we already have a rationing system in place—one based not on need but on ability to pay. A new study in the *Journal of the American Medical Association (JAMA)* found that the uninsured were 25 to 75 percent less likely to undergo each of five high-cost, discretionary procedures, including certain biopsies, colonoscopies, and CAT scans. Even after controlling for the severity of illness at the time of admission, the study discovered that the uninsured were far more likely than the insured to die before leaving the hospital. Coincidence? Not likely. Take the MRI again. The AHA explicitly recommends that MRI centers keep an eye on what's called the "funding mix"—in other words, making the MRI more available to those more able to pay.

So there's a strong social justice argument to be made for the rational rationing of health care. So what? That high-minded reasoning would be mighty small comfort if you found yourself waiting six months to get your hip replaced, like the Canadians do. It's rare that a procedure performed in the U.S. is not covered at all in the Canadian health care system. Instead, where rationing shows its dark side in Canada is in the wait you must endure for non-emergency care. Some cheerleaders for the Canadian system gloss over this problem, but no patient should have to wait six times longer to get his hip replaced under a new health care system than he would today at Georgetown University Hospital. Under our modification of the Canadian plan, no one—including those Americans who today have no hope of ever receiving the treatment in the first place—will have to.

PAPER TIGERS

How is that possible? Because for once, more government involvement means less paperwork. Consider D.C. General Hospital, where armed guards escort men in shackles to the overtaxed HIV clinic. Ninety percent of the men and women who come through the doors lack health insurance—not to mention jobs, homes, and families. Dying or not, they wait more than an hour to see a doctor for 10 minutes. If there seem to be few staff members in this massive complex, take a turn down the stairs and through the hall. There are hundreds of health care workers here at D.C. General. Unfortunately, most of them are filling out forms.

Patients here have enough to worry about without paperwork. But the Medicaid forms they're required to fill out are so complicated that many just can't keep up. One U.S. government estimate states that about a million Medicare enrollees a year don't seek reimbursement because they find the forms too complicated. And don't think just the poor get confused. A recent *Washington Post* editorial lamented that you need a personal CPA to keep track of all the forms that pour in when you suffer from a serious illness—the health insurance claim forms, the hospital bills, doctor bills, the abstruse notices from Medicare that need deciphering to find out what's covered. This paperwork isn't just tiresome for would-be patients—it's incredibly expensive. Thankfully, the Canadian national health program actually involves *less*—much, much less—bureaucracy than ours.

Think about it. Since every citizen is automatically covered in Canada, there's no need to employ armies of people to determine whether Mamie's diabetes is a "pre-existing condition"—there's no such thing. Fewer people are needed to work in doctors' or hospitals' billing departments, because those facilities bill the government directly for all services. Doctors aren't forced to hire professional staff to manage the intricacies of insurance status and the collections process. They don't have to keep track of exactly how many Tylenol tablets one patient swallowed during a hospital stay in order to bill him for them later; they need only track how many Tylenol tablets are being dispensed at the hospital on the whole, which requires a lot less paperwork.

Here's the bottom line: In Canada, just 11 cents out of every dollar spent on health care goes to administrative costs; across the border in the U.S., up to 24 *cents* goes to billing, form filing, and other advanced forms of paper shuffling performed by health administrators, whose ranks swelled nearly 400 percent from 1970 to 1987. In 1991 alone, we can expect to waste from $115 to $136 billion on health administration—money we could be spending on health *care*.

Steffie Woolhandler and David Himmelstein, Harvard-based physicians who work with Physicians for a National Health Program, have estimated that as much as $83 billion could be saved in paperwork costs alone if the U.S. switched to a national health plan. The General Accounting Office (GAO) estimate is a little more conservative: $68 billion. Yet even that amount is more than enough to pay for basic health coverage for *all* the uninsured people in the United States, with enough left over to do more besides.

The key thing to remember about these estimates is that they cover administrative savings alone. They don't include any of the other cost-saving measures already discussed, such as cutting back on unnecessary procedures or starting up a rational rationing system. And they assume—this is crucial—that Americans *will not* start waiting longer for their heart or kidney transplant operations, or for anything else. The GAO points out that with the equipment we've already got, we'll be able to provide high-tech treatments for everyone without resorting to Canadian-style queuing.

Once that's understood, the question becomes: What do we do with the savings? The first thing, of course, is to extend the same level of care that insured Americans now receive to the uninsured; Himmelstein and Woolhandler estimate in a May *JAMA* article that this change would run us about $12 billion. If you take the GAO's $68 billion as a con-

servative estimate of administrative savings and subtract that $12 billion, then you're left with a full $56 billion for other goodies. What should we do with it?

Well, just to calm fears, let's take the worst case scenario, assume that we'll need to pay out some more money to fund high-tech treatments for all who need them, and do some seat-of-the-pants calculations. Consider the example of shock wave lithotripsy, a process that breaks up kidney stones. Canadians wait about six weeks to receive lithotripsy, while the average Washingtonian can get it in about three weeks at Georgetown University Hospital. Right now in the U.S., about 23,000 people get lithotripsies per year. Assuming that most of these people have health insurance, we can divide 23,000 by the number of insured Americans—214 million—and come up with a rough ratio showing how many lithotripsies should be performed per population. Then take that ratio, multiply it by the 35 million uninsured, and we get a rough number for how many lithotripsies we need to do if we want to cover the poor. Multiply that number by how much physicians earn for performing the procedure in Canada—U.S.$241—and voilà, we've got a figure for how much we would need to chop off the $56 billion savings budget—$906,642. Now, that figure underestimates some costs (it doesn't take into account hospitalization, for example) and overestimates others (it assumes that all Americans who now receive lithotripsy have health insurance, while some undoubtedly don't). So, just to be conservative, let's multiply by 10.

We can use the same formula for kidney, heart, and heart and lung transplants. Multiply by 10 and tack on the lithotripsy cost, and you get about $31,387,750—just 0.5 percent of the money we've got to spend. That $56 billion could go an awfully long way.

If you're an economist or a hypochondriac, you may well be thinking: All that's fine, but what about improving on the quality of treatments already offered? With the government trying to hold down costs, what incentive will there be for the kind of daring research and development only good old American capitalism can foster? One reason Canada is able to control its health care costs, some critics point out, is that it can rely on the United States to invest in coming up with new treatments and equipment. With the U.S. also going to a national system, health care could stagnate.

In the first place, there's still plenty of incentive for a truly daring health care entrepreneur to hit the laboratory; after all, if he can convince the American health care system to offer his treatment, he'll be a millionaire. But let's suppose that private corporations after nationalization do lose the will to invest in R&D. Who needs 'em? The federal government already plans to spend $8.7 billion in 1991 to fund health research—that amounts to 44 percent of all such research performed in the U.S. last year. Double that investment, kiss the private money goodbye, and we'll still have tens of billions of dollars in savings to spend on wart removal or herbal treatments or lollipops for the kids who don't cry.

NORTHERN LIGHT

Right now there are almost as many piecemeal health reform proposals floating around Capitol Hill as there are congressmen. The most inventive program the Democratic leadership has come up with is more of what we've already got:

expansion of employer mandates and government programs in a "play or pay" scheme. Such a patchwork approach would actually be more expensive than our current system, let alone a Canada-type plan, because it adds benefits without cutting costs; estimates range from $24 to $60 billion worth of new taxes, much of which would go for more administrative bloat. This lack of vision springs partly from blind fear—a patent unwillingness to fight the AMA and an insurance industry facing annihilation. This is why the final thing we must take from Canada is courage.

The situation Canada faced back in 1964, right before the government enacted the universal program, may sound familiar. The Canadian Medical Association wasn't any more pleased with national health care proposals than the AMA is now—and neither were Canadian health insurance companies. Meanwhile, inflation was rising and the federal deficit worsening.

When the Medical Care Insurance Bill was introduced in July of that year, the parliamentary debate was fierce. "So strident were the tones, so angry the voices, and so vehement the opposition that one journalist summed up, 'The federal government's proposed legislation lies torn, tattered, and politically rejected,' " writes Malcolm Taylor, a public policy professor at York University and a former Canadian official. Yet the bill passed in the end, partly because of the boost it received from an official commission report, requested by the Canadian Medical Association, that to the doctors' chagrin came out in favor of a national program.

Congress should listen less to campaign contributors and more to the facts. We *can* provide both basic, preventative medicine and sophisticated high-tech care to every American—for less money than we now spend to coddle the few while leaving tens of millions vulnerable.

In fact, with some political courage and a little hard work, we could probably teach Canada a thing or two about the right way to run a national health care program.

NO

John C. Goodman

AN EXPENSIVE WAY TO DIE

Countries with national health insurance spend less on health care than the U.S. does. It is all too easy to assume that the U.S. can therefore control health-care costs through national health insurance without any loss of benefits. And this mistake is encouraged by a number of myths.

Myth #1: Although the United States spends more on health care per capita than countries with national health insurance, the U.S. does not get better health care for the extra dollars it spends.

This myth rests upon the fact that life expectancy hardly differs among the developed countries and that infant mortality in the U.S. is actually higher than in most other developed countries.

In fact, a population's general mortality is affected by a great many factors over which doctors and hospitals have little influence. For those diseases and injuries for which modern medicine can affect the outcome, however, which country the patient lives in really matters. Life expectancy is not the same among developed countries for premature babies, for children born with spina bifida, or for people who have cancer, a brain tumor, heart disease, or chronic renal failure. Their chances of survival are best in the United States.

Consider the availability of modern technology in the U.S. and in Canada, a country with comprehensive national health insurance. There are eight times more magnetic-resonance-imaging units (the latest improvement on X-rays), seven times more radiation-therapy units (used in the treatment of cancer), about six times more lithoptripsy units (used for nonsurgical removal of kidney stones), and about three times more open-heart surgery units and cardiac-catheterization units per capita in the United States than in Canada.

It is sometimes argued that countries with national health insurance delay the purchase of expensive technology in order to see if it really works and is cost-effective. Even if true, patients will be denied access to life-saving treatment while government bureaucracies evaluate it. For example, during the 1970s, life-saving innovations were made in the fields of renal dialysis,

From John C. Goodman, "An Expensive Way to Die," *National Review* (April 16, 1990). Copyright © 1990 by National Review, Inc., 150 East 35th Street, New York, NY 10016. Reprinted by permission.

Table 1

Use of Modern Medical Technology in the 1970s

Country	Pacemakers Per 100,000 Population, 1976	CAT Scanners Per Million Population, 1979	Kidney Dialysis And/ Or Transplants Per Million Population, 1976
Australia	7.3	1.9	65.8
Canada	2.3	1.7	73.4
France	22.6	0.6	111.3
West Germany	34.6	2.6	105.0
Italy	18.8	NA	102.0
Japan	2.7	4.6	NA
United Kingdom	9.8	1.0	71.2
United States	44.2	5.7	120.0

Source: National Center for Policy Analysis

CAT-scan technology, and pacemaker technology. Yet the implant rate of pacemakers in the U.S. during the mid 1970s was more than four times the rate in Britain, and almost twenty times the rate in Canada (see Table 1). The availability of CAT scanners in the U.S. was more than three times that in Canada and almost six times that in Britain. The treatment rate of kidney patients in the U.S. was more than 60 per cent greater than in Canada and Britain.

There is considerable evidence that cost effectiveness is not what drives the bias against modern medical technology abroad. CAT-scan technology was invented in Britain, and until recently Britain exported about half the CAT scanners used in the world. Yet the British government has purchased only a handful of CAT scanners for use in the National Health Service [NHS]. British scientists also co-developed kidney dialysis. Yet Britain has one of the lowest dialysis rates in all of Europe, and as many as

nine thousand British kidney patients per year are denied the treatment.

In the United States we pay more for health care. But we also get more. And what we get saves lives.

Myth #2: Countries with national health insurance have solved the problem of access to health care.

In Britain and New Zealand, hospital services are completely paid for by government. Yet both countries have long waiting lists for hospital surgery. In Britain, with a population of about 55 million, the number of people waiting for surgery is almost eight hundred thousand. In New Zealand, with a population of three million, the waiting list is about fifty thousand. In both countries, elderly patients in need of a hip replacement can wait in pain for years. Patients waiting for heart surgery are often at risk of their lives.

In response to rationing by waiting, both Britain and New Zealand have witnessed a growing market in private health insurance—where citizens willingly pay for prompt private surgery, rather than wait for "free" surgery in public hospitals. In Britain, the number of people with private insurance has more than doubled in the last ten years, to about 12 per cent of the population. In New Zealand, one-third of the population has private health insurance, and private hospitals now perform 25 per cent of all surgical procedures.

Canada has had a national-health program for only a few decades. But because the demand for health care has proved insatiable, and because the Canadian government has resolutely refused to increase spending beyond about 8.5 per cent of GNP, the waiting lines have been growing. In Newfoundland the wait for a hip replacement is about six to ten months, the wait for cataract surgery is two months, for pap smears up to five months, for "urgent" pap smears two months (see Table 2). All over Canada, heart patients must wait for coronary bypass surgery, and the Canadian press frequently reports episodes of heart patients dying while on the waiting list. Unlike Britain and New Zealand, however, Canada does not allow patients to turn to the private sector, although Canadian patients who can afford to do so sometimes travel to the U.S. for medical services they cannot get in their own country.

Myth #3: Countries with national health insurance hold down costs by operating more efficiently.

By and large, countries that have succeeded in slowing the growth of health-care spending have done so by *denying people services*, not by making efficient use of resources.

Table 2

Average Waiting Time in Newfoundland 1988

Procedure	Average Wait
Mammogram	2^{1}/$_2$ months
Bone scan	1–1^{1}/$_2$ months
Myelogram	3–4 months
Brain shunt	5 months
Hip replacement	6–10 months
Cataract surgery	2 months
CAT scan	2 months
Pap smear	2–5 months
Urgent pap smear	2 months

Based on physician surveys by the Fraser Institute. Michael Walker, "From Canada: A Different Viewpoint," *Health Management Quarterly*, Vol. XI, No. 1, 1989, p. 12.

How much does it cost a hospital to perform an appendectomy? Outside the U.S. it is doubtful that there is a public hospital anywhere in the world that could answer that question. One reason for [former British prime minister] Margaret Thatcher's health-care reforms is that even Britain's best hospitals did not keep adequate records, and it was not uncommon for the head of a hospital department to be unaware of how many people his department employed.

What about bed management? Consider that while fifty thousand people wait for surgery in New Zealand, one out of every five hospital beds is empty. While nearly eight hundred thousand people wait for surgery in Britain, at any point in time about one out of every four hospital beds is empty. In both Britain and New Zealand, about 25 per cent of all acute beds, desperately needed for surgery, are clogged by chronically ill patients who are using the hospitals as nursing homes—often at six times the cost of alternative facilities. In Ontario about 25 per cent of hospital beds are occupied by elderly chronic patients. Hospital administrators apparently believe chronic patients are less expensive than acute patients (because they mainly use the "hotel" services of the hospital), and thus are less of a drain on limited budgets.

Myth #4: Under national health insurance money is allocated so that it has the greatest impact on health.

Even when resources are organized efficiently, they are still distributed with random extravagance under systems of national health insurance. These systems take millions of dollars that could be spent to save lives and cure diseases, and spend this money to provide a vast array of services to people who are not seriously ill. Take the ambulance service. English "patients" take more than 21 million ambulance rides each year-about one ride for every two people in all of England. About 91 per cent of these rides are for non-emergency purposes (such as taking an elderly person to a pharmacy) and amount to little more than a free taxi service. Yet for genuine emergencies, the typical British ambulance has little of the life-saving equipment considered standard in most large American cities.

While tens of thousands who are classified as in "urgent need" of surgery wait for hospital beds, the NHS spends millions on items that have only marginal effects on health and which could well be financed either by charges on the patients or by a low-cost limited private insurance. On the average, the NHS spends more than $70 million each year on tranquilizers, sedatives, and sleeping pills; almost $19 million on antacids; and about $21 million on cough medicine. If

the NHS did nothing more than charge patients the full costs of the sleeping pills and tranquilizers they consume, enough money would be freed to treat ten thousand to 15,000 additional cancer patients each year and save the lives of an additional three thousand kidney patients.

Myth #5: Under national health insurance the elderly in the U.S. will receive at least the same benefits they now receive under Medicare.

The elderly have the most to lose from the adoption of national health insurance. Take chronic kidney failure. Across Europe generally, in the late 1970s, 22 per cent of dialysis centers reported that they refused to treat patients over 55 years of age. In Britain in 1978, 35 per cent of the dialysis centers refused to treat patients over the age of 55; 45 per cent refused to treat patients over the age of 65; and patients over the age of 75 rarely received treatment at all for this disease.

How pervasive is denial of life-saving medical technology to elderly patients in other countries? Lacking hard data, one can only speculate. However, a white 65-year-old male in the U.S. can expect to live 1.3 years longer than a 65-year-old British male. A white 65-year-old female in the U.S. can expect to live 1.4 years longer than a 65-year-old British female. For middle-aged males, U.S. mortality rates are higher than European ones. During the retirement years, however, when medical intervention can make much more of a difference, the U.S. mortality rate is significantly below that of European countries.

Myth #6: The defects of national-health-insurance schemes in other countries could be easily remedied by a few reforms.

The characteristics described above are not accidental byproducts of government-run health-care systems. Instead, they are the natural and inevitable consequences of politicizing medical practice.

Why are elderly and poor patients discriminated against in the rationing of acute care under national health insurance? Because national health insurance is always and everywhere a middle-class phenomenon. Prior to the introduction of national health insurance, every country had some government-funded program to meet the health-care needs of the poor. The middle-class working population not only had to pay for its own health care, but it was also paying taxes to fund health care for the poor. National insurance extends the "free ride" to the middle-class working population, and it is designed to serve the interests of this population.

Why do national-health-insurance schemes skimp on expensive services to the seriously ill while providing a multitude of inexpensive services to those who are only marginally ill? Because numerous services provided to the marginally ill create benefits for millions of people (read: millions of voters), while acute and intensive care services concentrate large amounts of money on a handful of patients (read: small number of voters). Democratic political pressures dictate the redistribution of resources from the few to the many.

Why are sensitive rationing decisions left to the hospital bureaucracies? Because the alternative is politically impossible. As a practical matter, no government can afford to make it a national policy that nine thousand people every year will be denied treatment for chronic kidney failure and die. Nor can any government announce that some people must wait for surgery so that elderly patients can use hospitals as surrogate nursing homes, or that elderly patients must be moved so that surgery can proceed. Budgetary decisions made by politicians and administrators are transformed into clinical decisions made by doctors.

Myth #7: Since national health insurance is very popular in other countries, it would also be popular in the United States.

National health insurance remains popular in other countries precisely because it does not function the way its advocates believe it should. It "works" in other countries for three reasons: 1) The wealthy, the powerful, and those who are most skilled at articulating their complaints find ways to maneuver to the front of the lines. 2) Those pushed to the end are generally unaware of the medical technologies denied to them. 3) There are no contingency fees, no generally recognized right of due process, and no lawyers willing to represent those who are systematically discriminated against—though these are beginning to develop, as, for instance, kidney patients learn the facts of their situation and organize into pressure groups on the AIDS model.

"Don't push me around" is a distinctively American phrase. In Europe, people have been pushed around for centuries. In the U.S. we have widespread access to information about modern medical technology, a legal system that encourages litigation, and a strong devotion to basic rights of due process. National health insurance, as it operates in other countries, would not survive the American cultural and legal system.

POSTSCRIPT

Does the United States Need Socialized Medicine?

If the American health care system is the patient, perhaps it is time for a complete check-up. There are those who argue that the system is in very good health and should be left alone. They may concede that strong medicine may be necessary in dealing with specific problems, as was the case with the creation of Medicare and Medicaid, but if such radical treatments as socialized medicine are prescribed for the system as a whole, the cure could be worse than the disease.

Former secretary of Health, Education, and Welfare Joseph A. Califano, Jr., believes that the system is not well, but in *America's Health Care Revolution: Who Lives? Who Dies? Who Pays?* (Random House, 1986), Califano argues that the movement to a sound health care system must be accomplished largely in the private sector. More critically, Charles J. Dougherty's *American Health Care: Realities, Rights, and Reforms* (Oxford University Press, 1988) is a sober examination of the moral right to health care, to which Americans do not always have ready access, and Dougherty proposes changes in the delivery system.

Others argue that radical surgery is necessary. One criticism is that the health care industry has lost the ability to control costs and that the present payment system must change. This view is argued in Dan C. Coddington, David J. Keen, Keith D. Moore, and Richard L. Clarke, *The Crisis in Health Care* (Jossey Bass, 1990). Similarly, Thomas H. Ainsworth, *Live or Die* (Macmillan, 1983), attacks escalating costs, restricted access, overspecialization, and technological overkill. Robert H. Blank, *Rationing Medicine* (Columbia University Press, 1988), examines the moral and economic implications of expensive procedures such as organ transplants, the treatment of seriously ill newborn babies, reproductive technologies, and fetal health. *Setting Limits* (Simon & Schuster, 1987) is a provocative examination of these issues by Daniel Callahan, director of the Hastings Center, that focuses upon moral issues in American society.

Some critics believe that medical costs have gotten out of hand, in part because expensive equipment and drugs tempt doctors and hospitals to prescribe unnecessary treatments and in part because modern medical technology can extend the life of a sick premature infant or a terminally ill person, but at costs that society simply cannot afford to pay. Given the finite limits that we must impose on medical costs, how do we choose what we are—and are not—prepared to pay for?

ISSUE 17

Was *Roe v. Wade* a Mistake?

YES: William H. Rehnquist, from Dissenting Opinion, *Planned Parenthood of Southeastern Pennsylvania v. Robert P. Casey,* U.S. Supreme Court (1992)

NO: Harry A. Blackmun, from Concurring Opinion, *Planned Parenthood of Southeastern Pennsylvania v. Robert P. Casey,* U.S. Supreme Court (1992)

ISSUE SUMMARY

YES: Supreme Court chief justice William H. Rehnquist believes that the Court wrongly decided *Roe v. Wade* and that states should have the right to establish their own abortion laws.

NO: Supreme Court justice Harry A. Blackmun believes that *Roe* was correctly decided, and he opposes any law that would limit a woman's access to an abortion beyond the limits set in that case.

Until 1973, the laws governing abortion were set by the states, most of which barred legal abortion except where pregnancy imperiled the life of the pregnant woman. In that year, the U.S. Supreme Court decided the controversial case of *Roe v. Wade.* The *Roe* decision acknowledged both a woman's "fundamental right" to terminate a pregnancy before fetal viability and the state's legitimate interest in protecting both the woman's health and the "potential life" of the fetus. It prohibited states from banning abortion to protect the fetus before the third trimester of a pregnancy, and it ruled that even during that final trimester, a woman could obtain an abortion if she could prove that her life or health would be endangered by carrying to term. (In a companion case to *Roe,* decided on the same day, the Court defined *health* broadly enough to include "all factors—physical, emotional, psychological, familial, and the woman's age—relevant to the well-being of the patient.") These holdings, together with the requirement that state regulation of abortion had to survive "strict scrutiny" and demonstrate a "compelling state interest," resulted in later decisions striking down mandatory 24-hour waiting periods, requirements that abortions be performed in hospitals, and so-called informed consent laws.

The Supreme Court did uphold state laws requiring parental notification and consent for minors (though it provided that minors could seek permission from a judge if they feared notifying their parents), as well as federal and state laws barring public funding for any abortion that is not necessary to save the woman's life. In 1989, in the case of *Webster v. Reproductive Health Services*, the Court went further, upholding provisions of a Missouri law that requires tests for viability on any fetus of more than 20 weeks gestation before performing an abortion and barring the use of public facilities or employees to perform an abortion that is not needed to save the pregnant woman's life.

The Supreme Court's 1992 decision in *Planned Parenthood of Southeastern Pennsylvania v. Robert P. Casey* was eagerly awaited, as it would determine how far the Supreme Court was prepared to go in constricting or overturning *Roe v. Wade*. As it turned out, neither side of the abortion issue was satisfied with the outcome. Four members of the Court were prepared to overturn *Roe* and give broad power to the states to restrict abortion as they choose. Two members of the Court wanted to return to the defense of abortion as originally set by *Roe*.

But three members of the Court sought what they perceived as a middle ground, although most advocates on the opposing sides would deny that such a middle ground exists. These justices were holding by the judicial rule of *stare decisis*, literally "to stand by things decided." The rule holds that long-settled constitutional interpretations on which people base their behavior should not be easily, if ever, overturned.

These three justices—Sandra Day O'Connor, Anthony M. Kennedy, and David H. Souter—wrote an unusual joint opinion in which they joined Justices Blackmun and John Paul Stevens III in affirming a woman's right to abortion free of "undue burdens" imposed by the state, such as the Pennsylvania requirement that a married woman must notify her husband before obtaining an abortion. At the same time, however, these three controlling justices joined Chief Justice Rehnquist and Justices Byron R. White, Antonin Scalia and Clarence Thomas in upholding Pennsylvania's requirements for informed consent, mandatory waiting periods, and parental consent or notification for minors.

Although public opinion polls usually show a majority of Americans supporting both a right to abortion in some circumstances and certain constraints on its exercise in others, millions of Americans on both sides of the issue believe that this is a profoundly moral question that should not be decided by polls or elections. Pro-life advocates favor a constitutional amendment outlawing abortion. Pro-choice advocates favor a federal freedom of choice act. On both sides, there is keen interest in the beliefs of future Supreme Court justices, who may be able to tip the closely divided Court in one direction or the other.

These deeply opposed views are best expressed in the opinions in the Pennsylvania case. Chief Justice William H. Rehnquist approved the Court's restrictions, but felt that the Court should go further and overturn *Roe*. Justice Harry A. Blackmun approved the Court's affirmation of the right of abortion, but believed that the Court had improperly inhibited that right by accepting many of the Pennsylvania requirements.

YES

William H. Rehnquist

OPINION OF WILLIAM H. REHNQUIST

CHIEF JUSTICE REHNQUIST, with whom JUSTICE WHITE, JUSTICE SCALIA, and JUSTICE THOMAS join, concurring in the judgment in part and dissenting in part.

The joint opinion, following its newly-minted variation on *stare decisis*, retains the outer shell of *Roe v. Wade*, 410 U.S. 113 (1973), but beats a wholesale retreat from the substance of that case. We believe that *Roe* was wrongly decided, and that it can and should be overruled consistently with our traditional approach to *stare decisis* in constitutional cases. We would adopt the approach of the plurality in *Webster v. Reproductive Health Services*, 492 U.S. 490 (1989), and uphold the challenged provisions of the Pennsylvania statute in their entirety. . . .

In *Roe v. Wade*, the Court recognized a "guarantee of personal privacy" which "is broad enough to encompass a woman's decision whether or not to terminate her pregnancy." We are now of the view that, in terming this right fundamental, the Court in *Roe* read the earlier opinions upon which it based its decision much too broadly. Unlike marriage, procreation and contraception, abortion "involves the purposeful termination of potential life." *Harris v. McRae*, 448 U.S. 297, 325 (1980). The abortion decision must therefore "be recognized as *sui generis*, different in kind from the others that the Court has protected under the rubric of personal or family privacy and autonomy." *Thornburgh v. American College of Obstetricians and Gynecologists, supra*, at 792 (WHITE, J., dissenting). One cannot ignore the fact that a woman is not isolated in her pregnancy, and that the decision to abort necessarily involves the destruction of a fetus. (To look "at the act which is assertedly the subject of a liberty interest in isolation from its effect upon other people [is] like inquiring whether there is a liberty interest in firing a gun where the case at hand happens to involve its discharge into another person's body").

Nor do the historical traditions of the American people support the view that the right to terminate one's pregnancy is "fundamental." The common law which we inherited from England made abortion after "quickening" an offense. At the time of the adoption of the Fourteenth Amendment, statutory

From *Planned Parenthood of Southeastern Pennsylvania et al. v. Robert P. Casey et al.*, 60 L.W. 4795 (1992). References and some case citations omitted.

prohibitions or restrictions on abortion were commonplace; in 1868, at least 28 of the then-37 States and 8 Territories had statutes banning or limiting abortion. By the turn of the century virtually every State had a law prohibiting or restricting abortion on its books. By the middle of the present century, a liberalization trend had set in. But 21 of the restrictive abortion laws in effect in 1868 were still in effect in 1973 when *Roe* was decided, and an overwhelming majority of the States prohibited abortion unless necessary to preserve the life or health of the mother. On this record, it can scarcely be said that any deeply rooted tradition of relatively unrestricted abortion in our history supported the classification of the right to abortion as "fundamental" under the Due Process Clause of the Fourteenth Amendment.

We think, therefore, both in view of this history and of our decided cases dealing with substantive liberty under the Due Process Clause, that the Court was mistaken in *Roe* when it classified a woman's decision to terminate her pregnancy as a "fundamental right" that could be abridged only in a manner which withstood "strict scrutiny." In so concluding, we repeat the observation made in *Bowers v. Hardwick*, 478 U.S. 186 (1986):

> "Nor are we inclined to take a more expansive view of our authority to discover new fundamental rights imbedded in the Due Process Clause. The Court is most vulnerable and comes nearest to illegitimacy when it deals with judge-made constitutional law having little or no cognizable roots in the language or design of the Constitution."

We believe that the sort of constitutionally imposed abortion code of the type illustrated by our decisions following *Roe* is inconsistent "with the notion of a Constitution cast in general terms, as ours is, and usually speaking in general principles, as ours does." *Webster v. Reproductive Health Services*, 492 U.S., at 518 (plurality opinion). . . .

II

The joint opinion of JUSTICES O'CONNOR, KENNEDY, and SOUTER cannot bring itself to say that *Roe* was correct as an original matter, but the authors are of the view that "the immediate question is not the soundness of *Roe's* resolution of the issue, but the precedential force that must be accorded to its holding." Instead of claiming that *Roe* was correct as a matter of original constitutional interpretation, the opinion therefore contains an elaborate discussion of *stare decisis*. This discussion of the principle of *stare decisis* appears to be almost entirely dicta, because the joint opinion does not apply that principle in dealing with *Roe*. *Roe* decided that a woman had a fundamental right to an abortion. The joint opinion rejects that view. *Roe* decided that abortion regulations were to be subjected to "strict scrutiny" and could be justified only in the light of "compelling state interests." The joint opinion rejects that view. *Roe* analyzed abortion regulation under a rigid trimester framework, a framework which has guided this Court's decisionmaking for 19 years. The joint opinion rejects that framework.

Stare decisis is defined in Black's Law Dictionary as meaning "to abide by, or adhere to, decided cases." Whatever the "central holding" of *Roe* that is left after the joint opinion finishes dissecting it is surely not the result of that principle. While purporting to adhere to precedent, the joint opinion instead revises it. *Roe* continues to exist, but only in the way a storefront on a western movie set exists: a mere facade to give the illusion of reality. . . .

In our view, authentic principles of *stare decisis* do not require that any portion of the reasoning in *Roe* be kept intact. "*Stare decisis* is not . . . a universal, inexorable command," especially in cases involving the interpretation of the Federal Constitution. *Burnet v. Coronado Oil & Gas Co.*, 285 U.S. 393, 405 (1932) (Brandeis, J., dissenting). Erroneous decisions in such constitutional cases are uniquely durable, because correction through legislative action, save for constitutional amendment, is impossible. It is therefore our duty to reconsider constitutional interpretations that "depar[t] from a proper understanding" of the Constitution. *Garcia v. San Antonio Metropolitan Transit Authority*, 469 U.S. at 557. Our constitutional watch does not cease merely because we have spoken before on an issue; when it becomes clear that a prior constitutional interpretation is unsound we are obliged to reexamine the question.

The joint opinion discusses several *stare decisis* factors which, it asserts, point toward retaining a portion of *Roe*. Two of these factors are that the main "factual underpinning" of *Roe* has remained the same, and that its doctrinal foundation is no weaker now than it was in 1973. Of course, what might be called the basic facts which gave rise to *Roe* have remained the same—women become pregnant, there is a point somewhere, depending on medical technology, where a fetus becomes viable, and women give birth to children. But this is only to say that the same facts which gave rise to *Roe* will continue to give rise to similar cases.

It is not a reason, in and of itself, why those cases must be decided in the same incorrect manner as was the first case to deal with the question. And surely there is no requirement, in considering whether to depart from *stare decisis* in a constitutional case, that a decision be more wrong now than it was at the time it was rendered. If that were true, the most outlandish constitutional decision could survive forever, based simply on the fact that it was no more outlandish later than it was when originally rendered. . . .

Apparently realizing that conventional *stare decisis* principles do not support its position, the joint opinion advances a belief that retaining a portion of *Roe* is necessary to protect the "legitimacy" of this Court. Because the Court must take care to render decisions "grounded truly in principle," and not simply as political and social compromises, the joint opinion properly declares it to be this Court's duty to ignore the public criticism and protest that may arise as a result of a decision. Few would quarrel with this statement, although it may be doubted that Members of this Court, holding their tenure as they do during constitutional "good behavior," are at all likely to be intimidated by such public protests.

But the joint opinion goes on to state that when the Court "resolve[s] the sort of intensely divisive controversy reflected in *Roe* and those rare, comparable cases," its decision is exempt from reconsideration under established principles of *stare decisis* in constitutional cases. This is so, the joint opinion contends, because in those "intensely divisive" cases the Court has "call[ed] the contending sides of a national controversy to end their national division by accepting a common mandate rooted in the Constitution," and must therefore take special care not to be perceived as "surrender[ing] to political pressure" and continued opposition. This is a truly novel principle, one which is contrary to both the Court's historical practice and to the Court's traditional willingness to tolerate criticism of its opinions. Under this principle, when the Court has ruled on a divisive issue, it is apparently prevented from overruling that decision for the sole reason that it was incorrect, *unless opposition to the original decision has died away.*

The first difficulty with this principle lies in its assumption that cases which are "intensely divisive" can be readily distinguished from those that are not. The question of whether a particular issue is "intensely divisive" enough to qualify for special protection is entirely subjective and dependent on the individual assumptions of the members of this Court. In addition, because the Court's duty is to ignore public opinion and criticism on issues that come before it, its members are in perhaps the worst position to judge whether a decision divides the Nation deeply enough to justify such uncommon protection. Although many of the Court's decisions divide the populace to a large degree, we have not previously on that account shied away from applying normal rules of *stare decisis* when urged to reconsider earlier decisions. Over the past 21 years, for example, the Court has overruled in whole or in part 34 of its previous constitutional decisions. . . .

There is also a suggestion in the joint opinion that the propriety of overruling a "divisive" decision depends in part on whether "most people" would now agree that it should be overruled. Either the demise of opposition or its progression to substantial popular agreement apparently is required to allow the Court to reconsider a divisive decision. How such agreement would be ascertained, short of a public opinion poll, the joint opinion does not say. But surely even the suggestion is totally at war with the idea of "legitimacy" in whose name it is invoked. The Judicial Branch derives its legitimacy, not from following public opinion, but from deciding by its best lights whether legislative enactments of the popular branches of Government comport with the Constitution. The doctrine of *stare decisis* is an adjunct of this duty, and should be no more subject to the vagaries of public opinion than is the basic judicial task.

There are other reasons why the joint opinion's discussion of legitimacy is unconvincing as well. In assuming that the Court is perceived as "surrender[ing] to political pressure" when it overrules a controversial decision, the joint opinion forgets that there are two sides to any controversy. The joint opinion asserts that, in order to protect its legitimacy, the Court must refrain from overruling a controversial decision lest it be viewed as favoring those who oppose the decision. But a decision to *adhere* to prior precedent is subject to the same criticism, for in such a case one can easily argue that the Court is responding to those who have demonstrated in favor of the original decision. The decision in *Roe* has engendered large demonstrations, including repeated marches on this Court and on Congress, both in opposition to and in support of that opinion. A decision either way on *Roe* can therefore be perceived as favoring one group or the other. But this perceived dilemma arises only if one assumes, as the joint opinion does, that the Court should make its decisions with a view toward speculative public perceptions. If one assumes instead . . . that the Court's legitimacy is enhanced by faithful interpretation of the Constitution irrespective of public opposition, such self-engendered difficulties may be put to one side.

Roe is not this Court's only decision to generate conflict. Our decisions in some recent capital cases, and in *Bowers v. Hardwick,* 478 U.S. 186 (1986), have also engendered demonstrations in opposition. The joint opinion's message to such protesters appears to be that they must cease their activities in order to serve their cause, because their protests will only cement in place a decision which by normal standards of *stare decisis* should be reconsidered. Nearly a century ago, Justice David J. Brewer of this Court, in an article discussing criticism of its decisions, observed that "many criticisms may be, like their authors, devoid of good taste, but better all sorts of criticism than no criticism at all." This was good advice to the Court then, as it is today. Strong and often misguided criticism of a decision should not render the decision immune from reconsideration, lest a fetish for legitimacy penalize freedom of expression.

The end result of the joint opinion's paeans of praise for legitimacy is the enunciation of a brand new standard for evaluating state regulation of a woman's right to abortion—the "undue burden" standard. As indicated above, *Roe v. Wade* adopted a "fundamental right" standard under which state regulations could survive only if they met the requirement of "strict scrutiny." While we disagree with that standard, it at least had a recognized basis in constitutional law at the time *Roe* was decided. The same cannot be said for the "undue burden" standard, which is created largely out of whole cloth by the authors of the joint opinion. It is a standard which even today does not command the support of a majority of this Court. And it will not, we believe, result in the sort of "simple limitation," easily applied, which the joint opinion anticipates. In sum, it is a standard which is not built to last.

In evaluating abortion regulations under that standard, judges will have to decide whether they place a "substantial obstacle" in the path of a woman seeking an abortion. In that this standard is based even more on a judge's subjective determinations than was the trimester framework, the standard will do nothing to prevent "judges from roaming at large in the constitutional field" guided only by their personal views. *Griswold v. Connecticut,* 381 U.S., at 502 (Harlan, J., concurring in judgment). Because the undue burden standard is plucked from nowhere, the question of what is a "substantial obstacle" to abortion will undoubtedly engender a variety of conflicting views. For example, in the very matter before us now, the authors of the joint opinion would uphold Pennsylvania's 24-hour waiting period, concluding that a "particular burden" on some women is not a substantial obstacle. But the authors would at the same time strike down Pennsylvania's spousal notice provision, after finding that in a "large fraction" of cases the provision will be a substantial obstacle. And, while the authors conclude that the informed consent provisions do not constitute an "undue burden," JUSTICE STEVENS would hold that they do.

Furthermore, while striking down the spousal *notice* regulation, the joint opinion would uphold a parental *consent* restriction that certainly places very substantial obstacles in the path of a minor's abortion choice. The joint opinion is forthright in admitting that it draws this distinction based on a policy judgment that parents will have the best interests of their children at heart, while the same is not necessarily true of husbands as to their wives. This may or may not be a correct judgment, but it is quintessentially a legislative one. The "undue burden" inquiry does not in any way supply the distinction between parental consent and spousal consent which the joint opinion adopts. Despite the efforts of the joint opinion, the undue burden standard presents nothing more workable than the trimester framework which it discards today. Under the guise of the Constitution, this Court will still impart its own preferences on the States in the form of a complex abortion code.

The sum of the joint opinion's labors in the name of *stare decisis* and "legitimacy" is this: *Roe v. Wade* stands as a sort of judicial Potemkin Village, which may be pointed out to passers by as a monument to the importance of adhering to precedent. But behind the facade, an entirely new method of analysis, without any roots in constitutional law, is imported to decide the constitutionality of state laws regulating abortion. Neither *stare decisis* nor "legitimacy" are truly served by such an effort.

We have stated above our belief that the Constitution does not subject state abortion regulations to heightened scrutiny. Accordingly, we think that the correct analysis is that set forth by the plurality opinion in *Webster*. A woman's interest in having an abortion is a form of liberty protected by the Due Process Clause, but States may regulate abortion procedures in ways rationally related to a legitimate state interest.

NO

Harry A. Blackmun

OPINION OF HARRY A. BLACKMUN

JUSTICE BLACKMUN, concurring in part, concurring in the judgment in part, and dissenting in part. . . .

Three years ago, in *Webster v. Reproductive Health Serv.*, 492 U.S. 490 (1989), four Members of this Court appeared poised to "cas[t] into darkness the hopes and visions of every woman in this country" who had come to believe that the Constitution guaranteed her the right to reproductive choice. (BLACKMUN, J., dissenting.) All that remained between the promise of *Roe* and the darkness of the plurality was a single, flickering flame. Decisions since *Webster* gave little reason to hope that this flame would cast much light. But now, just when so many expected the darkness to fall, the flame has grown bright.

I do not underestimate the significance of today's joint opinion. Yet I remain steadfast in my belief that the right to reproductive choice is entitled to the full protection afforded by this Court before *Webster*. And I fear for the darkness as four Justices anxiously await the single vote necessary to extinguish the light.

I

Make no mistake, the joint opinion of JUSTICES O'CONNOR, KENNEDY, and SOUTER is an act of personal courage and constitutional principle. In contrast to previous decisions in which JUSTICES O'CONNOR and KENNEDY postponed reconsideration of *Roe v. Wade*, 410 U.S. 113 (1973), the authors of the joint opinion today join JUSTICE STEVENS and me in concluding that "the essential holding of *Roe* should be retained and once again reaffirmed." In brief, five Members of this Court today recognize that "the Constitution protects a woman's right to terminate her pregnancy in its early stages."

A fervent view of individual liberty and the force of *stare decisis* have led the Court to this conclusion. Today a majority reaffirms that the Due Process Clause of the Fourteenth Amendment establishes "a realm of personal

From *Planned Parenthood of Southeastern Pennsylvania et al. v. Robert P. Casey et al.*, 60 L.W. 4795 (1992). Some notes and case citations omitted.

liberty which the government may not enter"—realm whose outer limits cannot be determined by interpretations of the Constitution that focus only on the specific practices of States at the time the Fourteenth Amendment was adopted. Included within this realm of liberty is "the right of the *individual*, married or single, to be free from unwarranted governmental intrusion into matters so fundamentally affecting a person as the decision whether to bear or beget a child." "These matters, involving the most intimate and personal choices a person may make in a lifetime, choices central to personal dignity and autonomy, are *central* to the liberty protected by the Fourteenth Amendment." (emphasis added). Finally, the Court today recognizes that in the case of abortion, "the liberty of the woman is at stake in a sense unique to the human condition and so unique to the law. The mother who carries a child to full term is subject to anxieties, to physical constraints, to pain that only she must bear."

The Court's reaffirmation of *Roe's* central holding is also based on the force of *stare decisis.* "[N]o erosion of principle going to liberty or personal autonomy has left *Roe's* central holding a doctrinal remnant; *Roe* portends no developments at odds with other precedent for the analysis of personal liberty; and no changes of fact have rendered viability more or less appropriate as the point at which the balance of interests tips." Indeed, the Court acknowledges that *Roe's* limitation on state power could not be removed "without serious inequity to those who have relied upon it or significant damage to the stability of the society governed by the rule in question." In the 19 years since *Roe* was decided, that case has shaped more than reproductive

planning—"an entire generation has come of age free to assume *Roe's* concept of liberty in defining the capacity of women to act in society and to make reproductive decisions." The Court understands that, having "call[ed] the contending sides . . . to end their national division by accepting a common mandate rooted in the Constitution," a decision to overrule *Roe* "would seriously weaken the Court's capacity to exercise the judicial power and to function as the Supreme Court of a Nation dedicated to the rule of law." What has happened today should serve as a model for future Justices and a warning to all who have tried to turn this Court into yet another political branch. . . .

II

Today, no less than yesterday, the Constitution and decisions of this Court require that a State's abortion restrictions be subjected to the strictest judicial scrutiny. Our precedents and the joint opinion's principles require us to subject all non-*de minimis* abortion regulations to strict scrutiny. Under this standard, the Pennsylvania statute's provisions requiring content-based counseling, a 24-hour delay, informed parental consent, and reporting of abortion-related information must be invalidated.

A

The Court today reaffirms the long recognized rights of privacy and bodily integrity. As early as 1891, the Court held, "[n]o right is held more sacred, or is more carefully guarded by the common-law, than the right of every individual to the possession and control of his own person, free from all restraint or interference of others. . . ." Throughout this century, this Court also has held that the fundamental right of privacy protects citizens against governmental intrusion in such intimate family matters as procreation, childrearing, marriage, and contraceptive choice. These cases embody the principle that personal decisions that profoundly affect bodily integrity, identity, and destiny should be largely beyond the reach of government. In *Roe v. Wade*, this Court correctly applied these principles to a woman's right to choose abortion.

State restrictions on abortion violate a woman's right of privacy in two ways. First, compelled continuation of a pregnancy infringes upon a woman's right to bodily integrity by imposing substantial physical intrusions and significant risks of physical harm. During pregnancy, women experience dramatic physical changes and a wide range of health consequences. Labor and delivery pose additional health risks and physical demands. In short, restrictive abortion laws force women to endure physical invasions far more substantial than those this Court has held to violate the constitutional principle of bodily integrity in other contexts. See, *e.g.*, *Winston v. Lee*, 470 U.S. 753 (1985) (invalidating surgical removal of bullet from murder suspect); *Rochin v. California*, 342 U.S. 165 (1952) (invalidating stomach-pumping).[1]

Further, when the State restricts a woman's right to terminate her pregnancy, it deprives a woman of the right to make her own decision about reproduction and family planning—critical life choices that this Court long has deemed central to the right to privacy. The decision to terminate or continue a pregnancy has no less an impact on a woman's life than decisions about contraception or mar-

riage. 410 U.S., at 153. Because motherhood has a dramatic impact on a woman's educational prospects, employment opportunities, and self-determination, restrictive abortion laws deprive her of basic control over her life. For these reasons, "the decision whether or not to beget or bear a child" lies at "the very heart of this cluster of constitutionally protected choices." *Carey v. Population Services, Int'l*, 431 U.S. 678 (1977).

A State's restrictions on a woman's right to terminate her pregnancy also implicate constitutional guarantees of gender equality. State restrictions on abortion compel women to continue pregnancies they otherwise might terminate. By restricting the right to terminate pregnancies, the State conscripts women's bodies into its service, forcing women to continue their pregnancies, suffer the pains of childbirth, and in most instances, provide years of maternal care. The State does not compensate women for their services; instead, it assumes that they owe this duty as a matter of course. This assumption—that women can simply be forced to accept the "natural" status and incidents of motherhood—appears to rest upon a conception of women's role that has triggered the protection of the Equal Protection Clause. The joint opinion recognizes that these assumptions about women's place in society "are no longer consistent with our understanding of the family, the individual, or the Constitution."

B

The Court has held that limitations on the right of privacy are permissible only if they survive "strict" constitutional scrutiny—that is, only if the governmental entity imposing the restriction can demonstrate that the limitation is both necessary and narrowly tailored to serve a compelling governmental interest. We have applied this principle specifically in the context of abortion regulations. *Roe v. Wade*, 410 U.S., at 155.[2]

Roe implemented these principles through a framework that was designed "to insure that the woman's right to choose not become so subordinate to the State's interest in promoting fetal life that her choice exists in theory but not in fact." *Roe* identified two relevant State interests: "an interest in preserving and protecting the health of the pregnant woman" and an interest in "protecting the potentiality of human life." With respect to the State's interest in the health of the mother, "the 'compelling' point . . . is at approximately the end of the first trimester," because it is at that point that the mortality rate in abortion approaches that in childbirth. *Roe*, 410 U.S., at 163. With respect to the State's interest in potential life, "the 'compelling' point is at viability," because it is at that point that the fetus "presumably has the capability of meaningful life outside the mother's womb." In order to fulfill the requirement of narrow tailoring, "the State is obligated to make a reasonable effort to limit the effect of its regulations to the period in the trimester during which its health interest will be furthered."

In my view, application of this analytical framework is no less warranted than when it was approved by seven Members of this Court in *Roe*. Strict scrutiny of state limitations on reproductive choice still offers the most secure protection of the woman's right to make her own reproductive decisions, free from state coercion. No majority of this Court has ever agreed upon an alternative approach. The factual premises of the trimester framework have not been undermined,

and the *Roe* framework is far more administrable, and far less manipulable, than the "undue burden" standard adopted by the joint opinion. . . .

III

At long last, THE CHIEF JUSTICE and those who have joined him admit it. Gone are the contentions that the issue need not be (or has not been) considered. There, on the first page, for all to see, is what was expected: "We believe that *Roe* was wrongly decided, and that it can and should be overruled consistently with our traditional approach to *stare decisis* in constitutional cases." If there is much reason to applaud the advances made by the joint opinion today, there is far more to fear from THE CHIEF JUSTICE's opinion.

THE CHIEF JUSTICE's criticism of *Roe* follows from his stunted conception of individual liberty. While recognizing that the Due Process Clause protects more than simple physical liberty, he then goes on to construe this Court's personal-liberty cases as establishing only a laundry list of particular rights, rather than a principled account of how these particular rights are grounded in a more general right of privacy. This constricted view is reinforced by THE CHIEF JUSTICE's exclusive reliance on tradition as a source of fundamental rights. He argues that the record in favor of a right to abortion is no stronger than the record in *Michael H. v. Gerald D.*, 491 U.S. 110 (1989), where the plurality found no fundamental right to visitation privileges by an adulterous father, or in *Bowers v. Hardwick*, 478 U.S. 186 (1986), where the Court found no fundamental right to engage in homosexual sodomy, or in a case involving the "firing of a gun . . . into another person's body."

In THE CHIEF JUSTICE's world, a woman considering whether to terminate a pregnancy is entitled to no more protection than adulterers, murderers, and so-called "sexual deviates."[3] Given THE CHIEF JUSTICE's exclusive reliance on tradition, people using contraceptives seem the next likely candidate for his list of outcasts.

Even more shocking than THE CHIEF JUSTICE's cramped notion of individual liberty is his complete omission of any discussion of the effects that compelled childbirth and motherhood have on women's lives. The only expression of concern with women's health is purely instrumental—for THE CHIEF JUSTICE, only women's *psychological* health is a concern, and only to the extent that he assumes that every woman who decides to have an abortion does so without serious consideration of the moral implications of her decision. In short, THE CHIEF JUSTICE's view of the State's compelling interest in maternal health has less to do with health than it does with compelling women to be maternal.

Nor does THE CHIEF JUSTICE give any serious consideration to the doctrine of *stare decisis.* For THE CHIEF JUSTICE, the facts that gave rise to *Roe* are surprisingly simple: "women become pregnant, there is a point somewhere, depending on medical technology, where a fetus becomes viable, and women give birth to children." This characterization of the issue thus allows THE CHIEF JUSTICE quickly to discard the joint opinion's reliance argument by asserting that "reproductive planning could take . . . virtually immediate account of a decision overruling *Roe.*"

THE CHIEF JUSTICE's narrow conception of individual liberty and *stare decisis* leads him to propose the same standard of review proposed by the plurality in *Webster.* "States may regulate abortion procedures in ways rationally related to a legitimate state interest. *Williamson v. Lee Optical Co.*, 348 U.S. 483, 491 (1955); cf. *Stanley v. Illinois*, 405 U.S. 645, 651–653 (1972)." *Post*, at 24. THE CHIEF JUSTICE then further weakens the test by providing an insurmountable requirement for facial challenges: petitioners must " 'show that no set of circumstances exists under which the [provision] would be valid.' " *Post*, at 30, quoting *Ohio v. Akron Center for Reproductive Health*, 497 U.S., at 514. In short, in his view, petitioners must prove that the statute cannot constitutionally be applied to *anyone.* Finally, in applying his standard to the spousal-notification provision, THE CHIEF JUSTICE contends that the record lacks any "hard evidence" to support the joint opinion's contention that a "large fraction" of women who prefer not to notify their husbands involve situations of battered women and unreported spousal assault. *Post*, at 31, n. 2. Yet throughout the explication of his standard, THE CHIEF JUSTICE never explains what hard evidence is, how large a fraction is required, or how a battered woman is supposed to pursue an as-applied challenge.

Under his standard, States can ban abortion if that ban is rationally related to a legitimate state interest—a standard which the United States calls "deferential, but not toothless." Yet when pressed at oral argument to describe the teeth, the best protection that the Solicitor General could offer to women was that a prohibition, enforced by criminal penalties, *with no exception for the life of the mother,* "could raise very serious questions." Perhaps, the Solicitor General offered, the failure to include an exemption for the life of the mother would be "arbitrary and capricious." If, as THE CHIEF JUSTICE contends, the undue burden test is made out of whole cloth, the so-called "arbitrary and capricious" limit is the Solicitor General's "new clothes."

Even if it is somehow "irrational" for a State to require a woman to risk her life for her child, what protection is offered for women who become pregnant through rape or incest? Is there anything arbitrary or capricious about a State's prohibiting the sins of the father from being visited upon his offspring?

But, we are reassured, there is always the protection of the democratic process. While there is much to be praised about our democracy, our country since its founding has recognized that there are certain fundamental liberties that are not to be left to the whims of an election. A woman's right to reproductive choice is one of those fundamental liberties. Accordingly, that liberty need not seek refuge at the ballot box.

IV

In one sense, the Court's approach is worlds apart from that of THE CHIEF JUSTICE and JUSTICE SCALIA. And yet, in another sense, the distance between the two approaches is short—the distance is but a single vote.

I am 83 years old. I cannot remain on this Court forever, and when I do step down, the confirmation process for my successor well may focus on the issue before us today. That, I regret, may be exactly where the choice between the two worlds will be made.

NOTES

1. As the joint opinion acknowledges, *ante,* at 15, this Court has recognized the vital liberty interest of persons in refusing unwanted medical treatment. *Cruzan v. Director, Missouri Dept. of Health,* _____ U.S. _____ (1990). Just as the Due Process Clause protects the deeply personal decision of the individual to *refuse* medical treatment, it also must protect the deeply personal decision to *obtain* medical treatment, including a woman's decision to terminate a pregnancy.

2. To say that restrictions on a right are subject to strict scrutiny is not to say that the right is absolute. Regulations can be upheld if they have no significant impact on the woman's exercise of her right and are justified by important state health objectives. See, *e.g., Planned Parenthood of Central Mo. v. Danforth,* 428 U.S. 52, 65–67, 79–81 (1976) (upholding requirements of a woman's written consent and record keeping). But the Court today reaffirms the essential principle of *Roe* that a woman has the right "to choose to have an abortion before viability and to obtain it without undue interference from the State." *Ante,* at 3. Under *Roe,* any more than de minimis interference is undue.

3. Obviously, I do not share the plurality's views of homosexuality as sexual deviance. See *Bowers,* 478 U.S., at 185–186, n. 2.

POSTSCRIPT

Was *Roe v. Wade* a Mistake?

Few issues in modern American society arouse anything like the moral passion and political fervor of the issue of abortion. Should women have the right to choose whether or not to carry a pregnancy to term, or should the "right to life" bar voluntary abortion? Where pro-choicers focus on the pregnant woman and speak of the "fetus," pro-lifers emphasize the "unborn child."

Antiabortionists ask: Do abortions cause pain to fetuses? Do women become psychologically scarred by abortion? Does legalized abortion produce insensitivity to human life? Pro-choicers in their turn ask: What harm is done to an unmarried teenage girl in bearing a baby? Who will raise and care for all the unwanted children? Will not prohibition produce, as it always has, countless unsafe back-alley abortions?

Public opinion appears to change depending upon the language used when the question is put. There are also substantive shifts of opinion depending in part on whether the pregnant woman simply exercises a preference not to have a child, considers economic hardship, is a minor, was raped, or was a victim of incest.

Heated discussion of the abortion issue continues: it is a part of many election campaigns at all levels of government, including the 1992 presidential election; Congress continues to consider both the Freedom of Choice Act, which would permit abortions, and a constitutional amendment that would forbid abortions; debate continues over restrictions on the sale of RU-486, an abortion-inducing drug that is available in Europe but banned in the United States.

Dozens of books have dealt with these questions since the Supreme Court's decision in *Roe v. Wade* in 1973. A comprehensive selection ranging from the pro-choice views of Dr. Alan Guttmacher to the pro-life position of Daniel Callahan can be found in J. Douglas Butler and David F. Walbert, eds., *Abortion, Medicine, and the Law,* 3rd ed. (Facts on File, 1986). Vigorous defense of the right to abortion will be found in Nanette J. Davis, *From Crime to Choice: The Transformation of Abortion in America* (Greenwood Press, 1985); Rosalind Petchesky, *Abortion and Woman's Choice: The State, Sexuality and Reproductive Freedom* (Northeastern University Press, 1984); and Beverly Wildung Harrison, *Our Right to Choose: Toward a New Ethic of Abortion* (Beacon Press, 1983). The opposition to abortion is thoughtfully expressed in James T. Burtchaell, *Rachel Weeping and Other Essays* (Andrews and McMeel, 1981) and in John Noonan's *A Private Choice* (Free Press, 1979).

Books that purport to establish a common ground or, as Lawrence Tribe put it, a "negotiated peace," include Tribe's *Abortion: The Clash of Absolutes*

(W. W. Norton, 1990) and Roger Rosenblatt, *Life Itself: Abortion in the American Mind* (Random House, 1992).

In 1992 the Democratic and Republican platforms took diametrically opposite positions on abortion. The Democrats endorsed the *Roe* decision, called for publicly funded abortions for those unable to pay, and backed the Freedom of Choice Act, then pending in Congress, a bill that would write into statute the principles of *Roe v. Wade* and—according to interpretations of some supporters and opponents—that might even strike down many of the abortion-related restrictions that the Court had already allowed under *Roe*, such as mandatory parental notification. If this position seemed extreme to many, so did that of the Republicans, which called for a "human life" amendment to the Constitution banning abortion and for congressional legislation extending the protection of "life" in the Fourteenth Amendment to that of "unborn children." The Republican platform contained no language that would provide for exceptions, either for rape, incest, or even the life of the woman, though both President Bush and Vice President Quayle endorsed exceptions in all three cases; almost all pro-lifers do agree that cases where the woman's life is endangered are special.

ISSUE 18

Should There Be a "Wall of Separation" Between Church and State?

YES: Edd Doerr, from "Does Religion Belong in Our Public Schools?" *USA Today Magazine,* a publication of the Society for the Advancement of Education (September 1987)

NO: George Goldberg, from *Reconsecrating America* (Wm. B. Eerdmans, 1984)

ISSUE SUMMARY

YES: Edd Doerr, executive director of Americans for Religious Liberty, believes that public schools should promote and reflect shared values, leaving religious instruction and celebration to the home and place of worship.
NO: George Goldberg, a writer and lawyer, holds that school prayer and the teaching of religion are permissible as long as all religions are accorded equal treatment.

The United States has more members (well in excess of 100 million) of more churches (more than 300,000) than any other country in the world. More than 95 percent of all Americans profess a belief in God. Recently, the growth of so-called cult religions and the increasing visibility of born-again Christians remind us that religion remains a powerful force in American society.

Because religious tolerance was a compelling issue when the United States was founded, the first clauses of the First Amendment to the Constitution deal with the relationship between the nation and religion. The Supreme Court now interprets these clauses to be binding upon the states as well as the national government.

The actual words are: "Congress shall make no law respecting an establishment of religion, or prohibiting the free exercise thereof." For the most part, the "free exercise" clause does not pose many constitutional controversies. The "establishment" clause does.

For the past 40 years, the U.S. Supreme Court has been examining and resolving church-state controversies. Sometimes it has appeared as if the Supreme Court supports the view of those who invoke Thomas Jefferson's famous metaphor about the necessary "wall of separation" between church and state. This appears to be the case in what has proven to be the most controversial church-state issue: the right of children and teachers to start their school day with a prayer.

In the case of *Engel v. Vitale* (1962), a 22-word prayer, recited daily in a number of public schools throughout the state of New York, became the center of a national controversy:

> Almighty God, we acknowledge our dependence upon Thee, and we beg Thy blessings upon us, our parents, our teachers, and our country.

This prayer, composed by the New York State Board of Regents (the governing body of the school system), was intended to be nondenominational. It was also voluntary, at least in the sense that the children were not required to recite it and could leave the room when it was recited. Nevertheless, the Court declared it unconstitutional, and in subsequent cases it also outlawed Bible reading and reciting the Lord's Prayer.

Other Supreme Court decisions have defended the right of the state to accommodate differing religious views. The Court has upheld a state's reimbursement of parents for the cost of sending their children to church-related schools on public buses, the loan of state-owned textbooks to parochial school students, and grants to church colleges for the construction of religiously neutral facilities. Public acknowledgment of religion is supported by such long-standing practices as having chaplains in the armed forces, tax exemptions for churches, and the motto "In God We Trust" on coins.

The Supreme Court has sought to define the constitutional boundaries of state support of religion by forbidding religious instruction in a public school class but permitting "release time" programs, which allow a student to be absent from public school in order to attend a religious class elsewhere. In 1990 the Supreme Court upheld the right of religious clubs to meet in public schools under the same conditions as other voluntary student organizations.

Those who advocate an impregnable wall of separation would forbid direct or indirect aid to religious bodies or religious causes. In direct opposition are those who have proposed a constitutional amendment to declare that the United States is a Christian nation and who would rewrite the laws and textbooks to reflect that conviction. Between these two extremes are a variety of accommodations made by legislatures and courts, compromises that probably fail to satisfy any of the advocates of absolutist views on the relations between church and state in America.

The irreconcilable conflict is posed here between Edd Doerr's support for stricter separation of church and state and George Goldberg's plea for government's increased accommodation to the needs of all religious groups.

YES

Edd Doerr

DOES RELIGION BELONG
IN OUR PUBLIC SCHOOLS?

Why can't children pray in school? Isn't creationism just as scientific as evolution and shouldn't it also be taught in public schools? If students can meet during school hours for other clubs, why can't they have a Bible discussion club? Aren't our public schools teaching "secular humanism," and isn't that why schools and textbooks rarely mention anything about Christianity?

These questions sum up much of the constant barrage of charges against American public schools, made mainly by such "New Religious Right" or "Radical Right" television evangelists as Jerry Falwell and Pat Robertson and their followers. Although the annual Gallup/Phi Delta Kappa polls of public attitudes toward public schools have not registered measurable popular support for the charges, they need to be examined because they have been put forth so vehemently and so extensively. The U.S. Supreme Court and lower courts have been and are being asked to rule on cases involving school prayer, "creationism," Bible clubs, and "secular humanism." The issues continually are being raised in Congress in proposed legislation and proposed constitutional amendments. Pres. Reagan, his administration, and his party's platforms have taken positions on these issues. Televangelists and columnists have made careers out of pressing the charges.

Tensions over religion have haunted public education in America since its humble beginnings in Massachusetts in the mid-17th century. Back when communities were more homogeneous than now, it was natural that the religion of the majority would permeate the curriculum, and there was little that minorities could do about it other than move to another community or start private schools. That is what many Catholics did in the 19th century, when the public schools tended to reflect a generalized, nondenominational Protestantism. However, over the generations, the growing pluralism of our society gradually smoothed over the religious rough edges in the schools, rendering them increasingly neutral with regard to religion and increasingly acceptable to families of nearly all religious persuasions.

It is significant that nonpublic school enrollment, a concrete measure of dissatisfaction with public education, peaked in the mid-1960's (at about 13% of total enrollment), both absolutely and proportionally. When Pres. Nixon's commission on nonpublic school finance, a body predisposed to favor tax aid to nonpublic schools, hired two Catholic universities to study the causes of enrollment decline in Catholic schools, which enrolled about nine-tenths of nonpublic students, the researchers concluded that the enrollment shift had little to do with ability to afford nonpublic schools and much to do with growing Catholic acceptance of public education. Between 1965 and the present, the proportion of Catholic students in nonpublic schools declined from about half to about one-quarter.

The increase in Protestant fundamentalist school enrollment in recent years has not equalled the decline in Catholic school enrollment. Primarily a response to racial integration of public schools originally, fundamentalist school enrollment now seems largely religiously motivated, a phenomenon related to the growth of what might be termed the "moral majoritarian" movement begun during the late 1970's.

The downturn in nonpublic enrollment began shortly after the Supreme Court's 1962 and 1963 school prayer rulings, which sharply punctuated a process of secularization that, before 1962, already had eliminated school-sponsored devotional activities from most schools. Critics of the Supreme Court's 1960's prayer rulings failed to grasp that Catholics had challenged Protestant prayers in public schools in the midwest at least two generations earlier.

Let us look at the specific problem areas cropping up in the courts:

School Prayer

Until 1962 and 1963, eastern and southern states tended to require and sponsor daily group prayers and/or Bible readings to open the school day. Lawsuits in New York, Pennsylvania, and Maryland brought by a variety of parents and students resulted in Supreme Court rulings to the effect that government-mandated or -sponsored devotions are incompatible with the religious neutrality required of public schools by the First Amendment clause barring laws "respecting an establishment of religion." That clause, like most of the Bill of Rights, is made applicable to state and local government by the Fourteenth Amendment.

Many people can't or won't understand that the Supreme Court in the *Engel* and *Schempp* rulings did not prevent individual students from praying or reading the Bible privately in the classroom; it only proscribed government-mandated, -sponsored, or -regimented devotions. Powerful movements of religious conservatives began pressuring Congress to amend the Constitution to allow government-sponsored group prayer in school. Civil libertarians and mainstream religious leaders rallied behind the Supreme Court, however, and all the proposed amendments were defeated, though not without many anxious moments for defenders of church-state separation. Perhaps the closest battle occurred in the House of Representatives in 1971, when a discharge petition brought a prayer amendment to the floor. Defeat of the amendment was largely due to the efforts of Rep. Robert Drinan, a Catholic priest who represented a mainly Catholic district in Massachusetts.

Advocates of school prayer amendments cite opinion polls which seem to show strong public support for their campaign. Nearly all of these polls, however, conveyed to respondents the false notion that students are denied the right to voluntary prayer, so the results are of questionable validity.

Preceding and setting the stage for the prayer rulings was a 1948 Supreme Court ruling (*McCollum*) holding that religious instruction could not be offered in public schools on a "released time" basis. Four years later, the Court ruled that schools could release students for up to an hour per week of religious instruction off the schools' grounds if there was no school pressure to get the students to attend. "Released time" religious instruction is no longer very common, though instances of *McCollum* violations continue to turn up in rural school districts.

TEACHING ABOUT RELIGION

In its school prayer rulings, the Supreme Court said that schools could and should offer objective, neutral instruction *about* religion. Yet, not a great deal of such instruction is taking place, for a variety of reasons. There is little demand for it from parents, educators, or religious groups, and there is some fear, partially justified, that such instruction could be converted too easily into proselytizing. Few states have any provision for training or certificating teachers to deal with a subject more complex and fraught with problems than any other. There is little agreement among educators, parents, scholars, and religious leaders about what should be taught and at what grade levels. Finally, those who are most concerned about getting some sort of religion into public education are not interested in objective, neutral education so much as in promoting their own particular viewpoints.

Related to this topic is the furor over a recent U.S. Department of Education study which shows that mention of religion is infrequent in textbooks, so infrequent as to lead to charges that the schools and textbook publishers are somehow hostile to religion. It is true that textbooks tend to overlook religion, but the reasons for this seldom are discussed. Textbook publishing is a highly profitable and competitive business. Our school populations are highly pluralistic, and religion is one of the touchiest subjects. In order to sell books, publishers have to avoid offending or making nervous the people responsible for selecting textbooks for local schools.

Can a textbook mention one religion or denomination without giving some sort of equal treatment to all? Should a textbook present only the positive side of religion and ignore the dark side? One critic bemoans texts which fail to discuss the reasons for the first Thanksgiving and the religious motives of the Puritan and Pilgrim settlers. Yet, a balanced treatment of religion in early New England would have to discuss the intolerance which led to the Salem witch trials, the execution of Mary Dyer for being a Quaker, and the exile of Anne Hutchinson for holding unauthorized religious meetings in her home. The Great Awakenings may be left out, but so too is the mention of religious support for slavery and religious insensitivity to other forms of social injustice. Schools and publishers evidently have found from generations of experience in hundreds, if not thousands, of communities that neglecting religion is safer than paying much attention to it.

Prof. Richard C. McMillan spoke for many experts in his excellent book, *Religion in the Public Schools*, in stating that, even though schools should offer objective instruction about religion, "it would be wise to restrict courses in religion studies to adolescents," and even then they should be electives. McMillan also puts the ball in the critics' court when he says that "A religious community should not request any form of religious instruction in the public schools until it may take pride in the quality of religious education provided by its own religious institutions."

Creationism and Evolution
In December, 1986, the Supreme Court heard an argument in the case involving a challenge to the Louisiana law which requires "balanced treatment" for "creationism" whenever evolution is taught in public schools. The lower Federal courts had found the law to violate the First Amendment's establishment clause. Advocates of "balanced treatment" contend that "creationism" and evolution are equally scientific, or equally unscientific, and therefore merit equal treatment. The scientific and educational communities, however, are in fairly solid agreement that "creationism" is essentially a fundamentalist religious doctrine, no matter how lawmakers might try to camouflage it. That was the view of the lower Federal courts when they struck down both Louisiana and Arkansas' "balanced treatment" laws.

The religious community is split on the issue, with fundamentalists supporting "balanced treatment" and mainstream Christianity and Judaism opposing it. Indeed, the plaintiffs in the Arkansas case were Catholic, Episcopal, United Methodist, Presbyterian, Baptist, Jewish, and Unitarian Universalist leaders and clergy.

("Creationism" follows a literal reading of Genesis and holds that our planet is not over 10,000 years old, that the fossil record was laid down by the biblical flood, that a deity created different "kinds" of plants and animals, and that humans were created separately from other animals. The consensus in science, however, is that the Earth is several billion years old, that all life forms evolved from earlier forms, that the fossil record was laid down over a vast span of time, and that humans evolved from primate ancestors and thus are related to other animals, most closely to the great apes. Scientists find little of scientific value in the writings of creationists. Many scientists are religious, while mainstream religious leaders do not find science hostile to religious values.)

Scientists, educators, and mainstream religious leaders believe that, if "balanced treatment" laws are upheld as constitutional, science education will be seriously damaged and American education will decline sharply in comparison with other advanced countries.

"Secular Humanism"
In mid-1986, an Alabama Federal judge presided over a trial in which a group of fundamentalist parents charged that public schools and textbooks teach the "religion of secular humanism." There are humanist or "secular humanist" organizations—such as the American Humanist Association, the Council for Democratic and Secular Humanism, the American Ethical Union, and the Society for Humanistic Judaism—but the charge that humanism or secular humanism is taught in public schools generally is accepted only by people of various funda-

mentalist persuasions. Whether humanism and secular humanism are religions or philosophies or "life stances" is irrelevant. What is relevant is whether what is distinctive about humanism is taught in the schools.

A typical argument of the accusers is that, since humanists believe in evolution and since schools teach evolution, therefore the schools teach humanism. Humanists also believe in democracy, but teaching democracy does not mean that the schools teach humanism. In the real world, the various currents of mainstream religion favor democracy and generally are not offended by evolution.

Whether humanism or secular humanism are religions or philosophies or life stances, their positions generally track Humanist Manifestoes I and II of 1933 and 1973 and the Secular Humanist Declaration of 1980. Apart from humanists' strong emphasis on philosophical naturalism, as contrasted with the supernaturalism of most forms of Christianity, for example, humanist views of moral and social issues are shared widely by Christian, Jewish, and other Americans.

In brief, humanism as a distinct philosophical or religious viewpoint is not taught in public schools. After all, our 16,000 public school districts are run by elected boards of local parents and voters. Our teachers and board members are a cross section of our population. To imagine that these tens of millions of voters, school board members, teachers, administrators, and parents are allowing humanism to be taught or promoted in their schools is to engage in paranoid fantasizing.

Nevertheless, it is becoming ever clearer that what fundamentalist critics call "secular humanism" is only a list of features of public education to which "moral ma-

joritarian" critics object, such as evolution, sex and family education, critical thinking, books containing thoughts or words offensive to the critics, and materials which do not consign women to "traditional" roles.

"Opting Out"

"Religious Right" attacks on public education took a new form in *Mozert v. Hawkins County Public Schools*, decided by a Tennessee Federal court in October, 1986. Finding for the fundamentalist plaintiffs, the judge held that their children should be allowed to "opt out" of an elementary reading program which allegedly conflicted with their "sincerely held" religious beliefs. Since no reading textbook series could satisfy the parents without raising establishment clause problems, the judge ordered that the children be allowed to study reading at home with the parents, subject to testing by school officials.

Critics of the ruling, now on appeal, point out that, if the ruling is not overturned, large numbers of fundamentalist and other parents may opt their children out of reading, social studies, science, and other classes to avoid having them exposed to any idea or utterance they regard as inconsistent with their religious beliefs. The resulting opt-outs would render much of public education chaotic and would put severe pressure on school administrators, teachers, and textbook publishers to exercise prior censorship over reading material and the content of class discussion. This in turn would render education sterile and very dull. The "moral majoritarians" who want public school curricula censored seem also to have a hidden agenda: They would like to create enough dissatisfaction with public education to generate popular support, now lacking, for tax support of sectarian private schools, which are free to permeate a curriculum with a particular sectarian point of view.

"Equal Access"

The early 1980's saw a sudden squall over whether "student-initiated" religious clubs could meet in public schools during or immediately before or after class hours. After several lower Federal courts held the practice unconstitutional, pressure was put on Congress to pass legislation to require all public schools accepting any Federal funds (as virtually all do) to allow religious groups "equal access" if schools allowed chess clubs or Young Democrats or Young Republicans to meet. Advocates of "equal access" held that it was discriminatory and a violation of free exercise for schools to allow all clubs except religious ones to operate.

Opponents replied that religion is singled out in the Constitution as special, that allowing religious clubs to operate in schools would be so close to government sponsorship as to violate the establishment clause, and that such clubs would generate sectarian divisiveness in schools. At one Congressional hearing on an "equal access" bill, I pointed out that "equal access" groups already were proselytizing and converting students, and doing so without the knowledge or consent of the parents of the targeted students. I urged defeat of the bill, or, failing that, that amendments be added to limit participation to older students (say, 16 or older), to require written parental permission for participation, and to prohibit "equal access" clubs from bringing in outside professional proselytizers. None of the safeguards was added to the bill and it was approved by Congress in 1984. While there seems to be no great

expansion of religious clubs in public schools, no data exist to show just how extensive they are.

"INVASION OF THE SOUL SNATCHERS"

The most overlooked problem in our public schools is what I have termed the "invasion of the soul snatchers." In 1983, an *Education Week* survey showed that some 4,500 adult professional missionaries were operating in public schools. Young Life had over 400 paid missionaries; Campus Life, the high school program of Youth for Christ, 800 missionaries; Bill Bright's Campus Crusade, 120 missionaries; Fellowship of Christian Athletes, 168 paid missionaries and 3,200 volunteer leaders and coaches, etc.

The problem only can have worsened after passage in 1984 of the "equal access" legislation, which specifically allows school religious clubs to bring in adult professionals. During the Congressional debate on "equal access," Moral Majority leader Rev. Jerry Falwell told *The Philadelphia Inquirer* that "We knew we couldn't win on school prayer [Pres. Reagan's proposed school prayer amendment had been defeated in the Senate in March, 1984] but equal access gets us what we wanted all along." What Falwell wanted was made clear in his *Fundamentalist Journal* in September, 1984, in a lead article describing the public schools as "a larger mission field than many countries."

The most successful single public school evangelist is probably Jerry Johnston, a 28-year-old preacher from Shawnee Mission, Kans., who claims to have spoken to over 2,000,000 students in more than 2,000 public schools. In a promotion piece for his "Life Public School Assembly" program, he states: "In the public junior and senior high school age bracket there are approximately 40,000,000 teenagers in the United States. This large group of young people represents one of the greatest virgin mission fields existent today and yet by and large, they are unreached by the Christian community." In the same promotion piece, Johnston urges fundamentalist "youth pastors" to use the "equal access" legislation to gain entry to public schools.

No one knows how successful these public school missionaries are, as there are no statistics on conversions. Astonishingly, the practice of allowing missionaries into schools has not been challenged in court, though it is unquestionably unconstitutional.

Holiday Observances

In New England before the American Revolution, Christmas observance, in school or anywhere else, was frowned upon as unbiblical and as too "high church" or "too papist." By the 20th century, however, Christmas and other observances became quite common. With the growth of pluralism and increased sensitivity toward the rights of religious minorities, sectarian activities began to recede. Yet, many holiday observances remain, and controversies continually flare up over school sanctioning of what religious minorities—including many Christians—regard as improper sectarian practices. Incidentally, many conservative Christians do not celebrate Dec. 25 religiously since they regard it as unbiblical.

Certainly, public schools may educate students *about* the traditions and festivals of various religions and cultures, but this should be done in an academic context. School-sponsored religious exhibits and ceremonies tend to be divisive, to slight whatever children in a school do not belong to the majority or plurality tradition, and raise not inconsequential First Amendment issues. The wisest course for public schools to follow is to provide religiously neutral education. They may and should promote the common democratic, civic, and civilized values shared by virtually all religious traditions, but religious instruction and celebration are best left to the home and to the church, synagogue, or mosque.

The best way to end this all too sketchy survey of the problems on the interface between religion and public education is to cite Justice William J. Brennan's remarks in his concurring opinion in the 1963 *Schempp* school prayer case:

> The public schools are supported entirely, in most communities, by public funds—funds exacted not only from parents, nor alone from those who hold particular religious views, nor indeed from those who subscribe to any creed at all. It is implicit in the history and character of American public education that the public schools serve a uniquely public function: the training of American citizens in an atmosphere free of parochial, divisive, or separatist influence of any sort—an atmosphere in which children may assimilate a heritage common to all American groups and religions. This is a heritage neither theistic nor atheistic, but simply civic and patriotic.

NO

RECONSECRATING AMERICA

The great mass of American people has watched the emotional debate [over church-state relations] with anxiety. They see the admirable and precious interfaith amiability of recent years disturbed by completely unnecessary lawsuits over issues as divisive as they are irrelevant to true religious freedom. To me, a Jew living in a country where almost everybody else is Christian, there is only one religious issue: equal treatment. If the New Testament is read in public schools, I want the Old Testament too. If Catholic parochial schools receive financial aid, I want yeshivas to get their fair share. If public employees get time off for Good Friday, I want them to get time off for Yom Kippur. If a crèche is displayed during the Christmas season on the lawn of the public library, I want to see a menorah nearby. . . .

THE ESSENCE OF RELIGIOUS FREEDOM IN A MULTISECTARIAN SOCIETY IS, AS OUR Founding Fathers perceived, twofold: (1) freedom from governmental compulsion to worship in any particular way, and (2) freedom to worship in one's own particular way. It was in recognition of this dual aspect of religious freedom that the federal government was explicitly forbidden to establish or disestablish any religion or to interfere with anyone's exercise of his faith. . . .

There is little question but that to the Founding Fathers "religion" did essentially have one meaning: the beliefs and practices associated with the worship of God, whether the Christian God, the Jewish God, nature's God, or Divine Providence. With that broad definition, and with the concomitant understanding, which the Founding Fathers also shared, that the only thing prohibited by the establishment clause of the First Amendment was *compulsion* of worship or the *preferential* treatment of one religion over competing religions, there would be little trouble today over interpretation and application of the establishment clause, and little "tension" between it and the free exercise clause.

But the Supreme Court greatly expanded both the definition of "religion" and the scope of the prohibitions of the establishment clause, with the result that an impasse, the classical irresistible force meeting immovable object, was created. As phrased by the Court, "tension inevitably exists between the Free Exercise and the Establishment clauses." But there was nothing inevitable about it.

There are good reasons for expanding the definition of "religion" to include virtually anything anybody deems sacred. The alternative puts the courts in the business of defining and assessing professed religious beliefs, a business for which they are neither equipped nor suited. If Henry David Thoreau occupies a place in a person's life comparable to that occupied by God in the life of a believer (the Supreme Court's phraseology in the conscientious objector cases), there seems no good reason why *Walden* should not enjoy all the protections accorded sacred scripture. But this special status extended to a writing under the free exercise clause will be a cruel joke if *as a consequence* it ends up on the establishment clause index.

Actually, if establishment continued to be defined as compulsion or preferential treatment, religion could be defined as broadly as might be desired. The "tension" only appears when the definition of religion is broadened for free exercise purposes *and* it is held that any governmental aid of religion, no matter how evenhanded, is prohibited by the establishment clause. *Then* it is inevitable that there will be tension between what the free exercise clause *requires* and what the establishment clause *forbids*.

The courts have become, if rather late in the day, fully aware of this dilemma. When in 1973 the Supreme Court struck down a New York plan to reimburse low-income families for parochial school tuition, it admitted that "it may often not be possible to promote the [free exercise clause] without offending the [establishment clause]." Similarly, when in 1980 the United States Court of Appeals for the Second Circuit held that the establishment clause required a public high school to deny the request of students to be allowed to hold prayer meetings on school grounds before the beginning of the school day, it conceded that the denial would violate their free exercise rights.

The preference of the courts for the establishment clause over the free exercise clause has given rise to much comment. It has been observed that free exercise is the goal of *both* of the religion clauses, the prohibition of establishment merely constituting a necessary means by which to realize it. According to this interpretation, whenever tension appears between the clauses, free exercise should prevail. . . .

That brings us to the central questions: (1) What is an establishment of religion? and (2) What is the free exercise thereof? It seems to me, after reading what Jefferson and Madison wrote on the subject, studying the cases, state and federal, and considering the observations of legal scholars of varying predilections, that there really should be no serious disagreement over the meaning of either of the religion clauses of the First Amendment.

The free exercise clause is perhaps the simpler one to understand, so I will consider it first. In essence it means that, consistent with public morals and an orderly society, every person should be allowed, and wherever possible helped, to worship whatever it is he deems sacred in whatever manner he deems appropriate. The qualifying phrase, "consistent with public morals and an orderly society," should and usually has been interpreted to require a showing of significant public harm to justify inhibiting a religious practice. Thus an Indian tribe was permitted to use an hallucinatory drug in its rituals despite its general proscription as a "controlled substance," Old Order Amish were permitted to remove their children from school at fourteen despite a law requiring school attendance until sixteen, and Jehovah's Witness children were permitted to abstain from pledging allegiance to the flag, which their religion held was a graven image, but no exemptions from the general laws were granted to polygamists or to Amish employers who did not wish to pay social security taxes for their employees. . . .

The free exercise clause, then, interpreted broadly and applied with common sense and goodwill, should not give rise to serious problems. Establishment clause cases are inherently more difficult; yet they too could be decided with relative ease with the application of a bit more common sense and goodwill than has been in evidence in judicial decisions striking down nondiscriminatory public assistance programs.

. . . The Supreme Court in 1983 upheld a state statute providing reimbursement of parochial school tuition. But the Court was obliged to accomplish this result by means of a disingenuous acceptance of a farfetched rationale of universality. But why shouldn't a nondiscriminatory program of public support of all schools within a jurisdiction, public, secular private, and church-sponsored, be allowed? In other words, let us consider the extreme case where a state offers its citizens educational vouchers redeemable at any school meeting state accreditation requirements. Such a system has been advocated, notably by Milton and Rose Fried-

man, and has been opposed with great vehemence by the educational establishment. Should the political processes by which such a program could be adopted or rejected be short-circuited by a judicial holding that it would be unconstitutional under the establishment clause because aid would be given to parochial schools along with public and secular private schools?

The issue of *compulsion* can be quickly disposed of. No one under a voucher program would be obliged to attend a parochial school. Indeed, the issue of school prayers, usually considered under the rubric of compulsion, would be significantly defused if children could attend any school they desired. If prayers were important, then, a child could be sent to a school which said them; and [an atheist's child] probably could go, with children of similarly minded parents, to a school which didn't.

The issue of *preferential treatment* of one religion over others would seem as easily disposed of. In a scheme of vouchers redeemable at any accredited school, no issue of preference could arise. The argument that such a scheme would primarily benefit the Catholic Church, because most parochial schools are Catholic, completely misconstrues the purpose of the establishment clause. It might as well be argued that maintaining the roads favors Catholics because they use them to go to church more often than Protestants, Jews, or Madalyn Murray O'Hair, or that lowering postal rates for books supports Southern Baptists who mail so many Bibles. As long as equal benefits are available to all religions, a scheme is not rendered unconstitutionally preferential because one or more religious groups choose not to take equal advantage of it.

There would thus appear to be *no* establishment clause reason why an educational voucher system should not be sponsored by a state. (There might be an equal protection clause reason if such a system tended to result in racially segregated schools, but that could be dealt with, as it was in the tuition reimbursement scheme allowed by the Court, by requiring that beneficiary schools agree to adhere to civil rights legislation.) Yet I fear that the Court, even as constituted today, would have difficulty in allowing such a program.

Why? Because of Justice Black's formulation of the establishment clause thirty-seven years ago:

The "establishment of religion" clause of the First Amendment means at least this: Neither a state nor the Federal Government can set up a church. Neither can pass laws which aid one religion, *aid all religions*, or prefer one religion over another.

The answer to Justice Black is that he was wrong, and that thirty-seven years of adherence by the Supreme Court to a wrong theory is enough. As stated by a leading American legal scholar:

The historical record shows beyond peradventure that the core idea of "an establishment of religion" comprises the idea of *preference*; and that any act of public authority favorable to religion in general cannot, without manifest falsification of history, be brought under the ban of that phrase.

There remains but one church-state issue to consider: religious activities in public schools—prayers, Bible recitations, hymn singing, Christmas and Hanukkah pageants, grace before milk and cookies. No discussion of church-state relations in America can be complete without a candid discussion of this difficult issue, and it should be noted at the outset that there are men and women of goodwill on both sides, and that reference to the Founding Fathers is of limited assistance since the first public school was founded in 1821 (in Boston) and public schools were not widespread in the United States until after the Civil War.

The arguments in favor of school religious exercises boil down to a belief that "spiritual" values must be inculcated in our children and that the home and the church are unequal to the job. The principal argument against is that religion in our pluralistic society is essentially divisive and must be kept out of the public schools which have been a major vehicle for creating a cohesive society. . . .

. . . It is fascinating how the same people who on certain occasions profess great sympathy for minorities and poor people turn into Marie Antoinette when confronted with school prayers: let them go to private school, or let their parents teach them religion. How can a person who in the context of aid to dependent children cites statistics of broken homes, rodent-infested apartments crowded beyond imagination, and children roaming the streets untended, in the context of school prayers conjure up warm families sitting around the fireside listening to the paterfamilias (50 percent of minority children in the United States live in fatherless homes) recite verses from the Bible with appropriate commentary?

But middle-class children from two-parent families may not receive much more religious training at home than ghetto children. For the image of the patriarchical family reading the Bible (or anything else) around the hearth is nearly as fanciful in the suburbs as in the central city. Only judges of venerable age and advanced myopia can suppose that there is time and occasion in the modern middle-class home for morning prayers. In the real world the weekday morning is a paradigm of chaos—of father racing about shaving, searching for the one tie he really likes with this suit, gulping a Danish and coffee, grabbing his briefcase, and rushing off to catch the 7:07; of mother trying to feed everyone (maybe even herself), dress herself and the five-year-old, search for the ten-year-old's math paper, assure the thirteen-year-old that she did not hide his sneakers, drive the children to school(s) and/or bus stop(s), and perhaps also get to her job on time (half of American mothers hold jobs outside the home). In this frenetic, frantic atmosphere, the possibility of stopping everything for three minutes to calm the spirit and give thanks to something beyond ourselves . . . is remote.

After-school opportunities for familial contemplation of eternity are even fewer. Extracurricular activities consume most of the children's time before dinner, shopping and cooking and perhaps her job consume all of mother's, and father is lucky if he makes it home for dinner. And then there is the ubiquitous television set by means of which the children will be taught that happiness may be found, may *only* be found, through the acquisition of nonessentials—a toy, a vacation, a car capable of going 120 mph in a country with a 55 mph speed limit. They see grown men and women exploding with joy because they guessed the price of an appliance they do not need and now will be given; they see fairytale children playing blissfully in an enchanted land and are told that their palpable joy derives from chewing a certain brand of gum; they see portrayals of

camaraderie, of intimacy and sharing among handsome men and lovely women untouched by sickness or human frailty in a pastoral idyll based solely on the consumption of a certain brand of beer. . . .

That, your Honor, is what children learn at home. Perhaps religious faith is a sham, "a chronic disease of the imagination contracted in childhood," the opium of the people. Perhaps Charlie's angels have more to offer than those Billy Graham writes about. But if you think so, why not say so? To pay lip service to the "spiritual needs of our young people" and then tell them that they must seek their fulfillment at home and only at home, is ignorant or dishonest or both.

Sex must be taught in the schools because parents are unequal to the task, but religious instruction is held to be within their competence. Surely the evidence compels the opposite conclusion.

The argument that, like Sergeant Friday in the old *Dragnet* series, schools are only concerned with *facts*, is equally untenable. The selection and presentation of the limitless supply of available observations, theories, and opinions determine the direction and meaning of the educational process. George Washington was born in 1732. So was Haydn. So, no doubt, were many other people, including saints and sadists and blasphemers and traitors. All *facts*, but which will you disinter and teach? Obviously it depends upon your animating principles. The Founding Fathers were animated by a belief in Divine Providence, a faith broad enough to take in theism and even, perhaps, pantheism, along with traditional religions. Some of us are still animated by similar beliefs, others are busy looking out for "Number 1," and still others are totally immersed in the beliefs and rituals of ancient religions. The one thing we should all be able to agree upon is that the courts should not take sides in the ongoing debate.

But *what about prayers*? The Court has now held that prayers may be said at the beginning of legislative and judicial sessions . . . [but] prayers are still banned from all public elementary and high schools in the country.

It should be understood that the ban is virtually total. For example, in 1982 the Tennessee legislature was considering a bill to allow (not require) public schools to set aside time for—well, for whatever the courts would allow. It had before it a statute drawn up by the Georgia legislature according to which a school could set aside up to three ten-minute periods a day—before school, after school, or during the lunch break—when students who so desired could use an empty classroom for prayers or silent meditation. The attorney general of Tennessee advised the legislature that the statute was unconstitutional. After several tries the legislature finally agreed on one minute of silence at the beginning of the school day and included in the statute a warning that teachers were not to suggest what the students should be thinking about during that minute. Even this statute was submitted to the attorney general for an opinion. He reviewed the cases, noted that "It is well-settled that the Establishment Clause forbids the state from requiring or even condoning perceptible religious exercises in public schools," and said that as long as the teachers did not encourage the students to say prayers during the minute of silence, the statute was constitutional.

Isn't that ridiculous? Any attempt to restrict the availability of obscene, racist novels in public school libraries is imme-

diately attacked as Nazism in the making; public school students are held to have a constitutional right to select their dress and hairstyles and to demonstrate in class against governmental policies of which they disapprove; but *God* has become so terrible a word that all the legal talent in the country must be mustered to exclude it absolutely from the public schools.

It is true that America's religions did not always live together in peace and harmony. The Puritans were not known for their tolerance of dissenters, anti-Catholic agitation once disfigured a large part of our public life, and no one named Goldberg is unaware of the history of anti-Semitism in America. But it is equally true that the tables have turned 180 degrees, and shields have been transformed into swords. . . .

Intolerance is ugly, no matter who practices it. When a minority practices it, it is also foolhardy, for intolerance breeds more intolerance, and minorities naturally suffer the most from an atmosphere of intolerance. With tolerance for the beliefs and practices of others, however foolish they may seem, and enlisting the aid of the courts not to prevent others from doing what they want but only to enforce one's own right to equal time, the issue of prayers in public school can be resolved without amending the Constitution.

POSTSCRIPT

Should There Be a "Wall of Separation" Between Church and State?

Few issues in American politics arouse such deep feelings as those relating to moral and religious convictions, and those deep feelings find expression in the preceding essays. Doerr is convinced that American public education can perform its function only if free of the parochial and divisive influence of opposing creeds. Goldberg is equally persuaded that this neutrality in theory is antireligion in practice, often effectively denying the exercise of religious belief.

What happens when religious views affect political policies? Richard G. Hutcheson, Jr., author of *God in the White House: How Religion Has Changed the Modern Presidency* (Macmillan, 1988), examines the impact of former president Jimmy Carter, a born-again Sunday-school-teaching Southern Baptist, and former president Ronald Reagan, who received strong support from religious conservatives for his antiabortion views and his views favoring school prayer.

The impact of religion on politics is not new. The influence of church policy on slavery, women's suffrage, Prohibition, and the civil rights movement is described in A. James Reichley's book, *Religion in American Public Life* (Brookings, 1985). Church-state relations and religious attitudes on abortion and nuclear disarmament are examined in Kenneth D. Wold's *Religion and Politics in the United States* (St. Martin's Press, 1987). A number of judicial decisions and legislative actions are considered in Richard P. McBrien's *Caesar's Coin: Religion and Politics in America* (Macmillan, 1987), a study that is sympathetic to, but not uncritical of, religious interests. A strongly separatist position is argued in Robert L. Maddox's *Separation of Church and State: Guarantor of Religious Freedom* (Crossroad, 1987).

James Davison Hunter's *Culture Wars: The Struggle to Define America* (Basic Books, 1991) explores church-state issues in America along a broader front: not merely that of religious sects but of profoundly different ways of looking at man and the universe. Hunter is convinced that a major cultural war is developing between "orthodox" and "progressive" combatants on such issues as school prayer, abortion, sex education, and gay rights. Hunter contends that this new war is developing not *between* religious denominations but *within* each religion. "In this," he believes, "the political relevance of the historical divisions between Protestant and Catholic and Christian and Jew has largely become defunct."

PART 4

America and the World

What is the role of the United States in world affairs? From what premise—realism or idealism—should American foreign policy proceed? What place in the world does America now occupy, and in what direction is it heading? American government does not operate in isolation from the world community, and the issues in this section are crucial ones indeed.

Should National Self-Interest Be the Basis of American Foreign Policy?

Is America Declining?

ISSUE 19

Should National Self-Interest Be the Basis of American Foreign Policy?

YES: Alan Tonelson, from "What Is the National Interest?" *The Atlantic* (July 1991)

NO: Joshua Muravchik, from *Exporting Democracy: Fulfilling America's Destiny* (AEI Press, 1991)

ISSUE SUMMARY

YES: Alan Tonelson, research director of the Economic Strategy Institute in Washington, D.C., advocates "interest-based" pragmatism in the formulation of American foreign policy and warns against utopian internationalism.
NO: Joshua Muravchik, a writer and scholar, warns against "the folly of realism" and argues that *interest* should be understood in the broadest sense, which includes an interest in democracy and human rights.

In the summer of 1992 Americans saw photographs of men, women, and children who resembled the living skeletons that were found in Nazi concentration camps at the end of World War II. They were Bosnians, most of them Muslim, who were imprisoned in Serbian "detention centers" in what was formerly the state of Yugoslavia on the Balkan Peninsula. Reports of massacres and torture, combined with the stated Serbian policy of "ethnic cleansing," further underscored the resemblance to the Holocaust. Meantime, Sarajevo, the former capital of Yugoslavia and now the capital of Bosnia-Herzegovina, seemed on the verge of falling to Serbian forces, the fate of its civilian population uncertain.

The United States and other nations protested this aggression, and the United Nations voted to impose sanctions against Serbia and began a humanitarian relief effort. From many quarters, however, came pleas for more active U.S. involvement. After all, the United States had not hesitated to lead other nations in a successful military intervention in the Middle East after Iraq invaded Kuwait in 1990. The expectation was that the United States would naturally lead an attack against the aggressor nation, as it had done less than two years before. The arguments against this option usually concentrated on the logistical differences between the Middle East and the Balkan Peninsula, but there was another major difference between the two areas that was less openly discussed: Bosnia-Herzegovina does not have very much oil underneath it. A Nazi-type regime could cause great human suffering, but its effects beyond the immediate area would probably be slight. A similar regime in control of the oil-rich Middle East could virtually paralyze Western industry and transportation.

To bring up such considerations may seem heartless and cynical, and there are good arguments for intervening militarily into such conflicts in order to save lives. Nevertheless, in the counsels of foreign policymakers, there are always some voices who ask this question about any proposed policy of intervention in another country: What's in it for us?

Those who put this question at the center of their deliberations call themselves *realists*. For them, the "vital interests" of their nation are what count. All other considerations, whether humanitarian, ideological, pacifistic, or militaristic, are irrelevant to making foreign policy. If a country threatens our vital interests, we should oppose it, by force if necessary, and ally ourselves with other states whose interests are similar to ours. When the danger to our vital interests passes, we then have no further reason to fight the country or ally ourselves with its enemies.

The realist school of thought has a long tradition in America. In his farewell address President George Washington warned against "foreign entanglements" that yield no concrete benefits for the country. In general, this view guided American foreign policy during the nineteenth century. Intervention in the affairs of other countries occurred only when it appeared that vital interests of the nation were at stake. But in this century, there have been periods when a very different line of thinking has been expressed by American statesmen. When the United States entered World War I, President Woodrow Wilson said that the purpose of the war was to "make the world safe for democracy," and at the war's end he proposed a generous peace for our former enemies and a new League of Nations to prevent further wars. Later presidents and other statesmen used language similar to Wilson's to announce the aims of American foreign policy. In his inaugural address President John F. Kennedy said that America would "pay any price, bear any burden . . . to assure the survival and success of liberty." For want of a better term, this approach to policy formulation is often called *idealism*, though its proponents insist that it is neither dreamy nor utopian. Their argument is that American foreign policy cannot forsake its own heritage of democracy and human rights. These, too, are among our vital interests, and if we ever forget that—if we think only in terms of power and resources and territory—we will lose whatever respect we have left in the world and thus jeopardize even our more tangible interests.

In the following selections, Alan Tonelson assumes the realist profile in his advocacy of "interest-based thinking," while Joshua Muravchik discusses the problems of realism and advocates a foreign policy based upon the ideals of democracy and human rights.

YES
Alan Tonelson

WHAT IS THE NATIONAL INTEREST?

For the first time since the end of the Second World War the United States faces the need to redefine the international requirements for its security and prosperity. Circumstances today demand that the United States rethink the ends of its foreign policy—that is to say, its national interests.

With the recent victories in the Cold War and the Gulf War, those who have been responsible for U.S. foreign policy are in a triumphant mood. There is little reason for it. The world continues to fray; ever more threatening weapons become ever more widely available. The gap between the stated ends of U.S. foreign policy and the means to achieve and pay for them remains wide and unbridgeable, as it has been for decades. Nor is it clear that the ends of U.S. foreign policy, when they are achieved, do more good than harm—for ourselves or for those we seek to assist. Perhaps more important, the recent victories have brought few benefits to the home front; indeed, they seem scarcely relevant to the daily lives and pressing concerns of most Americans today, or to the economic and social problems that bedevil the nation. The disconnection between the nation's needs at home and its ambitions abroad is at once bizarre and dangerous.

And yet, faced with all these facts, much of the nation's foreign-policy elite has chosen variously to ignore them or to berate those who have called attention to them.

Since the end of the Second World War, Americans have by and large defined their foreign-policy objectives in what may be called globalist or internationalist terms. Internationalism has been protean enough—liberal and conservative, hawkish and dovish, unilateralist and multilateralist—to have commanded the loyalty of figures as different as Ronald Reagan and Jimmy Carter. But its essence springs from three crucial lessons learned by most Americans and their leaders from the Great Depression and the rise of fascism during the 1930s, from the global conflagration that those events helped produce, and from the emergence of a new totalitarian threat almost immediately after that war.

The first lesson was that the United States would never know genuine security, lasting peace, and sustained prosperity unless the rest of the world also became secure, peaceful, and prosperous. The second lesson was that international security was indivisible—that the discontent that produced political extremism and, inevitably, aggression was highly contagious and bound to spread around the world no matter where it broke out. The third lesson was that the only way to achieve these fundamental goals and prevent these deadly dangers was to eliminate the conditions that breed extremism wherever they exist, and somehow to impose norms of peaceful behavior on all states.

The result of all this was a global definition of vital U.S. foreign-policy interests, with globalist international-security and economic structures to back it up. The United States supported the United Nations and forged alliances with scores of countries to guarantee security in all major regions and to deter aggression everywhere. In the process Washington expanded the definition of the U.S. defense perimeter to encompass literally every country outside the Communist world. At the same time, the imperative of resisting subversion as well as aggression everywhere in the world created an equally vital interest in the political and economic health of all these countries, which was fostered by U.S. foreign-aid programs and by an international economic system built on such mechanisms as the International Monetary Fund, the World Bank, and the General Agreement on Tariffs and Trade.

The internationalist approach led U.S. foreign-policy makers to insist that no corner of the world was so remote or insignificant that it could be ignored. Of course, not all parts of the world were given equal attention or resources. But disparities emerged not because foreign-policy makers viewed certain regions as expendable but because they perceived no serious threat either to these regions per se or to crucial international norms at the moment. Whenever a serious threat did appear, America's leaders usually favored a prompt response. The power of internationalist impulses has been underscored by military interventions, paramilitary operations, peace-keeping missions, and diplomatic initiatives in marginal countries and regions such as Angola, the horn of Africa, and Lebanon, and also by a foreign-aid program that continuously sprinkles funds on virtually every Third World mini-state, micro-state, and basket case that has won its independence since 1945.

Internationalism has insisted that U.S. foreign policy should aim at manipulating and shaping the global environment, as a whole rather than at securing or protecting a finite number of assets within that environment. It has yoked America's safety and well-being not to surviving and prospering in the here and now but to turning the world into something significantly better in the indefinite future—into a place where the forces that drive nations to clash in the first place no longer exist. Internationalism, moreover, has insisted that America has no choice but to "pay any price, bear any burden" to achieve these conditions, even though humanity has never come close to bringing them about. In so doing internationalism has sidestepped all questions of risk and cost. In fact, it has defined them out of existence.

YET EVEN BEFORE THE GORBACHEV REVOlution in Soviet foreign policy—during the Cold War years, when the case could be made for a total response to the ostensibly total Soviet threat—the problems created by the internationalist approach to foreign policy were beginning to loom as large as those that it was meant to solve. Militarily and strategically, internationalism identified America's foreign-policy challenges in such a way as to turn any instance of aggression into an intolerable threat to America's own security, whether or not tangible U.S. interests were at stake, and no matter how greatly the costs of intervention may have outweighed any specific benefits that the United States could plausibly have realized. Vietnam is the classic example. Internationalism also drew America into nuclear alliances—notably, in Europe—deliberately structured to entrap the country in nuclear conflict even in cases when our own national security had not been directly affected.

Economically, as early as the late 1960s internationalism showed signs of turning into a formula for exhaustion. Richard Nixon brought the post–Second World War international monetary system to an end, in 1971, precisely because America could no longer meet its foreign-policy obligations and its domestic obligations simultaneously. Politically, the internationalist strategies and rhetoric employed by U.S. leaders throughout the post-war era generated tremendous pressures on these same leaders to follow through. Remembering the political fire storms that followed the "losses" of China and Cuba, they repeatedly resolved to prove the nation's mettle when the next outbreak of trouble occurred, reducing to almost nil the possibility that noninvolvement would even be considered as an option, much less chosen.

Now, in the post–Cold War era, internationalism has become even more problematic. As our chronic budget gap shows, our foreign policy is politically unaffordable in today's America—as opposed to the America of the 1950s, when popular satisfaction with the barest skeleton of a welfare state and the country's economic predominance permitted levels of military spending two and three times as high as those of today (as a proportion of total federal spending). Internationalism continues to deny us a strategic basis for selectivity, a way of thinking about our international goals that would enable our leaders to resist the temptation to plunge into every crisis and right every wrong that life brings along, and to stand aside without being perceived by the American people as impotent or callous.

In fact, internationalism dismisses as morally reprehensible questions that other nations ask routinely in order to inject some discipline into their decision-making: What is it that we need to do in the world to secure a certain level of material and psychological well-being? What is it that we simply would like to do in the world? What are we able to do? How can we pursue our objectives without wrecking our economy, overloading our political system, or convulsing our society?

At best, post–Cold War internationalism is a recipe for intense, genuinely worrisome domestic political frustrations. Repeated failure to achieve declared foreign-policy goals and especially to avert foreign-policy outcomes officially characterized as intolerable or disastrous could poison and destabilize American politics and democracy. A string of such failures could bring calamitous international consequences by undermining America's ability to conduct a minimally responsible, rational foreign policy. At worst, internationalism raises the threat of drawing the nation into dangerous conflicts for the slightest of stakes. And even if such political and military disasters are somehow avoided, internationalism will continue to drain the nation to its core, especially if U.S. allies do not lend enough help.

Internationalism has not only locked the foreign policy of this nation of self-avowed pragmatists into a utopian mold; it has led directly to the primacy of foreign policy in American life and to the consequent neglect of domestic problems which has characterized the past fifty years. Internationalism encourages us to think more about the possible world of tomorrow than about the real world of today. Thus the strange irrelevance of our recent foreign policy, and even its victories, to the concerns of most Americans.

A NEW FOREIGN-POLICY BLUEPRINT

If internationalism is no longer an acceptable guide for U.S. foreign policy, what should take its place? What *can* take its place? Assuming that the means available to U.S. foreign-policy makers will not change significantly anytime soon—that American scientists will not devise a new ultimate weapon and preserve monopoly control of it; that U.S. allies will remain reluctant to increase their military and foreign-aid spending dramatically or to compensate the United States for its leadership role in other ways; that the American public will remain unwilling to make the sacrifices needed to carry out an internationalist foreign policy effectively (through some combination of higher taxes, reduced consumption, and reduced demand for public services); and that the unprecedented increases in national economic productivity needed to finance such a foreign policy soundly will remain nowhere in sight—the United

States will have to make some profound adjustments.

If the United States cannot hope to achieve the desired level of security and prosperity by underwriting the security and prosperity of countries all over the world, and by enforcing whatever global norms of economic and political behavior this ambition requires, then it must anchor its security and prosperity in a less-than-utopian set of objectives. It must therefore distinguish between what it must do that is absolutely essential for achieving this more modest set of objectives and those things it might do that are not essential. It must, in other words, begin to think in terms not of the whole world's well-being but rather of purely national interests.

The adjustments that are required would produce a foreign policy largely unrecognizable to Americans today. The U.S. government would still be a major force in world affairs, and the American people would still trade with, invest in, work in, and travel to other lands. But the preferred instruments of the new foreign policy would differ radically from those of internationalism. And the policy itself would spring from a completely different vision of America, of its strengths and weaknesses and, most important, its basic purposes. The new orientation, moreover, would reflect the manifest (if seldom articulated) wishes of the great majority of Americans, rather than those of the small, privileged caste of government officials, former government officials, professors, think-tank denizens, and journalists whose dreamy agenda has long dominated foreign-policy decision-making in America. For surely American foreign policy has been conducted with utter disregard for the home front largely because it has been made by people whose lives and needs have al-most nothing in common with those of the mass of their countrymen.

Unlike internationalism, interest-based thinking rests on a series of assumptions drawn both from common sense and from classical strategic maxims; and it can help prevent counterproductive outcomes by forcing decisionmakers continually to examine the impact of their policies on national security and well-being within a finite time frame. In the first place, a foreign policy derived from interest-based thinking would accept today's anarchic system of competing nation-states as a given. It would neither seek to change the nature of this system nor assume the system's imminent transformation. Instead, the new policy would confine itself to securing certain specific objectives that are intrinsically important to America's security and welfare—for example, the protection of regions that are important sources of raw materials or critical manufactured goods, those that are major loci of investment or prime markets, and those that by virtue of their location are strategically vital.

Interest-based thinking holds that in such a world U.S. national interests can and must be distinguished from the interests of the international system itself and from those of other individual states. This is just common sense. Because states differ in location, size, strength, natural wealth, historical experience, values, economic systems, degree and type of social organization, and many other particulars, their foreign-policy needs and wants—their interests—cannot always be identical or harmonious, and will in fact sometimes clash with those of certain other countries and those of whatever larger international community those states are supposed to belong to. Interna-tionalism's assumption of an ultimate harmony of interests among states and between states and the larger system often obscures these critical truths.

In addition, interest-based thinking assumes that since the world lacks a commonly accepted referee or means of resolving clashes of interests, states cannot count on other states or entities to define their interests or to protect them. States therefore need the means to accomplish these tasks on their own. Interest-based thinking assumes that because countries can in the end rely only on their own devices, national self-reliance and freedom of action are intrinsic goods. With an internationalist foreign policy, these imperatives tend to get lost in the shuffle.

Further, interest-based thinking maintains that because resources are always relatively scarce (if they were not, the discipline of economics would not exist), once foreign policy moves beyond the quest for what strategists call core security—the nation's physical, biological survival, and the preservation of its territorial integrity and political independence—the specific, concrete benefits sought must be brought into some sustainable alignment with the policy's economic, social, and political costs. And the payoff of policies cannot be put off into the long-term future. A country with finite available resources simply does not have the luxury of infinite patience.

THUS AN INTEREST-BASED FOREIGN POLICY would tend to rule out economic initiatives deemed necessary for the international system's health if those initiatives wound up siphoning more wealth out of this country (in the form of net investment, interest on debt, military expenditures, foreign aid, trade credits, jobs destroyed by imports versus those created by exports, and so forth) than they brought in. Similarly, it would oppose economic policies that actually destroyed wealth—for example, by stimulating inflation, by committing excessive resources to economically unproductive military spending and research and development, by necessitating excessive currency devaluations, by requiring exorbitant interest rates that discourage productive investment, or by blithely accepting the loss of industries that have been technology and productivity leaders for the sake of free-trade ideology or alliance unity.

Unlike internationalism, an interest-based foreign policy would not emphasize alliances and multilateral institutions, or promote worldwide economic efficiency to the point at which U.S. dependence on other countries is seen as a good in and of itself. Rather, the new policy would recognize the importance of maintaining the maximum degree of freedom of action and self-reliance in a still dangerous world. Indeed, an interest-based policy would also recognize that the related realms of economics and technology are as nakedly strategic as the military-political realm. While the Cold War was raging, internationalists viewed economic initiatives and technology as little more than assets to deny the Communist world or as a collection of baubles, to be doled out periodically as political favors to allies and neutrals. The end of the Cold War has produced many acknowledgments by internationalists of the rising importance of economic power. But even this outlook still tends to be nonstrategic. Internationalists still assume that, economically speaking, winning and losing have no meaning whatever—unless one cares about national pride—so long as the competition takes place

among nonhostile states. And they continue to believe that economic competition can always be kept reasonable and constructive, as if it were an athletic contest.

Despite its heightened sensitivity to questions involving resources, the new foreign policy would proceed from an assumption of American strength, not weakness. While conceding that the United States is neither powerful nor wealthy enough to remake the world in its own image, or to achieve security and prosperity for itself by securing these benefits for every country on the planet, it would recognize that America is powerful, wealthy, and geopolitically secure enough to flourish without carrying out this ambitious agenda. And it would understand that the cultivation of America's economic and military strength, not the creation of international institutions or global norms of behavior, is the best guarantor of national independence and well-being over the long run. The emergence of transnational threats such as environmental destruction and drug trafficking does nothing to reduce the importance of national power. The nations whose preferred solutions are adopted will be those bringing the most chips to the table.

PERHAPS MOST IMPORTANT, AN INTEREST-based U.S. foreign policy would firmly subordinate international activism and the drive for world leadership to domestic concerns. Indeed, it would spring from new and more realistic ideas about what can be expected of a country's official foreign policy in the first place. The new approach would acknowledge that the modest policy tools actually at a government's command—weapons, money, and suasion—cannot build a fundamentally new and more benign or congenial world political order, or change the millennia-old patterns of poverty, tradition, and misrule in which so much of humanity is trapped. Such changes can occur only on the organic level of international relations, as the result of informal social, cultural, and economic interactions over long stretches of time. And even if modern science and technology have greatly accelerated the pace of change, there is little reason to think that change can be controlled or manipulated at the operational level of international relations—by a state's day-to-day foreign policy.

The interest-based approach would also eschew any notion of foreign policy as first and foremost a vehicle for spreading American values, for building national character, for expressing any individual's or group's emotional, philosophical, or political preferences, or for carrying out any of a series of additional overseas missions that, however appealing, bear only marginally on protecting and enriching the nation: promoting peace, stability, democracy, and development around the world; protecting human rights; establishing international law; building collective security; exercising something called leadership; creating a new world order; competing globally with the Soviets (or whomever) for power and influence. None of these sweeping, inspiring, quintessentially internationalist goals can serve as guides for U.S. foreign policy. They are simply free-floating ideals. From time to time they may represent ways of advancing particular and advanceable American interests. But first we have to know what interests we want to advance. An interest-based approach would also reject the idea that meeting a set of global responsibilities can be the lodestar of U.S. foreign policy. Whose

definition of this unavoidably subjective notion would be chosen? And on what basis?

Nevertheless, the interest-based approach would recognize that in a democracy such views—that is, simple national preferences—frequently influence foreign policy. That is to say, Americans from time to time favor a course of action (invading Grenada, for example, or aiding the Kurds) not because it serves vital national interests but simply because they like it. An interest-based foreign policy would acknowledge that the citizens of a democracy have every right to choose whatever foreign policy they please; certainly they are answerable to no one but themselves. And it would hold that there is nothing intrinsically wrong with sometimes basing a foreign policy on the whim or preference of the majority. The new approach would insist, however, that the American public be willing to finance its whims soundly—something the United States government has not done for decades. If the public favors aid to insurgents around the world, or fighting poverty in developing countries, or helping new democracies in Eastern Europe or Latin America, or defending certain parts of the world because of a shared cultural heritage, then it should be willing to raise the revenues needed to pay for these policies. If the revenues are not forthcoming, the whims are probably not very strong to begin with and are probably best ignored.

The new foreign policy certainly would not preclude acting on principle. But it would greatly de-emphasize conforming to abstract standards of behavior. In fact, the new foreign policy would shy away from any overarching strategy of or conceptual approach to international relations. Unlike isolationism, for instance, it would not elevate nonintervention to the status of a commandment. And it would view other popular doctrines of American foreign policy—containment, détente, multilateralism, unilateralism, idealism, realism, the achievement of a global balance of power—with skepticism. It would be free to use whatever approach or combination of approaches seemed likeliest to achieve the best ends for the United States in a given situation. Its only rule of thumb would be "whatever works" to preserve or enhance America's security and prosperity and—provided that Americans are willing to pay the bills—what the country collectively wishes to define as its psychological well-being.

Internationalists worrying about this policy's potential lack of moral content might think harder about channeling more of their compassion into good works at home—where there is no shortage of grievous wrongs to be righted and where, as is not the case in many other countries, the social and institutional wherewithal for successful reform actually exists.

As for the issue of defining the ends of U.S. foreign policy beyond core security, there are no magic formulas to rely on. Once national survival and independence are assured, all the major objectives of U.S. foreign policy must be subjected to a rigorous cost-risk analysis. If objectives are truly vital—if physical survival or the continuance of America's democratic values and institutions are at stake—costs and risks can never exceed benefits. But if objectives are less than vital, costs and risks can exceed benefits. For a country with America's built-in geopolitical and economic advantages— with its capacity for achieving security, prosperity, and independence—the top priority is not to settle on a fixed defini-

tion of vital interests. It is much more important to learn to think rigorously and strategically about foreign policy, in order to ensure that whatever set of interests is chosen is not so ambitious that it exposes the country to more risks than it repulses, drains it of more strength than it adds, and makes Americans feel bad about themselves and their nation more than it makes them feel good.

The new policy's aversion to grand doctrines and frameworks would be in keeping with the conviction that the fundamental purpose of U.S. foreign policy should be nothing more glamorous than attempting to cope with whatever discrete developments arise abroad that could endanger American security and prosperity. The stress would not be on comprehensive initiatives to get at the root causes of the world's ills and conflicts, on promoting greater international cooperation or integration, or on getting on the right side of history—for these favorite internationalist aims entail enormous costs and offer scant promise of success. In a perilous strategic world, it is usually a mistake to consider foreign policy to be an activist instrument at all. Rather, Americans should start thinking of foreign policy in terms of avoiding problems, reducing vulnerabilities and costs, maximizing options, buying time, and muddling through—objectives that may be uninspiring but that are well suited to a strong, wealthy, geographically isolated country.

NO

Joshua Muravchik

THE FOLLY OF REALISM

In contrast to isolationism and pacifist idealism, realism suffers no disrepute. It even is enjoying something of a vogue. Foreign policy advocates of many different stripes today cloak themselves in its mantle.

Realism's roots go all the way back to Alexander Hamilton's argument with Thomas Jefferson over honoring the 1778 treaty of alliance with France. Jefferson emphasized America's contractual obligation and its ideological affinity for republican France over monarchical England. Hamilton, favoring neutrality, argued that a small nation such as ours could not afford to quarrel with either major European power. That insistence on putting self-interest first is the essence of realism. Policy must be guided by interest, says the realist, and not by sentiment, ideology, or abstract principles.

Often in our history the counsel of realism has been forwarded against the democratic idealist impulse, as when democratic enthusiasts in the 1820s sought some form of American aid to the Greek patriots fighting for independence from Turkey. John Quincy Adams's response is quoted by realists to this day. America, he said, "goes not abroad, in search of monsters to destroy. She is the well-wisher to the freedom and independence of all. She is the champion and vindicator only of her own."

Even when realism has not advocated a different course from democratic idealism, it has often sought a different spirit. Thus while Theodore Roosevelt did not demur from the decision to enter World War I, he did object to President Woodrow Wilson's rhetoric about fighting to make the world safe for democracy. Roosevelt's tart riposte stands as another classic expression of the realist sensibility: "First and foremost we are to make the world safe for ourselves." . . .

REALISM VERSUS DEMOCRATIC IDEALISM

It is easy to see then why a foreign policy that devotes itself in large measure to advancing the democratic cause is anathema to realists. They argue first that America cannot carry out such a foreign policy even if it wishes to do so

From Joshua Muravchik, *Exporting Democracy: Fulfilling America's Destiny* (The AEI Press, 1991). Copyright © 1991 by the American Enterprise Institute. Reprinted by permission. Notes omitted.

because its foreign policy is ineluctably dictated by its interests. Second, to the extent that America attempts to freight its foreign policy with such ideological content, the realists say, it is asking for trouble because it is deviating from its concrete interests. Such moral crusades in the past have been the bane of U.S. policy, they say. Third, a foreign policy that focuses on the advancement of democracy knows no geographic limits and carries American attention far from home rather than focusing on those regions that are strategically vital to the United States. Finally, they say, such a foreign policy is morally flawed because it seeks to impose our values on cultures that are different from our own.

The realist arguments, however, do not bear scrutiny. Do states inevitably behave as the realists describe? The realists' own lack of confidence in this cardinal tenet of their faith is betrayed by the insistence with which they criticize past foreign policies of the United States (and other countries) and prescribe for the future. If states behave only as geography and human nature ordain they must, then why criticize and why prescribe? Yet this logically fatal contradiction seems to trouble the realists no more than the analogous contradiction troubles Marxists or Calvinists. (If history itself intends the triumph of the proletariat, why should Marxists labor on its behalf? If God himself has predetermined the fate of each person, then why strive to demonstrate grace?)

The Impact of Humanitarianism

Not only is the realist argument thus self-evidently flawed in its logic, it is also refuted by a mound of empirical evidence. Although many state actions aim to defend interests, many do not. Some

are motivated by altruism. The United States rushes aid to the victims of flood, famine, or other catastrophe wherever these occur for no motive other than human sympathy. Several other countries do the same. Various states offer asylum to the persecuted, provide good offices for the mediation of distant disputes, and even contribute troops to international peacekeeping forces, all for reasons that are essentially humanitarian. . . .

What Is "Interest"?

In sum a variety of factors besides interest help to shape foreign policy. But this is not the only flaw in the realist argument. For even to the extent that realists are right in asserting that interests determine policy, they only beg the question of what interest is. Each state has an interest in defending itself from attack. By obvious extension each has an interest in avoiding a preponderance of antagonistic power being amassed on its borders. And by slightly further extension, topography, economics, and history may give a state an enduring interest in certain pieces of geography. Thus Russia, whether ruled by czars or commissars, craves a warm water port and therefore covets the Dardanelles. Moreover Russia, both under czars and commissars, has been a self-aggrandizing power pushing outward to subdue or despoil others.

Such continuities, say the realists, show that states behave not as they will but as they must, driven by immutable laws. But for every continuity there is a discontinuity, and the realists cannot account for these. In the 1960s America intervened heavily in Vietnam; in the 1970s it withdrew from Vietnam. From George Washington through Franklin Roosevelt, America remained aloof from European affairs; since World War II it has maintained permanent military deployments in Europe. In the nineteenth century Britain built the world's greatest empire; in the twentieth century Britain withdrew from empire. In the 1930s Japan became a paragon of militarism and conquered much of the Pacific; since regaining its independence from the occupation in 1952, Japan has refused to rearm and remains the world's only constitutionally pacifist state.

Under the rule of Anastasio Somoza Nicaragua sought to make itself America's most loyal ally; under the Sandinistas Nicaragua made itself the bastion of anti-Americanism on the American mainland. Under Gamal Abdel Nasser Egypt sought to lead a pan-Arab revolution whose first target was the state of Israel; under Anwar Sadat Egypt turned its back on the rest of the Arab world to make peace with Israel. Under Haile Selassie Ethiopia allied with the West; under Mengistu Haile Mariam it allies with the East. In the early 1950s China allied with the Soviet Union against the United States; in the 1970s China allied with the United States against the Soviet Union. Even the USSR, whose continuities of policy are so integral to the realist catechism, withdrew from Afghanistan under Mikhail Gorbachev, after invading it under Leonid Brezhnev, and in 1989 disgorged its East European empire, the same empire whose conquest and defense had been the centerpiece of Soviet policy for the preceding forty years.

The statesmen who formulated each of the acts and policies mentioned here—and one could go on with this list ad infinitum—believed they were acting in their country's interests. To different leaders at different times, however, the national interest seems to demand different things. (Indeed this may be said of different leaders at the same time, or even of the same leader at different times.) The reason is not hard to fathom. For most states, defense against the threat of imminent attack occupies only a small part of the total energy devoted to foreign affairs. A greater share goes to enhancing security for the longer term. But the exact form and direction of future dangers can be foreseen only imperfectly.

In that sense international politics is something like chess, with statesmen constantly seeking to gauge the effect of the loss of a pawn here, the movement of a rook there. The problem is that in chess the number of permutations is virtually infinite, and so is the number of possible strategies. This is all the more true in international politics, which has more pieces than a chess game, a board that is unbounded, and no fixed rules governing how each piece may move. Each statesman has an infinite choice of moves and a vast menu of strategies for advancing a nation's interests. Therefore to discover a law of politics saying that states will behave according to their interests is to discover almost nothing about how any state will actually behave. . . .

THE CRITIQUE OF IDEALISM

So much for the realist tenet that states behave simply as they must. What about the contrary realist argument . . . acknowledging that states are free to choose their own behavior but holding that American policy has suffered from excesses of idealism when it ought to have grounded itself in the firm soil of interest? Plentiful evidence exists to buttress this line of argument. In the hopes it invested in the League of Nations and the United Nations and in the outlawry of war and arms control, U.S. policy has indeed exhibited naiveté. But these visionary schemes were all excesses of pacifist idealism, not of democratic idealism. They were designed to keep the world's peace, not to make the world democratic. It is harder to find examples where an excess of democratic idealism led America astray.

To be sure, Americans have been naive as well about the democratic prospect, such as in the casual assumption after World War II that newly independent states of the third world would naturally evolve to democracy. But this has had no consequences for the United States more severe than disappointment. Are there instances in which democratic idealism has actually harmed us?

The prime exhibit in the realists' indictment of idealism is Woodrow Wilson's handling of peacemaking after World War I. Wilson's approach embodied both pacifist idealism and democratic idealism. The former expressed itself in his quest for a peace without victory (or at least a peace in which the victors did not aggrandize themselves and the vanquished were not subjugated) and his insistence on the creation of the League of Nations. His democratic idealism expressed itself in the principle of national self-determination, which he championed. The peace of Versailles was indeed flawed, lasting only twenty years before giving way to a conflagration still more terrible than the one it had brought to conclusion. And Wilson's performance as a peacemaker no doubt deserves criticism. But on what score? It is far from obvious that those elements of the peace that were motivated by democratic idealism were the harmful ones.

It is easy to imagine scenarios in which a different Versailles Treaty might have yielded a more secure peace and ended less tragically: had the terms given to Germany been more generous, or conversely had they been more Carthaginian; had the league not been created and more attention paid instead to ensuring a balance of power; or had Wilson not failed to secure U.S. entry into the league. But in what scenario would the peace have endured had it only been shorn of the principle of self-determination? To be sure, the story of the various republics of Central and Eastern Europe born at Versailles is a sorry one. Most soon lapsed into dictatorship of one kind or another, and their instability contributed to the instability of Europe.

But what should have been done with Poland or with the nations that had constituted Austria-Hungary? The empire could not have been put back together. Its advanced decrepitude had precipitated the war. If not given independence, to whom should these nations have been subjected, and how would this have made Europe more stable or the peace more secure? World War II may have broken out in Central Europe, but Central Europe's instabilities were not its cause. Its cause was German aggression and allied appeasement, an appeasement whose main ingredients were U.S. isolationism, British pacifism, and French realism. . . .

THE ILLOGIC OF CULTURAL RELATIVISM

Finally, the realists are left with the argument that it is wrong to foist our ways—that is, democracy—on others. In saying this the realists suddenly are arguing in moral terms. Their point, however, entails a logical fallacy. The reason it is wrong to impose something on others, presumably, is because it violates their will. But, absent democracy, how can their will be known? Moreover, why care about violating people's will unless one begins with the democratic premise that popular will ought to be sovereign?

This argument implies that people prefer to be ruled by an indigenous dictator than to be liberated through foreign influence. The realists will have a hard time explaining this to the people of Panama who danced in the streets when U.S. invaders ousted dictator Manuel Noriega or to Aleksandr Solzhenitsyn, who wrote:

> On our crowded planet there are no longer any "internal affairs." The Communist leaders say, "Don't interfere in our internal affairs. Let us strangle our citizens in peace and quiet." But I tell you: Interfere more and more. Interfere as much as you can. We beg you to come and interfere.

The examples of Panama, Japan, Germany, the Dominican Republic, and Grenada notwithstanding, to foist democracy on others does not ordinarily mean to impose it by force. Nor does it mean to seek carbon copies of American institutions. No serious advocate of democracy believes that each country ought to have a president rather than a prime minister, a two-house legislature rather than a single chamber, a two-party system rather than multiple parties, a triangular separation of powers rather than a bifurcation, quadrennial elections rather than some other schedule, federalism rather than a unitary system, or any of the other peculiarities of the American way. Belief in democracy as a universal value boils down to the conviction that adult human beings ought not to be governed without their consent. (And since universal consent on the choice of governors is impossible, its closest approximation is a system in which everyone may partici-

pate in the choice, even though not everyone's preferences are satisfied.)

This belief, it must be confessed, rests ultimately on premises about human dignity that are unprovable axioms. That human beings prefer not to be subjected arbitrarily to the rule of others is demonstrable, but that this preference ought to be honored is a value, not a truth. It is no more true than the contrary proposition that people ought to be ruled by the vanguard party or by the corporate state or by the religious authorities. But to argue . . . against democratic universalism on the grounds of cultural relativism is self-contradictory. It is logically unassailable (although repugnant) to argue against democracy on the ground that Lenin or Mussolini or Khomeini ought to rule. It is, however, incoherent to argue against democracy on the ground that people somewhere do not want it, for that argument is an appeal to democratic criteria. When realists resort to such pseudomoralism, they reveal only a lack of confidence in the essence of their own position, which is the rejection of morality in foreign policy.

In drawing a sharp distinction between the morality of individuals and that of states, the realists speak as if morality and self-interest were incompatible. But what form of personal ethics demands complete self-abnegation? Even Christianity, whose messiah is the apotheosis of self-sacrifice, does not enjoin its faithful to forgo self-preservation. It and every other major creed and ethical system recognizes self-preservation as a legitimate goal of the individual. Idealism or morality insists only that self-interest is bounded, that it is not infinite. Legitimate self-regard must be balanced against sensitivity to the well-being of others and must be pursued through honorable means. Why should the same not hold for the nation? Why can't national policy attempt to combine respect for the requisites of self-preservation with adherence to honorable means and with respect for the legitimate claims of other nations?

Perhaps the mixture between regard for self and for others differs somewhat in countries and individuals, but this is a difference of degree, not of kind. National policy may require more caution than some individuals choose in governing their own lives. The realists would be on far stronger ground if they asserted only that foreign policy must be guided by an inherent conservatism, that we must keep our powder dry and be mindful of our safety. . . .

The radical distinction that realists draw between the morality of individuals and that of states fails on a second ground as well. If individuals are obliged to abide by certain moral rules, can they be exempted from those rules when they act collectively with others in the name of the nation?

Those who argue yes sometimes point out that although we exalt the sixth commandment, we send soldiers off to kill. But the contradiction here is not explained by the contrast between personal behavior and national behavior. The contradiction is between killing and killing in self-defense. Most people condone killing done in defense of one's own life. In condoning military acts we assume, or we ought to, that they are conducted in self-defense. For a nation to wage aggressive war, to engage in acts of killing for self-aggrandizement rather than self-defense is no more justifiable than homicide.

Granted, self-defense for the nation is defined more broadly than for the private individual. We condone an individual's killing in self-defense only in dire emergencies. Anyone receiving a threatening telephone call is expected to call the police, not to kill the caller. A nation cannot call the police. Thus its legitimate acts of self-defense may include acts of deterrence or collective self-defense. In acknowledging the need for a broader definition of self-defense in the case of the nation, we are acknowledging that the universe in which it acts is not precisely analogous to the universe in which the individual acts. We can acknowledge too that some acts of war may be borderline between aggression and self-defense. But that does not amount to a total inability to distinguish between self-defense and aggression, or more broadly between right and wrong.

However difficult the judgments may be on occasion, some nexus must remain between the moral principles that govern an individual acting in a personal capacity and those that govern one acting as part of a nation. That is the judgment that the civilized world rendered in the Nuremberg trials. It is one we would reverse at our peril.

POSTSCRIPT

Should National Self-Interest Be the Basis of American Foreign Policy?

As Muravchik's essay makes clear, *national interest* is a term of uncertain content. Was it in our national interest to become involved in supporting the government of South Vietnam in the 1960s? At the time it seemed so to many Americans, but by the end of the decade some who had supported U.S. involvement on grounds of national interest thought that our interest would best be served by withdrawal. The same pro and con arguments, both based on national self-interest, can be applied to America's invasion of Panama, its involvement in the Persian Gulf War, and the contemplated involvement in the Balkans. Still, using national self-interest as a litmus test is likely to concentrate the mind in a certain manner. In the calculus of the interest-minded policymaker, there is always a balance sheet where the costs of intervention are weighed against the benefits. The idea that a nation might "pay any price, bear any burden" to protect liberty someplace else in the world would be unthinkable to an interest-minded policymaker, but not necessarily to an idealist. This does not mean that idealists are foolhardy, only that they are ready, when they consider it necessary, to play for high stakes.

In 1793, George Washington's administration proclaimed American neutrality in the war then raging between France and Great Britain, setting off a furious debate. Some American friends of France thought the United States should join France in the war because of a treaty made with it 15 years earlier and that the United States should be grateful to France for its help during the American Revolution. Defending Washington's policy, Alexander Hamilton wrote what has become a classic realist tract under the pen name "Pacifus." There is nothing in this war for us, Hamilton said, and to enter it out of gratitude would be folly. *Individuals* can do selfless things out of gratitude, but leaders of nations have others to think of besides themselves. "Existing millions, and for the most part future generations, are concerned in the present measure of a government."

The contemporary classic formulation of the doctrine of national self-interest is Hans Morgenthau's *Politics Among Nations* (Alfred A. Knopf, 1954). For an equally enduring critique of Morgenthau, see William Appleman Williams, *The Tragedy of American Diplomacy*, rev. ed. (Dell, 1972). Leading policymakers in American administrations from Kennedy to Bush have contributed informed essays to Edward K. Hamilton, ed., *America's Global Interests: A New Agenda* (W. W. Norton, 1989). Most of them proceed from the premise of national self-interest. For a viewpoint closer to that of Muravchik, see Stanley Kober, "Idealpolitik," *Foreign Policy* (Summer 1990). John Spanier, *American Foreign Policy Since World War II*, 12th ed. (Congressional Quarterly, 1991) is a useful treatment of the period up to the collapse of the Soviet Union.

It is hard to know in what direction American foreign policy is headed. With the breakup of the Soviet Union, many who once idealistically called for American support of freedom fighters throughout the world have become neoisolationists, while other former realists who once warned against Vietnam-type quagmires now seem ready to support American military involvement on behalf of human rights. At some deeper level each side may be philosophically consistent, but on the surface it appears as though each has its own peculiar mix of realist and idealist reflexes, joined together not logically but kaleidoscopically, their arrangement subject to the twists and turns of events.

ISSUE 20

Is America Declining?

YES: Edward N. Luttwak, from "Is America on the Way Down? Yes," *Commentary* (March 1992)

NO: Robert L. Bartley, from "Is America on the Way Down? No," *Commentary* (March 1992)

ISSUE SUMMARY

YES: Foreign policy strategist Edward N. Luttwak believes that Japan and Europe will soon be richer than the United States because of the failure of America's economic policies and social programs.
NO: *Wall Street Journal* editor Robert L. Bartley asserts that America is, and will remain, the wealthiest country and that it will continue to play the role of world leader.

After World War II the United States emerged as the most powerful nation in the world. In part this was because of the cumulative economic costs of two world wars for Germany, Great Britain, Japan, and the Soviet Union. America escaped the physical devastation that these nations suffered, and its economy boomed during and after the wars. With its unequalled prosperity and power, the United States assumed international leadership in armaments, investments, and aid.

Changing circumstances have raised serious questions regarding that leadership role. *Is it necessary?* Many Americans believe that, with the dissolution of the Soviet Union, sharp cuts in America's military forces and commitments abroad are possible. *Can we afford it?* America is no longer clearly the world's most prosperous nation. Between 1980 and 1992, its national debt more than quadrupled, from $900 billion to more than $4 trillion. America must make hard choices, and when unemployment is high and the economic future not promising, domestic needs are likely to receive the highest priority.

Even though public opinion polls show some pessimism, it is difficult for Americans to accept the view that this nation's power and influence will not endure. Yet historians have always noted the rise and fall of great powers, as has contemporary historian Paul Kennedy in his widely acclaimed and much debated 1987 book, *The Rise and Fall of the Great Powers.* Kennedy summarized his thesis thusly: "The historical record suggests that there is a very clear connection *in the long run* between an individual Great Power's economic rise and fall and its growth and decline as an important military power (or world empire)." Nations must spend to create the armies and navies that protect their wealth and security; but if they spend too much, they weaken their economic competitiveness. "Imperial overstretch" is Kennedy's term for the tendency of great powers to commit too much wealth to overseas commitments and too little to domestic economic growth.

Kennedy identified the loss of power with the decline of economic competitiveness. In his account, the most powerful nations in the last five centuries—successively, Spain, the Netherlands, France, and England—were unable or unwilling to tax themselves sufficiently to pay for their armed forces and empires, and the United States now finds itself in a comparable position. The greater the power of a state, the greater the expenditure that must be made to support it.

There is an almost instinctive American rejection of any theory that even suggests that historical forces determine our fates independent of our wills. Public rhetoric expresses a conviction that there is little that Americans cannot achieve, if they will it and work to achieve it. The qualities that made it possible for earlier American generations to settle a subcontinent and make it prosper—idealism, dedication to a common purpose, a willingness to sacrifice for significant long-range goals—can enable this generation to keep America prosperous and powerful into the future.

A further objection is that Kennedy's generalizations confuse different cases. After all, the United States has not created an international empire similar to those established by Spain, France, or England. To be sure, the United States, by virtue of its military and economic power, has exercised leadership; but that is very different from direct domination. American support for the United Nations, economic aid to rebuild war-torn Europe, and mutual security acts with the non-communist nations of Europe and Asia have been the acts of an ally, not a conqueror.

The collapse of the Soviet Union and its communist allies appears to leave the United States as the only superpower, rebutting predictions of America's decline. However, if the measure of power is now economic and not military, Japan and a newly united Europe emerge as formidable challengers to American dominance and leadership.

The issue of decline cuts across ideological lines. In the following selections, two conservatives, Edward N. Luttwak and Robert L. Bartley, reach opposite conclusions based on their interpretations of America's role in early 1992.

YES

Edward N. Luttwak

IS AMERICA ON THE WAY DOWN?

When will the United States become a third-world country? One estimate would place the date as close as the year 2020. A more optimistic projection might add another ten or fifteen years. Either way, if present trends simply continue, all but a small minority of Americans will be impoverished soon enough, left to yearn hopelessly for the lost golden age of American prosperity.

Nor can American decline remain only economic. The arts and sciences cannot flower and grow without the prosperity that pays for universities, research centers, libraries, museums, the theater, orchestras, ballet companies. It was the ample earnings of Italian traders and bankers that fed the scholars, painters, sculptors, architects, and poets who gave us the Renaissance. When Italy was by-passed by the new flows of oceangoing trade, its impoverished merchants and bankrupt financiers could no longer commission artists or keep scholars at their work, so that economic decline was followed in short order by the bleak downfall of Italian art and scholarship.

Finally, democracy too must become fragile once better hopes are worn away by bitter disappointment. What Americans have in common are their shared beliefs, above all in equality of opportunity in the pursuit of affluence. It would be too much to expect that democratic governance would long survive the impoverishment of all Americans except for a small privileged minority of inheritors, agents of foreign interests, and assorted financial manipulators.

When Buenos Aires was still a leading world metropolis, when the people of Argentina still enjoyed their famous steak-at-every-meal abundance that lasted into the 1950's, they would never have believed that their future would be a 40-year slide into poverty. Equally, the citizens of the U.S., still today by far the richest country in the world, steadfastly refuse to recognize what future is in store for them unless they can alter the course they are now on. Yet the simplest numbers confirm the slide, and suggest the chilling forecast.

IN 1970, AMERICANS WERE TWO-AND-A-HALF TIMES AS PRODUCTIVE AS THE Japanese, and twice as productive as the citizens of the European Community on average. By 1980, the pattern of decline had already set in. The United States was still well ahead of the European Community and Japan, but its edge has been cut in half in a mere ten years, while West Germany had actually overtaken it.

At that point, in 1980, a simple straight-line projection of the sort that professional economists deplore as much too simplistic would have suggested that in one more decade the United States would be overtaken by the richer Europeans and by Japan. And that is exactly what happened.

This being a 20-year trend and not just a brief downturn, it is perfectly reasonable to calculate what the future numbers would be if the United States were to remain on its present path. Already in the year 2000, Japan's gross national product per person would be twice that of America, while the richer European countries would have a 50-percent edge over the United States. Ten years after that, Japan would be more than three times as productive per person as the United States, and the richer European countries would be almost twice as productive per person as the United States.

Finally in 2020, when the children of today's middle-aged Americans will themselves be middle-aged, the richest Europeans would be more than twice as productive, while the gap between Japanese and Americans at 5-to-1 would be just about the same as the 1980 gap between Americans and Brazilians. At that point, the United States would definitely have become a third-world country—at least by Japanese standards. Certainly Americans would no longer be in the same class as West Europeans. . . .

THERE IS NO DOUBT THAT TO PROJECT THE future by simply extending the past is a procedure truly simplistic, because unexpected changes can always outweigh continuities. But so far, at least, the path seems straight enough—and straight downhill. It is also true that international comparisons can easily be distorted by abrupt exchange-rate fluctuations: one reason Switzerland reached the astounding gross national product of $30,270 per person in 1989 was that the Swiss franc happened to be very high during that year. Moreover, all fluctuations aside, exchange rates routinely deform comparisons because they reflect only the *international* supply and demand for capital, goods, and services denominated in any particular currency (as well as speculation and central-bank manipulations), and not the much greater amount of purely domestic transactions. Hence currencies can be greatly overvalued or undervalued as compared to their purchasing power at home.

Because the United States has chosen to open its markets to imports to a much greater extent than most other countries, let alone famously import-phobic Japan and Korea, the great outflow of dollars reduces the exchange rate far below the dollar's purchasing power at home. If we rely on a measure based on purchasing-power parities, we find that the United States scores much higher in international comparisons. Yet while purchasing-power values can depict living standards more or less realistically, it is only comparisons based on straight exchange rates that determine the "who-does-what-to-whom" of the international economy—including the little matter of which parties can buy attractive pieces of other (open-door) economies, and which parties can only sell them off. And that, of course, can make the enjoyment of even splendid living standards somewhat ephemeral.

Finally, if we switch to the purchasing-power plus gross-domestic-product criterion, we find that although the United States is still ahead, the trend is just as unfavorable as it is with other measures, and the pattern of relative decline just as evident.

To be sure, both the gross national product and the gross domestic product are indeed gross measures: a car accident increases both of them by the amount of ambulance, hospital, and bodyshop bills, while a healthy drop in cigarette smoking reduces them as sales and excise taxes go down. Nor can any international comparison be free of all sorts of distortions, large and small, no matter what criterion is employed, if only because the different consumption preferences prevalent in different countries are hard to equate. And yet, after all possible objections and all proper reservations are listed, it cannot finally be denied that the totality of all the relevant numbers contains irrefutable evidence that the American economy has long been in severe decline by world standards—and still is.

MANY OBSERVERS WOULD REACH THE SAME verdict without need of any numbers. Follow a traveler from Tokyo to New York—though it would be much the same if he came from Zurich, Amsterdam, or Singapore. After leaving his taxi at Tokyo's downtown City Air Terminal—a perfectly ordinary Tokyo taxi and therefore shiny clean, in perfect condition, its neatly dressed driver in white gloves—our traveler will find himself aboard an equally spotless airport bus in five minutes flat, with his baggage already checked in, boarding card issued, and passport stamped by the seemingly effortless teamwork of quick, careful porters who refuse tips, airline clerks who can actually use computers at computer speed, passport officers who act as if it were their job to expedite travel, and bus crews who sell tickets, load baggage, and courteously help the encumbered while strictly keeping to departure schedules timed to the exact minute.

Then, after an hour's bus ride over the crowded expressway to the gleaming halls of Tokyo's Narita international airport, and after the long trans-Pacific flight, when our traveler finally arrives, he will be confronted by sights and sounds that would not be out of place in Lagos or Bombay. He has landed at New York's John F. Kennedy airport.

Instead of the elegance of Narita, or Frankfurt, or Amsterdam, or Singapore, arriving travelers at one of the several JFK terminals that belong to near-bankrupt airlines will find themselves walking down dingy corridors in need of paint, over frayed carpets, often struggling up and down narrow stairways alongside out-of-order escalators. Those are JFK's substitutes for the constantly updated facilities of first-world airports. The rough, cheap remodeling of sadly outdated buildings with naked plywood and unfinished gypsum board proclaims the shortage of long-term money to build with, of invested capital. Equally, the frayed carpets, those defective escalators, and the pervasive minor dirt reveal how day-to-day money is being saved: by deferred maintenance—the most perfect sign of third-world conditions, the instantly recognizable background of South Asian, African, and Latin American street scenes, with their potholed streets, dilapidated buildings, crudely painted signs, and decrepit buses.

If the sheer lack of capital to provide proper facilities is the first third-world trait, the second is undoubtedly the lack of skill and diligence in the labor force. This phenomenon will be brutally obvious as soon as our traveler arrives in the customs hall, where baggage is contemptuously thrown off the incoming belts in full view of the hapless passengers. By then he will be too exhausted to complain: after a long flight, he is likely to have waited for hours to have his passport examined.

In due course, if our traveler transfers to a domestic flight, he may well encounter airline porters already paid to place suitcases on conveyor belts who nevertheless ask for tips in brusque undertones, just as in Nairobi or Karachi, sometimes hinting that the baggage might not arrive safely if no money changes hands. And he will in all probability then be trapped in slow lines while imminent flight departures are called out, waiting to be checked in by untrained clerks who tap on computer keyboards very slowly, with one finger.

Here, then, is the final trait typical of the third world—the chronic disorganization of perfectly routine procedures.

If our traveler is headed for a Manhattan hotel, he can choose between a dirty, battered, and possibly unsafe bus, or a dirtier and more battered taxi, usually driven by an unkempt lout who resembles his counterparts in Islamabad or Kinshasa rather than in London or Tokyo, where licensing requirements are strict and dress codes are enforced. At that point, a first-time visitor may still believe that both airport and taxi are glaring exceptions to the America he had always imagined—clean, modern, efficient. If so, he will immediately be disillusioned by the jolting drive over potholed highways and crumbling bridges, through miles of slums or miserable public housing.

Not as colorful as in Jakarta or Madras, the passing scene will still amaze those who come from the many European and even Asian cities where slums are now reduced to isolated survivals in remote parts of town (New York tour guides report a growing demand for the thrills of the South Bronx from European tourists quite uninterested in its pleasant greenery or the zoo, but eager to see open-air drug dealing at street corners, and the rows of burned-out buildings). After this unsettling encounter with an America already in full third-world conditions, an affluent tourist will next reach the luxurious glitter of a Manhattan hotel, but even there beggars may be standing near the door, just as in New Delhi or Lima.

IT SEEMS ONLY YESTERDAY THAT THE PROfessional optimists among us were still pointing to the continued American dominance of the world's entertainment, biotechnology, and aviation industries to reassure us that all was well, in spite of the virtual extinction of the U.S. consumer-electronics industry, the steady retreat of the auto industry, the drastic decline of the steel industry, and the widespread collapse of the machine-tool industry, still very much the foundation of all other industries.

Since then, Columbia Pictures has been sold to Sony, which had already purchased CBS Records in a previous transaction; the multimedia industry leader MCA has been sold off to Matsushita; Time-Warner, which includes HBO, has been partly sold to Toshiba and C. Itoh for $1 billion; and other notable names now belong to French and Italian interests. Word has it that it is only a matter of time before the remaining entertainment giants will go on the block in full or in part. Even hugely successful Disney, long the toast of Wall Street, chose to sell off the ownership of the hugely profitable Disneylands in France and Japan to local investors, in a typical exercise of capitalism-without-capital in the New American style.

Thus, Michael Jackson records may still sell by the millions all over the world, and American films may continue to dominate the global market, but the profits and the resulting opportunity for further capital accumulation now accrue to foreign owners.

Then there is the biotechnology industry, the *locus classicus* of the dynamic creativity and bold entrepreneurship that are supposed to compensate for all the other weaknesses of the American economy. The names of both buyers and sellers are far more obscure than in the Hollywood pairings, and the deals are much smaller (e.g., Chugai's $100 million purchase of Gen-Probe), but the great sell-off is under way just the same.

The pattern is by now well established. Americans still do most of the inventing, but because they cannot find capital at home to build the required facilities, they sell out to Japanese and European companies, receiving millions in license fees for products whose sales can eventually earn billions. Unfortunately, it is only those millions—and not the billions that will be earned mainly by foreign companies—that can be taxed to pay for basic research as well as all other government expenditures. As it is, the United States spent $5 billion on biotechnology research in 1990 as compared with only $1.7 billion for Japan, and less for Europe, but it is the Japanese and Europeans who are prospering, in great part by selling products originally developed in the U.S., mostly at the taxpayers' expense. . . .

WHEN A FARMER IS REDUCED TO SELLING off his broad acres rather than only his crops, his ultimate fate is not in doubt. Of course the analogy should be false because instead of a waning stock of acres, there is the unending flow of new technology that comes from the constantly celebrated creativity of our pluralist, multi-ethnic, undisciplined but ever-dynamic society.

Note, however, the small print that accompanied the dramatic announcement of the very latest example of that famous creativity. As soon as the suitably Korean-born chief developer of digital High-Definition (HD) TV revealed that the suitably small company he works for had totally overtaken the Japanese giants and their merely analog HD-TV, the company's owner, General Instrument, let it be known that it would not even try to raise the capital needed to produce and market the new invention, preferring to license production to established TV manufacturers, i.e., the Japanese TV giants.

In a manner literally pathetic, for pathos is the emotion evoked in the spectators to an inevitable downfall, a company spokesman hopefully speculated that if 20 million HD-TV sets were sold annually, its royalties at $10 per set could amount to as much as $200 million a year, a nice bit of change as they say—but truly mere change as compared to the $20–25 *billion* that the actual producers would earn each year, largely, no doubt, by exports to the United States.

But that is by now standard operating procedure, given our bootless capitalism-without-capital. It was Ampex, a U.S. company, which first developed the video-recorder technology that was then licensed for mere change to Matsushita, Sony, and the rest of those vigorous exporters—though of course their VCR export earnings did come back to the United States, through the purchase of CBS Records, Columbia Pictures, and MCA.

It is all very well to speak of the "globalization of industry" and to deride concerns for the nationality of production in an era of "transnational manufacturing," but when Taiwan acquires 40 percent of Douglas, or Japan's consortium has 20 percent of the next Boeing airliner, they assume no such responsibility for funding future U.S. aviation research, or Medicare for that matter—and the future earnings from those efforts will accrue to their balance of payments, and not ours.

WHAT IS HAPPENING TO THE U.S. AVIAtion industry in particular exposes the embarrassingly wide gap between the realities of what I have labeled geoeconomics, and the free-trade-plus-globalization fantasy that remains unchallenged dogma for so many Americans, not least in the Bush White House.

To begin with, the American aviation industry's only significant foreign competitor is the European consortium Airbus Industrie, which has been very successful of late even against Boeing, by selling its government-subsidized aircraft with the aid of government-subsidized loans at low interest. Similarly, Taiwan Aerospace is a government-guaranteed company, no more exposed to the vagaries of the free market than the Vatican; as such, it will always be able to count on government subsidies to underbid Douglas subcontractors, thereby taking over specialized manufactures conducive to its own planned growth into an independent maker of civilian airliners.

The wider meaning of such narrowly-aimed industrial subsidies and "national technology programs" is plain enough. Just as past generations were put in uniform to be marched off in pursuit of geopolitical schemes of territorial conquest, today's taxpayers in Europe and elsewhere have been persuaded to subsidize geo-economic schemes of industrial conquest. The free-trade true believers smile at such foolish generosity, and invite us to enjoy the resulting subsidy of our own consumption. Thus they safeguard the interests of the citizen-as-consumer, while ignoring the interests of the citizen-as-producer, but of the two roles it is only the latter that comports with the satisfactions of achievement and the dignity of employment. Moreover, the benefits of subsidized consumption that displaces our own production can only last so long as we still have acreage, famous buildings, golf courses, industries, and new technologies to sell off.

As for globalization, while 40 percent of Douglas can freely be bought by Taiwan, or 40 percent of Boeing could be bought by Japan at any time, a U.S. buyer would have rather greater chances of being allowed to acquire 40 percent of the Sistine Chapel than 40 percent of Mitsubishi Industries.

It is this flat refusal of reciprocity that justifies concerns over the scope of Japanese direct investment in U.S. manufacturing and research companies—far more consequential acquisitions than Rockefeller Center or any number of golf courses. At the last count, total European direct investment in the U.S. was still very much larger, at $262 billion, than Japan's $69.7 billion. But it is not racism that accounts for the widespread concern over the latter and not the former, as even well-informed Japanese sincerely believe. Almost all European countries positively encourage almost all U.S. acquisitions and almost all forms of U.S. investment, while in Japan, as in Korea, only the likes of soft-drink bottling plants can be established or acquired without hindrance.

For free-trade-plus-globalization true believers, this entire discussion of foreign investment in the U.S., and of the barriers to U.S. investment in Japan and Korea, misses the point entirely. Foreign investment, they ceaselessly point out, brings jobs, thereby neatly offsetting the consequence of their other article of faith: import-caused unemployment. Equally, U.S. investment abroad exports jobs, and if other countries are foolish enough to keep it out, the loss of optimal earnings for capital is compensated by the retention of employment within the United States. Both claims are perfectly valid, but to leave it at that, as many do, ignores the wider implications of foreign investment on both sides.

In the first place, when U.S. auto production, for example, is displaced by the output of foreign-owned "transplants," the complete employment pyramid of technical designers, development engineers, stylists, corporate managers, and sundry ancillary professionals is decapitated, leaving only the base of assembly-line workers with a few junior-executive positions thrown in.

And this is precisely the object of the geo-economic competition that is increasingly dominating the main arena of world affairs, now that geopolitics is being provincialized to the unfortunate lands where armed conflict is still plausible, if not actually under way. The goal of geo-economics is not to accumulate gold, as in mercantilism, for it is not kings in need of coin to pay their regiments who

are the protagonists, but rather corporate executives and their bureaucratic allies. Their aim is not territorial security or territorial expansion but its geo-economic equivalent: the conquest of the more desirable roles in the world economy.

Thus geo-economics is the very appropriate expression of meritocratic ambitions projected onto the world scene, just as geopolitics once expressed quintessentially aristocratic ambitions. Transplants do replace some of the jobs lost to imports, but what jobs? Are they the jobs that we would want for our children?

NONE OF THIS IS TO SAY THAT JAPANESE corporate expansionism, or foreign interests in general, are responsible for the woes of the American economy. Decades of unilateral market access have undoubtedly weakened American businesses and contributed to their decapitalization. But it would obviously be foolish to blame foreigners for our own policies, and our own delusions. I do not recall any commandos from Japan's Ministry of International Trade and Industry (MITI) descending on Washington to impose unreciprocated Japanese access to American markets and American technology. Nor can Toyota or Hyundai be blamed if the U.S. government simply fails to insist on reciprocity, trusting instead in the gentle conduct of interminable negotiations that yield insignificant results.

Certainly neither our European competitors nor the Japanese can be blamed for the long list of self-inflicted wounds that have been engendering the third-worldization of America.

They did not arrange the regulatory and business-culture changes that brought the mores and urgencies of Las Vegas to Wall Street and corporate boardrooms across the land, to subordinate both future growth and current employment to immediate payoffs for well-placed principals.

They had no say in the most original invention of American statecraft: representation without taxation to extract "entitlements" galore, so that savings, already scant, have been absorbed in Treasury paper, instead of modern factories or updated infrastructure.

They did not seize control of our classrooms, to discredit the discipline and absolute standards that are the prerequisites of all education, nor lately appoint the "multiculturalism" inspectors who equate arithmetic with racism, and who annex the study of history to group therapy.

Nor did foreigners devise our spectacularly antisocial "social" programs, by now most nefariously entangled in both racial politics and the crudest racism. There are very few Afro-Swedes, yet because Sweden is very generous to unmarried mothers, such mothers account for 50.9 percent of all births, as opposed to 25.7 percent in the less generous United States, and only 1 percent in notably ungenerous Japan, where 99 percent of all children are still compelled to grow up with both fathers and mothers. That, no doubt, is yet another of those exotic Japanese practices devised by the sinister MITI—certainly nothing enhances a country's competitive position more than a population properly brought up in stable families.

The list is by no means complete. The many new perversions of the administration of justice could add an entire list of their own, from ruinous product-liability awards against the manufacturers of 50-year-old machinery for one-year-old accidents, to the abandonment of the loitering laws, which leaves policemen powerless against urban predators. But even the few dysfunctions listed above would have been sufficient to propel our rapid slide into third-world conditions, complete with an entire generation of children as doomed as the street waifs of Rio de Janeiro. The newborn son of a long-gone teenage father and fifteen-year-old mother, with a grandmother in her thirties and a great-grandmother in her forties—all of them unmarried, uneducated, and unemployed—has become a rather common American type, destined from birth to roam the streets in between episodes of casual labor, crime, addiction, and imprisonment.

A search for the deeper sources of all the blatantly obvious diseases of American society would take us very far—though it might be said in passing that Anglo-Saxon style individualism could only be successful so long as there was still enough Calvinism to go around. But at least the immediate causes of our third-worldization are simply economic, a matter of capital and labor. And while the inadequate diligence of our labor force obviously has no simple cause, the immediate reason for our disastrous shortage of capital is plain enough. Americans have little to invest because they save so little.

Obviously, it is possible to invest without saving, if others lend the necessary money. And of course the United States has borrowed hugely in recent years, and also absorbed a vast amount of foreign investment. Yet given the size of the American economy, even the huge inflow of money from abroad could not possibly remedy the disastrous difference between our rate of savings and those of our competitors.

IN ANY CASE, THE RELENTLESS EROSION OF the entire economic base of American society is revealed by undisputed statistics that have none of the flaws of international comparisons. During the last 20 years—half a working lifetime—American "non-farm, non-supervisory" employees actually earned slightly less, year by year. As a matter of fact, by 1990 their real earnings (corrected for inflation) had regressed to the 1965 level. Will they regress further—perhaps to the 1960 level by 1995, and then to the 1955 level by the year 2000? It seems distinctly possible. Given the lack of invested capital, it is only with ever-cheaper labor that we can compete internationally. Therein lies our own path to Bangladesh.

Who are these poor unfortunates whose real earnings have been declining since 1965? Are they perhaps some small and peculiar minority? Not so. In November 1990, the last month for which those statistics are complete, they numbered 74,888,000, or just over 81 percent of all non-farm employees—that is, more than eight out of ten of all Americans who are not self-employed, from corporate executives earning hundreds or even thousands of dollars per hour, to those working at the minimum wage.

Far from being a minority whose fate cannot affect the base of American society, then, they *are* the base of American society, the vast majority of the labor force of manufacturing, mining, construction, transport, utility, wholesale and retail trade, finance, insurance, real estate, all other service enterprises, and government employees.

How can the entire structure of American affluence and advancement from luxurious living to scientific laboratories *not* decline when the vast majority of all working Americans are earning less and less? And how can the U.S. not slide toward third-world conditions if this absolute decline continues while in both Western Europe and East Asia real earnings continue to increase?

Inevitably, the most telling comparison is with Japan. In 1970, Japanese manufacturing employees earned only just over a quarter (or more precisely 27 percent) as much as their American counterparts. In 1988, they earned 7 percent more. If the trend were to continue straight on both sides, in 18 more years American earnings would be reduced to less than a quarter (23 percent) of the Japanese level, almost the same proportion as now obtains between Brazilian and American hourly wages in manufacturing.

It stands to reason that by then the United States would become Japan's Brazil, an amusing, sometimes unsettling country of vast expanses with a cheerful but impoverished third-world population. The casual banter that nowadays greets errors of blatant incompetence in American offices, factories, and shops; the patient silence evoked even by acts of willful negligence and aggressive apathy; the learned ability to ignore unkempt urban vagrants and all their importunings; and generally our increasing acceptance of breakdowns, delays, and all forms of physical decay—all this shows that we are indeed adapting to our fate, by acquiring the necessary third-world traits of fatalistic detachment. But they, of course, ensure that the slide will continue.

NO

Robert L. Bartley

IS AMERICA ON THE WAY DOWN?

To the ordinary, everyday sense of mankind, America has not declined, it has prevailed. Its foe of two generations has collapsed and now even seeks to adopt American institutions of democracy and market economics.

Though to people who use their eyes and ears it is obvious that American influence in the world is on the rise, we have not been able to put the notion of decline behind us. For a segment of American opinion refuses to use its eyes and ears. Instead, proponents of decline confuse themselves with statistics they do not understand, or in some cases willingly distort. They invoke jingoism by turning international trade into some kind of combat, instead of a series of mutually beneficial arrangements among consenting adults.

The notion of decline has recently been a fad of the Left, in alliance with a coterie of nonideological special interests. It is instructive to remember, though, that as the 1980's opened decline was a theme of the Right. Conservatives, notably but far from solely Jean-François Revel, warned that the West was falling behind in the military competition with the Soviet Sparta. It found itself manipulated by Soviet campaigns like the one that stopped the neutron bomb. The United States, the natural leader of the alliance, was wracked by inflation and stagnant productivity at home, preoccupied with hostages held by a primitive cleric, and unable even to fly six helicopters across the desert.

In those days, conservatives worried that the West lacked the will to use its superior economic resources even to defend itself. They can take heart that their warnings were heeded, that free peoples found the will to resist, that fear of Communist arms did not stunt them into self-doubt and inaction. But American will is now being tested in a more subtle way by the theme of decline, another recipe for confusion and self-destruction. If America generally falls prey to this delusion, it may throw away its birthright as the hub of a new and progressive world civilization.

On the Right, the notion of decline faded as Ronald Reagan filled the military spare-parts bins, frankly labeled the Soviet Union an "evil empire," invaded Grenada, bombed Libya, revived the option of missile defense. The diplomatic turning point was 1983, when the West withstood a determined Soviet campaign, including street demonstrations and the suspension of arms negotiations, to stop the deployment of Pershing missiles in Europe. At the same time, the United States was curbing its inflation with Paul Volcker's monetary policy and reviving economic growth with Ronald Reagan's tax cuts. Seven years of uninterrupted economic expansion did wonders for military preparedness, diplomatic creativity, and public morale. The economic revival that started in the United States and quickly spread to Europe proved the final undoing of the totalitarian challenge.

The containment policy the West had patiently pursued for two generations predicted that under steady pressure the Soviet empire would mellow or crack. Then it happened at a stroke. In 1989 the Berlin Wall was breached, and by 1991 the Communist remnants proved themselves inept even at coup-making. Meanwhile, an American-led attack decimated the world's fourth-largest army in six weeks of combat and at the cost of 148 Americans lost in action. The world's new military balance was clear, leaving only the mysteries of why President Bush stopped short of Baghdad and how the hysterical Cassandras who had predicted a desert debacle managed to retain their *bona fides* as military experts.

Nor is American predominance merely or even primarily a matter of military power. American ideals of democratic pluralism and market economics were spreading not only in the former Soviet Union but throughout South America, Eastern Europe, and even Africa. America remains the favored destination of the world's refugees and immigrants. Its

university system (despite the political-correctness plague) is unparalleled: it graduates many foreign nationals in science and engineering, of course, but many of them choose to stay in the U.S. For all the accomplishments of the industrious Japanese, America still dominates scientific innovation. Many transnational corporations, even if based in Germany or Switzerland, locate their research divisions in New Jersey or North Carolina. Japanese auto companies open design labs in Los Angeles. Above all, the U.S. utterly dominates the single capstone technology of our era, which in every language is called "software."

WHATEVER THE MOMENTARY ECONOMIC UPS and downs, too, the plain fact is that the United States is the wealthiest society in the history of mankind. Or at least this is plain to the economically literate, who understand that no meaningful comparison can be based on momentary exchange rates among different national currencies. In translating among currencies to make international comparisons, the only meaningful basis is purchasing-power parity (PPP), the exchange rate at which two currencies would each buy the same basket of goods. The Organization for Economic Cooperation and Development spends endless hours of tedious calculation to churn out PPP rates precisely for the purpose of facilitating such comparisons.

Under the current regime of floating exchange rates, currencies can vary widely from their purchasing-power parity. This distorts comparisons and above all trends—for temporary and reversible variations in exchange rates are likely to swamp any changes in underlying fundamentals. As recently as 1985, the dollar was well over its PPP rate, exaggerating the American standard of living. In later years, the dollar has been below PPP, making America look less wealthy than it actually is.

So current comparisons built on current exchange rates show America falling behind, but properly adjusting the comparisons to PPP makes the picture entirely different. *The Economist Book of Vital World Statistics*, for example, found that at 1988 figures and exchange rates, the United States ranked only ninth in the world in gross domestic product per capita—behind Switzerland, Japan, and the Scandinavian countries. But it also reported that at PPP exchange rates, the American standard of living was far above other advanced nations. With the U.S. at 100, Canada rated 92.5 and Switzerland 87.0. Then came the Scandinavian nations and some small countries, including Kuwait. West Germany rated tenth at 78.6, and Japan twelfth at 71.5. Other developed nations trailed.

In short, the American standard of living is substantially above that of Japan and most of Europe.

This is confirmed by physical measures. American automobile ownership, for example, is one car for every 1.8 persons. Iceland has two people for each car, while Canada, New Zealand, and West Germany have 2.2. France has 2.5, the United Kingdom 2.8, and Japan 4.2. Similarly, there are 1.2 Americans per television set, compared to 1.7 Japanese and 2.4 Germans. The United States is also one of the world's great undeveloped countries, with 26.3 persons per square mile, compared to 102.1 in France, 233.8 in the United Kingdom, 246.1 in West Germany, 324.5 in Japan, and 395.8 in the Netherlands. While I have no figures handy, the American standard of living is most evident of all in housing; the Japa-

nese measure apartment sizes in tatami mats.

As for the recent trends, the American economy led the world out of the economic crisis of the late 1970's by staging so remarkable a boom between 1983 and 1990 that it is now hard to remember such bywords as "stagflation" or "malaise" or "Euro-pessimism." In this expansion, the U.S. economy grew by 31 percent after adjustment for inflation, about equivalent to building 1982 West Germany from scratch. Real disposable income per capita rose by 18 percent. Productivity resumed growth after stagnating in the 1970's, and in fact surged in manufacturing. Manufacturing output grew faster than GNP, and exports leapt by more than 92 percent. More than eighteen million new jobs were created, even while the *Fortune* 500 companies pared their payrolls. Tax revenues kept pace with GNP growth and, since this was supposedly a decade of greed, it should be noted that charitable giving grew at 5.1 percent a year, compared with 3.5 percent a year over the previous 25 years.

Again, a remarkable leap in living standards is confirmed by physical measures. In 1980, hard as it may be to remember, only 1 percent of American households owned a videocassette recorder. By 1989, the figure was more than 58 percent. For all practical purposes, every video rental shop in the nation was started during the seven fat years. In 1980, cable-television systems reached 15 percent of American households, mostly in remote areas with difficult reception. At the end of the decade, half of all homes were wired. In 1981, when the Apple II was a hackers' toy, a little over two million personal computers were in use in the whole country. That year, IBM introduced its first PC, and Apple followed with the Macintosh in 1984. By 1988, the two million PC's had exploded to 45 million. Of this number, roughly half were in homes.

THE MOST REMARKABLE FEATURE OF THE 1980's, though, was economic globalization. The 24-hour trading markets were stitched together; dollars circled the world at electronic speed. Rock-and-roll invaded Prague and Moscow, and Japanese auto companies built plants in Tennessee (Nissan), Ohio (Honda), and Kentucky (Toyota). "Interdependence" became the new byword, though one inadequate to describe the evolution of the world economy into an organic whole.

As the U.S. economy led the world out of the doldrums of 1982, the world voted with its money. In 1979, foreigners invested $38.7 billion in the United States; in 1980 this number was $58.1 billion. But investment inflows soared to $83.0 billion in 1981, $93.7 billion in 1982, $130.0 billion in 1985, and $229.8 billion in 1987. With the Volcker monetary policy and the Reagan tax cuts, America was where the world's investors saw the most promising return. And demand in America created the export markets that led Europe out of its pessimism.

A great source of the confusion about the American economy, and a great source of the current poor-mouthing, is that the United States has still not come to terms with its integration into the world economy. Thus America's sages gazed on the developments sketched above and decided the sky was falling. In sending their money here those perfidious foreigners expected to get paid back. Indeed, the whole reason they were sending their money here was that they anticipated a higher return here than they could get at home. Their eagerness to invest in America instead of at home was turning us into—shame!—a debtor nation. And, of course, the American purchases that stimulated the European revival were reflected in—horrors!—a trade deficit.

In 1976 an official U.S. government advisory committee studying the international statistics suggested that

the words "surplus" and "deficit" be avoided insofar as possible. . . . These words are frequently taken to mean that the developments are "good" or "bad" respectively. Since that interpretation is often incorrect, the terms may be widely misunderstood and used in lieu of analysis.

Following the committee's recommendations, the Commerce Department stopped publishing most of what had up to then been a plethora of different "balances"—the current accounts balance, the basic balance, the net liquidity balance, the official settlements balance. Because the bureaucrats thought they had to publish something, they kept the merchandise trade balance, which has been used in lieu of analysis ever since.

What the advisory committee understood, and what cannot be emphasized too much, is that international statistics are an accounting identity; they will balance tautologically, by definition. After all, for every buyer there has to be a seller. The various trade balances are only different stopping places in a great circle of transactions. Except for zero, there is no bottom line.

The most constructive way to look at the international accounts is to divide them into three parts, which must by definition net out to zero. The two big halves are, first, trade in goods and services, and, second, investment. These are essentially two sides of the same coin; normally a trade deficit is financed by an investment surplus, or inflow. And a trade surplus will accompany investment outflows. The third part of the international accounts is called "official financing"; if trade and investment do not offset each other, the central banks have to step in and act as balance wheel— this can represent a problem if, as happened with U.S. accounts in the mid 1970's, there are simultaneous outflows of trade and investment.

In the normal investment-trade see-saw, though, a zero trade balance is not normal or even desirable. The U.S. ran a trade deficit for nearly all of its first 100 years, and generated trade surpluses under the Smoot-Hawley Tariff in the midst of the Great Depression. Normally, a rapidly growing economy will demand more of the world's supply of real resources and run a trade deficit. It will also provide attractive investment opportunities and attract capital inflows. In a healthy world, the two will offset each other, for periods of perhaps a century.

Yet somehow we have come to measure our nationhood by the one statistic of the trade balance. The real mystery is why we even collect it; if we kept similar statistics for Manhattan island, Park Avenue would lie awake at night worrying about its trade deficit. We have even come to view trade as some kind of nationalistic competition. Winning, apparently, is selling more to the rest of the world than we buy from it. Leaving aside the fact that this is ultimately impossible, why? If we could do it, what would we do with the proceeds, bury them in Fort Knox?

. . . [F]AR FROM SINKING INTO DECLINE, America is now at the center of one of the great, exciting moments in mankind's economic history. A second industrial revo-

lution is remaking world society. Not since the industrial revolution itself has technological advance been so breathtaking, or more pregnant with changes in the way mankind lives and thinks of itself.

More breathtaking now, probably, than even then. James Watt's steam engine pales beside what our generation has already seen: the splitting of the atom, the decoding of the gene, and the invention of the transistor and the computers it spawned. These are not only magnificent leaps of the technological imagination, they are potential precursors of currently unimaginable economic advance. Atomic power, unless cold fusion turns out to be real after all, has perhaps not realized what we once thought of as its potential. The first fruits of biotechnology are just now entering the markets. But already the transistor and the rest are changing the world.

Indeed, we live every day with the electronic revolution. As the first industrial revolution changed an agricultural economy into an industrial economy, a second industrial revolution is changing an industrial economy into a service economy. More specifically, into an information economy, in which the predominant activity is collecting, processing, and communicating information. We are headed toward a world in which everyone on the globe is in instant communication with everyone else.

It is this web of instant communication that has stitched the world into increasing interdependence. In fact, throughout this century the world economy has been more interdependent than anyone realized: the Great Depression, for example, was preeminently a world event, and its origins lay in disturbances in the international economy. But with today's 24 hour financial markets and transnational corporations, economic interdependence is hard to miss.

The same web of instant communication is responsible for the political developments that have rocked our age. Orwell, in his *Nineteen Eighty-Four,* saw information technology as an instrument of Big Brother. We are now seeing clearly that it is quite the opposite. The onslaught of the information age played a key role in liberating Eastern Europe and in spreading democratic currents through the Soviet Union and the developing world. The totalitarians have found they cannot control a people in touch with the outside. In Albert Wohlstetter's phrase, *the fax shall make you free.* Big Brother can of course build a society without computers, but that society will not be able to compete in the modern world, as China seems to be learning after Tiananmen Square.

The precision weapons demonstrated with such effect in the Gulf War are also an aspect of information technology. They promise to make combat once again the province of professional warrior against professional warrior; no longer need philosophers talk about "mutual assured destruction"—the targeting of women and children with nuclear missiles. Once we fully understand this, it will redound to the benefit of civilians everywhere.

Naturally our time and our nation have their problems. Americans should take education more seriously, instead of subordinating it to goals like racial balance and asbestos removal. Our legal system should let police enforce the law against vagrants, and should stop inflicting a parasitic tort-bar industry upon us. Our political system is so frozen it seems unable to address these everyday problems.

More broadly, there is such a thing as being too liberated, having too many options. We are still learning to live with our new freedoms. The onslaught of modernity has not been good for institutions such as the family. We are overly susceptible to fads—health scares, for example—and for that matter the fad of declinism.

For all these problems, what mostly needs to be explained is not what is wrong with America, but how so much of our articulate elite can so completely mistake reality. A great part of the answer is that progress is unsettling, as rapid change always is. Looking back over history, indeed, we see that ages of economic advance have often been ages of pessimism.

In particular, history's all-time champion economic pessimist, Thomas Malthus, published his first essay on population in 1798; this was 29 years after James Watt's first patent in connection with the steam engine. The first industrial revolution, in other words, was the venue for Malthus's gloomy theorizing. He was explaining why economic progress was impossible just as mankind was taking the greatest economic leap in history.

Not surprisingly, the Malthus paradox attracted the attention of Joseph A. Schumpeter, our century's greatest economic historian and one of its greatest economists. One chapter in his massive *History of Economic Analysis* relates how ancient societies were worried about overpopulation, but after about 1600 this changed completely. The prevailing attitude was that "increasing population was the most important symptom of wealth; it was the chief cause of wealth; it was wealth itself."

"It is quite a problem to explain why the opposite attitude," Schumpeter wrote, "should have asserted itself among economists from the middle of the 18th century on. Why was it that economists took fright at a scarecrow?" Malthusian pessimism did not develop despite the progress of the industrial revolution, Schumpeter concluded. It developed because of the progress.

Long-run progress, Schumpeter pointed out, causes short-run problems, and

> in the industrial revolution of the last decades of the 18th century, these short-run vicissitudes grew more serious than they had been before, precisely because the pace of economic development quickened.

This is not to say that the short-run problems were imaginary. In the short run, technological advance destroyed agricultural jobs faster than it created manufacturing jobs, especially since guilds and the like created bottlenecks. A type of mass unemployment arose that had been unknown in the Middle Ages, and with it urban slums, gin mills, and great social debates over the Poor Laws. Malthus's pessimism was echoed a few decades later by Dickens. But we now know that during the lives of both men mankind was rapidly building wealth.

If, then, we are currently experiencing a second industrial revolution, it is not surprising to hear such Malthusian themes as overpopulation and the exhaustion of resources echoing through our public discourse. From the primitive technology of a wooden sailing ship, the earth's forces look overwhelming. Now that we have the technological prowess to put men on the moon, the earth looks like a fragile flower, puny beside our own powers.

The rapid change of the second industrial revolution, moreover, upsets established institutions and established elites. As instant information and instant markets erode the power of governments, so too they erode the power of corporate chieftains and labor bosses. We can now all watch the poor chairman of Exxon writhing over an oil spill in Alaska. Many chief executives find themselves displaced, albeit with golden parachutes: half of *Fortune's* top 500 corporations in 1980 were gone from the list in 1990. Under the force of industrial competition and information on wages and working conditions, labor unions find their private-sector membership declining.

So too with intellectual elites, who find their skills fading in relevance and their positions endangered. Perhaps political correctness in the academy is best seen as a brand of Luddism. And surely much of our articulate class feels threatened in a deeply personal way by the notion that a historic corner was turned under a simple-minded movie actor.

This mixture of neurosis, special pleading, ideological hostility, ignorance, and confusion is obviously a phenomenon to be reckoned with. Indeed, even an unbridled optimist has to admit that there is after all one way America actually could decline. To wit, if this neurotic pessimism becomes a self-realizing prophecy.

THIS WOULD BE A HISTORIC TRAGEDY, FOR the confluence of the second industrial revolution and the collapse of totalitarianism presents the human race with an unparalleled opportunity. The decade of the 1990's is not a time for pessimism, but a time for large thoughts and large ambitions. The tide in the affairs of men is running, and we must take the current when it serves. The brightest hope for mankind today is that the breaching of the Berlin Wall on November 9, 1989 marked the end of a beastly era that started with the assassination of Archduke Francis Ferdinand in Sarajevo on June 28, 1914.

The consciousness of everyone alive today was forged in an abnormal era, a century of world war, revolution, and totalitarianism. While mankind has always suffered wars and other miseries, our century ranks with the most wretched in history. Technology turned battle from a contest of knights into an assault on whole civilian populations. A Great Depression sank the world economy. With the rise of Hitler and Stalin, the human soul was under siege. World War II dissolved into a worldwide confrontation between the West and Communism.

At issue was the nature of man—a cog in the great dialectical machine of history, or an autonomous individual capable of free will and self-government? If reform succeeds in Russia, or even survives, all this will be history. We will have a new era to define.

The skyline of Paris is dominated by the great monument to an earlier and less gruesome era. The Eiffel Tower was erected for the Paris Exposition of 1889 to celebrate the scientific and engineering prowess of *La Belle Epoque*. *La Belle Epoque*, of course is typically associated with *fin de siècle* Paris, the Paris of Toulouse-Lautrec. It was an age of extraordinary flowering of the arts, when Manet, Degas, and Monet fought the battles that led to the *Salon des Refusés*. It was also an age of extraordinary science, with the likes of Louis Pasteur and Madame Curie. Most of all, it was an age of faith in human progress. Even the dour Emile Zola invoked "a century of science and democracy."

The hub of this civilization was Great Britain. With the Corn Laws it practiced free trade *unilaterally*, to the benefit of its own consumers and the advancement of underdeveloped nations. With the Royal Navy it protected freedom of the seas (and suppressed the slave trade). With the pound sterling, it was the anchor of an exceptionally efficient international monetary mechanism known as the gold standard. Goods, labor, and capital moved freely to their most productive uses throughout an integrated economy spanning two continents and more.

The biggest beneficiary of this system was the United States of America. Open immigration peopled its lands. Open markets in Europe took its grain, at the expense of agricultural interests in Europe and especially England. Despite these sales, its hunger for capital goods was such that it ran trade deficits year after year, but this mattered little because of consistent investment inflows. For, most important of all, the London financial markets mobilized the capital of the civilization as a whole for the prodigious and exciting task of developing the North American continent.

TODAY WE ARE IN A POSITION TO BUILD A new version of the institutions of the *Belle Epoque* and rekindle its spirit. We can hope, too, to avoid another Sarajevo, for the technology of the second industrial revolution is less threatening than that of the first. The Eiffel Tower was the product of a master engineer, in its way a monument to central planning. The smelting of steel and the building of railroads were enterprises that demanded central planning and the mobilization of massive capital. Napoleon had demonstrated how to conscript whole societies for war, and in the ensuing century the experience of mankind taught it efficient logistics and bureaucratic order. The very advance of science led philosophers like Marx to think of "laws of history." In 1914 this technology, combined of course with the recurrent follies of mankind, marched the world into war.

Ever since, we have been struggling to tame the impact of technology and the mindset it engenders. As the assembly line turned men into interchangeable cogs, the centralized, bureaucratic state became a breeding ground of totalitarianism. But the technology of the second industrial revolution empowers the governed rather than the governors. In its constant churning today's technology has a dark side to be conquered, but its bright side offers the hope of a liberating era.

Certainly technology is not everything. Its opportunities must be exploited by the human spirit. Our dilemma is that all of us living in the 1990's have been taught from the cradle not to believe in dreams. We are cynical about politicians, and they live down to our expectations. Instead of a century of science and democracy we have Andy Warhol proclaiming that everyone will be famous for fifteen minutes. Instead of Toulouse-Lautrec we have Robert Mapplethorpe.

And instead of the promise of world cooperation led by the United States, we have the gloomy apostles of decline, alarmed because goods and capital move across lines someone drew on maps, trying to manufacture conflict out of the peaceful and mutually beneficial intercourse among peoples.

The last time the will of the West was tested, it rose to the challenge. In particular, the American electorate understood that the threat was Soviet Communism, not the military-industrial complex. With the more subtle test of a litany of decline coming out of Cambridge, Detroit, and Washington, there will again be confusion and apparent close calls, but in the end the delusion will not sell. Indeed, given any sort of intellectual and political leadership to frame the challenge, the American nation will rise to the rich opportunity before it.

POSTSCRIPT

Is America Declining?

The publication of Paul Kennedy's *The Rise and Fall of the Great Powers* (Random House, 1987) provided the historical framework for national soul-searching regarding America's future role in the world. Despite the disagreement between Luttwak and Bartley over whether or not the United States is declining, there is no doubt that other nations have been growing and will likely continue to grow in productivity, military power, and international influence.

This likelihood is examined in Lester C. Thurow, *Head to Head: Coming Economic Battles Among Japan, Europe and America* (William Morrow, 1992). Thurow argues that a united Western Europe will abandon traditional free trade for trading blocs and managed trade, while Japan will enjoy the economic advantages of momentum, a high rate of investment, and a cohesive internal culture. Confronted by these challenges, the United States must recognize the need to change from individualistic to communitarian capitalism.

Pessimism regarding America's chances of remaining the world's most prosperous and most powerful nation is sometimes tempered with hope. Walter Russell Mead urges cutbacks in American commitments in *Mortal Splendor: The American Empire in Transition* (Houghton Mifflin, 1987). Like Kennedy, Mead traces parallels with past empires and concludes that decline is inevitable, but Mead maintains that America can shape its postimperial future.

Steven Schlosstein, *The End of the American Century* (Congdon & Weed, 1989), concludes that the United States has declined economically because it has become inferior to Japanese society with respect to the quality of education, the stability of family life, the balance between personal and collective welfare, and other social and economic factors.

Pessimism regarding America's power and influence in the post–cold war world is rejected by analysts who believe that the nation has the ability and the will to continue to play a leading role under changing conditions. This is the position of Joseph S. Nye, Jr., *Bound to Lead: The Changing Nature of American Power* (Basic Books, 1990). Nye argues that only the United States possesses great resources of land, population, military power, economic capacity, scientific discovery, and technology.

Kennedy's decline thesis is also rejected by Richard McKenzie, "The Decline of America: Myth or Fate?" *Society* (November/December 1989), and Owen Harries, "The Rise of American Decline," *Commentary* (May 1988). For Norman Podhoretz, the issue is not overstretching or overspending but national will. In *The Present Danger* (Simon & Schuster, 1980), he poses the question: "Do we have the will to reverse the decline of American power?"

Whatever our conclusions, the debate prompted by the theory of decline compels us to examine the nature and consequences of American values and goals in relation to the rest of the world.

CONTRIBUTORS
TO THIS VOLUME

EDITORS

GEORGE McKENNA received his bachelor's degree from the University of Chicago in 1959, his M.A. from the University of Massachusetts in 1962, and his Ph.D. from Fordham University in 1967. He has been teaching political science at City College of New York since 1963, and is currently chair of the Department of Political Science. Professor McKenna has written many books and articles on American government and political theory, including *American Populism* (Putnam, 1974) and *American Politics: Ideals and Realities* (McGraw-Hill, 1976). His most recent textbook is *The Drama of Democracy: American Government and Politics* (The Dushkin Publishing Group, 1990).

STANLEY FEINGOLD was born in New York City in 1926. He attended high school in the city and received his bachelor's degree from the City College of New York. He received his graduate education at Columbia University and taught political science at City College. From 1970 to 1974, he was given a special appointment as Visiting Professor of Politics at the University of Leeds, England. At present he is a professor at Westchester Community College, a unit of the State University of New York.

STAFF

Marguerite L. Egan   Program Manager
Brenda S. Filley   Production Manager
Whit Vye   Designer
Libra Ann Cusack   Typesetting Supervisor
Juliana Arbo   Typesetter
David Brackley   Copy Editor
David Dean   Administrative Assistant
Diane Barker   Editorial Assistant

AUTHORS

HERBERT E. ALEXANDER is the director of the Citizens Research Foundation in Los Angeles, California, and a professor of political science at the University of Southern California.

ROBERT L. BARTLEY, the recipient of the 1980 Pulitzer Prize for editorial writing, is the editor and vice president of the *Wall Street Journal*, with primary responsibility for the editorial page. He is a member of the Council on Foreign Relations and the American Political Science Association, and he holds honorary doctor of laws degrees from Macalester College and Babson College.

WALTER BERNS received his Ph.D. from the University of Chicago in 1953. He taught at the University of Toronto, Cornell University, and Yale University before becoming the John M. Olin Professor of Government at Georgetown University in Washington, D.C. He is also the author of more than 40 articles and 7 books, including *Taking the Constitution Seriously* (Simon & Schuster, 1987). He has held a Guggenheim Fellowship, a Fulbright Fellowship, and a Rockefeller Fellowship, among other honors.

HARRY A. BLACKMUN has been an associate justice of the U.S. Supreme Court since his appointment by former president Nixon in 1970. He wrote the Court's decision in the landmark *Roe v. Wade* case.

DAVID BOLLIER is a journalist and a consultant specializing in politics, law, the media, and consumer affairs. He graduated from Yale Law School in 1985, and he is the coauthor, with Henry S. Cohn, of *The Great Hartford Circus Fire* (Yale University Press, 1991).

ROBERT H. BORK, a former U.S. Court of Appeals judge for the District of Columbia Circuit, is the John M. Olin Scholar in Legal Studies at the American Enterprise Institute in Washington, D.C., a privately funded public policy research organization.

STANLEY C. BRUBAKER is a professor of political science in the Department of Government at Colgate University in Hamilton, New York, and the director of Colgate University's Washington Study Group.

STEPHEN L. CARTER is a professor of law at Yale University Law School and the author of *Reflections of an Affirmative Action Baby* (Basic Books, 1991).

NOAM CHOMSKY is the Institute Professor in the Department of Linguistics and Philosophy at the Massachusetts Institute of Technology, where he has been teaching since 1976. He is the recipient of the 1984 American Psychological Association Distinguished Scientific Contribution Award and the author of *Necessary Illusions: Thought Control in Democratic Societies* (South End Press, 1989) and *Deterring Democracy* (Verso Publications, 1991).

JOAN CLAYBROOK is the president of Public Citizen, a public interest group in Washington, D.C., and a former administrator of the National Highway Traffic Safety Administration. She received her bachelor's degree from Goucher College in Baltimore, Maryland, and her J.D. from Georgetown University Law Center.

WILLIAM J. CROTTY is a professor of political science at Northwestern University, where he has been teaching since 1966. A member and former president of the Policy Studies Organization and the American Political Science Association, he was a project director for the National Municipal League's American Political Project. His publications include *Party Reform* (Longman, 1983) and *The Party Game* (W. H. Freeman, 1985).

EDD DOERR is the executive director of Americans for Religious Liberty in Silver Spring, Maryland.

PAULA DWYER is a Washington correspondent for *Business Week* magazine.

THOMAS BYRNE EDSALL is a political reporter for the *Washington Post*. His publications include *Chain Reaction: The Impact of Race, Rights, and Taxes on American Politics* (W. W. Norton, 1991).

BARBARA EHRENREICH, a writer and a contributing editor to *Ms.* magazine, is a fellow of the Institute for Policy Studies and an associate fellow of the New York Institute for the Humanities. An outspoken feminist and socialist party leader, she has authored or coauthored numerous books and articles, including *The Worst Years of Our Lives: Irreverent Notes from a Decade of Greed* (Pantheon Books, 1990).

STANLEY FISH is the chairman of the Department of English at Duke University and a professor of law in the Duke University School of Law. Considered to be a pioneering literary theorist, he is the author of more than 75 publications, most recently *Doing What Comes Naturally: Change, Rhetoric, and the Practice of Theory in Legal and Literary Studies* (Duke University Press, 1989).

BENJAMIN M. FRIEDMAN is the William Joseph Maier Professor of Political Economics at Harvard University in Cambridge, Massachusetts. He is the coeditor of *Handbook of Monetary Economics* (North-Holland, 1990), with Frank H. Hahn, and a coauthor of *Does Debt Management Matter?* (Oxford University Press, 1992), with Jonas Agell and Mats Persson.

GEORGE GOLDBERG is an author and a member of the New York State Bar. He has written a number of books, including *A Lawyer's Guide to Commercial Arbitration* (American Law Institute, 1983) and *Church, State, and the Constitution*, rev. ed. (Regnery Gateway, 1987), which examines church-state relations in the United States.

JOHN C. GOODMAN is the president of the National Center for Policy Analysis, a Dallas-based research organization founded in February 1983, and the author of six books and numerous articles published in professional journals. He received a Ph.D. in economics from Columbia University, and in 1988 he won the Duncan Black award for the best scholarly article on public choice economics.

DOUGLAS HARBRECHT is a Washington correspondent for *Business Week* magazine.

NAT HENTOFF is a writer and an adjunct associate professor at New York University. He is a regular contributor to such publications as the *Washington Post, The Progressive, The Village Voice,* and *The New Yorker,* and he is the author of several books on public policy, including *The First Freedom: The Tumultuous History of Free Speech in America* (Delacorte, 1980).

EDWARD S. HERMAN is a professor emeritus of finance at the University of Pennsylvania Wharton School of Business. His publications include *The Terrorism Industry: The Experts and Institutions that Shape Our View of Terror* (Pantheon Books, 1990).

HERBERT HILL, a former labor director of the National Association for the Advancement of Colored People, is a professor of African American studies and a professor of industrial relations at the University of Wisconsin–Madison.

LEONARD W. LEVY was the Andrew W. Mellon All-Claremont Professor of Humanities and the chairman of the Graduate Faculty of History at the Claremont Graduate School until his retirement in 1990. His publications include *The Origins of the Fifth Amendment* (Macmillan, 1969), winner of the 1969 Pulitzer Prize in history, and *The Establishment Clause: Religion and the First Amendment* (Collier Macmillan, 1986).

EDWARD N. LUTTWAK is the director of geo-economics and holds the Arleigh Burke Chair in Strategy at the Center for Strategic and International Studies in Washington, D.C. He is also a member of the board of editors for *Orbis: A Journal of World Affairs.*

MARY MEEHAN is a free-lance writer based in Washington, D.C., who has contributed articles on social issues to a variety of periodicals.

THOMAS GALE MOORE, economist and educator, is a senior fellow of the Hoover Institution on War, Revolution, and Peace. He is also an adjunct fellow of both the American Enterprise Institute and the CATO Institute, and he is a member of the advisory board for the Reason Foundation.

JOSHUA MURAVCHIK is a resident scholar at the American Enterprise Institute. His publications include *The Senate and National Security: A New Mood* (Sage Publications, 1980) and *News Coverage of the Sandinista Revolution* (AEI Press, 1988).

ETHAN A. NADELMANN is an assistant professor of politics and public affairs at the Princeton University Woodrow Wilson School of Public and International Affairs. He was a founding coordinator of the Harvard Study Group on Organized Crime and has been a consultant to the Public Agenda Foundation's National Issues Forum and to the Department of State's Bureau of International Narcotics Matters. He is an assistant editor of the *Journal of Drug Issues* and a contributing editor of the *International Journal on Drug Policy*.

RICHARD P. NATHAN is the director of the Rockefeller Institute of Government at the State University of New York at Albany and a provost of the Rockefeller College of Public Affairs and Policy. He has also been a professor at Princeton University, a researcher at the Brookings Institution, and a federal government official. His publications include *Reagan and the States* (Princeton University Press, 1987), coauthored with Fred Dolittle, and *Social Science in Government: Uses and Misuses* (Basic Books, 1988).

NELSON W. POLSBY is a professor of political science and the director of the Institute of Governmental Studies at the University of California, Berkeley, where he has been teaching since 1969. He is also the president of the Yale University Council and a member of the Academic Advisory Board of the American Enterprise Institute in Washington, D.C. He has held Guggenheim fellowships twice and fellowships at the Center for Advanced Study in the Behavioral Sciences twice, among other honors.

ROBERT RECTOR is a policy analyst for social, welfare, and family issues at The Heritage Foundation, a public policy research and education institute whose programs are intended to apply a conservative philosophy to current policy questions.

WILLIAM H. REHNQUIST became the 16th chief justice of the U.S. Supreme Court in 1986. He has been a justice in the Supreme Court since his appointment by former president Nixon in 1972.

LINDA ROCAWICH is the managing editor of *The Progressive*. She is a former staff member of the National Council on Crime and Delinquency.

WILLIAM A. RUSHER, a former publisher of the *National Review*, is a senior fellow at the Claremont Institute for the Study of Statesmanship and Political Philosophy, a research and education institution that focuses on contemporary issues in Asian studies, American history, political philosophy, modern economics, and foreign policy.

JAMES L. SUNDQUIST is a senior fellow emeritus and a former director of the Governmental Studies Program at the Brookings Institution, a private nonprofit organization devoted to research, education, and publication in economics, government, foreign policy, and the social sciences. His publications include *The Decline and Resurgence of Congress* (Brookings, 1981) and *Constitutional Reform and Effective Government* (Brookings, 1992).

ALAN TONELSON is the research director of the Economic Strategy Institute in Washington, D.C., a research organization that focuses on U.S. economics, technology, and national security policy. His essays on American politics and foreign policy have appeared in numerous publications, including the *New York Times, Foreign Policy,* and *Harvard Business Review,* and he is the author of a forthcoming book on U.S. foreign policy.

DAVID VOGEL is a professor of business administration in the Haas School of Business at the University of California, Berkeley. He is the author of *Fluctuating Fortunes: The Political Power of Business in America* (Basic Books, 1989).

NANCY WATZMAN, a writer whose articles have appeared in *The New Republic, The Nation, The Washington Monthly,* and other publications, is a policy analyst for Public Citizen, a public interest group in Washington, D.C.

FRED WERTHEIMER is the president of Common Cause, a citizen's lobbying organization. A graduate of the University of Michigan and Harvard Law School and a former fellow of Harvard University's Kennedy Institute of Politics, he is the author of numerous law review articles on campaign finance reform

and a series of Common Cause investigative studies on the role of money in American politics.

TOM WICKER is a former political columnist for the *New York Times.* His publications include *Unto This Hour* (Berkeley Publishing, 1985) and *One of Us: The Age of Richard Nixon* (Random House, 1989).

JAMES Q. WILSON is the James Collins Professor of Management and Public Policy at the University of California, Los Angeles, where he has been teaching since 1985. He is also the chairman of the board of directors of the Police Foundation and a member of the American Academy of Arts and Sciences. He has authored, coauthored, or edited numerous books on crime, government, and politics, including *Politics of Regulation* (Basic Books, 1982) and *Bureaucracy: What Government Agencies Do and Why They Do It* (Basic Books, 1989).

INDEX

376